JACKIE
AFTER
JACK

*Also by Christopher Andersen
in Large Print:*

An Affair to Remember:
  The Remarkable Love Story of
  Katharine Hepburn and Spencer Tracy
Jack and Jackie:
  Portrait of an American Marriage
Young Kate:
  The Remarkable Hepburns and the
  Shaping of an American Legend

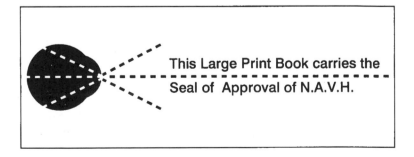

This Large Print Book carries the
Seal of Approval of N.A.V.H.

JACKIE AFTER JACK

PORTRAIT OF THE LADY

Christopher Andersen

Thorndike Press • Thorndike, Maine

Grateful acknowledgment is made to the following for permission to use the photographs in this book:

AP/Wide World Photos: 10, 11, 13, 14, 15, 19, 24, 28, 36, 42, 50, 60
Archive Photos: 2, 3, 9, 16, 20, 23, 25, 26, 38, 39, 45, 62
David McGough/DMI: 47, 48, 51
Globe Photos: 17, 31, 32, 33, 34, 37, 46, 59
Mark Shaw/Photo Researchers: 1
Reuters/Corbis-Bettmann: 52, 56, 57, 58
Reuters/Gary Hershorn/Archive Photos: 61
Rex: 53, 54, 55
UPI/Corbis-Bettman: title page, 4, 5, 6, 7, 8, 12, 18, 21, 22, 27, 29, 30, 35, 40, 41, 43, 44, 49

Published in 1998 by arrangement with William Morrow & Co. Inc.

Thorndike Large Print ® Americana Series.

The tree indicium is a trademark of Thorndike Press.

The text of this Large Print edition is unabridged. Other aspects of the book may vary from the original edition.

Set in 16 pt. Plantin by Minnie B. Raven.

Printed in the United States on permanent paper.

Library of Congress Cataloging in Publication Data

Andersen, Christopher P.
   Jackie after Jack : portrait of the lady / Christopher Andersen.
     p. (large print) cm.
   Originally published: New York : William Morrow, c1998.
   Includes bibliographical references.
   ISBN 0-7862-1501-1 (lg. print : hc : alk. paper)
   ISBN 0-7862-1502-X (lg. print : sc : alk. paper)
   1. Onassis, Jacqueline Kennedy, 1929– . 2. Celebrities — United States — Biography. 3. Presidents' spouses — United States — Biography. I. Title.
   [CT275.O552A64 1998b]
   973.922′092—dc21
   [B]   98-17240

For my magnificent Kate

What is my proudest accomplishment? I went through some pretty difficult times, and I kept my sanity.

— *Jackie*

PREFACE

From the very beginning, theirs was destined to be one of the most celebrated unions of the twentieth century: he the handsome, charismatic young standard-bearer of one of America's most powerful families, she the darkly beautiful thoroughbred. By the time it ended with gunshots in Dallas, John Fitzgerald Kennedy and his wife, Jacqueline, were indisputably the First Couple of the World.

— *Jack and Jackie: Portrait of an American Marriage*

The fairy tale may have ended with JFK's assassination on November 22, 1963, but not the legend. The President's thirty-four-year-old widow would soon rise Phoenix-like from the ashes to become the most talked-about, written-about, and speculated-about figure of her generation — arguably, with the possible exception of Princess Diana, the most famous woman in modern times.

Together, Jack and Jackie had survived his life-threatening illness (during their marriage he was given last rites three times *before* Dallas), his rampant infidelity, the death of one parent and the incapacitating stroke of another, a miscarriage, a stillbirth, and the loss of their son Patrick. Alone, she was left to bear the heaviest burden of all.

In the days and weeks following Dallas, Jackie's quiet strength and natural dignity were the glue that held together a nation. If she could hold her head high, what right did we have to fall apart? She was just as determined that we not forget what her husband had stood for. The haunting sound of muffled drums had scarcely faded away when Jackie began laying the groundwork for Camelot — a bit of revisionist history she hoped would endure for generations.

It did not. Barely a decade had passed before cracks began appearing in the Kennedy myth. Soon the torrent of scandalous revelations concerning the family's underhanded political practices and the slain President's reckless private life had all but washed away what little remained of Jackie's fairy-tale kingdom.

Conversely, the Legend of Jackie only seemed to grow with each passing decade. Even after she committed what many considered the ultimate betrayal — marrying Greek shipping tycoon Aristotle Onassis —

Jackie's public was still willing to forgive. During the last two decades of her life, she remained an object of endless fascination: aloof, inaccessible, mysterious — an abiding symbol of money, power, style, elegance, and dignity.

When she died after a short battle with cancer on May 19, 1994, Americans felt a profound sense of loss. As long as most of us could remember, Jackie had been a larger-than-life figure, and her too-sudden death signaled the end of an era. Yet there remained that nagging feeling that we never really *knew* Jackie. She was a global icon, a creature of mystique and mystery more than a living, breathing human being.

Therein lies the true irony. For Jackie's legacy far transcends the narrow boundaries of wealth and glamour. She was the young wife who had finally bridged the emotional chasm between herself and her husband only to have him cruelly snatched from her, the young mother left to raise their young children alone, the intensely private woman fated to live her life center stage.

So singular was her place in history that no one can ever really know what it was like to *be* Jackie. She was, in every sense of the word, unique. She was also flawed. The product of a bitter divorce, Jackie had worshiped her alcoholic, womanizing father but also listened to her mother, who prized money and social status above all else.

Yet there was something about Jackie — a certain valor — that transcended her shortcomings. Ultimately, she chose to embrace the world rather than be defeated by it, to go on loving and being loved, and to live her life on her own terms. Jacqueline Bouvier Kennedy Onassis proved that she was one thing above all else: an American Original.

JACKIE: Where will we be buried
when we die, Jack?

JACK: Hyannis, I guess.
We'll all be there.

JACKIE: Well, I don't think you should
be buried in Hyannis.
I think you should be buried at
Arlington.
You just belong to all the country . . .

Afterwards, I was really
in my own shell of grief.
— *Jackie*

ONE

"Jack, Jack, Jack, can you hear me? I love you, Jack." Jackie was cradling her husband's head in her lap, pressing down on the top, she would later explain with an almost chilling detachment, "to keep the brains in." Sprawled on top of her, trying to shield both the President and the First Lady with his 190-pound bulk, was stone-faced Secret Service agent Clint Hill.

Only moments before, Jackie and Jack had exchanged one final glance as the first of the three shots hit him in the back of the neck, severed his windpipe, and exited his throat. She thought it was a motorcycle backfiring, until she heard Texas Governor John Connally, riding in the jump seat directly in front of the President, shouting "Oh, no, no, no . . . My God, they're going to kill us all."

The expression on Jack's handsome, forty-six-year-old face that moment the first bullet struck would haunt Jackie's dreams for the rest of her life. "He looked puzzled. I remember he looked as if he just had a slight headache," she later said. "I could see a piece of his skull coming off. It was flesh-colored, not white. I can see this perfectly

15

clean piece detaching itself from his head. Then he slumped in my lap." Connally was also shot. He and his wife, Nellie, were both sprayed with gore from the head wound to the President. "I have his brains," Nellie Connally could hear Jackie say, "in my hands!"

Jackie stared at Jack in disbelief for a full seven seconds before frantically climbing onto the slippery trunk of the Lincoln. Jackie would later say she had no memory of crawling out onto the trunk, or any idea why she did it. Had she been reaching to help Agent Hill, who had been riding in the backup car and now jumped up onto the rear bumper of the presidential limousine? Was she merely trying to escape the horror? Hill knew precisely what she was doing. The First Lady was trying frantically to retrieve the largest piece of the President's skull that had been blown off. Instead, Hill helplessly watched the palm-sized bone fragment bounce off the rear fender and land in the street.

"He's dead, he's dead," Jackie could hear people yelling as the motorcade raced to Parkland Memorial Hospital six miles away. Her trademark pillbox hat was pushed down over her forehead by the wind; she ripped it off — the hatpin that had held it in place took a handful of her hair with it — and threw it to the floor. Only inches from him, cradling his head in her white-gloved hands, she could see "the pink-rose ridges" on the inside of his shattered skull. But from his hairline down, she later said, "his head was so beautiful. I tried to hold the top of his head down, maybe I could keep it in . . . but I knew he was dead."

She would always remember the roses. Three times that day she had been presented with the yellow roses of Texas. "Only in Dallas, I was given red roses," Jackie later said. "How funny, I thought — red roses for me." And now their car was full of blood and red roses — an image that remained indelibly etched in her mind.

The driver floored the accelerator and suddenly Jackie felt "a sensation of enormous speed." Still, Jackie said of the seven-minute dash to Parkland, "it just seemed an eternity." But when the presidential limousine pulled up to the emergency room entrance, Jackie, still caressing Jack's head, refused to let them take her husband inside. "Please, Mrs. Kennedy," Clint Hill pleaded, "we must get the President to a doctor." Hill could see that Jack's blue eyes were open in a fixed stare. The seat and floor were strewn with blood-soaked rose petals, crushed remnants of the bouquet that had been lying on the seat between them. "I'm not letting him go, Mr. Hill," she said. "You know he's dead. Leave me alone."

Realizing that Jackie did not want anyone to see that a sizable portion of Jack's skull had been blown away, Hill whipped off the jacket of his regulation black suit and wrapped it around the President's head. Satisfied that this small portion of JFK's dignity had been preserved, she allowed Hill, Jack's longtime aide Dave Powers, and another Secret Service agent, Roy Kellerman, to gently move Jack to a waiting stretcher. As they lifted the President, the coat began to slide away, and Jackie rushed to hold it in place. "It wasn't repulsive to me for one moment," Jackie would recall of the blood and gray brain matter that covered her dress, legs, and arms. She ran alongside the stretcher, making sure the jacket did not slip again. "Nothing was repulsive to me — and I was running behind with the coat covering it . . ."

Others were not so brave: When it struck him that the odd blotches on Jackie's pink wool suit were his friend's blood and brain matter, Dave Powers burst out sobbing. (Later, Powers pulled aside one of the priests who had been summoned to give Jack the last rites. Powers, convinced he was suffering a coronary, wanted the cleric to hear his confession.)

As they stepped inside the hospital, Jackie chanted the same mantra to herself: "I'm not going to leave him, I'm not going to leave him." But "these big Texas interns" had other ideas. "Mrs. Kennedy," they said as they tried to pull her away from Jack, "you come with us."

"They wanted to take me away from him," she recalled. "They kept trying to get me, they kept trying to grab me. But I said, 'I'm not leaving.' Doctors are so bossy . . . They boss you around." She remembered how she had been kept from him when he nearly died during an operation on his spine nine years before. "They're never going to keep me away from him again," she vowed to herself.

Dr. Marion Jenkins, head of Parkland's anesthesiology department, noticed that Jackie was "carrying one hand cupped over the other hand. She nudged me with her left elbow," Dr. Jenkins recalled, "and then with her right hand handed me a good-sized chunk of the President's brain. She didn't say a word. I handed it to the nurse."

Eight minutes after he was shot, Jack was admitted to the hospital simply as "Case 24740, white male, gunshot wound." Incredibly, the President still had a faint heartbeat and was still breathing when he reached Parkland. Doctors immediately began giving him massive blood transfusions. Jackie stood outside Trauma Room 1 (Connally, who would recover from his wound, was taken to Trauma Room 2) in the narrow corridor,

19

puffing on a cigarette given to her by a Dallas patrolman, her eyes wide with shock. She was still wearing her white kid gloves, now drenched in Jack's blood.

After ten minutes, the police officer brought over folding chairs for Jackie and Nellie Connally. Both women watched in anxious silence as interns and nurses raced in and out of the trauma rooms with bottles of saline solution, syringes, and whole blood. "We never spoke a word to each other," Nellie Connally remembered. "Not a word. It only dawned on me then how strong she was. Jackie was a strong woman — a very, very, very strong woman." (Ironically, Jackie had told her husband earlier that day that she "hated" John Connally. She complained of Connally's "petulant, self-indulgent mouth. If a man's good-looking enough, it seems to be something ruinous. They almost get soft. I just can't bear his weak mouth and his sitting there saying all these great things about himself. I really hate him.")

Soon Powers and Kenneth O'Donnell, JFK's Chief of Staff, were pacing the corridor, watching the expression on Jackie's face but "too numb" to talk to her. For a moment she allowed herself to think that "maybe he isn't dead — he's going to live!" She turned to O'Donnell. "Ken," she asked, "do you think he still has a chance?"

"Of course," O'Donnell replied automatically, without believing it for a minute.

It dawned on her then that if by some miracle Jack did pull through — he had come close to death at least three times before Dallas and somehow survived — he would be severely brain-damaged. When his father, Joseph Kennedy, had been incapacitated by a stroke, Jack told Jackie, "Don't let that happen to me." Still, she was not ready to let him go. "I'll take care of him every day of his life," she told herself, "I'll make him happy . . ."

He can't die, she told herself. Not *now*. When their infant son, Patrick, succumbed to respiratory problems just four months earlier, Jackie and Jack broke down in each other's arms. "Oh, Jack, oh, Jack," she had cried. "There is only one thing I could not bear now — if I ever lost you."

They had been through so much together during their decade-long marriage: They had weathered the private crises — the back surgeries that nearly ended Jack's life, his father's stroke, her father's death, the miscarriage, the stillbirth, John Jr.'s difficult delivery, the loss of little Patrick — and the public ones: the Bay of Pigs, Berlin, the Cuban Missile Crisis.

Yet Jack had never changed his womanizing ways, and although he loved Jackie in his own way, husband and wife had never managed to bridge the emotional gap between them. Their close friend Ben Bradlee described both Jackie and Jack as "remote and independent" people who hid their true feelings from each other, and even the First Lady referred to herself and the President as "two icebergs." The writer Theodore H. White, who later spoke to Jackie about the impact Patrick's death had on their relationship, observed that "there had always been this wall between them. But their shared grief [over Patrick] tore that wall down."

Now, as Jack lay dying, Jackie realized they had never been more in love. She decided that it wasn't enough that she wait outside; she had to be with him, at his side. But when she moved toward the door, Head Nurse Doris Nelson literally blocked her path. "You can't come in here," she said, grabbing the First Lady by the shoulders.

Jackie tried to shove the large woman out of the way. "I'm going to get in that room," she told the nurse. Rear Admiral George Burkley, the President's personal physician, emerged from the room. He was shaking. "Mrs. Kennedy," he said, "you need a sedative."

"No, I want to be in there when he dies."

With Jackie in tow, Dr. Burkley pushed his way into the crowded trauma room. "Get her out of here," blurted the chief operating surgeon, Dr. Malcolm Perry, but Burkley stood his ground. "It's her prerogative," he declared. "It's her prerogative." When Dr. Perry kept insisting she leave, Jackie grew angry. "It's my husband," she said. "His blood, his brains, are all over me."

The floor, indeed, was covered with the President's blood. Jackie sank to one knee in it and said a brief prayer before rising to watch the doctors trying desperately to resuscitate her husband. At one o'clock, one of the attending physicians, Dr. Kemp Clark, told Jackie that it was over. Her husband was dead. Father Oscar Huber had been summoned from nearby Holy Trinity Church to perform the last rites.

A sheet had been pulled up to cover Jack's face, leaving one of his feet exposed. The foot, Jackie observed, "was whiter than the sheet." She took the foot in her hand and gently kissed it. Then she pulled the sheet down, exposing his face. "His mouth was so *beautiful*," she recalled. "His eyes were open." Dr. Jenkins remembered that "she started kissing him. She kissed his foot, his leg, thigh, chest, and then his lips. She didn't say a word." One of the doctors found his hand under the sheet and guided hers to it. She held his hand while Father Huber gave Jack Extreme Unction.

Given the circumstances of the President's sudden death and the priest's own condition — Father Huber feared he could collapse at

23

any moment — he offered the abbreviated version of the last rites, using his thumb to anoint Jack's forehead with holy oil as he recited in Latin. The ceremony ended with the Apostolic Blessing: "I, by the faculty given to me by the Apostolic See, grant to you plenary indulgence and remission of all sins, and I bless you. In the name of the Father, and of the Son, and of the Holy Ghost. Amen."

Jackie appeared satisfied, but Dr. Burkley, the only other Roman Catholic in the trauma room, was not. "Is that *all?*" Dr. Burkley demanded. Surely a tragedy of this magnitude called for more than the priest's shorthand version. At Burkley's insistence, Father Huber recited the Lord's Prayer and the Hail Mary. The priest then used a cotton swab to wipe the holy oil from JFK's face, recoiling when he realized that the cotton ball, too, was now drenched in blood. Only Jackie seemed unfazed. "Eternal rest grant unto him, O Lord," Huber said. "And let perpetual light shine upon him," Jackie answered.

Jackie returned to her folding chair in the corridor, smoking another cigarette while the nurses and orderlies cleaned her husband's body. Suddenly, it looked as if she might faint. A nurse rushed to her side with a cold towel, which Jackie pressed to her forehead.

She was determined not to lose consciousness — not now. Jackie had insisted on seeing Jack one more time before he was placed in the bronze casket for the trip back to Washington. "You just make sure I get in there before they close the coffin," she said. When the nurses and orderlies were finished, she went back into the trauma room with Kenny O'Donnell and watched as they lifted the President's naked body off the operating table and placed it gently in the coffin. She was surprised by how small he looked, how fragile.

Her white kid gloves had now stiffened with Jack's blood, and she turned to a uniformed Dallas policeman who helped her pull them off. Then she took off her gold wedding band — it, too, was smeared with blood — and slipped it on the President's finger. O'Donnell assured her that it was the right thing to do at the time, but removed the ring from Jack's finger later that night at Bethesda Naval Hospital when she began having doubts.

O'Donnell had other things on his mind. The new President, Lyndon Johnson, was in a near-panic wondering if this wasn't a "Communist conspiracy" to wipe out the entire top tier of government. O'Donnell urged LBJ to fly out of Love Field and return to Washington immediately — Jackie and JFK's body would follow. "You take good care of that fine lady," Johnson told O'Donnell.

Getting back to Washington would not be so easy for Jack and Jackie. Dallas County Medical Examiner Earl Rose insisted that state laws required that the President's body not be removed from Parkland Hospital until an autopsy had been performed. Dr. Rose was told that a proper autopsy would be performed as soon as they reached Bethesda, but the medical examiner refused to budge. Rose was supported by a local judge, who loudly informed Jackie and anyone else in earshot that as far as he was concerned, JFK's death was "just another homicide."

Jackie, presidential aides Powers, O'Donnell, Larry O'Brien, General Godfrey McHugh, and a handful of others now formed a protective ring around the casket. Dr. Rose shouted at all of them — JFK's widow included — demanding that President Kennedy's body not be moved. Even in death, they seemed determined to separate Jack and Jackie. She turned to O'Donnell and said quietly, "I'm not going to leave here without Jack."

Finally, after endless phone calls and wrangling, they forced their way past the irate Dr. Rose and loaded the casket into a waiting white hearse. Jackie got in the back with the coffin, sitting next to it on a jump seat as the hearse sped off with Secret Service agent Andy Berger behind the wheel. During the short ride to Love Field, O'Donnell and Powers expected to hear sirens any minute — the sound of Dallas police cars coming to intercept the hearse and reclaim the body.

Caught up with the others in this improbable getaway, Jackie kept thinking that she had to get home with her Jack. The hearse pulled up to Love Field, and Jackie poured out the back with the others. Powers, O'Donnell, and the Secret Service agents hurriedly slid the heavy bronze coffin out of the hearse and lugged it up the gangway of *Air Force One*. A dozen seats at the back of the plane had been removed to accommodate it. When she went to her compartment toward the front of the plane to splash water on her face, Jackie was dumbfounded to see Lyndon Johnson perched on her bed. She returned to the spot in the tail section near her husband's coffin.

Why hadn't Johnson already left on *Air Force Two*? O'Donnell wanted to know. Didn't he realize that by remaining behind unnecessarily he put himself — and perhaps the nation — in grave peril? There was always the possibility that this was indeed part of a larger conspiracy, and now added to that was the fact that Texas authorities might show up any minute, guns drawn, to prevent *Air Force One* from taking off.

But Johnson had no intention of leaving until he was sworn in as President — a needless formality that could easily have taken place at a later time, once everyone was out of harm's way. He had placed a call to Federal District Judge Sarah Hughes, and now everyone was forced to sit in the sweltering afternoon heat — the air-conditioning could not be turned on until the engines were started — waiting for Judge Hughes to arrive.

Johnson, meantime, was cracking. General McHugh, who at first had no idea that LBJ was even on the plane, claimed that at one point he discovered Johnson cowering in the closet of the President's cabin. "They're going to kill us," he whimpered. "They're going to shoot down the plane, they're going to kill us all." It was then, McHugh said, that he actually got LBJ to "snap out of it" by slapping him. McHugh, in turn, was observed by others on the plane as dashing up and down the center aisle a half dozen times, wild-eyed and rambling.

Neither man was a picture of composure. Nor were most of the others aboard *Air Force One* that day. JFK's devoted secretary Evelyn Lincoln, who had gone to work for Jack years before he met Jackie, wept softly. Jackie's private secretary, Mary Gallagher, fingered her rosary. Pamela Turnure, the Jackie lookalike who was both secretary to the First Lady and lover to the President, sat by the coffin, tears streaming down her cheeks. Lady Bird Johnson choked back sobs as she fingered her choker of pearls.

Among them, Jackie seemed to dwell in an odd oasis of comparative calm. Sitting alone less than a foot from the coffin on the rear starboard side of the aircraft, she spoke only to complain about the heat. "It's so hot," she said. "Let's leave."

Johnson, in the interim, had downed a bowl of vegetable soup, changed his shirt, washed his face, and dictated a letter to his secretary before finally vacating the bedroom so Jackie could freshen up. Once she stepped inside, Jackie saw that someone had laid out a fresh outfit on one of the two beds — the white suit and black shoes she was to have worn at Jack's next scheduled stop, in Austin. Within moments, there was a knock on the door. LBJ and a stricken Lady Bird walked in to offer their condolences. They sat on the bed on either side of Jackie. Johnson enveloped her hand in his. Lady Bird said, "Oh, Jackie, you know, we never wanted to be Vice President. And now, dear God, it's come to this!"

"Oh, what if I hadn't been there!" Jackie said as if to reassure Lady Bird. "I was so glad I was there."

The new First Lady looked stricken. "What wounds me most of all," Lady Bird blurted out, "is that this should happen in my beloved state of Texas!" Jackie stared back blankly. Lady Bird regretted the remark the instant she uttered it.

Johnson explained to Jackie that he wanted to be sworn in on the plane, and that a judge was on her way to perform the ceremony. Jackie nodded. Lady Bird asked if she didn't want to change out of her clothes? No, Jackie replied, not now. Perhaps all she needed was a little time alone . . .

Once the Johnsons were gone, Jackie lit up a Salem, her brand of choice. She paced nervously, then went into the powder room. She was staring blankly into the mirror and combing her hair when Kenny O'Donnell gently pushed open the door. The judge had arrived and everyone was waiting, he told Jackie, but she really did not have to participate if she didn't feel up to it. Always with an eye toward posterity, she told him she wanted to be present for the ceremony. "In the light of history," she explained, "it would be better if I was there." Like Lady Bird, O'Donnell asked if she didn't want to change out of her bloodstained suit. "No," she replied.

"Everybody kept saying to me put a cold towel around my head and wipe the blood off," Jackie later said. "I saw myself in the mirror, my whole face splattered with blood and hair. I wiped it off with Kleenex. History! I thought, no one really wants me there. Then one second later I thought, Why did I wash the blood off? . . . If I'd just had the blood and caked hair when they took the picture . . ."

In truth, no one wanted Jackie there to witness the ceremony more than Lyndon Johnson. Her presence would convey to the world her support for the new President. While everyone stood in the center of the plane waiting for Jackie to materialize, Pam Turnure wondered, "How can they ask her to do this?"

The door to the bedroom opened, and Jackie emerged. Johnson stepped forward to take her hand. "This is," he said solemnly, "the saddest moment in my life." Jackie took her place at the Johnsons' side. White House photographer Cecil Stoughton, who had taken countless photographs of JFK and his young family, was now perched on a seat just a few feet from the President, telling people where to stand and where to look, as if arranging a wedding photo.

Judge Hughes had already begun the oath when JFK advisor Larry O'Brien handed her JFK's personal, monogrammed copy of the Holy Scriptures. She started again, this time with LBJ's left hand resting on the Bible that had belonged to his slain predecessor. During the twenty-eight-second oath, Stoughton used two cameras — a Hasselblad and an Alpha Reflex — to snap sixteen pictures.

31

"We're just like characters in a play," Lady Bird thought as she stood at her husband's right side. "We're stepping into a strange new world. It has the quality of a dream, and yet it isn't a dream at all . . ." Kenny O'Donnell could only think of Jackie. "She's being used," he said to himself. *"She's being used."*

Jackie, drenched in sweat yet unwilling to remove her wool suit coat, stood at LBJ's left, staring numbly at Judge Hughes. "At least," she kept thinking, "they'll see Jack's blood. They'll see what they did." She was unaware that Stoughton had been instructed to shoot her at an angle where the bloodstains on the front of her skirt were not visible.

LBJ hugged Lady Bird, then Mrs. Kennedy. Within minutes, *Air Force One* was taxiing down the runway. It was 2:47 P.M. Dallas time — just two hours and seventeen minutes after the fatal shots were fired.

Jackie sat with the new First Couple, but when LBJ ordered another bowl of soup from the galley, she had to excuse herself. "I've got to be back there with Jack," she thought, and dashed to the rear of the plane to be with the coffin. She took a seat next to O'Donnell, just opposite the casket.

Dr. Burkley ventured back and asked if now, perhaps, she might wish to change out of her bloody clothes? "No!" she shot back.

"Let them see what they've done. I want them to see what they've done."

The admiral returned to the front of the plane, and Jackie turned to O'Donnell. "We looked at each other," he recalled, "and she finally lost it — *for the very first time that day she allowed herself to cry.*" Others in the cabin could hear her sobs over the engines. It was ten minutes or more before she could finally regain enough control to speak. "Oh, it's happened," she said.

"It's happened," O'Donnell replied resignedly.

More sobs. "Oh, Kenny, what's going to happen?"

"You want to know something, Jackie?" O'Donnell said. "I don't give a damn."

"Oh, you're right, you know. You're right. Just nothing matters but what you've lost . . ."

O'Donnell said he was going to have a stiff drink — a Scotch — and suggested she have one, too. Like her husband, Jackie was not much of a drinker — although she had a taste for champagne, wine, and an occasional daiquiri. But she had always considered whiskey in any of its forms to be too intimidating. She had, she told O'Donnell, never even tasted Scotch.

Jackie brushed away a tear and thought for a moment. "Now," she said, "is as good a time as any to start." O'Donnell handed her a triple. She drank it, all the while staring at "that long, long coffin." Then she downed another. Nearly everyone on board, with the obvious exception of the flight crew, began drinking — whiskey, gin, vodka. No matter. The emotions of the moment were so overwhelming that alcohol seemed to have no effect at all.

O'Donnell was convinced that his boss must have had some sort of premonition that the end was near. A month earlier, when Jack had visited his father, Joseph P. Kennedy, for what would turn out to be the last time at the Kennedy family compound at Hyannis Port, Jack kissed his father on the cheek, walked toward his waiting helicopter — and then turned to kiss him a second time "as if to say good-bye."

The night before, Jack had turned to Powers and O'Donnell and for no apparent reason said, "Last night would have been the best night to assassinate a President." O'Donnell asked Jackie, "Can you tell me why we were talking about that? I've never discussed that with him in my life." And on the thirteen-minute flight from Fort Worth to Dallas that very morning, Jack showed his wife a black-bordered, full-page ad in *The Dallas News* denouncing his "ultra-Leftist" policies. "We're heading into nut country today," he had said. "But, Jackie, if somebody wants to shoot me through a window with a rifle, nobody can stop it, so why worry about it?"

While the Kennedy faction was still reeling from the unreality of it all, those in the forward section of the plane were tightening their grasp on government. There was, in fact, already a sharp division between the Texans who huddled around their leader and the members of Jack's fabled "Irish Mafia" who shunned LBJ and sat aft with "their" president. Understandably, several Kennedy staffers had a difficult time concealing their resentment of the State of Texas and its drawling inhabitants. "It was undeniably very, very sick," Clint Hill said of the atmosphere in the cabin, "with a great deal of tension between the Kennedy people and the Johnson people." Johnson aide Bill Moyers was sent back to summon O'Donnell and Powers for a meeting with the new President; LBJ was already planning a gathering of his congressional leadership. The two Kennedy men told Moyers they did not want to leave Jackie.

The internecine strain was palpable to everyone but Jackie. Knowing that those around her were too destroyed to say much of anything, she called on her inner reserves to comfort them. "Oh, Dave, you've been with Jack all these years," she told Powers. "What will you do now?" She knew Clint Hill would spend the rest of his life blaming himself, but "Lace" (Jackie's code name) wanted him to know that she could never hold him responsible; in fact, she told the devastated Secret Service agent that she and her husband had always regarded him as "one of the family."

Powers and O'Donnell began to reminisce with Jackie. They recalled how just a month earlier, Jack was in Boston attending a Harvard-Columbia football game when at halftime he suddenly turned to them and said he wanted to visit the grave of his infant son, Patrick, who had died the previous August. He wanted to go "alone," so they ducked out, eluded the press, and drove to the cemetery. The Secret Service detail kept a respectful distance while the President walked slowly up to the headstone simply marked KENNEDY. "He seems," Jack had said sadly, "so alone here."

Jackie understood. "I'll bring them together now," she said. Not in Massachusetts, as Powers and O'Donnell assumed, but at Arlington. Mentally, she was already making funeral plans.

Those inside *Air Force One* were both the focus of the world's attention and to some degree insulated from the anxieties the assassination had triggered. LBJ was not the only high-government official who worried that this might be part of a larger conspiracy

— Communist or otherwise — perhaps even a coup. For one thing, practically the entire cabinet was out of Washington. In a plane thirty-five thousand feet over the Pacific, Press Secretary Pierre Salinger, Presidential Assistant McGeorge Bundy, Secretary of State Dean Rusk, Treasury Secretary C. Douglas Dillon, and four other cabinet members were on their way to an economic conference in Tokyo.

Salinger listened to the news crackling over the radio in short bursts — at first that "Lancer" (JFK's code name) was shot. Then that the wounds were fatal. Tears coursing down his crimson cheeks, Salinger informed Rusk and the other cabinet members that the President was dead. "It was the worst moment you can imagine," he said. "The most sickening, devastating feeling. But there was also real fear that this might be a coup. We wondered if we were at war. Afraid? I was never more afraid in my entire life."

To counter the fear and grief as they turned back for Honolulu, Salinger, Rusk, and the others played a surreal game of poker. "It seems strange, of course," Salinger said, "but it was the only way I could come up with to keep our minds off the horror of the moment. After all, there was nothing, absolutely nothing we could do. Periodically, one of us would sort of just turn away and start crying, and then return to the game."

Salinger, who by that night would be back in Washington, had particular reason to be upset. He knew the President was wary of making the trip to Dallas — Adlai Stevenson had been spat on by an angry mob there just a few weeks earlier and had pleaded with Kennedy to stay away from Texas — but Salinger dismissed the warnings. "Don't worry about it," he told JFK, "it's going to be a great trip and you're going to draw the biggest crowds ever. Going with Mrs. Kennedy will be terrific."

Salinger was only one of many who felt they shouldered some of the blame. Listening to the news reports in a Jacksonville air terminal, Florida Senator George Smathers felt queasy recalling the conversation he had had with his old friend three days earlier. "How do I get out of it?" Jack had asked him.

"You can't get out of it, Mr. President. You've got to go. You're doing the right thing." Now and for the rest of his life, Smathers would say over and over to himself, "I wish to God I hadn't said it."

Attorney General Robert F. Kennedy had been having lunch by the pool with wife, Ethel, and several guests when, just minutes after the shots were fired, FBI Director

J. Edgar Hoover called.

"I have news for you," the Director said, almost casually.

"What?" Bobby asked.

"The President has been shot."

"What? Oh," Bobby sputtered. He was clearly in shock. "I — Is it serious? I —"

"I think it's serious," Hoover said coldly. "I'm endeavoring to get details. I'll call you back when I find out more."

Within minutes, the Attorney General had called CIA Director John McCone and told him to make the five-minute drive from CIA headquarters to Hickory Hill, Bobby's estate in Virginia. McCone arrived even before Hoover called with the matter-of-fact confirmation that the President had died. Bobby would later remember that Hoover would have sounded more excited if he were reporting that he had "discovered a Communist on the faculty of Howard University." At one point Bobby went outside for a breath of fresh air with Ed Guthman, a key advisor in the young Attorney General's crusade to root out Mob influence in organized labor. "I thought they'd get one of us," Bobby said, "but Jack, after all he'd been through, never worried about it. I thought it would be me."

The reason for Hoover's curt response — and for the fact that Bobby spent much of the first hour following his brother's assassination being briefed by CIA Director McCone — would remain secret for decades. One of the first things Bobby asked McCone was, "Did the CIA kill my brother?" "No," McCone answered. Yet what all three men did know about the "they" who killed JFK would have a profound and lasting impact on Bobby's personal sense of responsibility, and on the depth of his feeling toward the President's young widow.

It was no small irony that the man and woman closest to Jack were now so supremely self-possessed. Aboard *Air Force One*, Jackie spoke warm words of comfort while sharing her plans for the funeral. Boston's craggy-voiced Richard Cardinal Cushing was practically the Kennedy clan's personal chaplain; he had married Jack and Jackie ten years earlier at Newport, Rhode Island, and had presided over the funeral service for little Patrick as well. He would say the Low Requiem Mass. "There was this wonderful tenor from Boston who sang at our wedding — his name is Luigi Vena — I want him to sing 'Ave Maria' and 'Agnus Dei,' " she told Powers and O'Donnell.

Just nine days earlier, Jack, Jackie, Caroline, and John-John listened to the legendary bagpipes of the Black Watch Regiment perform on the South Lawn of the White House — the last time the First Family was together. "How he loved them," Jackie said wistfully. "They must be at the funeral, too."

Bobby, meanwhile, had taken charge of things on the ground. The rest of the family responded with numb disbelief. Jean Kennedy Smith was window-shopping on Fifth Avenue when a woman ran up to her screaming, "Haven't you heard the news?" A group had gathered next to a parked car to hear the bulletins over the radio. Rather than rushing to a nearby television or jumping in a cab for her home, she numbly walked the twenty blocks to her Park Avenue apartment. Of all the Kennedy women, Jean was the closest to Jackie; she boarded the shuttle to Washington to be at her sister-in-law's side.

Eunice and her husband, Peace Corps Director Sargent Shriver, were in the dining room of Washington's Lafayette Hotel and had just been handed their menus when they were told of the shooting. They went on to order and inhaled a bowl of soup before the enormity of it all hit them.

In Hyannis Port, Rose, the iron-willed matriarch of the Kennedy clan, was about to settle in for her daily afternoon nap when the news of the shooting first flashed over the TV. She paced the house, assuring those around her that everything would be "just fine — you'll see." When her son's death was confirmed, she went for a walk on the grounds with her nephew Joey Gargan. "Joey, we must go on living," she told him. "We can't look back. We must go on, Joey. We must."

Bobby sent his last remaining brother, Ted, to Hyannis to tell their father. Joe, suffering from a stroke and confined to a wheelchair, had not been informed. The servants unplugged the television set and told him it was out of order. This ruse continued for two days until, according to the elder Kennedy's private nurse, Rita Dallas, Ted stood by as Eunice tried to break the news to her father. "Daddy, Daddy, there's been an accident," she stumbled. "But Jack's okay. Jack was in an accident, Daddy. Oh, Daddy, Jack's dead. He's dead but he's in heaven. Oh God, Daddy, Jack's okay, isn't he?"

The nurse's monitor next to Joe's bed had been turned off, so none of the staff heard what was going on inside his room. "But I'll tell you," said Ham Brown, the Secret Service agent assigned to protect JFK's father, "there wasn't a dry eye among all of us standing out in the hall. When they came out, they were all crying."

At the Santa Monica Beach house Pat Kennedy Lawford shared with her then-husband, Peter Lawford, an inebriated Judy Garland was telling the sister of the fallen

President, "Oh my God, I'll never sing 'Over the Rainbow' to him again." The Lawfords, like the rest of the Kennedy clan, were thinking of Jackie now. In the evening the couple boarded an American Airlines flight for Washington, bringing along their daughter Sydney, age seven, for the express purpose of keeping her cousin Caroline company during her terrible ordeal.

"Those poor children!" Ethel had cried when Bobby told her they were now fatherless. That afternoon "Lyric" (Caroline's code name; John-John was "Lark") chatted away animatedly in the backseat of a family friend's station wagon, on her way to her very first sleep-over. An unmarked Secret Service car with a single agent followed at a discreet distance. When the first news flash came over the car radio, the mother of Caroline's girlfriend switched it off immediately. She was confident that Caroline, clutching her pink teddy bear and chatting with her daughter, had heard nothing.

But she had. Within minutes, they had pulled over to the side of the highway and transferred Caroline from the station wagon to the Secret Service car. Sitting in the passenger seat next to the agent, the President's daughter clutched her pink teddy bear and her small suitcase as they sped back to the White House. "There was no way of knowing," the agent said, "if someone was out to

43

kill the whole First Family. We couldn't take the chance."

Incredibly, another motorist thought the same thing. Spotting Caroline in the unmarked black Ford, an anonymous driver, who may well have thought the First Daughter was being kidnapped, began to pursue the car. After a breakneck chase through Washington streets during which the car carrying Caroline swerved in and out of heavy midday traffic, John F. Kennedy's little girl was deposited safely back at the White House.

As soon as all the Kennedys were informed, Bobby phoned Jackie's sister, Lee Radziwill, at her home in London. With the help of the U.S. Embassy, she would get the first available flight out the following morning. Their mother, Janet Auchincloss, had just finished a few rounds of golf and was resting at the Auchincloss mansion on Washington's O Street when the call came. Although she claimed "someone" had called her with instructions to take the children, the notoriously controlling Mrs. Auchincloss made a unilateral decision to have Caroline and John Jr. brought to her house to spend the night.

Jackie's sixteen-year-old half-brother, Jamie Auchincloss, was scurrying between classes when a teacher told him that his brother-in-law had been shot. When he arrived at the house on O Street, he found Caroline and John Jr. waiting for him in the living room, "expecting to spend a playful late afternoon with their uncle Jamie." Neither child had yet been told what had happened.

"Usually when we got together a lot of the chitchat revolved around the interesting things Daddy and Mommy did," Jamie said. "This time I steered them away from the subject — though with all the excitement I'm sure Caroline must have known something was up. While we played on the floor of the living room, several of the Secret Service men were huddled around the TV set in the kitchen. I tried to keep her away from the news but at one point Caroline jumped up and ran into the kitchen for a cookie. The Secret Service men jumped up and switched off the set, but I think in that fleeting moment Caroline saw what was going on. When she came back into the room, we picked up where we'd left off, but her mood had changed. She turned very quiet."

As *Air Force One* prepared to land at Andrews Air Force Base shortly after 6 P.M., General McHugh made one last attempt to get Jackie to change her dress. Again, she refused. She made an exception for the pillbox hat, however, which she held in her hand. The hat was splattered with bits of gray, and that, she seemed to agree, was excessively gruesome. McHugh quickly cleaned off the hat and returned it to her.

No sooner had the plane come to a halt than Bobby Kennedy bounded aboard, ignoring LBJ's outstretched hand as he ran straight to Jackie. They embraced. They had apprehended the killer, Bobby told her — a small-time Marxist. He did not bother mentioning Lee Harvey Oswald's name, nor the fact that he suspected that Oswald had not acted alone. "He didn't even have the satisfaction of being killed for Civil Rights," Jackie said. "It had to be some silly little Communist. It even robs his death of any meaning."

Millions of her countrymen sat transfixed in front of their television sets that night, watching as Jackie was helped off *Air Force One* and the coffin bearing her husband loaded into a waiting hearse. Jackie, still unwilling to leave her husband's side, slid in the back with Bobby. Again, she poured out the grisly details of the assassination during the forty-minute ride to Bethesda Naval Hospital.

At Bethesda, as she had on the plane, Jackie consoled those who had come to console *her*. Jack and Jackie's old friends and neighbors Tony and Ben Bradlee and Martha and Charlie Bartlett were there — two of only a handful of married couples who could claim to be close friends of the First Couple. So were Secretary of Defense Robert McNamara, Jackie's mother, Janet, and stepfather, Hugh D. "Uncle Hughdie" Auchincloss, and Nancy Tuckerman, Jackie's pal since girlhood and the First Lady's new social secretary. "Poor Tucky," Jackie said. "You came all the way down from New York to take this job and now it's all over. It's so sad. You will stick with me for a little while, won't you?"

When Pam Turnure could not contain her tears, Jackie hugged her. "Oh, Pam," Jackie said to the woman she rightly suspected of having an affair with her husband, "what are you going to do now?"

Jackie, her eyes "still wide open in horror" as Ben Bradlee recalled, "fell into our arms in silence."

"Oh, Benny, do you want to hear what happened?" she asked. Her grief was not so great that she forgot she was talking to *Newsweek*'s Washington bureau chief. "But not as a reporter for *Newsweek*, okay?"

Bradlee was so stunned by the calculated warning that he heard "almost nothing" she said. "I can remember now only the strangely graceful arc she described with her right arm as she told us that part of the President's head had been blown away by one bullet. She moved in a trance to talk to each of us, ignoring the advice of doctors to

47

get some sleep and change out of her bloody clothes."

While the autopsy continued behind closed doors, Jackie indeed seemed willing to relive the moment again and again for any friend or family member who would stop to listen. "She never broke down. The veneer never cracked," Charlie Bartlett said. "She was in complete control, remarkably poised — just unbelievable. She talked about the most horrifying details of the assassination, and even if you didn't want to hear it you knew she had to tell it."

Again, Jackie talked of the roses — red, not yellow as they had been at every other stop in Texas. Dr. Burkley had given her two blood-soaked roses that had slipped down Jack's shirt after the shots were fired. Now Jackie handed one of them back to Burkley. "This," he said, holding the blossom in the palm of his hand, "is the greatest treasure of my life." (Burkley also retrieved another treasured item for Jackie. Knowing that Jackie was having second thoughts about giving up her wedding ring, Ken O'Donnell instructed the physician to remove it from JFK's finger and return it to her.)

As cathartic as the process of reliving Jack's murder may have been, it was also a clear sign to many that Jackie was still in shock. Hours had passed, yet she still rejected all attempts to change out of her clothes. "It's as though," Martha Bartlett whispered to her husband, "she doesn't want the day to end."

At one point, after berating herself once again for wiping Jack's blood off her face with Kleenex before the swearing-in ceremony aboard *Air Force One*, she turned to Bobby. "What's the line," she asked him, "between history and drama?" Bobby, taken aback, proffered no answer.

The Attorney General, meantime, was preoccupied with making sure that the autopsy did not give rise to any conspiracy theories. He barred the presence of a forensic pathologist and insisted that the tissue, blood, and organ samples taken during the autopsy be handed over to his Justice Department. Later, Jackie told Bobby that she wanted all this material — including the President's brain — destroyed, and all the photographs and X rays taken at the autopsy sealed.

It was only now that Jackie, still running on adrenaline, asked about the children. When Janet Auchincloss told her that Caroline and John Jr. had been taken to their grandparents' house on O Street, Jackie stiffened. "What are they doing there?" she asked.

"Jackie, I had a message that you had sent from the plane that you wanted them to come there and to sleep there," Janet replied without skipping a beat. Jackie looked, Mrs. Auchincloss recalled later, "absolutely amazed."

"But I never sent such a message."

"You don't want them there, then?"

"No, I don't," Jackie said firmly. "The best thing for them would be to stay in their own rooms with their own things so their lives can be as normal as possible. Mummy, my God, those poor children. Their lives shouldn't be disrupted, now of all times!"

Janet rushed to the phone and called the children's British nanny, Maud Shaw. "Fortunately they hadn't gone to bed yet," Janet said. "So they thought they had just simply come to have supper with their grandmother." The children were bundled into their winter coats and whisked back to the White House. "She was right, of course," a chastened Janet Auchincloss later conceded. "When it came to her children, Jackie was always right."

Ben and Tony Bradlee were at the White House when the children arrived. Before they left the White House to meet Jackie at Bethesda, they wondered aloud if it wasn't time someone broke the news of their father's death to the children. "I'm going to tell them myself," Bradlee had said, only to be pulled back by his wife at the last minute. Instead, the journalist did his best to distract the children.

"Tell me a story! Tell me a story," demanded John-John, jumping up and down. Bradlee told him a story, and then another. The boy wanted more.

Bradlee thought for a minute. "Chase me around the house," Bradlee ordered John-John. Delighted to oblige, the President's son did chase Bradlee — around the Yellow Oval Room, down the hall, into the West Sitting Room, the family dining room, the kitchen, and back — squealing with joy the entire time.

Back at Bethesda, the children's grandmother asked Jackie point-blank, "Who do you want to tell the children?"

Jackie paused for a moment, weighing her thoughts carefully. John was too young to understand what was happening, but what if Caroline was told by one of her little friends? Jackie took a long drag on her cigarette. "I think Miss Shaw should do exactly what she feels she should do," she stated. Her tone was businesslike, but that was just a defense. The very thought of having to look into the eyes of her children and tell them their father was gone was too much for her. This was one burden someone else would have to shoulder for her. "Miss Shaw will have to judge how much the children have seen or heard or whether they are wondering. She will just have to use her own judgment."

51

Maud Shaw was the logical choice. Caroline was only eleven days old and still in the hospital with her mother when Maud began caring for her; given the demands on the President and First Lady, Miss Shaw was the most constant presence in their lives. Needless to say, as she watched the children play in the family quarters of the White House, she dreaded the assignment handed to her. Things got worse as more and more dignitaries arrived and departed via helicopter and limousine. Each time a chopper touched down, the children leapt to their feet shouting, "Daddy's home! Daddy's home!"

Maud had broken the news of their little brother Patrick's death only four months before. But this she found impossible to do. "I haven't the heart to tell them," the nanny kept saying. "Why can't someone else do this? I can't . . . I can't . . ." She tucked little John in his crib without mentioning anything about his father's death; that, it was agreed, could wait until morning.

After Caroline changed into her pajamas and climbed under the covers, Miss Shaw sat down on the edge of the bed and held the little girl's hand. There were tears in the woman's eyes. "I can't help crying, Caroline, because I have some very sad news to tell you," she said. "Your father has been shot. They took him to a hospital but they couldn't make him better. He's gone to look after Patrick. Patrick was so lonely in heaven. He didn't know anyone there. Now he has the best friend anyone could have. And your father will be so very glad to see Patrick."

Caroline burst into tears. "But what will Daddy do in heaven?" she asked.

"I am sure God is giving him enough things to do because he was always such a busy man. God has made your daddy a guardian angel for you and for Mommy and for John."

Caroline was inconsolable. Miss Shaw stayed with the child over the next hour as she buried her head in her pillow and cried herself to sleep. She was confident that she had made the right decision in not waiting until morning. "It's better for children Caroline's age to get a sadness and a shock before they go to sleep at night," the nanny later told Jackie. "That way it won't hit them hard when they wake up in the morning."

John-John, however, was told the next morning. "Did Daddy take his big plane with him?" the boy asked Miss Shaw. Yes, the nanny replied. "I wonder," he said, "when he's coming back."

Sleep was something Jackie should have craved as she paced the halls at Bethesda, cigarette in hand, until 4 A.M. Television sets flickered in nearly every waiting room and alcove. Like millions of her fellow citizens, Jackie now watched footage of herself being helped off *Air Force One*, and of Lyndon Johnson stepping before waiting television cameras to make his first official statement as President. "This is a sad time for all people," Johnson drawled solemnly. "We have suffered a loss that cannot be weighed. For me it is a deep personal tragedy. I know the world shares the sorrow that Mrs. Kennedy and her family bear. I will do my best. That is all I can do. I ask for your help — and God's."

Jackie had already been at Bethesda for hours when her trusted obstetrician, Dr. John Walsh, arrived. She had repeatedly waved aside any suggestion that she return to the White House without Jack's body. "I'm not leaving here until Jack goes," Jackie declared, "and I won't cry until it's all over."

But Walsh was concerned. She needed her rest, not only to recuperate from all that had already transpired but also to make it through the emotionally draining days ahead. She agreed to take a nap at the hospital, and to be administered a shot of the powerful sedative Visatril. Rather than succumbing to the drug and sleeping for several hours straight as Dr. Walsh fully expected she would, Jackie returned to the group asking if someone had a cigarette. The drug had not even slowed her down. By the time the night was over, Jackie had smoked several packs.

In the predawn hours of Saturday, November 23, Jackie finally returned home to the White House with her husband. While somber guards looked on, she walked alongside the casket as it was carried by representatives of each of the armed services up the stairs of the North Portico. Bobby Kennedy had put Sargent Shriver in charge of making all funeral arrangements, and Shriver in turn had consulted with the Kennedys' longtime artist friend William Walton. Jackie wanted the funeral of another martyr to serve as the model for her husband's. "Find out how Lincoln was buried," she told Bobby, and White House protocol chief Angier Biddle Duke scrambled to get all the information he could on the pomp and ceremony that had surrounded that event ninety-eight years earlier.

In the East Room, Shriver, Duke, and Walton had been huddling over books hastily fetched from the Library of Congress, showing how the White House looked after Lincoln's death. "We spent a great deal of time putting up this black crepe paper around the mantelpiece," Nancy Tuckerman recalled, "and workmen were up with ladders putting it around chandeliers, and it took forever."

Once the honor guard had entered the East Room and placed the flag-draped coffin on the hastily erected catafalque, everyone bowed their heads as Father John Kuhn of St. Matthew's Church said a few words of prayer. As Kennedy advisor Arthur Schlesinger Jr. recalled, Jackie then stepped up to the coffin, knelt down, and "buried her head in the flag. Soon she walked away. The rest of us waited for a little while . . . We were beyond consolation."

But Jackie tried. She walked up to Salinger and put her arm around him. "Pierre, I can *see* this has been a terrible day for you," she said. "You look exhausted. I want you to spend the night here in the White House." Along with O'Donnell and Larry O'Brien, Salinger trekked up to the bedrooms on the third floor, directly above the second-floor family quarters, and desperately tried to fall asleep.

Jackie had also asked her mother and stepfather to stay at the White House that night, in the President's bedroom. JFK's sleeping quarters were separated from Jackie's bedroom by a walk-in closet that contained their stereo system. They would be only steps away. "This touched me very much," Janet Auchincloss later recalled. "I knew she didn't want to be alone."

Not surprisingly, the Auchinclosses found it impossible to sleep in the blue-and-white room where the slain President's presence was still palpable. Everywhere were signs of the back problems that had plagued him since college. In a corner, below Childe Hassam's *Flag Day*, was the Carolina rocking chair Jackie had padded and upholstered. On the nightstand, a heating pad. Spread out on a table at the foot of his large mahogany four-poster was JFK's favorite reading material: *The New York Times*, *Time*, *Newsweek*, *The Washington Post*, *History Today*. Even if the circumstances had been different, it was unlikely that the Auchinclosses would ever have been comfortable here: The cattletail mattress prescribed by another of the President's physicians, Dr. Janet Travell, was rock-hard.

It was nearly 5 A.M., and, finally, Jackie was changing out of the bloodstained pink wool suit — a "gory emblem," as Salinger put it, "of everyone's loss." Her longtime personal maid, Providencia "Provi" Parédes, had already drawn a bath for her. While her mistress's sobs echoed from the tile-walled bathroom, Provi hastily folded the clothes and packed them in a cardboard box. Then, through her own tears, she stashed the box in a linen closet. A few days later Provi turned the box over to Janet Auchincloss, who in turn scrawled "NOV. 22, 1963" on the lid and hid it in the attic on top of another box containing Jackie's wedding dress. There it would remain for the next twenty years. (In 1997, the wedding dress was placed on display at the John F. Kennedy Library; the famous pink suit Jackie wore in Dallas, still bearing the President's bloodstains, is stored at the National Archives in Washington.)

Dr. Walsh, who tried and failed to put his patient under at Bethesda, knocked on the door of Jackie's bedroom. He gave her 500 milligrams of another potent sleep-inducing drug, Amytal. Once again confident that she would soon pass out, Dr. Walsh bid her good night and departed. This time, Jackie began to feel the drug taking hold. Rather than surrender to it quite yet, she got up, walked into the hall, and knocked on her husband's bedroom door. "Uncle Hugh," she said softly, "I don't want to sleep alone." Since her own father, the notorious "Black Jack" Bouvier, had passed away six years before, Jackie and Hugh had grown close. Now he did not hesitate to do whatever he could to comfort her. Uncle Hugh lay down on the bed and, cradling her in his arms, rocked Jackie gently as she cried herself to sleep.

It had been the longest day of her life, and now she could hardly imagine beyond this moment. Jacqueline Bouvier Kennedy, the most celebrated First Lady America had ever known, was only thirty-four years old.

Those three years we spent in the White House were really the happiest time for us, the closest, and now it's all gone. Now there is nothing, nothing.

— *Jackie*

Worlds were closing in around her.

— *Clark Clifford,* friend

TWO

It all had been a dream, just a strange dream, Caroline thought as she climbed out of bed and grabbed the big stuffed giraffe Daddy had given her. The little girl in the pink pajamas raced down the hallway toward her father's room with John-John in hot pursuit. The President was almost always up by now, and would normally have consumed a big breakfast — soft-boiled eggs with bacon and toast, orange juice, and coffee — by the time Maud Shaw brought the children in to see him. They would jump into Daddy's arms, and then Caroline would switch on the television and sit on the floor, watching cartoons while the President read the papers. At 9 A.M. Jack LaLanne would come on, and the kids would do jumping jacks while Daddy, invariably near hysterics, clapped along.

Today the children were too excited to wait for Miss Shaw, so they bounded into Daddy's room on their own. Grandmother and Uncle Hugh, who had returned from Jackie's room, were propped up in bed, unable to sleep. The smile vanished from Caroline's face. Pushing the giraffe ahead of her — "sort of to ease her entrance," Janet Auchincloss recalled — she inched her way into the room. John-John followed, pulling a toy.

On the bed was a copy of *The New York Times* with JFK's black-bordered picture covering the entire front page.

"Who is that?" Caroline asked.

"Oh, Caroline," her grandmother replied sadly, "you know that's your daddy."

The little girl looked up. "He's dead, isn't he? A man shot him, didn't he?"

For once, Janet was speechless. "Her little face was so extraordinary," she said. "It's hard for Caroline to . . . she's a very, very affectionate little girl and she's a very thoughtful child. And I think that the behavior of both the children through the next days was a remarkable tribute to the way the President and Jackie had brought them up."

Pierre Salinger knew how Caroline felt. He had managed to doze off for about an hour when, at 7 A.M., the phone jangled him awake. "Mr. Salinger," said the White House operator, "the President is calling." "Thank God," he thought. "Jack." He allowed himself "one brief moment of joy" before the person on the other end spoke. "Pierre," said the caller, "this is Lyndon Johnson."

While LBJ was busy Saturday morning contacting all of JFK's assistants, advisors, and staff members with precisely the same heartfelt line — "Pierre/Kenny/Larry/ Evelyn/Sarge/Bobby, I need you more than he needed you" — Jackie put on the only black dress she owned.

There was to be a brief Mass for family and friends that morning at the White House. Father John J. Cavanaugh, a former president of Notre Dame University and a longtime Kennedy family friend, knocked on the door of Jackie's bedroom at 9:30 A.M. — just twenty hours after Jack was shot — and asked to hear her confession.

"Confession? What am I supposed to confess, Father?" she asked. Instead, she demanded to know how a caring God could "let something like this happen."

Then Maud Shaw brought in Caroline and John-John. It was the first time Jackie had seen them since their father's murder. She hugged each child, then took them by the hand and marched downstairs. She was directed, uncomprehending, to the small family dining room, where everyone was seated on folding wooden chairs. No, she said firmly, the Mass must be held with the casket in the East Room.

As each person picked up a chair and moved into the East Room, Jack's old Navy buddy Paul "Red" Fay approached Jack's widow. "She looked totally, completely devastated — in a complete daze," Fay recalled.

"There was nothing I could say. All I could do was put my arms around her and hug her. Then I went over behind this drape and cried my eyes out. She was an amazing woman. Her strength and sense of what was right and her dignity through the whole thing — she carried a lot of us who weren't as strong as she was . . ." Another friend and admirer of Jack's, journalist Theodore White, also choked back tears. "One mourned," he said, "for the gaiety, the elegance, the graces he and his lady had brought into this house."

Seeing the flag-draped sarcophagus for the first time, Caroline leaned over to Miss Shaw and asked how her father could possibly fit inside. "Daddy's too big for that," she said. "How's he lying? Are his knees under his chin?" She wanted to see her father one more time, but that was impossible: Jackie decreed that the coffin would remain closed while her husband lay in state, after Bill Walton said the undertaker had made JFK look "like a waxworks dummy — something you'd see at Madame Tussaud's."

When the ceremony in the East Room was over, Jackie walked over to the elevator that would take her upstairs to the family quarters. White House usher J. B. West was standing, ashen-faced, outside his office. Jackie went up and threw her arms around him. "*Poor* Mr. West," she said.

"I couldn't speak," West recalled. "It was all I could do to stand. I just held her for a moment."

A short time later, West walked Jackie over to the Oval Office for a final look. Johnson had already begun giving orders as President from temporary offices in the Executive Office Building next door to the White House. As soon as they returned to Washington, LBJ assured Jackie, "Honey, you stay in the White House as long as you like." Workmen had in fact begun crating the Kennedy family's belongings even before she returned from Dallas. At 9 A.M. Saturday they had begun moving the President's things out of the Oval Office — the paintings, the desk, his rocking chair. By noon, all that would remain were the two stark-white opposing sofas next to the fireplace.

But most of the furniture was still there when Jackie made her final, unannounced visit. "Evelyn Lincoln stood, bewildered, in the middle of the room," West said. Then Jackie, "eyes like saucers," memorized the Oval Office — "the walls, the desk we had found in the basement, the small pictures of Caroline and John — then she walked out of John F. Kennedy's office for the last time."

From there, they walked over to the Cabinet Room and sat down. "She searched my face," West said, "as if she might find the truth there."

"My children," Jackie said, "they're good children, aren't they, Mr. West?"

"They certainly are."

"They're not spoiled?"

"No, indeed."

Jackie stared into West's eyes. "Mr. West, will you be my friend for life?" West could only manage to nod.

Despite the Johnsons' eagerness to move into the White House, Jacqueline would remain at the Executive Mansion a full — and to Johnson, galling — eleven days. The wife of the last President to die in office, Eleanor Roosevelt, had left the White House the same day.

Jackie realized the next seventy-two hours would take all the energy she and those around her could muster. She told her own emotionally drained staff to "try and be strong — three days from now we'll all collapse." Following her own advice, the First Lady, who in three short years had left her own indelible stamp on the White House, busied herself with the funeral arrangements rather than focus on her own incalculable loss. She sat down at her desk and, pausing occasionally to take a drag on a Salem, dictated scores of memos to Mary Gallagher. No detail was too small to escape the Vassar-educated perfectionist's eye. She ordered sympathy cards and designed the black-bordered "In Memorium" Mass card with a

Jacques Lowe photo of Jack taken in 1959 as its centerpiece (the photo, which shows JFK in profile, would also be used on a number of commemorative stamps). She wrote out the inscription for the Mass card: "Dear God, Please take care of your servant, John Fitzgerald Kennedy."

She had been too upset to talk to the widow of J. D. Tippit, the Dallas patrolman shot and killed by Lee Harvey Oswald just forty-five minutes after the assassination. But Jackie did take the time to send Marie Tippit an inscribed photograph of the Kennedy family. "There is another bond we share," Jackie wrote. "We must remind our children all the time what brave men their fathers were."

Jackie asked her friend Bunny Mellon, wife of the philanthropist Paul Mellon and overseer of the White House Rose Garden, to arrange the flowers on the President's grave. She went through her husband's things and culled mementos for her husband's friends to remember him by — a leather cigar case with the JFK monogram for the stogie-chomping Salinger, Navy dog tags to Cardinal Cushing, a favorite kelly green tie to Kenny O'Donnell — and dashed off a personal note to accompany each item.

Jack's belongings were being moved out of the Oval Office when Jackie remembered that a month earlier he had promised to give his desk phone to the Army Signal Corps of Fort Monmouth, New Jersey, because he had used it to inaugurate the Army's Syncom satellite. She asked that the phone be sent to Fort Monmouth immediately.

Jackie even found the time to write a highly personal note to her husband's opponent in the hard-fought 1960 presidential campaign, Richard Nixon. In it, she basically told Nixon, who had actually been friends with Jack when the two men served in the Senate, to be thankful that he hadn't won. "You two young men — colleagues in Congress — adversaries in 1960 — and look what happened," she wrote. "Whoever thought such a hideous thing could happen in this country. I know how you must feel — so closely missing the greatest prize. And now for you the question comes up again — and you must commit all your and your family's hopes and efforts again. Just one thing I would say to you — if it does not work out as you have hoped for so long, please be consoled by what you already have — your life and your family.

"We never value life enough when we have it," she went on in her letter to Nixon, "and I would not have had Jack live his life any other way, though I know his death could have been prevented and I will never cease to torture myself with that . . . But

. . . please think of all that you have."

In turn, Jackie was moved by the letters Lyndon Johnson had written to her children the night before. "It will be many years before you understand fully what a great man your father was," the new President wrote to JFK's not-yet-three-year-old son. "His loss is a deep personal tragedy for all of us, but I wanted you particularly to know that I share your grief — You can always be proud of him."

To Caroline, he scrawled, "Your father's death has been a great tragedy for the Nation, as well as for you, and I wanted you to know how much my thoughts are of you at this time. He was a wise and devoted man. You can always be proud of what he did for his country. Affectionately, Lyndon B. Johnson."

Now Jackie wanted her children to do the same for their father. "You must write a letter to Daddy now," she instructed Caroline, "and tell him how much you love him."

"DEAR DADDY," Caroline printed in large block letters, "WE ARE ALL GOING TO MISS YOU. DADDY, I LOVE YOU VERY MUCH, CAROLINE." John scrawled an *X* on his sister's letter.

Her own remarkable stamina notwithstanding, none of this could have been accomplished without the pharmaceuticals supplied by Dr. Max Jacobson. "Dr. Feelgood," as Jacobson came to be known, already had a patient list that included Yul Brynner, Eddie Fisher, Alan Jay Lerner, Zero Mostel, Johnny Mathis, and Winston Churchill, among others. Jacobson began injecting Jack with amphetamine "cocktails" (mostly Dexedrine) before the televised Kennedy-Nixon debates of 1960, just to give him an edge against his formidable Republican opponent. Throughout JFK's presidency, both the President and the First Lady (along with several key members of the administration) relied on Jacobson's shots of what is commonly known as speed to get through a variety of stressful situations — including the Bay of Pigs Invasion, the Steel Crisis, the disastrous summit with Soviet Chairman Nikita Khrushchev in Vienna, the mobilization of the National Guard to desegregate the University of Mississippi, the triumphant visits to Paris and Berlin, and the Cuban Missile Crisis.

JFK's longtime friend Chuck Spalding recalled that Jacobson was "a strange man — a mad scientist type." He also said that initially Jacobson's shots made him feel "wonderful, full of energy — capable of doing just about anything. I didn't know exactly what he was giving me, but it was a magic potion as far as I was concerned." Spalding would soon learn on his own that, in addition to imbuing the user with a sense of power and well-being, these stimulants were highly addictive. They could also lead to depression and even trigger symptoms of paranoid schizophrenia.

Amphetamines were not the only dangerous drug in Dr. Max's arsenal. At Bobby Kennedy's insistence, the Food and Drug Administration analyzed fifteen vials of the substance routinely being injected into the veins of the President and the First Lady. FDA scientists determined that the mixture contained not only speed, but substantial quantities of steroids as well. Given what was known at the time, neither of these perfectly legal drugs was judged to be either addictive or harmful.

Yet at the time of her husband's death, both the President and the First Lady were, unknowingly, addicted to speed. "I don't think Jackie could have made it through that week without it," Spalding conceded. And what of the steroids? It would be decades before the medical community established that steroids — particularly the kind used back then — were carcinogenic. Yet, commonly, the cancer itself might not surface for as long as thirty years. Among the types of cancer linked to steroid use: lymphoma.

Blissfully unaware of the possible long-term cost, many of Jacobson's patients found themselves coping with the tragedy in Dallas by popping two or three times their usual number of "pep" pills. When it became evident that the sedative Pat Lawford had taken before boarding her flight from L.A. to Washington was not working, a friend handed her one of Jacobson's favorite pills. Don Weis, who gave JFK's sister the pill, remembered that "she got very happy on it. It was shocking. She acted silly. It was not the trip back you would expect from Pat Lawford. But it wasn't her fault. I gave her the pill."

Jacobson himself flew directly to Washington from New York as soon as he heard the news. As they had dozens of times before, Secret Service agents ushered Dr. Feelgood directly to the family quarters as soon as he arrived. Jackie rolled up the sleeve of her black mourning dress at the White House and averted her eyes from the needle as Jacobson injected the potent upper into her veins.

"Jackie was crushed, as we all were," said Spalding. It was Spalding who introduced Jack to Jacobson in 1960. "She had also been unable to sleep and was just wrung out, totally exhausted. There was no way she could have done all that she had to do in those days after the assassination *without* those shots from Dr. Max. No way." For the next few days, Jacobson remained in the shadows, discreetly within reach of the grieving widow.

That Saturday night, Dr. Walsh added to the mix by giving Jackie a double dose of Amytal. It could not, however, fully counteract the effects of the amphetamines she had been given. So Jackie stayed up all night at the small writing desk in her room, scribbling a rambling letter to her husband. It was dawn before she finished pouring out her heart, and the letter, which now stretched to five pages, was drenched in her tears. Jackie folded the letter, placed it in an envelope, and sealed it.

Bobby had shown little emotion thus far. He was, Ben Bradlee observed, "almost catatonic, glued to Jackie's side, as he was to be for the next days." Yet at one point a family friend, Milt Ebbins, saw Bobby go up to the coffin, throw his arms around it, and begin talking to his dead brother. "It broke my heart," Ebbins said.

The next day Jackie, with Bobby at her side, went to the East Room. Before the casket was moved to the Capitol Rotunda, where more than a quarter million mourners would come to pay their last respects, Mrs. Kennedy needed to see Mr. Kennedy one last time. The Honor Guard representing each of the four armed services — the Army, Navy, Marines, and Air Force — was marched to the far end of the room and the soldiers ordered to look away as General

Godfrey McHugh unlatched the coffin and slowly lifted the heavy lid. Jack was dressed in the clothes Dave Powers had picked out for him — a blue-gray single-breasted suit, black shoes, white shirt with a subtle JFK monogram on the cuff, and a blue tie with small white polka dots. A handkerchief was tucked neatly into his breast pocket. A rosary had been placed in his folded hands.

Jackie hated the way he looked. In an effort to make the President presentable, even "if the casket were opened a thousand years from now," the overzealous undertaker had gone too far. The late President's face was a mask of pancake, rouge, and lipstick. He looked like a mannequin.

Jackie stood and placed the letters she and the children had written into the coffin, along with a pair of gold cuff links she had given him and a favorite piece of scrimshaw — the presidential seal carved on a whale's tooth — which had also been a present from Jackie. To this Bobby added a silver rosary that had been a gift from Ethel, the gold PT-109 tie clip Jack had given him, and a clip of his own hair. Someone brought a pair of scissors, and Jackie carefully cut off a lock of her husband's hair. Then she turned to Bobby. "It isn't Jack," she said. *"It isn't Jack."*

As the coffin lid came down for one final time, Bobby and Jackie were oblivious to the fact that millions of their countrymen sat glued to their television sets, mouths agape. They had just seen Dallas nightclub owner Jack Ruby lurch forward and shoot Lee Harvey Oswald in the basement of the Dallas County Jail.

"Just one more awful thing," Jackie later said when Bobby told her the news. Her brother-in-law did not tell her that Ruby claimed he had killed Oswald to avenge the Kennedy children and to spare Jackie from having to relive those horrible moments at Oswald's murder trial. Strangely, in Chicago, where he was a small-time operator with underworld connections, Ruby was known to have despised Jack Kennedy. How Ruby used his cozy relationship with Dallas cops to gain access to the basement was already being debated. What the public was not told about at the time was the presence of another unidentified man who leapt on Oswald's chest and began giving him coronary pulmonary resuscitation — the worst possible kind of treatment for abdominal injuries. While Oswald gasped and screamed, the stranger literally pumped the lifeblood out of him through his punctured aorta.

The millions of families sitting dazed before their black-and-white television sets watched the drama of two Americas unfold — one as sacred as the other was profane. Ten minutes after Oswald was pronounced dead, Jackie leaned over and said softly to her daughter, "We're going to say good-bye to Daddy now, and we're going to kiss him good-bye, and tell Daddy how much we love him and how much we'll always miss him." Then they walked up to the catafalque, silently knelt, and in a gesture that would unleash what was left of America's tears, took the flag that covered the coffin in their gloved hands and tenderly kissed it.

For these days, so fraught with emotion, the eyes of the nation would be riveted on the beautiful widow and her equally beautiful children. Jackie wore the only black dress she owned — the same one she'd worn the night he announced his presidential candidacy — but she wanted Caroline and John-John to *look* their age as much as possible and not like miniature adults. Toward that end, she dressed them in powder blue children's coats and red shoes instead of somber mourning attire. "It was wise not to put them in dark clothes and hats," Jackie's mother said. "They looked and behaved perfectly naturally, not like some wind-up dolls. That's what Jackie wanted."

Later that day, Jackie's younger sister, Lee, arrived from London with her husband, Prince Stanislas Radziwill. When JFK's closest friend, Lemoyne "Lem" Billings, told her it was nice that she could make it, Lee exploded, "How can you say that? Did you think I *wouldn't?*" For his part, Stas (pronounced "Stash") Radziwill looked around and said the White House looked like "Versailles after the King had died."

Notwithstanding Billings's innocent welcoming remark to Lee, eyes justifiably widened when Aristotle Onassis showed up at the White House less than forty-eight hours after JFK's assassination. It was because of the Greek shipping magnate that Jackie had accompanied her husband to Dallas in the first place, and his presence in their midst now offended several Kennedy intimates.

After the death of Patrick, Lee had been looking for ways to buoy her sister's spirits, and Onassis had invited them both on an Aegean cruise aboard his luxurious 325-foot-yacht, *Christina*. The opera diva Maria Callas had been Ari's lover for years, but now Lee was rumored to have set her sights on the Greek tycoon. JFK, who knew Onassis and disliked him, suspected his sister-in-law was just trying to impress Ari by delivering America's First Lady as a shipboard companion.

"Lee had a sort of romance going with Onassis," Evelyn Lincoln said. "At first Jack didn't like the idea [of Jackie going along on the *Christina*] but then he thought maybe it would do her some good."

When their Aegean idyll ended, Ari presented Jackie with a magnificent diamond-

and-ruby necklace that could be converted into two bracelets. Lee wrote to Jack with a tongue-in-cheek complaint about the special attention Ari was showing Jackie. "Ari has showered Jackie with so many presents I can't stand it. All I've got is three dinky little bracelets that Caroline wouldn't even wear to her own birthday party."

"Onassis fell for Jackie," Lincoln said, "and then it turned out that he became more than just a friend." Lincoln believed Jackie and Ari had started an affair during that first cruise after Patrick's death. "I think so, yes. Jackie loved money. Ari had money. That might have been what she saw in him. And she didn't like President Kennedy's political friends. She didn't like that kind of life."

At a dinner party with the Bradlees shortly after her return, Jackie apologized for the negative publicity her cruise aboard the notorious Onassis yacht created. With an eye toward a second term in the White House, Jack told her that Ari would not be welcome to return to the United States until after the 1964 elections.

Kennedy had also exploited Jackie's residual guilt feelings over Ari. Always resentful of Jack's political "Irish Mafia" (or "Murphia," as she sometimes called it), the President's wife had all but refused to campaign with him. At the same time, she did not hesitate to make thirteen trips to such foreign locales as France, England, Italy, Austria, India, Pakistan, and several Latin American countries. This time, she agreed to accompany her husband to Dallas. "You know how I hate that sort of thing," she told Tuckerman. "But if he wants me there, then that's all that matters. It's a tiny sacrifice on my part."

"Jackie must have felt very guilty," said Clare Boothe Luce, who had been a close friend of Joe Kennedy. "Everyone knew how much she hated going out on the campaign trail with Jack." Concurred Kenny O'Donnell: "I almost fell over when he told me Jackie was coming with us."

Now, on the eve of her husband's state funeral, Jackie drew Onassis to her side — or at least as close to her side as she could without alienating Bobby. While Jackie dined with Bobby and Lee in the West Sitting Room, Ari joined the Lawfords, the Shrivers, Secretary of Defense McNamara, Dave Powers, and a handful of others in the family dining room.

He was aware that Irish wakes could be raucous affairs, but even the fun-loving Ari was astonished at the mood inside the White House. In fact, the Kennedys had begun resorting to their celebrated horseplay the day before. Just a few hours after Jack's body was brought back to the White House to lie in state, somebody snatched the blond wig off Ethel Kennedy's head and tossed it from one guest to the next until it landed on McNamara's balding pate.

Powers, always regarded as JFK's resident court jester, had been so close to the President that he took nude dips with the leader of the Free World every day in the White House pool. Now he kept up everyone's spirits with stories of the early days campaigning in Boston. "For the first time," Bradlee said, "even Jackie laughed."

"You'd never know there was a funeral," said Milt Ebbins, who dined in the White House that Saturday, Sunday, and Monday. "Jokes were being told at the table. Ethel was very funny. I tried to tell Pat [Lawford] about seeing Bobby crying in the East Room and she curtly cut me off — 'We don't want to hear about that.' "

Pat's husband, Peter Lawford, was also taken aback at first. "Everybody was up," he recalled, "drinking and smiling and trying to make the best of it." They even kidded each other about all the mourning coats and black veils they were now forced to buy. "Not being Irish," Lawford said, "I tried to get in the swing of it, but I was thoroughly destroyed. Looking back, I realize the way President Kennedy's death was handled was really the best way, even with the bad jokes. I think John F. would have looked on too much grief as unproductive."

"The average American was at home crying in his mashed potatoes," one Secret Service agent observed, "but inside the White House that night it was party time." According to Lem Billings, "when Onassis arrived we all piled into a sports car and raced to Arlington, and later we all laughed and sang and carried on with great hilarity back to the White House."

There, the French wine and Scotch whiskey flowed as those dearest to Jack tried to top one another's stories about their fallen leader. Ted, understandably drunk, led everyone in several choruses of "That Old Gang of Mine" and "When Irish Eyes Are Smiling."

Onassis inadvertently provided the entertainment for the remainder of the evening. After Bobby joined the rest of the family for coffee, they all began needling Ari about his ostentatious lifestyle and his mysterious past. Then the Attorney General of the United States abruptly disappeared. He returned with a contract stipulating that half the Onassis fortune would be donated to the poor people of Latin America. After all, Bobby pointed out, it was in Argentina that Ari made his first million. Onassis went along, and with a flourish signed the ersatz document in Greek. It would be four years before the press learned that Onassis was in

Washington for the funeral, much less inside the White House as the grieving widow's personal guest.

Jackie was not particularly fond of the Kennedy women — she called Jack's boisterous sisters the "Rah-Rah Girls" — and she had a particular disdain for in-law Ethel, whom she chided for being "more Kennedy than thou." But Jackie also understood that their jubilant behavior, which on the surface seemed shockingly inappropriate, was in direct proportion to the depth of their grief.

"It's a very Irish thing," said Chuck Spalding, who also slept over at the White House that night. "They make bad jokes and drink too much just to keep from going crazy. It's how they cope. Jack had lost so many of the important people in his life — his brother Joe, his sister Kathleen, little Patrick — he knew better than anyone how important it is to laugh at times like these. Now, Jackie was a completely different type. It didn't come naturally to her, but she understood the whole Irish thing and tried to be a part of it."

Bradlee remembers Jackie as being "extraordinary" that evening. "Sometimes she seemed completely detached, as if she were someone else watching the ceremony of that other person's grief. Sometimes she was silent, obviously torn. Often she would turn to a friend and reminisce, and everyone would join in with their remembrance of things forever past."

Periodically, she would wander into another room and stare at the endless television coverage of the funeral. Lawford remembered how "odd it was to watch her face as she watched herself marching behind the President's coffin on television." Later, Jackie would confide to a friend that "it all seemed like it was happening to somebody else."

Although Jackie was also half Irish — Janet's dirt-poor grandparents had emigrated to the United States during the potato famine — she was definitely a Bouvier in temperament. In the midst of all the revelry, Jackie told Bobby she wanted to return to the Capitol Rotunda. At about 9 P.M., they walked in so quietly that the thousands of mourners filing silently past the coffin were at first oblivious to their presence. Jackie again knelt beside the coffin for a few minutes, and, once again, pressed her lips to the flag.

The night had turned cold, and Jackie was not wearing a coat. Bobby led her toward their waiting limousine, but Jackie pulled away. "Let me walk, let me walk," she said. They had gone only a short distance in the darkness when a woman came up and threw her arms around Jackie. They hugged for a few moments, never saying a word to each other. Then Jackie stopped to talk to a group of nuns waiting to pay their respects. Only then did the rest of the crowd begin to realize that JFK's widow was in their midst. Responding to pleas from the justifiably concerned Secret Service agents, Jackie finally returned to the car.

Jackie returned to the White House and promptly decreed that Lee would sleep with her and assigned Stas Radziwill to the President's room. Lee's husband wound up dozing on a cot at the end of the mammoth four-poster; unlike the Auchinclosses, he could not bring himself to sleep in JFK's bed.

She was so distracted by the week's momentous events that it was only at the last minute Maud Shaw realized that Monday, the day of his father's funeral, was also John-John's third birthday. Caroline turned six two days later, and it had been agreed there would be a joint birthday midway between the two dates. But over breakfast that Monday, Caroline and the nanny sang "Happy Birthday to You" to young John and handed him two presents — a children's book from Miss Shaw and a toy helicopter from his sister.

By now almost anyone else would have collapsed under the strain, but Jackie was propelled forward by an abiding sense of duty to Jack's memory. "She felt he should be in the pantheon of great leaders, alongside Lincoln and FDR," Theodore White said, "and the state funeral was an important step in that direction."

Indeed, no one was more keenly attuned to the importance of appearances than Jackie. It was Jackie who, by kicking off her shoes during the West Virginia primaries and speaking flawless Spanish to Puerto Rican immigrants in New York, had helped win the presidency for her husband. Moreover, she had single-handedly transformed the White House interior — Jackie described it upon her arrival as looking like, among other things, "a cheap hotel" — into a showcase of American period furnishings.

She also set the tone of the Kennedy administration by celebrating culture to an unprecedented degree. Stars of the Metropolitan Opera, Shakespearean actors, and the greatest classical artists of the time were invited to perform for visiting heads of state. In their short time in the White House, Jack and Jackie hosted no fewer than sixty-six state dinners and receptions. And with her elaborate bouffant coifs and shimmering haute couture gowns, no one had had a greater impact on fashion in the 1960s than Jackie. That impact extended beyond U.S. borders: From Paris to New Delhi, millions poured into the streets to cheer the American First Lady.

Relying on her own finely honed sense of style and showmanship, she had created an American Versailles and taken it on the road. If Jack's state funeral was to be the grand finale, then Jackie wanted it to reflect the pomp, grandeur, and glamour that had characterized their reign in the White House.

There was also a desire to impress on the American people the magnitude of the nation's loss. "She deeply believed, as a lot of us did, that her husband was a great man, and that he was on the verge of doing truly great things for the country and for the world," Arthur Schlesinger said. Jackie wanted to mark a fitting end to the era. "There will be other great presidents," she said. "But things will never be the same."

On Monday morning, the caisson that had carried FDR's coffin was drawn by three pairs of matched gray horses from the White House to St. Matthews Cathedral. Following close behind was the traditional "riderless horse," named Black Jack (coincidentally, the moniker that had long ago been bestowed on Jackie's father, "Black Jack" Bouvier).

To the eerie, unforgettable cadence of muffled drums, Jackie and the family walked behind the coffin as it made its way up 17th

Street. They were followed by a cortege that included 220 representatives from 102 nations, including French President Charles De Gaulle, Ethiopian Emperor Haile Selassie, West German Chancellor Ludwig Erhard, Britain's Prince Philip, Irish President Eamon de Valera, Israel's Foreign Minister Golda Meir, and Soviet Deputy Premier Anastas Mikoyan.

Inside the cathedral, Cardinal Cushing was conducting the Mass in Latin when suddenly he surprised himself and everyone else by switching to English. "May the angels, dear Jack, lead you into Paradise," the Cardinal intoned in the unmistakable gravelly voice he himself once described as "death warmed over." Cushing continued, his voice breaking, "May the martyrs receive you at your coming. May the spirit of God embrace you, and mayest thou, with all those who made the supreme sacrifice of dying for others, receive eternal rest and peace. Amen."

The impact was immediate and dramatic. Jackie broke down and began to sob uncontrollably. "You'll be all right, Mommy, don't cry," Caroline said, reaching up to wipe away her mother's tears. "I'll take care of you." With that, Jackie regained her composure.

"Caroline — she held my hand like a soldier," Jackie said a few days later. "She's my helper. She's mine now . . . But John-John is going to belong to the men now. Caroline asked me, what kind of prayer should I say? And I told her to say either 'Please, God, take care of Daddy' or 'Please, God, be nice to Daddy.' "

The most heart-tugging moment for the American people came as the family stood outside the cathedral, watching the flag-draped coffin leave for the final journey to Arlington. One month earlier, John-John had marched into Caroline's catechism class with a stick on his shoulder. "He thinks he's a soldier," Caroline had said, "and he doesn't even know how to salute."

Today, mimicking the real soldiers he saw all around him, John-John snapped to attention and, arm at precisely the right angle, snapped off a salute that melted the hearts of millions. "Like everyone else I cried when I saw him standing there saluting his father's coffin," said Caroline's religion teacher, Sister Joanne Frey. "It was a *perfect* salute."

The three-mile-long procession slowly made its way across the Potomac to the grave site. Ironically, only six months earlier JFK had visited Arlington and strolled on the grass just below the Custis-Lee Mansion, where Robert E. Lee once lived. JFK and his daughter marveled at the view. "I could stay here," he said then, "forever."

As taps played, General De Gaulle and

Haile Selassie saluted the coffin. A formation of fifty jet fighters roared overhead, followed by *Air Force One*, which dipped its wings in a final salute. While the Marine Band played the Navy hymn, the pallbearers ceremoniously folded the flag that had covered the coffin into the familiar, neat triangle. "Mrs. Kennedy," said Arlington Superintendent Jack Metzler, "this flag is presented to you in the name of a most mournful nation." Jackie took the flag and clutched it to her. Metzler could see that, behind the veil, her eyes were welling with tears.

One more significant gesture remained. Jackie had been so impressed by the eternal flame that burned at Paris's Arc de Triomphe in honor of the Unknown Soldier that she wanted one for Jack's grave. Now someone handed her a taper. She leaned over and held the flame to the wick, igniting it. Jackie passed the candle to Bobby, who repeated the ritual before handing it to Teddy in turn. Standing a few feet away, Cardinal Cushing kept asking himself, "How could this happen in the United States? Why? Why? Why?"

It was over. "The funny thing is," Spalding said, "Jack would probably have hated the whole thing. He would have thought it was all just too much. There was a great fatalistic streak in him, you know, a feeling that when you're dead you're dead and let's not make a big deal out of it. But he would have been in awe of Jackie for pulling it all off."

She probably could not have seen it to the end had it not been for Bobby's constant presence at her side. "Through it all Bobby was a rock," recalled Letitia "Tish" Baldridge, Jackie's previous White House Social Secretary. Within hours of the assassination, Baldridge had flown in from her new home in Chicago to help Sargent Shriver arrange the funeral. "During that time Bobby held everyone together in the family quarters. Jackie was incredibly strong, but she couldn't have made it through those horrible days without Bobby. There were times when she looked terribly lost, and he would take her arm and steer her in the right direction, whispering in her ear. His strength and gentleness were superhuman."

After the funeral, Jackie returned to the White House and stood in a receiving line while more than two hundred foreign dignitaries filed past. "How can she stand to do this?" White House photographer Cecil Stoughton asked himself. Still, according to John Kenneth Galbraith, who was then Ambassador to India, Jackie looked far from distraught. "She was," he said, "in perfect control as usual."

Jackie wanted to use the occasion to try

and perform some diplomatic miracles of her own. Franco-American relations had been strained to the limit by the imperious De Gaulle, who cared more for Madame Kennedy than he did for her husband. Jackie, who had such long-standing affection for the General that she named her poodle "Gaullie" after him, nevertheless did not want to give him the satisfaction of knowing that she preferred the French Impressionists to all other painters. Before the funeral, she had instructed White House Curator James Ketchum to replace the Cézannes hanging in the upstairs Yellow Oval Room with prints of Philadelphia, Baltimore, and Washington. "I want President De Gaulle to be aware of the heritage of the United States."

Greeting De Gaulle warmly, she took the General aside and told him that Jack might have been frustrated but "was never bitter" about France's independent foreign policy. "Come," she then said, taking De Gaulle by the hand, "let me show you where your beautiful commode is." A vase brimming with fresh flowers sat atop the antique chest of drawers, and Jackie handed one, a daisy, to the French president. "I want you to take this as a last remembrance of the President," she said, and the General, holding the flower and looking quite confused, departed.

JFK's widow then turned her attention to the Russians. She asked Soviet Deputy Premier Mikoyan to tell Khrushchev that "he and my husband worked together for a peaceful world, and now he and you must carry on my husband's work."

Leaving nothing so important to chance, a week later Jackie sat down and wrote directly to the Soviet Chairman, explaining that she had tried to give Mikoyan a message

but as it was such a terrible day for me, I do not know if my words came out as I meant them to . . .

So now, in one of the last nights I will spend in the White House, in one of the last letters I will write on this paper at the White House, I would like to write you my message.

You and he were adversaries, but you were allied in a determination that the world should not be blown up. You respected each other and could deal with each other. I know that President Johnson will make every effort to establish the same relationship with you.

The danger that troubled my husband was that war might not be started so much by the big men as by the little ones.

While big men know the needs for self-control and restraint — little men are sometimes moved more by fear and pride. If only in the future the big men can continue to make the little ones sit down and talk, before they start to fight . . .

I send this letter because I know so deeply of the importance of the relationship which existed between you and my husband, and also because of your kindness, and that of Mrs. Khrushchev in Vienna. I read that she had tears in her eyes when she left the American Embassy in Moscow, after signing the book of mourning. Please thank her for that.

While her mother charmed the unprecedented assemblage of world leaders at the White House, Caroline's religion teacher, Sister Joanne Frey, was preparing for the afternoon class. "I was told by the White House that there would be a class," Sister Joanne said, "but of course that Caroline would not be there." Then, without warning, "in walked Caroline and a Secret Service man. Caroline was wearing a little trench coat."

"Sister, I know I'm early," Caroline said apologetically, "but we were just riding around and we didn't have any place to go."

Caroline looked so lost and alone, even with the hulking Secret Service agent standing in the doorway. "Oh, I'm glad you're here," Sister Joanne replied. "I have so many things to do to get the class ready — you can help me!"

As Caroline began to take off her trench coat, her teacher caught sight of a large medal hanging around her neck. Suddenly Caroline closed the coat. "I've got something to show you," she said, and then with a flourish opened her coat again to show Sister Joanne the medal.

"Oh, that's very, very nice, Caroline," the Sister said.

Then, very matter-of-factly, Caroline said, "Haile Selassie gave it to me."

"Can you imagine?" Sister Joanne said. " 'Haile Selassie gave it to me' — just as casually as that."

Then Caroline pulled out her religion book. "My mommy had lots of things to do, and I know I'm not supposed to, but she told me I could go ahead a few pages and work in my religion book. I'm sorry. Everybody else was so busy. I just needed something to do."

"Of course it's fine, Caroline," Sister Joanne said. The nun was moved by how alone the little girl seemed, but she was also struck by the activity her mother had chosen to keep her busy. "Here it was the day of the President's funeral — her husband's funeral — and Jackie could have told Caroline to do anything. But she wants Caroline to do something involving religion. It really says a lot about the woman, and how much she cared about the kind of people her children would become." During that year, Caroline missed only one week of religion class.

Later that same day, there was a small party celebrating John-John's birthday in the family dining room. There was a little table piled high with packages, ice cream, and a cake with three candles on it. With his sister's help, John-John blew out the candles, and then he proceeded to tear the brightly colored wrapping paper off gift after gift.

Dave Powers led everyone in a cappella renditions of "That Old Gang of Mine" and "Heart of My Heart," and, as Jamie Auchincloss recalled, "everyone's emotions were strained to the very limit." For Bobby, hearing "Heart of My Heart," one of Jack's favorite tunes, was unbearable. He fled the room.

At one point in the festivities, Jackie and Rose were having coffee in the Yellow Oval Room when Caroline ran up to her mother. "Mommy," she asked, "did they love Daddy?"

"Oh, yes. They did love Daddy," Jackie replied.

"No, Mommy," Caroline objected, shaking her head. "They couldn't have loved Daddy. If they had loved him, they wouldn't have done what they did to him."

Jackie could think of nothing to say. Then Caroline, looking concerned, asked, "Mommy, do they love you?"

It was obvious the question had been preying on the little girl's mind. "Well, I think so, at least some," Jackie said. Seeing the look of confusion on her daughter's face, Jackie continued, "Maybe I should have told you that not everybody loved Dad. Many more loved Daddy than loved me. But I think some of them love me, too."

Caroline still looked less than satisfied with the answers she was getting. "After all," Jackie said, "not everybody loved Jesus, did they?" That was enough for the little girl, and she scampered back to the party.

Shortly before midnight, Jackie grabbed a bunch of lilies from a hall table and went with Bobby to Arlington. There, with the Attorney General kneeling at her side, she carefully placed the flowers on her husband's fresh grave. Then Bobby took her hand in his, and together they walked across the wet grass into the still, cold night.

Jack was the love of my life. No one will ever know a big part of me died with him.

— *Jackie*

She had performed flawlessly, superbly. I know now she wanted to cry, and she could not.

— *Theodore H. White*

I feel like a wounded animal. What I really want to do is crawl into a corner and hide.

— *Jackie*

THREE

Four days after she held what was left of her husband's head in her lap, Jackie invited Lady Bird Johnson to the White House for tea. "Some of the happiest years of my marriage have been spent here," she told the new First Lady. "You will be happy here."

That same day, the former First Lady made an appearance in the East Room to stand beside the new President as he addressed Latin American leaders. LBJ wanted to reassure them that he intended to continue Kennedy's firm anti-Communist policies in the region — something they were eager to hear now that Lee Harvey Oswald was widely being described as a pro-Castro Communist.

Although she once broke up her husband by calling the Johnsons "Colonel Cornpone and his little pork chop," Jackie now felt a genuine affection for them. After LBJ's speech in the East Room, Jackie returned to her quarters and wrote a letter to Johnson thanking him for "walking yesterday — behind Jack" during the funeral procession.

You did not have to do that. I am

sure many people forbade you to take such a risk, but you did it anyway . . . Thank you for your letters to my children. What those letters will mean to them later you can imagine.

It was strange last night. I was wandering through this house. It was the night after the funeral . . . Late last night, a moving man asked me if I wanted Jack's ship pictures left on the wall for you. They were clearing the office for you. I said no because I remembered all the fun Jack had those first days hanging the pictures of things he liked, setting out his collection of whale's teeth . . . I thought you would want to put things from Texas in it. I picture some gleaming longhorns. I hope you put them somewhere. It cannot be very much help to you your first day in office to hear children out on the lawn at recess. It is one more example of your kindness that you let them stay. I promise they will be gone soon. Thank you Mr. President.

Two days later she would call to personally wish LBJ a happy Thanksgiving. Given all she had gone through the previous week, LBJ was deeply moved by the call. He was also unnerved by the fact that she insisted on calling him "Mr. President" — a formality that sounded unnatural coming from her.

"Dear Jackie," Johnson wrote back. "How could you possibly have found that extra moment — that extra ounce of strength — to call me . . . You have been magnificent and have won a warm place in the heart of history."

Perhaps. But as willing as she now was to ease the transition by visibly supporting the new Chief Executive, Jackie soon made it clear she would do so on her own terms. "I will tell you one thing," she told Charles Bartlett. "They will never drag me out like a little old widow like they did Mrs. Wilson when President Wilson died. I will never be used that way."

In the days after the funeral, Jackie continued to astound everyone with her take-charge attitude. This was particularly true in the family quarters, where Mary Gallagher described the atmosphere as "sheer bedlam." Even before JFK's body was brought back to the White House, books, furniture, toys, and other household items had been packed away in wooden crates.

Now Jackie — unwilling to turn over the job to anyone else — took upon herself the heartbreaking task of sifting through Jack's personal effects and files. (His presidential papers, ultimately bound for the John F. Kennedy Memorial Library in Boston, were warehoused separately.) "It's so much easier

101

doing it while you're here," she told her secretary, "than at night when I'm alone. I just drown my sorrows in vodka."

With the help of Gallagher, Provi the maid, and Jack's valet, George Thomas, she pulled suits and ties from closets, cleaned out cabinets, and combed through dresser drawers. At times, she would hold something — his razor, a shoe — and stare off into the distance, lost in her own thoughts. More than once, she buried her face in one of his shirts and rocked back and forth, beyond consolation.

"Why did Jack have to die so young?" she asked Gallagher. "Even when you're sixty, you like to know your husband is there. It's so hard for the children. Please, Mary, don't ever leave. Get yourself fixed for salary on my government appropriation — just don't leave me!"

She reached out to old friends — for practical advice at first — but these conversations invariably turned morose. There was, recalled Washington power broker and confidant Clark Clifford, "an unutterable loneliness descending on her."

Still, she was not yet ready to surrender completely to her grief. There simply remained too much to do, and an astonishingly short amount of time in which to do it. Jackie and the children flew to Hyannis Port to spend Thanksgiving with the rest of the Kennedy clan. Arriving with the folded flag that had covered Jack's casket, Jackie went straight to her father-in-law's room.

"He was in bed," recalled Secret Service agent Ham Brown, "and even given the horrible circumstances, he smiled when Jackie entered the room. He and Jackie were buddies."

To be sure, during her courtship with Jack, Jackie had made winning over the old man her first order of business. She had embodied all the traits that so aggravated the rough-and-tumble "Rah-Rah Girls" — her supposedly aristocratic French pedigree; her days at Miss Porter's School, Vassar, and the Sorbonne; her family ties to the blue-blooded Auchinclosses. She was easily the most intelligent and polished of Jack's girlfriends, but what charmed Joe Sr. most was Jackie's cutting wit. Of all the beautiful young women Jack had brought home, Jackie had been the only one with guts enough to talk back to the clan's intimidating chieftain. "A girl with a mind of her own," Joe beamed, "just like us."

Even before she officially became his daughter-in-law, Jackie commanded Joe's attention to an extent that no other woman — not even Rose — did. While Jack and his brothers and sisters roughhoused on the lawn, played football, or sailed, Joe and

Jackie sat on the porch at Hyannis "talking about everything," she recalled, "from classical music to the movies . . . He never got angry with me for talking straight to him; on the contrary, he seemed to enjoy it." When Jack's rampant infidelities brought them to the brink of divorce in 1955, it was Joe who paid Jackie $1 million in cash to give his philandering son another chance.

On Thanksgiving Day of all days, Jackie now sat with Joe and, as she had always done, gave it to him straight. "They stayed in that room talking for about an hour," Secret Service agent Ham Brown said. Just as they had the previous Sunday, when Eunice and Ted first broke the news to their father, "everybody in the hall was sobbing. Tears everywhere. Secretaries, nurses, Secret Service agents. We were all a mess. When Jackie opened the door to leave, I looked inside and there was this sad, sad sight of Joe just sitting upright in bed, the triangle of flag still in his lap."

Later, Joe fell asleep and someone, reaching for a blanket in the dark, unfolded the flag and spread it over him. When he woke up at 3 A.M., Joe looked down at the flag and cried out for help. "He thought," said one of the agents, "that he was the one lying in state."

One task was too painful even for Jackie.

As she told Ken O'Donnell and Dave Powers on *Air Force One* on the return trip from Dallas, Jackie wanted her son Patrick, who had lived just forty hours, to join Jack at Arlington. She also wanted their unnamed baby girl, who had arrived stillborn in 1956, to be reburied at Arlington.

At her daughter's request, Janet Auchincloss set out to unite both babies with their slain father. Accompanied by Cardinal Cushing and Father Hillary of the Portsmouth Priory, Janet first went to the Kennedy family plot in Brookline, Massachusetts. There the two prelates performed the Catholic rites over the body of Patrick as he was disinterred.

Then they flew to Newport, Rhode Island, to pick up the body of the little girl. Again, Cushing and Father Hillary performed the necessary rites of the Church as the casket was lifted from the ground. To avoid creating a circus atmosphere, everything had been done in total secrecy. But when it looked as if the press might get wind of Janet's mission, the schedule was moved up a day.

At Quonset, Rhode Island, the tiny white coffins were loaded on to the *Caroline*, the Kennedy family DC-3, which had been discreetly parked at a far corner of the airfield. There, Ted Kennedy joined Janet, Cushing, and Father Hillary for the two-hour flight to Washington.

In the early morning hours, Janet and the priests arrived at Arlington with the hearse bearing the Kennedys' two dead children. At 8:40 that evening, Janet, Jack's brothers, Jamie Auchincloss, and a few other close friends and relatives stood with Jackie for a private twenty-minute burial service. "It was dark, except for the eerie, flickering light from the Eternal Flame," Jamie Auchincloss said. "It was incredibly touching, but Jackie had that look of resolve. She wanted to bring them all together again, and she did."

Still, there remained thousands of small, distracting details to attend to. It had long been a tradition of outgoing Presidents to leave behind one work of art to add to the permanent collection at the White House. When it came time to select the painting that would be presented to the White House in Jack's name, Jackie asked a half dozen major galleries to send over their most treasured works. Finally, the woman who had so painstakingly filled the Executive Mansion with the finest American antiques picked a French Impressionist work to hang in the Green Room: Claude Monet's *Morning on the Seine*. The accompanying plaque read: "In memory of John F. Kennedy by his Family."

As her time at 1600 Pennsylvania Avenue drew to a close, Jackie ordered that another plaque be placed over the mantel in the

First Lady's bedroom. This one, engraved in bronze, read: "In this room lived John Fitzgerald Kennedy with his wife Jacqueline — during the two years, ten months and two days he was President of the United States — January 20, 1961–November 22, 1963."

Above it was another plaque: "In this room Abraham Lincoln slept during his occupancy at the White House as President of the United States, March 3, 1861–April 13, 1865."

The Lincoln Bedroom was the one place in the house where Jackie went when she felt overwhelmed. It was, she said, "the one room in the White House with a link to the past. It gave me great comfort . . . When you see that great bed, it's like a cathedral. To touch something I knew he had touched was a real link with him. I used to sit in the Lincoln Room and I could really feel his strength. I'd sort of be talking with him. Jefferson is the President with whom I have the most affinity. But Lincoln is the one I love." Now, in Jackie's waning days in the White House, she closed herself off in the Lincoln Room for hours at a time. White House staff members could hear her, behind the closed doors, having animated — if decidedly one-sided — conversations with the ghost of the Great Emancipator.

It seems incomprehensible now, but at the

time Jackie was gripped by the fear that Jack would be forgotten. Even as she waited in Bethesda for the autopsy to be concluded, she had paid close attention to what television commentators were saying about her husband. "In that first wave of reporting," Teddy White said, "Kennedy's youth — the fact that he had been cut down in his prime, before he could accomplish the great deeds he had set out to achieve — these were the things that were emphasized. This made his death all the more tragic, after all. But Jackie interpreted that as meaning he hadn't been in office long enough to have a lasting impact, and that left her deeply troubled."

Convinced that her husband would soon become nothing more than a historical footnote, she dashed off scores of notes and letters to friends, ending with the same sad, almost desperate exhortation: "Please never forget him."

Jackie later conceded that she was not acting altogether rationally. "It's funny what you do in a state of shock," she said. "I remember going over to the Oval Office to ask him [LBJ] for two things. One was to name the space center in Florida 'Cape Kennedy.' Now that I think back on it that was so wrong, and if I'd known Cape Canaveral was the name from the time of Columbus, it would be the last thing that Jack would have wanted. The reason I asked was, I can remember this first speech Jack made in Texas was that there would be a rocket one day that would go to the moon. I kept thinking, 'That's going to be forgotten, and his dreams are going to be forgotten.' I had this terrible fear then that he'd be forgotten, and I thought, 'Well, maybe they'll remember some day this man did dream that.' "

The second favor she asked of Johnson was that he continue the commission she had begun for the renovation of Washington. Not only did he continue the commission, he established the new Committee for the Preservation of the White House and appointed Jackie to it. Moreover, Lady Bird adopted the beautification project as her own. Jackie spent one of her long, lonely, final evenings at the White House drafting a detailed eleven-page letter to the new First Lady. In it she described all the antiques, paintings, sculptures, and decorative objects she had, through a combination of detective work and diplomacy, managed to track down and then acquire for the White House.

"It may seem odd that Jackie could take the time to write a letter about artworks and antiques when her husband had just died," White observed. "But it was her way of getting her mind off herself, and the sheer horror of what she had just experienced. Besides, she had a very definite sense of her place in history. She did not want her contributions to be forgotten, either." Lady Bird's Press Secretary, Liz Carpenter, agreed that these objects in the White House had a special meaning for Jackie and that writing about them was probably "therapeutic" for her. But the idea that Jackie could invest hours jotting down a laundry list of acquisitions when her husband had just been murdered right before her eyes struck Carpenter as "pretty grim — rather ghoulish."

Knowing that he was now to be the Democrats' standard-bearer in the coming election, Johnson was eager to keep Jackie in his corner. It was hard to imagine at the time that anyone had more clout with the American electorate. Toward that end, Johnson asked Congress to allocate $17 million toward the construction of a new national cultural center, and to name it the John F. Kennedy Center for the Performing Arts.

Less than two weeks after the assassination, Johnson told Pierre Salinger, "I want to do something nice for Jackie — I'll name her Ambassador to France!" Salinger relayed the offer to Jackie, who turned it down flat. "Ambassador to Mexico, then?" LBJ persisted. Johnson knew Jackie spoke Spanish as well as French fluently, and had been a huge hit when she visited Mexico City as First Lady. But Jackie declined that offer, too.

"President Johnson said I could have anything I wanted," she told Charlie Bartlett. "I would like to work for someone, but one is expecting someone to come home every weekend, but no one is . . ."

The new President's election-year overtures, though heartfelt, rankled Jackie. "She had always treated the Johnsons well when Jack was President," Spalding said, "and she knew LBJ was genuinely grateful for that. As much as Johnson hated Bobby, he got along well with Jack and Jackie. But Jackie wasn't stupid. She knew Johnson wanted her in his corner in the next election, and there were times when she resented the pressure from the Johnson camp."

"I don't want to go out on a Kennedy driveway to a Kennedy airport to visit a Kennedy school," Jackie said. "I'm not going around accepting plaques. I don't want medals for Jack. I don't want to be seen by crowds."

Of all the symbols and gestures, Jackie was most grateful for something quite small — the light from the flame that flickered on Jack's grave. "Whenever you drive across the bridge from Washington into Virginia, you see the Lee Mansion on the side of the hill in the distance," she said. "When Caroline was very little, the mansion was one of the first things she learned to recognize. Now, at night you can see the flame beneath the mansion from miles away."

Yet Jack's widow could not shake the belief that he would soon fade from the memory of a fickle American public. So, in typical Jackie Kennedy fashion, she took a bold step to forever enshrine her husband in the thoughts of his countrymen.

The morning after Thanksgiving, she called Teddy White from Hyannis Port. "I have something I want *Life* magazine to say to the country," she told him, "and you must do it." She lashed out at the "bitter people" who were already writing that he had been in office too short a time to make a lasting impact.

Jackie told White she would be sending a Secret Service car to pick him up at his home in New York and drive him to Hyannis. But when White called the Secret Service, he was told that Jackie was no longer First Lady and in no position to be giving the Secret Service orders. To complicate matters further, White's mother, who was staying with him over the Thanksgiving holiday, suffered a heart attack. Faced with staying at his stricken mother's bedside or driving in a thunderstorm to talk to Jackie, White headed north to Hyannis Port.

The next day, exactly one week after the assassination, White was ushered into the living room of Joseph Kennedy's house. "We were all there — Dave Powers, Franklin Roosevelt Jr., Jack's sister Pat Lawford —

trying to keep up Jackie's spirits," Chuck Spalding recalled. "When Teddy White came in she asked the rest of us to leave. Everyone knew he had been Jack's friend, so none of us felt the need to stick around and protect her. Besides, we were all so damned tired at that point." (The only one among them who seemed to understand that White was concerned about his own mother, the writer observed, was Roosevelt. The Kennedys were, said Spalding, "never all that concerned about other people's relatives.")

White took his place on the sofa opposite Jackie. Dressed in a beige pullover sweater and black slacks, smoke swirling from her ever-present cigarette, she was calm, composed, and "beautiful," he later recalled, "with eyes wider than pools." She was also, White said, "without tears, drained, white of face." White did not know that Dr. Max Jacobson had been giving Jackie Valium in addition to her usual amphetamine injections.

Jacobson had been a phantom presence during the period surrounding the funeral — standing with Florida Congressman Claude Pepper directly behind Jackie as she and Caroline knelt by the coffin in the Capitol Rotunda, and only a few steps away from Jackie as she lit the Eternal Flame at the President's grave site.

Gore Vidal, who had known both Jackie and Jack well, had warned Jackie to stay away from Jacobson. Vidal's mother had been married to Hugh Auchincloss prior to his marrying Janet Bouvier, and Auchincloss was the father of Vidal's half-sister, Nina. "I knew Max well — all of us in Hollywood and in show business knew what he was all about," Vidal said. At the time, Vidal knew Jack had been getting the amphetamine shots, but he was unaware that Jackie was getting them too. In retrospect, Vidal realized how she managed to find "the energy to stay up for several days straight after Dallas planning the state funeral and chatting with De Gaulle . . . Jackie was a strong woman with an overwhelming need for control, but I think even she would have collapsed without that extra boost from good old Max."

From 8:30 P.M. until midnight, Teddy White scribbled notes as Jackie described in riveting, often shockingly gruesome detail the assassination itself. Throughout, she fidgeted with the gold wedding ring Kenny O'Donnell had removed from JFK's finger at Bethesda. On her pinkie finger she wore a small gold ring with emerald chips — green for Patrick — which Kennedy had given her to remember their tiny son.

Much of the time, she seemed to be lost in her own world as she spoke of the moments leading up to the gunshots. It was "hot, wild — like Mexico and Vienna," she said, referring to two of the trips she had made abroad with Jack. "The sun was so strong in our faces. I couldn't put on sunglasses. Then we saw this tunnel ahead. I thought it would be cool in the tunnel . . . then there was one noise . . . I thought it was a backfire."

White sat "paralyzed," as he put it, listening to her describe how the fatal shot tore away a piece of Jack's skull, how his brain matter was sprayed over her, and how she cradled his head as they raced to Parkland. Most of the time, it seemed to White as if she were in trance, not seeing him at all.

When her eyes did focus on the journalist, it was to stress the reason she had asked him to Hyannis Port in the first place. Jackie confessed that until she met her husband, she had always thought of history as something "bitter old men wrote." Then, she went on, "I realized history made Jack what he was. You must think of him as this little boy, sick so much of the time, reading in bed, reading history, reading the Knights of the Round Table, reading Marlborough. For Jack, history was full of heroes. And if it made him this way — if it made him see the heroes — maybe other little boys will see.

"Men are such a combination of good and bad," she said, rambling now. "He was such a simple man. But he was so complex, too. Jack had this hero idea of history, the idealistic view, but then he had that other side, the pragmatic side. His friends were his old friends. He loved his Irish Mafia."

Then she returned to the point that she was there to make. "There's this one thing I kept thinking of," she said. "Oh, I'm so ashamed of myself. Jack, everything he ever quoted was Greek or Roman — don't protect me now — this line from a musical comedy keeps going through my mind. I kept saying to Bobby, 'I've got to talk to somebody, to see somebody' . . . I want to say this one thing, it's almost been an obsession with me, all I keep thinking of is this line from a musical comedy, it's been an obsession with me."

Jackie told White that at night, when Jack's back pain made it hard for him to sleep, she would play his favorite record — the cast album from *Camelot*. The song he loved most, sung by Richard Burton, was the very last cut on the record. And his favorite line was the very last one in the song — the line that had been running relentlessly through Jackie's fevered mind. The melancholy lyric had been written by Jack's old friend and Harvard classmate Alan Jay Lerner:

> Don't let it be forgot,
> That once there was a spot
> For one brief shining moment
> That was known as Camelot.

"There'll never be another Camelot," she said wistfully. "There will be great Presidents again — and the Johnsons are wonderful, they've been wonderful to me — but there'll never be another Camelot again." In the course of their conversation, Jackie blasted the "bitter old men" who write history almost as many times as she equated Jack's administration with the romantic paradigm of Camelot.

As White dictated his story over a phone in the kitchen to *Life*'s editors back in New York, Jackie hovered over him, resisting any efforts to downplay the Camelot analogy.

"It was no accident," he later said. "She was a keenly intelligent woman who had obviously thought long and hard about how she wanted her handsome, heroic young husband remembered. She had always been described as a fairy-tale princess, and now she wanted Jack Kennedy to take his place in history as a modern King Arthur."

As White later pointed out, Jackie's twentieth-century Camelot was a "misreading" of history. But at least on the surface, the comparison worked. The Kennedy White House *was* a "magic moment in American history" when "gallant men danced with beautiful women . . . when artists, writers, and poets met at the White House." As soon as *Life* hit the stands with White's story the following Monday, the

American public eagerly embraced Jackie's evocation of Camelot. It would become an enduring metaphor for the Kennedys' thousand days in office.

As terrified as she was that Jack would be relegated to "dusty history books," for a few fleeting moments Jackie seemed to recognize the danger in obsession. "I said to myself," she allowed, " 'You must never forget Jack, but you mustn't be morbid.' "

But what of history as it really was? For all her concern about Jack's legacy, Jackie asked few questions about the man or men responsible for his death. No one can ever recall hearing her speak the name Lee Harvey Oswald.

Conversely, when Bobby Kennedy first told her JFK's murder was committed by a small-time Communist acting alone, Jackie said she wished it *had* been a conspiracy because that would have lent some larger meaning to Jack's death. Why didn't she press the issue?

"She trusted Bobby completely," said Oleg Cassini, a close friend of both Jack and Jackie and the First Lady's designer during the White House years. "Most people were so numb, so shocked by the assassination that it was a relief to be told it was just one isolated nut and not some larger conspiracy." Concurred Pierre Salinger: "It was a very dangerous time. The Cuban Missile Crisis, when we had been pushed to the brink of nuclear war, had happened just the year before. Frankly, my first thought when I heard the news was that we could be at war."

At the Justice Department, Deputy Attorney General Nicholas Katzenbach was now running things; Bobby, overcome with grief and focusing much of his attention on Jackie and her children, would not return to work for months. Katzenbach, who along with FBI Director J. Edgar Hoover was eager to forestall any talk of conspiracy, wrote to Johnson on November 24 — even before Ruby shot Oswald. "The public must be satisfied that Oswald was the assassin," Katzenbach wrote, "that he did not have confederates who are still at large; and that the evidence was such that he would have been convicted at trial."

The next day, Hoover announced that "not one shred of evidence has been developed to link any other person in a conspiracy with Oswald to assassinate President Kennedy." To rubber-stamp this finding, Johnson appointed the bipartisan seven-member Warren Commission, headed by Chief Justice Earl Warren. Only one member, former CIA Director Allen Dulles, would take an active hand in shaping the commission's findings that Oswald acted alone.

It would be sixteen years before the U.S. House of Representatives Select Committee on Assassinations (HSCA), following clear leads that were never followed on direct orders from Hoover, concluded that there had been a conspiracy to kill President Kennedy. Based on the testimony of hundreds of witnesses, previously suppressed government documents, and hundreds of wiretaps, the following scenario unfolded:

Beginning with Joseph Sr., who made millions as a rumrunner during the Depression, the Kennedy family had had links to organized crime. When JFK ran for President in 1960, it was Chicago mobster Sam Giancana who, by falsifying election returns, helped put Illinois in the Democrat's column. Giancana and the President even shared a mistress, Judith Campbell.

The Mob's loose alliance with the Kennedys continued after Jack took office. Acting on behalf of the CIA and as a favor to Jack, the Mob made several attempts on Cuban President Fidel Castro's life. They kept failing because mafioso Santos Trafficante, who had once operated casinos in Havana, was acting as a double agent. In return for warning Castro before each attempted hit, Trafficante was paid off for the mob-owned casinos Castro had closed down.

Meanwhile, Jack's younger brother was cracking down on the very underworld leaders who had helped elect his brother President. Only thirty-five organized crime members had been brought to trial in the last year of the Eisenhower administration. In 1963 alone, Bobby had succeeded in indicting 288.

Around the country, Mob kingpins vowed revenge — most notably New Orleans godfather Carlos Marcello. Bobby had even had Marcello kidnapped and deported to Guatemala. After Marcello sneaked back into the United States, the Attorney General charged him with perjury, illegal entry, and fraud.

Jack Kennedy knew all too well how dangerous the situation was for Bobby; frequently he told others in the administration that he worried about his little brother. But when Marcello told associates that he planned on using a "nut" to get rid of Kennedy, he was talking about Jack, not Bobby. "The dog will keep biting if you only cut off its tail," Marcello said, adding that he feared JFK would retaliate with the Army if Bobby were killed.

Months before Dallas, Trafficante and another enemy of Bobby's, Teamster boss Jimmy Hoffa, were telling associates of a planned Kennedy assassination. Trafficante bluntly stated to friends that "the President is going to be hit." FBI bugs revealed that in fact Mob leaders from one end of the country to the other were complaining bitterly about the Kennedys and discussing how to "remove them."

Things came to a head in September when the CIA finally caught on to the fact that Trafficante was working for Castro and cut off his information. No longer able to count on Trafficante's warnings, a worried Castro told the Associated Press that "the CIA is trying to kill certain Cuban leaders."

Without his pipeline to the CIA, Castro felt cornered. According to Mob boss Johnny Roselli, who was executed gangland style after telling his story to veteran journalist Jack Anderson, the Cuban dictator instructed Trafficante to take out a contract on the life of the President of the United States.

"The same three Mob assassins who had been sent to kill Castro," Anderson said, "were then sent to kill JFK. Since Dallas was in Carlos Marcello's jurisdiction, he was all too glad to oblige. On November 22, it so happened Marcello arranged to be in court — perfect alibi." In 1979 the HSCA would finally learn that Castro sympathizer Lee Harvey Oswald had ties to Marcello (Oswald's mother, Marguerite, had had a long-standing affair with Marcello's driver, Sam Termine). They also uncovered evidence that Jack Ruby had not only been an underling of the old Al Capone gang in Chicago but had run casino money from Havana to Miami for Trafficante. If Ruby killed

Oswald to revenge the death of his beloved JFK, that came as news to all who knew him. "Like the rest of the Mob — and he was on the fringes of organized crime — Ruby was widely quoted as *hating* Kennedy, not loving him."

In late 1997, the National Security Agency declassified documents showing that "an emotional and uneasy" Fidel Castro mobilized his armed forces and went on Cuban national television immediately after Kennedy's assassination to deny any link between Cuba and Oswald. At least one U.S. ambassador, unnamed in the report, went on record as saying he was certain Castro was behind the assassination.

The day after the assassination, CIA Director John McCone had met with Bobby Kennedy, President Johnson, and presidential advisor McGeorge Bundy. "McCone told Johnson about the whole plot to kill Castro and how it had backfired," Anderson said. "He also told the new President the public must not know. If they found out, McCone argued, the American people would rise up and demand military action against Castro. In turn Khrushchev, who was still on the ropes in the Kremlin after his Cuban Missile Crisis defeat, might be forced to push the button this time." According to Anderson, McCone told Johnson that the resulting nuclear exchange would cost an estimated forty million to forty-two million American lives.

Within minutes, LBJ was on the phone to J. Edgar Hoover.

"Edgar, I want you to serve your country by doing the right thing," Johnson said.

"What do you want me to do, Mr. President?"

"I want you to save forty-two million American lives. The way you do this is to keep Castro from being mentioned in the investigation. It could force Khrushchev to act and lead to World War Three."

Hoover eagerly obliged. The Warren Commission, all the while, "investigated *nothing*. Lyndon was a complete tyrant, a one-man band, he made sure they knew nothing. I had known Lyndon Johnson for many years," Anderson went on. "I knew him *well*. He was always worried that somebody might get to the Warren Commission, that is why he appointed Allen Dulles to it." The former CIA director, fully apprised of Castro's involvement, was LBJ's "ace in the hole. Dulles, aided by Hoover, was the chief advocate of the one-assassin theory."

Several years after he left office, LBJ was sitting down to be interviewed by ABC anchor Howard K. Smith. Chatting before the camera went on, Johnson suddenly blurted out, "Kennedy tried to kill Castro but Castro got him first."

Smith nearly fell off his chair. LBJ, suddenly realizing what he had said, refused to repeat it before the cameras. Significantly, he did not retract the statement, either.

Even those who were not privy to the facts found it hard to believe that Oswald acted alone. Jackie's own mother believed it was no coincidence that the assassination took place in Dallas. "Mother always felt Johnson was behind Jack's assassination," Jamie Auchincloss said. "She never stopped believing it."

By the late 1970s, Ted Kennedy would privately lean toward the conspiracy theory, as would Bobby's eldest son, Joe, and several other Kennedy cousins. But in the years immediately following Dallas, the Kennedys would support the findings of the Warren Commission. So did the vast majority of Americans, too shell-shocked to entertain the possibility of something as sinister as an international conspiracy.

Jackie, however, went along with the party line. "To tell you the truth," she later said, "everything that happened that caused the Warren Commission to exist — you know, I don't think I really sat and thought, 'Hmmm. Let me look at the makeup of the Warren Commission.' Somehow I had this feeling of, What did it matter what they found out? They could never bring back the person who was gone."

Both publicly and privately, she never questioned the findings of the Warren Commission or commented on the investigation or any evidence in the case. "Kennedys — that includes Jackie — don't like to stir up skeletons of any kind," Anderson pointed out. "They know where that can lead."

David Halberstam, who wrote extensively about the Kennedy White House in *The Best and the Brightest* and whose own brother was a murder victim, felt that Jackie's reluctance to dig deeper was "perfectly understandable. If you've ever lost a loved one under circumstances like that, you know that it is just too painful to keep reliving the moment. You want to put the horror behind you as quickly as you can and move on with your life. For Jackie, I'm sure it was a matter of survival — not only for herself but also for her children. From their standpoint, who cared if Oswald acted alone? Their father was dead."

Bobby knew that his aggressive pursuit of the Mob had contributed to Jack's death, and that made his feelings toward Jackie that much more intense. "Jack was killed because of Bobby, I'm convinced of that," a close friend of Jack, Jackie, and Bobby said. "Bobby must have felt that, too. The guilt really must have been almost unbearable. As the heir apparent in the family, he would have comforted Jackie. Because he felt partly responsible for Jack's murder, Bobby went overboard. You couldn't pry him from Jackie's side in those first few months. Jackie didn't mind — she was totally dependent on him in the beginning — but after a while Ethel sure did."

As a means of coping with his own grief, Bobby organized a touch football game at the Kennedy family compound in Palm Beach, Florida. "It was the roughest, wildest game I have ever seen," Salinger said. "Everybody was trying to get the anger out of their systems. Bobby was absolutely relentless. He attacked the man with the ball like a tiger — slamming, bruising, and crushing — and so did everybody else. One guy broke a leg, and you couldn't count the bloodied noses. It was murder."

The last night they were to spend together in the Executive Mansion as a family, Jackie threw the promised joint birthday party for Caroline and John-John. There was another cake — a big one this time — and the children took turns tearing open their presents. Caroline's favorite was a stuffed bear, John-John's a model of *Air Force One*.

One of the problems that had confronted Jackie immediately upon returning to Washington with her husband's body was the issue of where she was going to live. At first she was intent on staying in Washington. It was home to her children, as well as to most members of the Kennedy and Auchincloss clans. The few close friends Jackie had were here, and it was in the nation's capital where Jack's presence would still be most keenly felt.

But where? "I'm *never* going to live in Europe," she insisted, putting an end to rumors that she would move to France. "I'm not going to 'travel extensively abroad.' That's a desecration. I'm going to live in the places I lived with Jack. In Georgetown, and with the Kennedys at the Cape. They're my family. I'm going to bring up my children. I want John to grow up to be a good boy."

The fact remained, however, that Jackie was in no position to go house-hunting. "In Washington, you cannot buy a house on the spur of the moment and move in," said John Kenneth Galbraith, who "took on" the job of finding his friend Jackie a new place to live. "It occurred to me that Averell Harriman, who had more real estate than he knew what to do with, could offer her his house." Galbraith described the Harriman mansion, which boasted its own swimming pool and a dining room that sat eighteen, as "a large comfortable house in the most agreeable part of Georgetown and has the particular advantage of some of the best Impressionist paintings in the world."

Galbraith broached the subject with Harriman, who at the time was serving as Under Secretary of State. Harriman called Jackie and made the offer, but only after being coaxed into making it by his colorful, outspoken wife, Marie. "It was one of her typical acts of generosity," recalled bandleader Peter Duchin, who for a time was raised by Marie Harriman. No one knew, Duchin said, about "the diplomatic skill she had employed getting Ave to move into a room in the Georgetown Inn for several weeks." At the time, Marie told Duchin that "all he does is complain about the goddamn bath being too short." Not that Marie was that happy at the inn herself. "Room service is awful," she said, "but poor Jackie. She needs the house more than we do."

In the two days before Jackic and her young family departed the White House, the Harrimans' seven-bedroom redbrick house was flooded with last-minute deliveries. There was a briefcase emblazoned with the initials JFK, a box marked "John's Toys — N Street," a bicycle, a tricycle, hatboxes, the children's two parakeet cages — one pink, the other blue — and several cases of French wine. Yellow chrysanthemums arrived from Washington's leading florist, and a maid appeared clutching an armload of manuals — the White House guidebooks that Jackie had published and sold to finance the renovation.

Shortly after noon on December 6, Jackie left the White House. A half hour later, a black White House limousine pulled up in front of the Harriman mansion and out stepped Jackie and her children, followed closely by Bobby and Ethel. The neighborhood was familiar: Only three blocks away at 3307 N Street was the Federal redbrick house she and then-Senator Kennedy moved into when Caroline was only three weeks old — "My sweet little house," Jackie had said then, "leans slightly to one side and the stairs creak. I love it."

Inside the Harriman house, Jackie and her in-laws gazed at the walls in something approaching disbelief. It was hard not to be impressed; wherever they looked, they saw works by Matisse, van Gogh, Toulouse-Lautrec, and Cézanne. A half hour after they arrived, Bobby and Ethel left the house and a smiling Jackie closed the front door behind them.

A few days earlier, Jackie had watched blankly as Treasury Secretary C. Douglas Dillon awarded his department's citation for exceptional bravery to Clint Hill. At first the law provided that she and her children continue to receive Secret Service protection for two years — a period that was eventually extended to a presidential widow until remarriage or death. Under the new provisions, all presidential offspring are entitled to protection until age sixteen.

Jackie required more than just the small army of dark-suited, sunglass-wearing agents encircling her Georgetown home. To begin with, she faced the prospect of answering the more than three hundred thousand letters and sympathy notes stacked six feet high in the East Wing of the White House. The flood continued for more than a month, at the rate of forty thousand letters *a day*. (Anyone who sent a contribution of $1,000 or more for the Kennedy Library received a personal response from Jackie.)

Congress, at LBJ's urging, appropriated $50,000 for her to hire Nancy Tuckerman and Pam Turnure as her private staff. This would prove to fall far short of her needs. The first year she overran her budget by $120,000, and Congress promptly voted to pick up the difference.

Outside the Harriman home, a carnival atmosphere prevailed. Drivers, hoping to catch a glimpse of Jackie or the children, slowed to a crawl in front of the house, clogging traffic for blocks. Sidewalks on both sides of N Street were packed shoulder to shoulder with gawkers. Those few close friends who dropped by to keep Jackie company and to make sure she was all right had to run the gauntlet of newspaper photographers and tourists.

Despite the obstacles, Bobby visited every day. Charles and Martha Bartlett, McGeorge Bundy, and a handful of others also made a point of coming for tea at least once a week. Still, Jackie could not help but feel trapped among the Harrimans' van Goghs and Cézannes.

On weekends, Jackie escaped to Wexford, the country house she and Jack had built in Atoka, Virginia. Two weeks before the assassination, Jack and Jackie had spent an idyllic autumn weekend there with Tony and Ben Bradlee, walking the fields, sipping Bloody Marys on the stone terrace, watching as Jackie rode and jumped. Now, without Jack, the dynamics of the friendship had changed.

Ben Bradlee recalled that these back-to-back weekends in December were spent "trying with no success to talk about something else, or someone else. Too soon and too emotional for healing, we proved only that the three of us had very little in common without the essential fourth."

Jackie could not stop reliving those moments in Dallas, or lamenting what might have been if only Jack had lived. The Bradlees, groping for something comforting to say, reminded Jackie that she was only thirty-four, that love and marriage could still be in her future.

Their host said nothing. But a few days later, the Bradlees received a note from

Jackie, dated December 20. "Something you said in the country stunned me so — that you hoped I would marry again," Jackie wrote. "You were close to us so many times. There is one thing that you must know. I consider that my life is over and I will spend the rest of it waiting for it really to be over."

During another weekend at Wexford, Jackie sat up until 3 A.M. pouring out her heart to Chuck Spalding's ex-wife, Betty. Jackie had no idea where she was going to live, or how she was going to manage raising Caroline and John-John alone. "No one knows what it's like, no one knows what it's like," she repeated like a mantra. Of course, she was right.

Determined to remain in Washington and anxious not to overstay her welcome at the Harrimans', Jackie recruited Tony Bradlee and her sister, Lee, to search for another smaller house in Georgetown. In addition to house-hunting, the holiday season provided yet another diversion for Jackie and the children. Jack had already done some Christmas shopping, ordering seventy-five bound copies of Inaugural Addresses that he intended to sign and give to cabinet members and friends. Instead, Jackie signed the copies and gave them — with a note explaining that this was a gift from both her and the late President.

Bobby gave Jackie the present Jack had intended to give her — a small sculpture of the Egyptian goddess Isis. Jackie, inspired by her husband's love of the classics, gave Bobby a copy of Edith Hamilton's *The Greek Way*. Grappling with his own grief, Bobby devoured the book, scribbling in the margins and underlining passages as if he were cramming for a final exam. He became obsessed with a particular passage from Herodotus: "All arrogance will reach a harvest rich in tears. God calls men in a heavy reckoning for overweening pride."

Bobby, according to those who knew him, may have at last begun to see the toll that hubris and recklessness had taken on his family. His eldest brother, Joseph Jr., had died in a World War II suicide mission over France trying to best the Pacific exploits of his war hero brother, Jack. His sister Kathleen "Kick" Kennedy, who had been excommunicated after marrying Billy Hartington, the Protestant eldest son of the Duke of Devonshire, became a widow when Hartington was shot by a German sniper. Four years later, Kick died when the plane that carried her and her married lover, Peter Fitzwilliam, crashed in France. And now Jack . . .

"The Kennedys had used the Mafia to get Jack elected and to try to assassinate Castro," Gore Vidal said. "Bobby was sort of the family bulldog, very accustomed to pushing people around and getting his way. He figured that once the Mafia had served its purpose he could turn on them as he had on so many other people, and that they would just take it. Apparently the Mob did not share that view."

"Bobby had been the Rock of Gibraltar for everyone — Jackie, his family, all of Jack's friends," said one of Jackie's closest friends. "A few days after the funeral, he turned to me and, choking back tears, said, 'God help me, I'm to blame for this. Jack would be alive today if it weren't for me.' I told him that of course he had nothing to do with his brother's murder, but he looked right into my eye and said, 'No, I mean it. *It should have been me.*' "

Unable to fully come to terms with Dallas, Bobby never spoke of the assassination directly. Instead, he and other family members would refer euphemistically to JFK's murder as "the events of November 22, 1963."

While Bobby agonized over the role he played in bringing about his adored brother's death, Jackie tried to make life as normal as possible for her young children. Caroline wrote a letter to Santa asking for a Nancy Nurse doll and rehearsed for her Christmas pageant. It would be the first one without her father in the audience. "Mrs. Kennedy wanted the pageant to go on as usual," Sister Joanne Frey said. "Angier Biddle Duke had been in Paris but he flew back to handle the guest list, and Jackie would come in every now and then — sometimes wearing riding clothes — just to see how everything was going. Jackie came with her sister, Lee, and the Auchinclosses, and everyone sang Christmas carols. But no one could forget that someone was missing."

Judging by the presents she picked out to give to friends and family, Caroline was already very much her mother's daughter. On a Christmas shopping expedition, Caroline picked out a set of van Gogh prints for Jackie, her brother, and her nanny, Maud Shaw.

Shortly after Christmas, Jackie paid $175,000 for a three-story, fourteen-room, beige brick colonial town house at 3017 N Street, not far from the Harrimans'. She had hoped to escape the prying eyes of the curious, but if anything the problem at her new home was worse.

From street level, all the rooms that faced the front of the house — the living room, the dining room, the study, several bedrooms and bathrooms — were plainly visible. Feeling as if she were on display, Jackie kept the drapes drawn tight, day and night. "They actually sit there and eat their lunch and throw sandwich wrappers on the ground," she complained of the crowds.

"I'm trapped in that house and can't get out. I can't even change my clothes in private because they look in my bedroom window."

"Outside the crowd of spectators grew and grew," said decorator Billy Baldwin, whom Jackie had hired to do the interior of her new home. "There was bumper-to-bumper traffic. The new Kennedy home had become a tourist site."

"It's very upsetting," Jackie told Baldwin. "Women are always breaking the police lines and trying to hug and kiss my children as they go in and out. The world is pouring terrible adoration at their feet and I fear for them. How can I bring them up normally? We never would have named John after his father if we had known."

Baldwin made one of his visits to the N Street house in the middle of a winter storm that rattled windows and snapped the branches off trees. They went to work unpacking box after box of books until the bookcases were filled. Then Jackie opened a box and beckoned Baldwin over to look at its contents. Inside were several small Greek and Roman antiquities that Jack had bought over the years — the beginnings of a collection. Jackie put one on the mantel, another on an end table, and she paused for a moment. "You know it's very sad, isn't it? It's like a young married couple going into a new home and unpacking things. I could never make the White House personal."

She wandered over to a window and looked at the gawkers huddled outside in the subfreezing temperatures. After a few quiet moments, she returned to Baldwin — this time with tears streaming down her face. "I'm afraid," she said, "I'm going to embarrass you." Then she fell onto the sofa, Baldwin remembered, "burying her face in her hands as she wept."

His first inclination was to put his arm around his friend and console her, but Baldwin was too stunned to move. "Billy, do you mind if I tell you something?" she asked, wiping her eyes with a handkerchief. "I know my husband was devoted to me. I know he was proud of me. It took a very long time for us to work everything out, but we did, and we were about to have a real life together."

"She had held on as long as she could," Baldwin said. "She had been like Joan of Arc from the time of Kennedy's death and through the funeral. But now she was surrounded by memories."

She confided in Baldwin that she felt "utterly alone. Can anyone possibly understand how it is to have lived in the White House, and then suddenly be living alone as the President's widow? As First Lady, I made maybe two friends."

Out of her overriding concern for her children, Jackie showed Baldwin photographs of their bedrooms at the White House and asked that he make their new rooms look identical. "She wanted their lives to be disrupted as little as possible," Baldwin said. "She was trying for some semblance of constancy, of continuity. Sadly, this was impossible."

By staying to supply a sympathetic ear, Baldwin earned Jackie's lasting gratitude. When she married Aristotle Onassis five years later, Jackie gave Baldwin the lucrative assignment of redecorating her villa on the Onassis-owned island of Skorpios.

The nation saw the same haunted look in Jackie's eyes when she appeared on television to thank the American people for their support. Sitting on a leather club chair in Bobby's Justice Department offices, a microphone hanging around her neck, she spoke in the same measured, slightly breathless whisper made famous by her televised White House tour two years before.

"The knowledge of the affection in which my husband was held by all of you has sustained me, and the warmth of these tributes is something I shall never forget," she said. "Whenever I can bear to read them . . . All his bright light gone from the world. All of you who have written to me know how much we all loved him and that he returned that love in full measure.

"It is my greatest wish that all of these letters be acknowledged. They will be, but it will take a long time to do so . . . I know you will understand. Each and every message is to be treasured," she continued, "not only for my children, but so that future generations will know how much our country and people in other nations thought of him. Your letters will be placed with his papers in the library to be erected in his memory in Boston, Massachusetts.

"I hope that in years to come many of you and your children will be able to visit the Kennedy Library. It will be, we hope, not only a memorial but a living center of study for you people and for scholars from all over the world."

Anyone who spent time with Jackie during this period walked away emotionally drained. Noting that she had become a "prisoner in her own home," Robert McNamara tried to take her out to lunch at a Washington bistro but was undone by the gaping stares of the other patrons. Chuck Spalding remembered that she was just "flattened, lost. You'd try to change the subject but she kept coming back to Jack."

In early December, Max Jacobson had returned to his practice in New York, leaving a variety of pills behind for Jackie to take.

But neither the sleeping pills nor the anti-depressants was working. There was no way she could keep from running the scene in Dallas over and over again in her mind, trying to figure out how things might have been different if the limousine driver had stepped on the gas the instant he heard gunshots, or if they had left the airport sooner, or if she had leaned to the left instead of the right . . .

Shortly before Christmas, she had called Jacobson in New York. "She sounded very depressed," Jacobson said. "There was nothing of the usual liveliness in her voice. She asked me to come to Georgetown to see her." This time, there were no Secret Service agents waiting at the airport to meet him. Jacobson hailed a cab.

"In a middle-class neighborhood, the driver stopped at a small building," Jacobson recalled. "I picked up my medical bag and rang the doorbell. A Secret Service man opened the door, and when I identified myself, announced me. I heard her voice from the second floor, asking me to come up.

"She came toward me, greeted me, and invited me into a dimly lit room. She seemed detached and somewhat vague. She sank into an upholstered chair, and with eyes wide open gazed at the wall."

He dug into his medical bag and pulled out a syringe and a vial. "My life is over,

Max," she said, offering her arm for one of his injections, "just empty, meaningless."

For the next forty-five minutes, Jacobson tried to convince her "that there were many important things that she could do in the future." He reminded her of "her previous profession — journalism — her interest in art and theater and sports, and especially of her obligation to her children . . . I tried my best to impress upon her that life would go on, eventually, and the sooner she realized it the better it would be. To continue to live is certainly what Jack would have wanted her to do."

Suddenly there were voices downstairs. "Jackie stood up abruptly and looked at me," Jacobson said. "With a sharp, clear voice, she said, 'I hear Bobby coming up the stairs. Please leave through this door.' "

"When Jack was alive, a lot of people at the White House were taking those shots — including Bobby," Spalding said. "But he was always suspicious of Jacobson and would have thrown him out on his ear if he caught him there."

Returning to New York, Jacobson prepared one of his "C.A.R.E. packages" to send to Jackie. As many as five hundred of these packages went out to his famous clients every week. In each was a vial containing Jacobson's potent amphetamine-steroid "cocktail" and ten disposable syringes. Before leaving her, Jacobson had carefully taught Jackie how to give herself the injections.

The drugs only made Jackie even more prone than usual to violent mood swings. According to her own half-brother, Jamie Auchincloss, "Jackie could be absolutely giddy and enchanting one moment, and then you'd turn around, and for no apparent reason, she'd just run off as if someone had flipped a switch." The Kennedys' photographer and friend Jacques Lowe observed the same behavior, adding that at times everybody — including the President — "walked on eggshells around her."

Feeling overwhelmed, Jackie now struck out at those closest at hand. Evelyn Lincoln's modest request for a larger office in which to display JFK's things triggered an angry outburst. "But these things are all *mine*," Jackie said. When her husband's secretary grumbled about overwork, Jackie countered, "Oh, Mrs. Lincoln, all this shouldn't be so hard for you, because you still have your husband. What do I have now? Just the library."

Jackie also quizzed JFK's devoted secretary about what it was she was actually doing. "Why, Mrs. Lincoln," she chided. "I could sit down and in a half-day index all these items on cards myself!"

Jackie's own secretary, Mary Gallagher, did not fare much better. Jackie complained

143

that Gallagher's annual salary of $12,000 was excessive. Combing over checkbooks to find ways to cut costs, Jackie became indignant when she discovered that Provi, her personal maid since the mid-1950s, was paid $900 in overtime.

"Overtime?" she snapped, unaware of the concept. "Do you mean to say that for every little thing extra someone does around here, I have to *pay* them?"

Gallagher nodded. "Yes, Jackie," she said. "That's usually the way it works."

In her husband's abrupt absence, Jackie may have been feeling guilty about her own spendthrift ways. When she and Jack did clash, it was often over the huge amounts of money she spent on clothes — upward of $20,000 a year (the equivalent in 1998 of more than $200,000). Jack would wave Jackie's clothing bills in the air and yell, "Goddammit, she's breaking my ass!"

"He'd get really worked up about it, turn purple with rage," Jack's friend George Smathers recalled. In the end, though, whatever she spent was "just a drop in the bucket as far as the Kennedys were concerned. So long as old Joe Kennedy paid for everything, Jackie knew she had nothing to worry about."

Jack's estate at the time of his death was valued at $1,890,646.45 (nearly $20 million in 1998 dollars) — and did not include addi-

144

tional millions placed in trust for his wife and children. Papers filed by Ted Kennedy, one of the executors of JFK's will, showed that his various checking accounts contained almost $114,000, and that he owned $715,239.23 worth of stocks and bonds. The balance was divided primarily among "mortgages, notes, and cash" ($116,377.37); the estimated value of copyrights on his writings ($275,000); "other miscellaneous intangible personal property" ($1,009,814.85); $21,615.23 from a trust set up for his late brother, Joseph P. Kennedy Jr.; $21,546.19 from a trust set up for his late sister, Kathleen "Kick" Kennedy Hartington; and $557,341 that represented Jack's share of the Kennedy-owned Merchandise Mart in Chicago.

Nevertheless, he did not leave Jackie a rich woman. She received a little less than $70,000 in cash — representing the salary owed for the month of November, Navy retirement pay, and Civil Service death benefits. The rest, about $10 million, was tied up in two trust funds for the widow and her children. Jackie was to be paid the income from one of the two funds — about $175,000 a year — as well as the standard presidential widow's pension of $10,000 a year and free lifetime use of the mails.

Jackie still sent her bills to the Kennedy family offices in New York, and they were taken care of as they had always been. But increasingly Jackie, who was always surrounded by great wealth while having only limited resources of her own, fretted about her financial future.

For all her worries, Jackie tried with the help of Jack's loyal "Murphia" to create a normal atmosphere at home for the children. Dave Powers dropped by every day to march around with John-John or carry him piggyback as he had done at the White House. Playing Davy Crockett to Dave Powers's grizzly bear, the three-year-old was blissfully unaware of his mother's sadness.

Caroline was another matter. She had always been sensitive, introspective, wise beyond her years. Now she was more somber, quieter than usual. "After Patrick's death," Sister Joanne Frey said, "the President brought home a little cocker spaniel puppy. When I asked Caroline why they named it Shannon, she said, 'Oh, Sister, you know it's the name of a river in Ireland.' " Another time, on a trip to St. Joseph's Church in Washington, Frey pointed to a statue of Sir Thomas More and asked if any of the children knew who the man was.

"I don't know who he is," Caroline said, studying the statue closely. "But I know he probably lived hundreds of years ago, and is wearing the robes of an Englishman in office."

"Here she is just six years old, and she

can recognize a sixteenth-century English cleric," Frey said. "Her mother read to her a great deal. They were always skipping way ahead in the text. She was a very, very bright little girl. After her father died, she picked up on everything that was going on around her. She was very much attuned to her mother's pain."

A few days before Christmas, Sister Joanne had asked her students to put their heads on the table and to think about Jesus. Then she asked them to share their thoughts. Caroline was the first to volunteer. "It made me think of how my mommy always watched cowboy movies with my daddy because my daddy always liked cowboy movies. My mommy doesn't like cowboy movies *at all,* but she watched them because she loved my daddy."

There were poignant moments when Caroline's own sense of loss bubbled to the surface. Sharing a wishbone with Jackie's teenage half-sister Janet Auchincloss, Caroline asked if she could have anything she wished for.

"Anything," her aunt Janet assured her.

"I want to see my daddy," Caroline said.

During a winter weekend at Hyannis, Joe's nurse, Rita Dallas, watched as six-year-old Caroline took a solitary walk on the beach, then sat down and gazed out over the water. Caroline "made a desolate picture huddled so alone in deep despair," said Dallas, who watched as Jackie joined her. They strolled together along the water's edge, and when the wind kicked up, Jackie wrapped her arms around her little girl to shield her from the bone-chilling cold.

As she had done that day on the beach, Dallas observed, Jackie would "provide the child with the strength that is necessary to suffer a great loss. She shielded her until the sharp pain had settled in to a dull, eternal ache. She set an example for her, and as the years passed, the little girl was able to pick up the task of living."

Yet it was her own mother's undisguised anguish that seemed to most disturb the little girl. In late January, Sister Joanne was teaching her catechism class about Mary Magdalene washing the feet of Christ when suddenly Caroline said, "My mommy cries all the time."

Frey returned to the story of Mary Magdalene, but Caroline insisted "My mommy cries *all* the time. My mommy cries all the time."

Frey tried again, but Caroline wanted to talk. So the sister stopped everything to listen. "After my daddy died, my mommy is always crying," Caroline said. "I go and get in bed with her and tell her everything is all right and tell her to stop crying. But she doesn't. My mommy is always crying . . ."

"Caroline wasn't crying when she said this — she didn't even seem that emotional," Frey explained. "She just had to tell somebody what was happening behind closed doors. It was a cry for help. Obviously the poor little girl didn't know what to do."

Even for the sake of her daughter, Jackie seemed to find it impossible to pull out of her deep depression. "I'm a living wound," she said. "My life is over. I'm dried up — I have nothing more to give and some days I can't even get out of bed. I cry all day and all night until I'm so exhausted I can't function. Then I drink."

Only one person could fully fathom the depth of Jackie's pain. Bobby was also, Chuck Spalding observed, "one of the walking wounded. As sad as Jackie looked, Bobby looked even worse." Pierre Salinger agreed. "Bobby was very tough — in many ways tougher than JFK," Salinger said. "But he worshiped his older brother, just idolized him. Everything he did he did for the President, and in a terrible instant it was all gone."

Unable to sleep, Jack's little brother would get out of bed in the middle of the night and drive around Washington for hours. Sometimes he visited Jackie at the N Street address, where they talked until sunrise, taking solace in their shared grief. "I think he is the most compassionate person I know,"

Jackie said, "but probably only the closest people around him — family, friends, and those who work for him — would see that. People of a private nature are often misunderstood because they are too shy and too proud to explain themselves."

Over the next six months, Bobby became a surrogate father to his brother's children. Nearly every day, Jackie took them to Hickory Hill to play with Bobby and Ethel's brood of eight.

"They think of Hickory Hill as their own home," Jackie later said. "Anything that comes up involving a father, like Father's Day at school, I always mention Bobby's name. Caroline shows him her report cards. She makes drawings at school marked 'To Uncle Bobby.'

"We used to think that if anything happened to us, we'd want to leave the children with Ethel and Bobby," Jackie added. "But we always felt they had their own big responsibilities. Now I want them to be part of that family. Bobby wants to look after his brother's children. There's John, with his brother's name. He's going to make sure John turns out as he should."

That meant lots of affection for Caroline, who unabashedly clung to her uncle whenever she visited Hickory Hill. "She's my pal," Bobby said of the quiet, introspective little girl. He could not help but be touched by her. "Every time I see her," he told Jack's best friend, Lem Billings, "I want to go somewhere and cry."

For John-John, too young to understand the tragedy of his father's death, there was a healthy dose of Kennedy roughhousing. "Jack made John the mischievous, independent boy he is," Jackie said. "Bobby is keeping that alive."

Soon, Jackie became so convinced that only Bobby could replace Jack in her children's lives that she asked him to legally adopt them. Ethel, growing jealous of the attention Bobby was giving the President's widow, suggested that that would not be a good idea.

Jackie was as fond of Ethel as Ethel was of her. "She drops kids like rabbits," Jackie once said of Bobby's prolific wife. She also derisively called Ethel "the baby-making machine — wind her up and she becomes pregnant."

Jackie may have felt her own life had been irreparably shattered, but she did everything she could to make certain her children did not suffer the same fate. The daily visits from Dave Powers continued, and occasionally old White House fixtures like Kenny O'Donnell and Pierre Salinger dropped in to check up on Caroline and John.

Jackie also asked White House Curator Jim Ketchum, who had been reading a book of Russian fairy tales to John-John, to come by the N Street house with the book around bedtime. After Ketchum had read to John-John, they all agreed to go out to Billy Martin's Carriage House, a popular Georgetown restaurant, for dinner.

There was a hitch — neither Ketchum or Tuckerman had any money. "No problem," said Jackie, who went upstairs and returned with a fistful of one-dollar bills snatched from the children's piggy bank.

It was the first time Jackie had ventured out in public for dinner, yet no one bothered her. When they had finished, Jackie said to Ketchum, "Jim, I'm going to put my hand under the table, and you put your hand under the table, and I'm going to give you the money and you pay the bill."

Ketchum stuck his hand under the table "and of course, she dropped the money. The next you know, I'm underneath the table of Jackie Kennedy, on my hands and knees gathering crumpled dollar bills." While everyone else in the restaurant "was just staring open-eyed," Jackie collapsed with laughter. "She was just loving it." Ketchum wondered if she had dropped the money so everyone would know she was paying for the meal, and not him, or if she "just wanted to laugh, even briefly."

Jackie returned to Billy Martin's a week later on the arm of Robert McNamara.

Jackie often told Jack that she felt McNamara was the most attractive man in his cabinet. "Men can't understand his sex appeal," she once commented to the Bradlees over dinner at the White House. "Look at them," she told Tony, pointing to Ben Bradlee and the President. "They look just like dogs that have had a plate of food grabbed from under their noses."

At Billy Martin's, Jackie, clearly intoxicated, was draped over McNamara, "hugging and kissing him," according to one witness. At one point Jackie got up and staggered toward the ladies' room. "Then she came out kind of weaving and terribly unsteady on her feet, and left." Everyone in the restaurant recognized her, but out of sympathy no one said a thing. The incident never made the papers.

Back on N Street, the crowds were becoming larger and more unruly. Busloads of tourists now drove by several times a day. "It was a complete circus," said NBC newswoman and Kennedy friend Nancy Dickerson, "there was no way anyone could tolerate it."

Although Bobby was clearly Jackie's main pillar of support in the family, Lee Radziwill had remained in Washington, thinking of ways to lift her sister's spirits. At Lee's urging, Jackie began to test the waters in the city where they were raised, New York. She spent two weekends at the Carlyle Hotel on Madison Avenue. During his presidency, Jack had used the Kennedys' suite at the Carlyle as a jumping-off point for several of his extramarital affairs. A secret labyrinth of subterranean passageways had made it possible for Jack to party with beautiful women at their East Side town houses without ever being detected by the press.

On her trip back to Manhattan, she spent time with old friends like Truman Capote and Leland Hayward's wife Pamela Churchill (later to become Mrs. Averell Harriman and eventually U.S. Ambassador to France). "Jackie couldn't go anywhere in Washington without being mobbed," Capote said, "but in New York they ignored her the way they ignore everyone else. We walked down Madison Avenue and no one said a thing. Not a thing."

By late February, Caroline also seemed a little less withdrawn. On President's Day, Sister Joanne Frey showed three pictures to her religion class. With each, she asked the class to identify the person. First, she held up a portrait of George Washington, then one of Lincoln. Finally, she held up a portrait of President Kennedy.

"Who can tell me who this is?" she asked. Frey remembered that "Caroline was just *vibrant*, but she didn't say anything. The other children started saying 'That's Caroline's daddy! That's Caroline's daddy!' Caroline just sat there beaming with pride."

Her own heartache aside, Jackie still went out of her way to boost the morale of those who had been close to her and Jack in the White House. When Pierre Salinger, drinking heavily and unhappy as Lyndon Johnson's press secretary, contemplated running for a U.S. Senate seat in his home state of California, the Irish Mafia discouraged him.

Bobby, the hard-nosed politico, told him to run "only if you can win" — and made it clear that he doubted if Salinger could. Ken O'Donnell told Pierre bluntly, "I don't think you've got the guts."

Disheartened, Salinger turned to "the one person whose opinion I valued even above Bobby Kennedy's. I paid a visit to Jackie in Georgetown. When I told Jackie I wanted to run for the Senate, she beamed. "I *know* you can win. If there is some quiet way I can help, please let me know."

Later that same night, Bobby dropped by Salinger's house and promised his help. Jackie had told Bobby she was backing Jack's old friend for the Senate regardless of the odds, and "that was apparently enough for Bobby. He told me," Salinger said, "I could count on his help."

On St. Patrick's Day, Sister Joanne Frey

had just finished teaching her religion class when Caroline came up to her and pointed to a magazine on her desk. It contained another photograph of JFK. "Can I take it home, Sister?" she asked. "My mommy saves every picture she can find of my daddy. She told me that whenever I see one I should bring it to her. Then she puts them in these big books. I don't know why, but it makes her smile."

From that point on, said Sister Joanne, "whenever there was a photo or picture of the President — even if it was only the size of a postage stamp — she'd take it home to her mother." The idea of Jackie sitting alone in her room pasting magazine cutouts in albums seemed "odd, to say the least," the nun said. "Particularly since you couldn't go ten minutes without seeing JFK's image — especially back then. He was *everywhere* — on a stamp, even on a fifty-cent piece! Perhaps it was therapeutic for her."

That afternoon, Sister Joanne was driving by Washington's Rock Creek Park when she spotted a familiar figure. "It was Mrs. Kennedy," she recalled. "I rolled down the window — there was no place I could park — and called out to her. I was wearing my habit, so she recognized me immediately and came over to the car. I looked around for a Secret Service agent, but didn't see anybody. She seemed to be just wandering through the park alone, lost in her thoughts."

"Caroline told me about the picture of my husband you showed in class," she told Sister Joanne. "I'm looking forward to seeing it."

Frey recalled that Jackie "looked so miserable, it was hard for me to concentrate on what she was saying. She wore a sort of babushka over her head, and no makeup — her eyes were red, her face was swollen, it was obvious she had been crying."

Sister Joanne went straight home, and "there in the paper was a picture of Mrs. Kennedy at Arlington putting a shamrock on the President's grave earlier in the day. She was wearing a mink coat, and looked beautiful in the photograph. Then it hit me: This is the face the public sees. I just saw the *real* Mrs. Kennedy — alone, sad, completely devastated."

Lee insisted it was time Jackie get away from all the painful memories. She had been lobbying to have her sister move with her to New York, arguing that there she would be free to move about the city without constant harassment from the press. Lee even paved the way by having Stas Radziwill purchase an eleven-room co-op at 969 Fifth Avenue.

Lee's concern for her sister belied an intense rivalry that had, in the words of their mutual friend Truman Capote, "left Lee feeling very, very lost and totally eclipsed by

Jackie." Capote first realized this in 1962, when he jotted down, "My God, how jealous Lee is of Jackie. I never knew." Yet, for the moment at least, her heart genuinely went out to Jackie.

That spring Jackie faced another soul-wrenching task. Secretly, she returned to Hammersmith Farm, the Auchincloss estate in Newport, to pick out the permanent marker for Jack's grave at Arlington. At her request, John Steven's Stone Masons in Newport selected a half dozen stones for her to choose from. These slabs, weighing hundreds of pounds each, were hauled to Hammersmith Farm, where they were laid in a semicircle in the Auchincloss garden. Jackie walked from stone to stone, running her hand over the marble surface, studying each for any imperfections.

"There was a sad symmetry to Jackie choosing the President's grave marker at Hammersmith," Jamie Auchincloss said. "It was where she and Jack were married, where Jackie had come of age, and was the site of the summer White House." Jackie "went about the whole process in a very business-like way," he said, "but everybody watching this — including the stonemasons — was fighting back tears."

During the Easter holiday, Jackie took Caroline and John-John to Stowe for a ski vacation with Bobby, Teddy, and their families. Then she left with Bobby, Chuck Spalding, and Lee and Stas Radziwill for a week at Bunny Mellon's hilltop villa in Antigua. They went sailing, water-skiing, and picnicking on some of the tiny uninhabited islands in the area. At night they had cocktails on the veranda and listened to records — "mostly Sinatra and Peggy Lee," Spalding remembered, which Bobby played over and over again at ear-splitting levels.

"Everybody was trying to drown out the bad memories any way they could," Spalding said, "to really try and get some fun out of life again." Toward that end, Jackie had brought along a supply of Dr. Max Jacobson's tablets.

It was also clear that the special bond between Bobby and Jackie was developing into something more than friendship. They held hands, huddled together in corners, and whispered confidences in each other's ears. "Bobby and Jackie were definitely a unit, a twosome," Spalding said. "She relied on him for everything, and he adored her. There was definitely an intimacy there."

That a romance might develop seemed only logical, given the longstanding Kennedy tradition of sharing girlfriends. Over the years women were passed from one brother to another, or from Joe Kennedy to his sons — or vice-versa. Bobby had, for instance, begun seeing Marilyn Monroe after his brother Jack ended his affair with her.

In his grief, Bobby also sought solace in the company of women other than Ethel. Joan Braden, who with her newspaperman-husband, Tom Braden, was the model for the television series *Eight Is Enough*, listened to Bobby pour out his heart about his dead brother one evening. "He had never seemed more vulnerable," Braden remembered. "When he asked me to go upstairs, I went. On the bed, we kissed. Then he got up to take off his tie. But I could not go through with it. He was hurt, silent, and angry."

There was someone else who, believing Bobby had softened considerably since Dallas, was spending intimate moments alone with him. A decade earlier, Lee's first husband, Michael Canfield, had listened in one room while his wife made love to Jack Kennedy in the next. Now Lee found herself falling for Jack's younger brother. In the early months of 1964, she threw two parties for the Attorney General in London, and to those present it was apparent that Lee had more than a passing interest in her guest of honor. "Lee wanted to sleep with Bobby," Capote said, "and Bobby, like all those Kennedy men, was not one to pass up the opportunity."

On May 29, what would have been Jack's forty-seventh birthday, Jackie and the children placed flowers on his grave, and after a mass at St. Matthew's Church flew north to Hyannis Port. There Jackie, still worried that her husband would be forgotten, made a televised pitch on behalf of the Kennedy Library that was broadcast on both sides of the Atlantic. "Many people in many countries have written to me, saying that he gave them new confidence in America," she said, "and in their own ability to solve their problems."

Echoing JFK's Inaugural Address, she added, "We should all do something to right the wrongs we see and not just complain about them. We owe that to our country." Then she went on to describe her vision for the JFK Library: "His office will be there. You can hear every speech he made, you can see all the manuscripts of his speeches and how he changed them."

Working tirelessly to find the right architect for the project, she had in fact already decided on a relative unknown named I. M. Pei. Overruling those who wanted an established architect like Philip Johnson or Mies van der Rohe for the job, Jackie said she felt "I.M.'s temperament was right. He was like a wonderful hunting dog when you clip the leash. I don't care if he hasn't done much. I just knew he was the one."

Once the TV broadcast on behalf of the JFK Library was over, Jackie again withdrew into her "shell of grief." Finally heeding

Lee's advice, Jackie went apartment hunting in New York with Nancy Tuckerman. To sidestep the press, Nancy Tuckerman played the role of prospective buyer while Jackie went along disguised as the nanny.

Nothing suited Jackie until longtime Kennedy friend Jayne Wrightsman, whose palatial oceanfront estate in Palm Beach served as JFK's winter White House, told her about a five-bedroom, five-bath apartment at 1040 Fifth Avenue that had just come on the market. The fifteenth-floor co-op, owned by Mrs. Lowell Weicker (her husband would serve both as Connecticut's Republican senator and as the state's governor), boasted its own elevator as well as sweeping views of Central Park and the reservoir.

Moreover, 1040 Fifth came with a built-in support group. In addition to Lee, who lived just down the block at 969 Fifth, in-laws Peter and Pat Lawford resided at 990 Fifth, Steven and Jean Kennedy Smith lived at 950 Fifth, and step-brother Hugh "Yusha" Auchincloss III lived nearby on Park Avenue.

She declared the co-op "perfect" for her needs, but would not meet the $200,000 asking price without first consulting her financial guru, Lazard Freres Director Andre Meyer. "If you think it's a good investment," she told the elderly Meyer, "I'll buy it." She did, and spent another $125,000 to have it decorated.

To make the move out of the Washington area complete, Jackie unloaded Wexford for a reported $130,000. She then leased a house not far from Bobby Kennedy's own summer rental in Glen Cove, Long Island. Soon Bobby, stung by Lyndon Johnson's decision not to put him on the 1964 ticket as his running mate, would also relocate permanently to New York and announce his candidacy for the U.S. Senate.

From a suite at the Carlyle Hotel, Jackie oversaw the small army of workmen who were transforming the somewhat frayed-at-the-edges Fifth Avenue apartment into a showplace. She was also busy trying to raise funds for the JFK Library. Using the same talent for persuasion that funded her historic White House restoration, Jackie charmed, cajoled, and shamed individuals and nations alike into contributing to the project.

Financier Meyer, who gave Jackie the green light to purchase the New York co-op, kicked in $250,000. Fiat Chairman Gianni Agnelli had made headlines when he and Jackie went swimming off his yacht anchored along the Amalfi Coast in 1962, prompting JFK to cable her "A LITTLE MORE CAROLINE AND LESS AGNELLI." Now the dashing Italian auto magnate was anteing up $100,000 for the Kennedy Library fund, as were the governments of Venezuela, Puerto Rico, and France.

She had not yet shaken her demons, if indeed she ever would. Yet Jackie, no longer pursued by the more aggressive Washington press corps and no longer surrounded by painful memories of her days as First Lady, was beginning to feel like a human being again. "New York gave her the one thing she so desperately needed," Nancy Dickerson said. "It gave her room to breathe."

More than six months after the assassination, the move also marked Jackie's sexual reawakening. "Some people thought Jackie was more of a voyeuse than a practitioner — that she liked to watch," Gore Vidal said. "I'm not at all convinced of that. She and Jack both loved gossip and could go on talking endlessly about other people's sex lives, but I always got the distinct impression that she was very interested in sex the same way that Jack was very interested in sex. It was a game for them, and they *both* played it."

While her feelings for Bobby intensified and deepened, she also became romantically involved with someone else — a brief, potentially shocking affair that both parties managed to keep secret. He was a year younger than Robert Kennedy, handsome, dynamic, rich — and a passionate crusader for Civil Rights. Like Jack and Bobby, he had had a torrid affair with Marilyn Monroe. But unlike the Kennedy brothers, whose peccadilloes were kept from the press and public, the new man in Jackie's life was an international sex symbol whose countless conquests offscreen as well as on were legendary. His name was Marlon Brando.

She's a fighter, for all her frail beauty.

> — *Frank Conniff,*
> family friend

I'd jump out of the window for him.

> — *Jackie,*
> speaking about her feelings for
> Bobby Kennedy, 1965

FOUR

By the time Jackie Kennedy and Marlon Brando first got together in early 1964, the Academy Award–winning star of *A Streetcar Named Desire* and *On the Waterfront* had already cut a wide swath through Hollywood. Brando was so promiscuous that he kept two abortionists on retainer to cope with the inevitable outcome of his recreational pursuits. Even Jackie's husband was impressed.

"I don't think," Brando conceded, "I was constructed to be monogamous . . . I've had far too many affairs to think of myself as a normal, rational man." Brando led what he described as a "Rolodex Life" when it came to women, but he also harbored a deep-seated grudge against womanizers like himself. He explained that he saw his middle age as "the 'Fuck You' years. If I met a man who had a certain kind of overt masculinity, he became my enemy." Victory, admitted Brando, "often took the form of sleeping with his wife."

During one drunken evening he shared with JFK in 1960, Kennedy became suddenly and inexplicably belligerent. Brando was still relatively sleek in 1960, but Kennedy discerned that the *Stella!*-shouting sex symbol was beginning to put on a few pounds. Sensing he had discovered Brando's Achilles' heel, he declared that the actor was "too fat for the part."

"What part?" a thoroughly perplexed Brando wanted to know.

"That's not important. It's the fat that's important."

"Are you kidding?" Brando countered. "Have you looked in a mirror lately? Your jowls won't even fit in the frame of the television screen. When they have to go in for a close-up, they lose half your face. You look like the moon on television. I can hardly see your face, it's so fat."

Jack insisted he weighed less than Brando, so the two men stumbled into the bathroom. When Jack got on the scale, Brando hooked his toe on the corner "and made him about twenty-five pounds heavier, so that he weighed more than I did."

"Let's go, Fatso," Brando told JFK, "you lost."

In late January, just a few weeks after her outing with Robert McNamara at Billy Martin's, Jackie joined her sister, Brando, and Brando's business manager, George Englund, for lunch at Washington's Jockey Club. They were forced to wade through a sea of reporters and photographers to get into the restaurant, but Jackie would later tell friends it was well worth the effort.

From the moment they met, Jackie was "totally smitten" with the charismatic, athletic, and still brutishly handsome Brando. For more than three hours he regaled Jackie and Lee with stories of his travels in the South Pacific while making *Mutiny on the Bounty*, as well as his crusades on behalf of Native Americans and India's "untouchables."

Jackie reciprocated with details of her triumphant visit to India where, except for a much-photographed elephant ride with her sister, Lee had kept a discreet distance while adoring mobs shouted *Jackie Ki Jai! Ameriki Rani!* ("Hail Jackie! Queen of America!") Among other things, Jackie told a transfixed Brando, "Prime Minister Nehru showed me how to stand on my head and meditate."

According to her friend Franklin Roosevelt Jr., Jackie was "enchanted" by Brando and found him "extremely attractive." Chuck Spalding agreed: "Like half the other women on the planet at the time, Jackie found Marlon Brando completely irresistible." When the lunch was over, Jackie had to run the press gauntlet again — another unnerving reminder that her life would never be her own as long as she remained in Washington.

Now that she had resettled in New York,

Jackie invited the fatally charming Brando to her suite at the Carlyle. Brando viewed Jack's widow, at this point the most admired woman in America, as a challenge. "The less likely I was to seduce a woman," Brando said, "the more I wanted to succeed."

One evening, after several drinks and in a sudden explosion of pent-up passion on both sides, Jackie and Brando made love. According to Random House editor Joe Fox, Brando wrote about his brief, torrid affair with Jackie in an original draft of his own memoirs. But Fox, a friend of Jackie's, convinced Brando to take out the reference.

Brando admitted to "a lot of extracurricular fucking during the early sixties," and his affair with Jackie was, typically, short-lived. "I have always been lucky with women," he conceded, "though I hardly ever spent more than a couple of minutes with any of them." (Brando appears to have had much the same laissez-faire attitude toward men. Truman Capote recalled that in 1956 Brando admitted he "went to bed with lots of men" but that he did not consider himself gay. Brando explained that these men were so attracted to him, "I just thought that I was doing them a favor.")

It is doubtful that Jackie, still very much involved with Bobby and also spending time with a number of handsome escorts, from Robert McNamara to former Deputy Defense Secretary Roswell Gilpatric, was interested in pursuing the relationship after it had been consummated. The affair was reminiscent of her brief romance with William Holden, in retaliation for Jack's 1953 premarital affair with Audrey Hepburn.

Jackie "had her share of affairs with the famous," Gore Vidal said, adding that at first he suspected "these couplings were motivated by revenge on Jack, not to mention just plain stamp collecting." Vidal claimed that "one common misconception about Jackie is that she was above it all, that she wasn't interested in movie stars and other garden-variety celebrities. But celebrities — including Jackie — are invariably celebrity-mad in the same way that liars always believe liars."

Try as she might to forge an entirely new life for herself in New York, Jackie was still tormented by the ghosts of the past. Early that summer of 1964, Jim and Minnie Astor Fosburgh invited a small group that included Jackie, the cartoonist Charles Addams, and Kitty Carlisle Hart for a weekend at their country home in Westchester County.

"We were all so sorry for Jackie and so determined for her to have a good time," Hart said. "Of course the assassination was still the number-one topic — there was still a great deal of discussion about it several months after the fact. But that weekend, everybody was desperately concerned not to say anything that might upset her."

One day when everyone was sitting around the pool, Hart recalled, "the conversation lagged a bit so I said, 'Let's all tell each other our Walter Mitty stories — what we'd like to be.' Charles Addams wanted to be a big band leader. I don't remember what I said I wanted to be . . ."

When it came to Jackie, there was total silence as she stared off into the distance, thinking. "I'd like," she said, "to be a *bird*."

"I understood exactly what she meant," Hart said. "She wanted to be free, gone, away." After their swim, Hart and Jackie went into the cabana changing room. "She started to talk about those last three minutes in the car in Dallas," Hart recalled, "and I just listened. She kept asking herself what she could have done differently — if she had moved just this much to the left, or that much to the right, would it have made a difference?

"Jackie maintained a social façade, but with me she was very different. I had lost my husband [playwright Moss Hart] only a year earlier, and I know how it feels to suddenly be left alone with young children. There was a kinship between us. I could sympathize."

Nonetheless, as Jackie detailed those same horrifying moments when the bullets ripped into her husband's head "over and over and over again," even Hart found it "unnerving. She was a woman possessed."

Tragedy struck the family yet again on June 19, 1964, when Ted Kennedy insisted on flying in bad weather to Springfield, Massachusetts, to accept his party's nomination for a second term in the Senate. The small plane crashed into an apple orchard, killing Ted's aide and the pilot. Ted's back was broken in the accident. Less than forty-eight hours later, Jackie joined Bobby at his younger brother's bedside. Later in the hospital cafeteria, she said, "Oh, Bobby, we have such rotten luck."

"Somebody up there," Bobby replied wryly, "doesn't like us."

The crash cemented the already strong bond between the two surviving Kennedy brothers. "The relationship between Teddy and Bob has become far deeper the last six months," Jackie said. "Teddy has become to him now what Bob was to Jack. They're like crossed fingers. They talk every morning, and every night, wherever they are."

With Jackie firmly entrenched in New York, Bobby now considered running for the Senate from that state. The week following Teddy's accident, Bobby posed for the cover of *Life* magazine with six of his extended brood climbing all over him. In the foreground, John-John, wearing shorts and missing his left front tooth, smiled broadly for the camera. The other children were all caught in various stages of hysteria, with one sad exception: Caroline, who sat silently on her uncle's knee wearing an expression that fell somewhere between wistful and melancholic.

In the *Life* piece, Bobby stated flatly that he would not run for the Senate — that Teddy's brush with death made it clear to him that his first responsibility was to the family. In truth, Bobby had already made up his mind to run for the Senate if LBJ — whom he loathed — did not pick him for his running mate. The *Life* cover story was a calculated attempt to garner public support and force Johnson's hand. Two days after Johnson told Bobby he had chosen Minnesota Senator Hubert Humphrey for the number-two spot, Kennedy announced his Senate candidacy and moved into a sprawling apartment in Manhattan's glass-sheathed United Nations Towers.

Bobby's ace in the hole was Jackie. "You knew that if you were in trouble, he'd always be there," she had said. Now she wanted to be there for him. "He is the one," she said, "that I would put my hand in the fire for."

Soon, she was doing for Bobby what she

176

had done for Jack during the 1960 presidential campaign, translating passages from Voltaire and providing quotes from Tennyson and Shakespeare to use in his speeches. Nonetheless Bobby, accused of carpetbagging and suffering from comparisons with his charismatic brother, quickly grew discouraged. After only a month of campaigning, he told Jackie he intended to quit. She responded with an impassioned letter urging him to stay in the race.

On July 7, Jackie's office issued the formal, belated announcement that the former First Lady was relocating to New York permanently. The next day her longtime secretary Mary Gallagher, whom Jackie had tearfully begged to never leave her side, received a call.

"I suppose by now you've read in the newspapers about my move to New York," Jackie said.

"Yes, Jackie," Gallagher answered, "I have, but . . ."

"Well, since my life is all changed now and my staff will be located in New York, I guess I really won't be needing you any more after September First."

Gallagher was in shock. "Well, Jackie, if that's your decision . . ."

"Oh, now, Mary," Jackie replied, "don't get huffy . . ."

Gallagher knew that someday Jackie

would no longer need her, but explained that "when the time would come for Jackie to announce she no longer needed me, it would be in a warm, face-to-face manner. Obviously, I had expected too much."

In August, Jackie returned to Europe for the first time since Jack's death. With her wealthy friends the Wrightsmans, she cruised Yugoslavia's Dalmatian coast on their yacht *Radiant II* before spending two weeks in Italy with Lee and Stas Radziwill. She returned in time for the Democratic National Convention in Atlantic City.

Concerned that sentiment for the Kennedys would sweep the convention, Johnson wisely arranged for the balloting to take place before Bobby introduced a twenty-minute film tribute to Jack. Welcomed with a thunderous ovation, Bobby brought the crowd to tears by quoting from *Romeo and Juliet*:

> When he shall die,
> Take him and cut him out in little stars,
> And he will make the face of heaven
>   so fine
> That all the world will be in love
>   with night,
> And pay no worship to the garish sun.

The passage, selected by Jackie, was a not-so-subtle swipe at Jack's garish successor in the White House.

Bobby notwithstanding, Jackie was still the star of the convention. At a reception in her honor at the Deauville Hotel, Jackie, wearing a sleeveless white dress, white gloves, and a fixed smile, shook the hands of five thousand delegates and alternates. Bobby and Lady Bird Johnson stood next to her for support.

"Eyes shining and always, always smiling," writer Shana Alexander said of Jackie, "she stood stiff — one hand pumped ceaselessly up and down like a lovely mechanical doll." Outside the ballroom, those without a pale blue invitation tried to push their way past security guards, shattering a plateglass door in the process. In the end, Alexander felt that "for all its air of unreality, Mrs. Kennedy's performance and the response it evoked was the most touchingly real event of the convention."

In case there was any doubt as to where her sympathies lay, Jackie did not go out of her way for the incumbent President. According to William Manchester, Jackie had always been "appalled by Johnson's earthiness." Once, when they were discussing Jackie's friend Adlai Stevenson, LBJ said, "You know, he squats to piss." Jackie was "horrified," Manchester said. "She didn't know what to say. She was stunned."

Bobby had gradually convinced her that LBJ was the enemy, and she now shared her brother-in-law's open contempt for the man. "Don't you know the Johnsons despise us?" she said to Mary Gallagher. "They won't even allow the Secret Service agents to wear their PT-boat tie clips anymore."

After the reception, Jackie headed directly for Newport and the Auchincloss summer home, Hammersmith Farm. Her half-brother, Jamie, was on board the plane with her waiting to take off.

"Jackie was exhausted, and really looking forward to going home. But we just sat there on the runway," Jamie said. "Finally, Jackie asked why we weren't taking off. It turned out that *Air Force One* was also there, and that President Johnson insisted that she come out and pose with him for pictures on the runway. She refused. Jackie did not want to be used that way."

LBJ would not take no for an answer, and for the next half hour the pilots radioed back and forth until Johnson himself got on the radio and talked to Jackie directly. Wouldn't she make this one gesture that could mean so much to him and to the Party in this election year? he pleaded. "She said, gently but firmly, no," Jamie said. "My sister could not be budged once her mind was made up, and the one thing she hated above all else was being exploited — even by the President."

With one major exception. Bobby felt he needed the endorsement of the *New York Post* if he had any hope of defeating New York's popular Senator Kenneth Keating, who had the backing of many influential liberals. Over tea at her Carlyle Hotel suite, Jackie tried to win over the *New York Post*'s publisher, Dorothy Schiff.

"He must win," Jackie told Schiff. "He will win. He must win. Or maybe it is just because one wants it so much that one thinks that. People say he is ruthless and cold. He isn't like the others. I think it was his place in the family, with four girls and being younger than two brothers and so much smaller. He hasn't got the graciousness they had. He is really very shy, but he has the kindest heart in the world."

Yet back in Washington a bizarre series of events threatened not only to derail Bobby's Senate campaign but to explode the Camelot myth in its infancy. Even Ben and Tony Bradlee professed to be shocked when they learned that Tony's sister, Mary Meyer, had carried on an affair with Jack for the final two years of his life.

"There was no way Jackie could have known about it," said Kennedy friend Nancy Dickerson, who was dating Mary's ex-husband, Cord Meyer, at the time. "So I was paying attention to those things. I knew Jack was fond of Mary Meyer, but nobody remotely suspected they were having an affair. None of us knew."

But J. Edgar Hoover knew and, by extension, so did his boss, Attorney General Robert F. Kennedy. In October 1964, while Jackie was trying to persuade Dorothy Schiff that Bobby could carry on the Kennedy legacy, Mary Meyer went for her usual stroll along the towpath by the canal in Georgetown. She was grabbed from behind and shot, execution style, once under her cheekbone. A young black man who had been seen in the area was charged with the murder of Mary Meyer and later acquitted.

Not long after Meyer's death, the Bradlees went to her house in search of her diary and discovered that CIA counterintelligence operative James Angleton had broken in. He, too, was looking for the diary, which described in considerable detail her affair with the President — including an evening when they both smoked marijuana inside the White House. The Bradlees turned the diary over to the CIA to be destroyed, but instead it surfaced in 1976. This time, the original was turned over to Tony Bradlee, who burned it.

Because Meyer's affair with JFK was unknown to the public and to the press — with the exception of Ben Bradlee — little was made of her mysterious, unsolved murder. Investigators at the time noted that Meyer's murder had all the markings of a Mafia execution. Were they worried that Meyer knew about the ongoing White House–CIA–Mafia plot to assassinate Castro and might talk?

If Bobby was shaken by Meyer's murder, he did not let on to anyone in his campaign. Because of Jackie's passionate intercession, he won the coveted endorsement from the *New York Post* and went on to win the election by 700,000 votes. Jackie's was not among them. She chose not to vote that year, a decision that infuriated many Democrats — just as she had in 1960 when she voted for only one candidate, her husband, so as not to "dilute" the experience.

"I know that LBJ was hurt that I didn't vote in 1964," Jackie later said. "People in my own family told me I should vote. I said, 'I'm not going to vote.' This is very emotional, but I'd never voted until I was married to Jack. I guess my first vote was probably for him for Senator . . . Then this vote would have been his — he would have been alive for that vote. And I thought, I'm not going to vote for anyone because this vote would have been his."

In mid-November, Jackie was still living at the Carlyle while Billy Baldwin commanded a small army of paperhangers and plasterers at 1040 Fifth. But she didn't mind the temporary quarters. "I think she saw her return to the city as coming home," Nancy Tuckerman recalled. "And more than anything she hoped — perhaps even expected — that in a city of such size and diversity, she'd be able to find the anonymity she longed for. But this was unrealistic, and intellectually she probably knew it."

Perhaps, but for a time she convinced herself that she might be able to assume the role of private citizen. Toward that end, she gave up her lifetime franking privilege, and complained bitterly about the ever-present Secret Service agents still assigned to guard her and the children.

Even at the White House, Jackie was very specific about what she would and would not tolerate from the agency assigned to guard her family. "Mrs. Kennedy feels very strongly," wrote the head of the Secret Service Children's Detail in a confidential memo, "that though there are two children to protect, it is 'bad' to see two agents 'hovering around' . . . If Mrs. Kennedy is driving the children, she still insists that the follow-up car not be seen by the children . . .

"Mrs. Kennedy is adamant in her contention that agents must not perform special favors for John Jr. and Caroline or wait upon them as servants. Agents are not to carry clothes, beach articles, sand buckets, baby carriages, strollers, handbags, suitcases etc., for Caroline and John Jr. and the children must carry their own clothing items, toys etc. . . . The agent must drift into the background quickly when arriving at a specific location, and remain aloof and invisible until moment of departure. . . .

"Mrs. Kennedy," the memo continued, "is inclined to believe that the agents are doing too much for the children, and feels 'it is bad for the children to see grown men waiting upon them. The agents must demand that Caroline pick up her own discarded clothes, shoes, toys, accessories, etc.' "

Jackie insisted on remaining her children's first line of defense at the beach. "Drowning is my responsibility," she told the agents, claiming that the Secret Service "is not responsible for any accident sustained by the children in the usual and normal play sessions." These were "the sole responsibility of Mrs. Kennedy."

Caroline's horseback riding presented another problem for the agents, who suggested that they get a horse of their own so they could follow her. According to the memo, Jackie replied that "the Kennedy children are better riders than the Secret Service agents, and that Caroline was probably safer riding with the other children than she would be with a Secret Service agent 'with a very limited knowledge of horses.' " Besides, Jackie pointed out that as a child she had broken her collarbone falling off a horse, and that she expected Caroline to "have her share of riding spills and accidents — how else will she learn?"

Jackie was also afraid that the children were becoming too attached to one particular agent as a father figure. Reluctantly, she asked that he be reassigned. As a token of their admiration and affection, Jackie and the children gave the departing agent, Charlie, one of their seven dogs.

What Jackie did want the Secret Service for was to serve as a bulwark against the general public. When she visited a Hyannis Port newsstand with John-John one day, the agent stood by while a small crowd of "harmless onlookers" — mostly "elderly ladies with cameras" tried to snap a few photos. Jackie, said the agent, "turned a cold shoulder and refused to permit any photographs." Later, she instructed the agent, "Do something when there are people around like that!"

But Jackie, as Tuckerman pointed out, "by this time was more than a household name. She was a public figure, and the press and the rest of the world were not about to let her forget it."

She moved into her Fifth Avenue apartment that autumn hoping that it would prove to be her refuge from the prying eyes of the public, her sanctum sanctorum. On moving day, Jackie and Tuckerman emptied cartons, put books on bookshelves, and hung paintings on the walls. At about 8 P.M., the doorbell rang and Jackie, wearing jeans and looking "quite disheveled," opened the door. "There stood two distinguished-looking couples in full evening attire," Tuckerman said. "When they recognized Jackie they were taken aback. They said they were expected for dinner at Mrs. Whitehouse's. It turned out that the elevator man, unnerved by the mere thought of Jackie's presence in the building, was unable to associate the name *Whitehouse* with anyone or anything but her."

The apartment itself would remain essentially unchanged for the next thirty years. "She was not in the habit of changing or rearranging furniture," Tuckerman said. "Once everything was in place, she kept it that way, replacing worn upholstery or slipcovers with identical materials."

At last she seemed to have much of her life under control. Caroline was enrolled in second grade at the prestigious Convent of the Sacred Heart just a few blocks up from her Fifth Avenue apartment at 91st Street. John-John, still a year away from entering St. David's School, rode his tricycle, visited the Central Park Zoo, and rode on the carousel while Secret Service agents watched from the sidelines.

For Caroline, the adjustment was difficult. She wondered why she was never asked to any of the other girls' birthday parties. Jackie got on the phone to another mother to find out why. "Of course we'd love to invite Caroline," the woman sputtered, "but we all felt that it might be presumptuous of us to ask."

By all means, Jackie replied, "Please invite Caroline to everything. She's dying to come!" From that point on, the little girl's social schedule rivaled her mother's.

Most days Jackie spent in her unmarked office at 200 Park Avenue sorting through the mail with Pam Turnure and Nancy Tuckerman. Yet Jackie found time to go on a few outings with the children — to the circus, to the World's Fair, to Serendipity off Third Avenue for butterscotch sundaes.

When Morocco's King Hassan II visited, Jackie threw a small birthday party at her apartment for the Crown Prince, who was turning four. She felt she owed it to Hassan, who had, after all, offered her her own Moorish palace in Marrakech (she initially accepted but then had second thoughts).

Aware that there were few things more taxing than children's birthday parties, Jackie asked Jamie Auchincloss, then seventeen, to lend a helping hand. "You've got to remember that little Muhammed was considered to be a direct descendant of the Prophet Muhammed," Jamie said, "and therefore a very, very big deal in the Moslem world."

When Jamie got there, "the birthday boy was sitting at the table and looking terrified.

There were several bodyguards standing around and a nanny who looked even more intimidating than the bodyguards. All of a sudden, Jackie came bursting out of the kitchen with a big birthday cake. She couldn't sing a note, and she knew it, but that didn't keep her from belting out this incredibly off-key version of 'Happy Birthday.'

"And just for fun she threw in all these titles, only some of which were little Muhammed's. 'Happy Birthday to you, Happy Birthday to you, Happy Birthday Dear Muhammed, Crown Prince, Lion of Judah . . .' We thought it was hysterical, but her guests weren't laughing."

Then, Jackie's half-brother remembered, Muhammed tried to blow out the four candles "and couldn't. No matter how hard he tried and how many times he blew, they wouldn't go out. Even when the nurse and the guards helped — nothing. Jackie had put trick candles on the cake, and was sure everybody would think it was funny. But the Prince was considered infallible in his part of the world, and so he started crying and the nurse started yelling at my sister — something she shouldn't have done. Jackie was not accustomed to be talked to that way — especially by a servant. So she basically told the woman it was her house and she'd do what she damn well pleased. I was very proud of her."

Over the next few months, Jackie's New York friends took turns inviting her to their town houses and Park Avenue triplexes for dinner. A frequent escort was the writer George Plimpton, whose friendship with Jackie dated back to her debutante days. "We would go to these small dinner parties — always groups of four or six, never more than that," Plimpton said. "In those days I used to go around to see her quite a lot. She was absolutely devoted to her children, and even with all that had happened she made sure they had a happy life. I always adored Caroline. She was really a very, very special person. Whenever I could I'd drop in and read her a story. When I was a boy I loved *Treasure Island*, but when I read it to her she'd be out by the time I got to the second page."

That November of 1964 it seemed to Plimpton that Jackie had "more or less come to terms with what had happened. I always felt the business about her strength during the funeral was overstated. It was a terribly, terribly sad occasion, certainly, but she was raised, as I was, to believe that you keep your chin up and you don't throw yourself on the coffin. However, Dr. Feelgood gave her the shots to get through it all."

The first anniversary of Dallas hit Jackie with unexpected force. "People tell me that time will heal," she told Dorothy Schiff. "How much time? Last week I forgot to cancel the newspaper and I picked them up and there was the publication of the Warren Report, so I canceled them for the rest of the week. But I went to the hairdresser and picked up *Life* magazine, and it was terrible."

Schiff was stunned at the toll all the anniversary press coverage seemed to be taking on Jackie in those weeks leading up to November 22, 1964. "It was hard talking to her," Schiff said. "She let silences go on. She is odd and different, very much less the queen than she was."

The memories flooded back as the anniversary drew nearer. "I should have known that it was too much to dream that I might have grown old with him," Jackie said. "On so many days — his birthday, an anniversary, watching his children running to the sea — I have thought, 'But this day last year was his last to see that.' Soon the final day will come around again . . .

"Learning to accept what was unthinkable when he was alive changes you. I don't think there is any consolation. What was lost cannot be replaced. Now I think that I should have known that he was magic all along. I did know it, but I should have guessed that it could not last . . . Now he is a legend when he would have preferred to be a man."

As the anniversary approached, black-bordered photographs of JFK went up in store windows everywhere. Walking down Fifth Avenue on the way to Kenneth's hair salon, Jackie passed a dozen or more of these sad reminders. Once inside the salon, she stood at the receptionist's and cried.

"I can't stand it," she told her hairdresser, Rosemary Sorrentino. "Why do they remember the assassination? Why can't they celebrate his birthday?" When November 22 finally arrived, she spent the day sitting on a bench in Central Park, she later recalled to a friend, "crying my eyes out."

She was grateful to Truman Capote when he marked the first anniversary by sending her a porcelain rose. "Dear Truman," she wrote, "thank you for thinking of me always — in times that are difficult for me with such beautiful things."

Only one person really understood her anguish, and by the winter of 1964, he and Jackie were lovers. In public, confident that they were both above reproach in the wake of Jack's assassination, Bobby and his brother's widow did little to hide their affection for each other. They continued embracing, kissing, holding hands.

Classified Secret Service files revealed that Jackie and Bobby were in each other's near-constant company throughout the latter half of 1964. One fairly typical evening, for example, Bobby and Jackie attended the Kennedy Foundation Board of Directors meeting at the Four Seasons Restaurant, went to a private club called L'Interdit, then spent the night together at the Smiths' apartment at 950 Fifth.

Over the next three years, Bobby and Jackie would be seen cozying up to each other in nightspots around New York and coming out of various hotel suites in the early-morning hours. While Ethel remained at Hickory Hill or Hyannis Port with her children, Bobby and Jackie vacationed together, sharing a bedroom at the Montego Bay estate of a friend.

Bobby's office was abuzz with speculation about the Senator and Jackie. "Jackie would call all the time and ask, 'Is Bobby there?' " a staffer recalled. "The word we got was that she was shell-shocked . . . I think they needed each other, both trying to recuperate. Bobby never smiled, and in private he would cry."

Even staunch Kennedy loyalists grudgingly admitted the probability of a romance between Bobby and Jackie. According to Red Fay, after Dallas Jackie went "into hibernation and Bobby was over there practically every day with her. She's a fascinating woman. If she'd throw her charm at you, why you'd be emotionally swayed. Bobby was a controlling individual, and I think that probably if Bobby felt something, why, she was going to go along."

At her country house in Glen Cove, Long Island, Jackie and Bobby were spotted together nearly every weekend, walking arm in arm or nuzzling in the back of some quiet bar. Bruce Balding, who owned the stable where Jackie boarded her horses, remembered that "many people often saw Jackie and Bobby off by themselves, heads together, or looking fondly at each other in various hotels in the area, so they got the idea."

At the time, Jackie's sister, Lee, was having an affair with journalist Taki Theodoracopulos, who shared an apartment with Peter Lawford at New York's Sherry-Netherland Hotel. "Jackie and Bobby used to come to the bar in the hotel sometimes and have a drink, quickly and rather discreetly," Theodoracopulos said, "and Lawford was telling me at the time — this was January 1965 — that Jackie was sleeping with Bobby. The press always knew about Jack's affairs, they just didn't reveal them. But Bobby played altar boy and the press bought it."

Lawford also told his wife, Patricia, that Bobby was filling in for Jack "in all departments." Clare Boothe Luce, who along with her husband, Henry Luce, had been a longtime friend of Joseph Kennedy, also knew of the affair. "Well, of course *everybody* knew Jackie and Bobby Kennedy were 'involved,' if that's the proper term for it," she said. "At least everyone who knew them were aware of what was going on between them."

Nancy Dickerson also claimed "Jackie and Bobby were definitely having an affair. You must remember that this was years before anyone even wrote about Jack's infidelities. When the stories about JFK and Marilyn Monroe started to surface, they were dismissed as preposterous. After Dallas, no one would have believed that St. Jackie and St. Bobby were sleeping together, no matter how obvious it was. It would have been considered sacrilege."

Gore Vidal began to believe that she came to love Bobby even more than Jack. "I suspect," he said, "that the one person she ever loved, if indeed she was capable of such an emotion, was Bobby Kennedy. As Lee had gone to bed with Jack, symmetry required her to do so with Bobby. But there was always something oddly intense in her voice when she mentioned him to me."

At least one friend was convinced that the love affair with Bobby saved Jackie's life. Around the time of the anniversary, Jackie admitted to a friend that she had considered suicide. "She said she had enough sleeping pills to do it," recalled Roswell Gilpatric, one of Jackie's closest confidants. "But of course she wouldn't because of the children. Everyone who loved her was very concerned about her state of mind. Nancy Tuckerman would call and say Jackie was in her room, too ill to keep our dinner date. All the terrible memories had flooded back, and Bobby was the only one who could pull her out of her depression."

Indeed, when Bobby was not around to provide emotional support, Jackie sometimes lashed out at those around her. This was nothing new. In the White House, Jackie had been famous for her displays of temper. George Smathers remembered that Jack "had a hell of a temper, but he never held a grudge. Now Jackie was something else entirely." As *Look* photographer Stanley Tretick put it, Jackie "had a kind of way about her that strikes terror in your heart."

By Christmas, the glamorous, self-assured Jackie of old began to reemerge. She was now ensconced at "1040," and the pale blue stationery bearing that address would become familiar to all who knew her. The paneled, parquet-floored apartment itself reminded Arthur Schlesinger of "a drawing room in London, old comfortable stuff, an ambience of total comfort." Nearly all the furnishings had been in the family quarters at the White House.

The private elevator opened on to a long entrance hall with gilt-framed mirrors and nineteeth-century French architectural studies hanging on the walls. A number of artifacts Jackie and Jack had collected over the years were displayed on a table: matching yellow porcelain jardinieres, a marble torso of a Roman god, a ceremonial sword.

In the living room, there were white sofas with floral throw pillows, velvet-upholstered Louis XVI chairs, various European prints, and on an ornate French chest a half dozen Greek and Roman busts — part of the antiquities collection begun by JFK. Displayed on an easel was John Singer Sargent's ethereal *Venetian Girl*; nearby, Sargent's *Head of an Arab* and a striking watercolor by Peter Paillon, *Study of a Snow Owl.* Caroline and John-John would proudly lead visitors by the hand to look at a world map covered with colored pins — each pin indicating a spot their father had visited during his presidency. From the wraparound terrace, the view was dominated by Central Park and the reservoir, with the Hudson River and New Jersey beyond.

Perhaps the warmest room of the house was the dining room, with its crimson damask wallpaper and matching drapes, bookcases, overstuffed couches, and a black baby grand piano. On either side of the marble fireplace were blue-and-white ginger jars filled with firewood.

Jackie's green-and-white corner bedroom

would eventually look down on the Metropolitan Museum's glass-enclosed Temple of Dendur, which Jackie had actually chosen when the government of Egypt offered one of its ancient ruins as a memorial to Jack. (The temple would be shipped from Egypt to its new home across from Jackie's apartment in 1975.) The master bedroom contained the only picture of JFK in the apartment — a simple silver-framed photograph she kept on her dresser.

Jackie's closets reflected her twin passions for shopping and for organization. Evening suits and day suits were separated; evening dresses were arranged by length; and all clothes were lined up, primary color and then shades of color. Hundreds of pairs of shoes were cataloged by style and by color.

An avid artist since her days at Miss Porter's School in Farmington, Connecticut, Jackie spent hours at the window trying to capture the spectacular view on canvas — and even more time spying on pedestrians and neighbors through a high-powered telescope. "She liked the idea of turning the tables," Charles Addams said, "and prying into *other peoples'* lives for a change."

Another frequent visitor to 1040 remembered Jackie's "wicked laugh" when she spotted something "naughty. Once she shouted for me to come and look through the telescope and there were two people making love in the park — right in broad daylight. They were stark naked, and sort of down in the bushes so that no one walking by could see them. But we sure could! Jackie was crying it was so funny."

World leaders and social lions alike beat a path to her door. Housewarming gifts included the collected works of Winston Churchill — forty-nine volumes in all — from his son Randolph, and a $17,000 Louis XV bed from Bunny Mellon. Among those coming to pay homage to the world's most famous widow: Morocco's King Hassan, President Johnson, Rudolf Nureyev, and the children's favorite, Haile Selassie.

The day after Christmas 1964, she took the children on another Kennedy family ski trip — this time to Aspen. Bobby asked Joan Braden to come along. "When we all went skiing," recalled Braden, "she said, 'There'll never be another Jack.' There were escorts, companions, and another husband, but there was never another Jack for her."

Despite repeated pleas from LBJ and even a few Kennedys, Jackie refused to attend the Inauguration in January. Instead, she embarked on a whirlwind schedule of parties and trips. In New York, she saw a Greenwich Village production of *Tartuffe* and, swathed in sable, attended a Metropolitan Opera gala performance of *Tosca*. Backstage,

Aristotle Onassis's future wife was introduced to Onassis's longtime mistress, Maria Callas. It would be their first and only cordial encounter.

The children went along on another ski trip, this time to the Catskills, before Jackie spent a week with the Radziwills in Acapulco, site of her honeymoon with Jack twelve years earlier. In March, she vacationed with Lee yet again, this time at Florida's Hobe Sound.

The following month, Jackie snubbed Lyndon Johnson once more, refusing to attend the dedication of the White House Rose Garden in her honor. Instead, Jackie sent her mother to fill in for her at the ceremony. "Our mother did not want to go. She would call Jackie up, practically in tears, begging her to go," Jamie Auchincloss recalled. "Mummy did not want to stand next to Lyndon Johnson because she believed Johnson killed JFK. Jackie may have felt that, too, though she wouldn't come out and say it."

Jackie's mother did go to the White House in her daughter's place, and even managed a few touching remarks. "President Kennedy loved gardens very much and planned this one with Jacqueline," she said. "I can't think of anything more meaningful to all the people who care about Jacqueline than to have this beautiful garden as a memorial to the years she shared with him here." For the remainder of the Johnson administration, Jackie received an official invitation to every state dinner and scores of other White House functions. No longer hiding the fact that she considered LBJ a coarse usurper, she did not bother to answer a single one.

While Lyndon and Lady Bird seethed, Jackie, Caroline, and John Jr. jumped aboard a Pepsi corporate jet and headed for another week of skiing in Keene, New Hampshire. Not long after, Jackie, dazzling in an Yves St. Laurent gown and on the arm of Averell Harriman, arrived at a dinner dance thrown by Lee "to brighten Jackie's day." Among the more than one hundred guests were Sammy Davis Jr., Leonard Bernstein, director Mike Nichols, Maurice Chevalier, movie producer Sam Spiegel, and Leopold Stokowski. According to one of the guests, Bobby, who was there without Ethel, "hovered around Jackie like he owned her. I saw her a hundred times with Jack, and Bobby and Jackie had the same sort of electricity between them."

In May, Jackie and the children traveled to England, where Queen Elizabeth dedicated a memorial to JFK at Runnymede, the meadow beside the Thames where the Magna Carta was signed in 1215. The ceremony, which reduced Jackie to tears, was followed by tea with the Queen at Windsor

Castle. They were accompanied by David Ormsby-Gore, an old friend of the Kennedy family and Britain's Ambassador to Washington during the Kennedy administration. At one point, Jackie took Ormsby-Gore (now Lord Harlech) aside and thanked him for all he and his wife, Sissie, had done for her after the assassination. In the dark days following the funeral, the Ormsby-Gores were among the few close friends who dropped by frequently at the N Street house to cheer her up.

Before they returned home from London, the children sat for Cecil Beaton, who later jotted down his impressions of their mother in his diaries. Jackie struck the noted photographer and artist as an "over-life-size caricature of herself. Huge baseball players' shoulders and haunches, big boyish hands and feet; very dark, beautiful, receptive eyes . . . a somewhat Negroid appearance; the suspicion of a mustache, and very dark hair."

The following month, Jackie caused a near-riot when she showed up at the Broadway opening of *Leonard Bernstein's Theater Songs*. Later she paid a visit to Ottawa before celebrating her thirty-sixth birthday with the Kennedys at Hyannis Port. A constant stream of dinners, parties, and benefits followed — one in Boston to honor Cardinal Cushing on his seventieth birthday, then fund-raisers for, among other cultural institutions, the Boston Symphony and New York's Asia House.

For these outings, Jackie called on various escorts, many of whom, but by no means all, were elderly, married, or gay. Longtime JFK friend Bill Walton, who had helped her with the White House restoration and in planning Jack's state funeral, fell into that final category. Ros Gilpatric, Bob McNamara, Arthur Schlesinger, Mike Nichols, Charles Addams, and Andre Meyer were among those available at a moment's notice to don black tie and pick her up at 1040 Fifth for a night on the town. Of these, Jackie was to become romantically involved with only two.

A notorious if dignified Lothario, Gilpatric had already had a brief romance with Jackie. "I loved my day in Maryland," she had written to him when she was still First Lady. "It made me happy for one whole week . . . But I know the spell will carry over until tomorrow . . ." When his third wife (out of five) finally filed for divorce in 1970, it was over his enduring devotion to Jackie. "They were certainly very, very close," Madelin Gilpatric said. "Just say it was a particularly close, warm, long-lasting relationship."

Gilpatric admitted in 1995 that in fact he and Jackie "loved each other. I suppose," he explained, "I filled a void in her life." Now that Jack was gone and they both lived in

New York, where he was a partner in one of the city's most powerful law firms, the bond between Jackie and Gilpatric only strengthened.

The sardonic, urbane *Addams Family* creator, Charles Addams, though less long-lived as a love interest, nevertheless was one. Jackie was enchanted by the ghoulish humor reflected in his thirteenth-floor (of course) penthouse, with its suits of armor, assorted medieval instruments of torture, and a coffee table that had once been an embalming board for soldiers killed in battle during the Civil War. "You see," he would say with gleeful malevolence, pointing to the holes drilled in the corners of the table, "that's where the blood drains out."

Despite the all-too-real horrors she had experienced firsthand, Jackie shared in Addams's macabre sense of humor. "I love Pugsly and Lurch, but my favorite is Morticia," Jackie told Addams with a wink. "She and I have a lot more in common than you might think."

There were times, however, when her actions left the cartoonist dazed and confused. "One minute she is very sweet and tender," he told a mutual friend, "and the next minute she is an iceberg. She may be the moodiest woman I've ever met. Don't ask me what the real Jackie Kennedy is like because I really haven't the faintest idea."

Night after night Jackie, invariably swathed in ermine or mink, emerged from restaurants, hotels, and nightclubs to a fusillade of popping flashbulbs. She soon became a glittering fixture on the social scene, flitting from La Caravelle (where Joe Kennedy used to grope starlets and chorus girls under the table) to Sardi's to the Russian Tea Room to Le Pavillon to Orsini's to La Côte Basque to the Colony to Le Mistral to La Grenouille to the Copacabana to the trendiest discotheque of the mid-1960s, Arthur. Even her mentor Bunny Mellon, no slouch when it came to incessant socializing, confessed that she became exhausted "just looking at Jackie's calendar."

Clearly, it was her intention to see and to be seen. "There are ten thousand wonderful, out-of-the-way restaurants in New York where she could have gone and no one would have noticed or cared," said her columnist friend Aileen Mehle, better known as Suzy. "But Jackie was making a statement. It was her way of saying, 'I'm back — and I'm bigger and more glamorous than ever.' She enjoyed the attention, of course." Social chronicler Stephen Birmingham wondered why, if she was interested in maintaining her privacy, she "wanted to be photographed outside fashionable restaurants wearing a miniskirt? It made her look bow-legged."

Jackie's new life left little room for old acquaintances. "After she left Washington we really didn't see her very often," Charlie Bartlett mused. "I suppose because it was always a foursome, the sight of us must have brought back old memories that were just too painful for her." The same went for the Bradlees, Kentucky Senator John Sherman Cooper and his wife, Lorraine, and Jack's old buddies like George Smathers and Red Fay.

"I've never known anyone," said Jamie Auchincloss, "who cut people off with such ease. The phrase 'Out of sight, out of mind' was invented for Jackie." Priscilla McMillan, who had begun observing Jackie when she was a teenage debutante and later befriended Jack, noted that "Jackie never seemed to have really close friends the way most people do. Aside from Jack and her father, whom she adored, I don't think she was emotionally tied to anyone — including Lee. She could be very charming, and she obviously loved to flirt, but that was all an act. She just never seemed to *need* anyone. She had a great presence, a tremendous sense of self. There was a grandeur about her that really sort of scared people off. It was her shield against any real emotional intimacy."

One of the old friends who did hang on was George Plimpton. In August of 1965, Jackie planned an elaborate party for Caroline

206

and forty of her daughter's friends at Hammersmith Farm. "Jackie wanted the party to be a treasure hunt, so she went to the Coast Guard station and got a longboat, then she went out and bought all this fake jewelry for the treasure and a big chest to put it in. Then she had me write this log that gave all these clues about where the treasure chest was buried on the beach. The log also had a warning — that the minute anyone opened up the chest, the pirates who had buried it there would come back to reclaim it."

While the children hunted for the treasure, Plimpton, Rhode Island Senator Claiborne Pell, and several other men decked out in pirate garb waited just out of sight aboard the longboat. "When the children found the treasure, Jackie gave the signal and we rowed into view shouting and yelling and waving our rubber swords."

The result was pandemonium. "A lot of the children began weeping," Plimpton remembered. "Others ran for the nannies. Caroline and John looked puzzled, but they didn't run away. I stepped off the boat, stumbled on a rock, and was completely soaked. Caroline walked up to me and said, 'I know who *you* are.' Nobody had more fun that day than Jackie. She was doubled over with laughter."

In retrospect, the theme made perfect sense to Plimpton. Jackie had always had a fondness for buccaneers — so much so that she displayed a Jolly Roger flag on the wall of her room at Hammersmith Farm.

"Jackie loved pirates," Plimpton said. "She had a lot of them in her life. Her father was a pirate, she married *two* pirates, and her father-in-law Joe Kennedy was probably the biggest pirate of them all."

Jackie herself remained a paragon of decorum — she donned black to greet Pope Paul VI at a U.N. reception, for example — but she was learning to enjoy life again. Not long after her papal encounter, she teamed up with one of Bobby Kennedy's aides, William vanden Heuvel, to throw a party for John Kenneth Galbraith at the Sign of the Dove restaurant on Third Avenue.

Wearing a sleeveless fur jacket over a slinky white silk gown, she danced the frug and the watusi with Ted Kennedy, Pierre Salinger, Arthur Schlesinger, and Truman Capote. The disco band Jackie hired for the occasion caused such a racket that neighbors, David Rockefeller and Irving Berlin among them, complained.

"It was just an evening of pure fun," Galbraith said. "Time had passed, and this was an expression of her enjoying herself again." One guest arrived to pay his respects to Jackie, and, so as to not attract undue attention, left after only a few minutes — Aristotle Onassis.

Once again, as the second anniversary of Jack's death approached, Jackie was plunged into a pit of despair. One evening Truman Capote returned home to his U.N. Plaza apartment to find Jackie sitting alone in his living room. She was holding the porcelain rose he had given her the year before. Sipping champagne and gazing out at the Manhattan skyline, the two talked until dawn.

This time, Jackie bounced back more quickly than she had the year before. Gradually, the battling Jackie who had made White House staffers tremble with her tantrums and demands began to emerge.

Employees, past and present, were the first to feel her wrath. Certain that the "they" who had killed her husband were now hell-bent on invading her privacy, she made it clear to everyone who worked for her that they were not to divulge even the smallest tidbit about her life, on pain of dismissal.

Nancy Tuckerman and Pam Turnure were told not to disclose what breed of dog she preferred, what books she was reading, what television programs she watched, or what movies she liked. A woman inadvertently mentioned to a reporter that she was Caroline's piano teacher and was fired the next day. Limousine drivers were rotated on a regular basis, so none would become too familiar with her comings and goings. They were instructed not to speak to Jackie unless spoken to.

Jackie's strict orders that everyone entering the building be carefully screened were wreaking havoc with her neighbors. Maids were being frisked by Secret Service agents in the laundry room. Delivery people were stopped, questioned, searched, and sometimes turned away.

Jackie's growing mistrust of her household staff extended to the kitchen. The cook made the mistake of mentioning that Jackie had dieted off twenty-five pounds. The young German chef who replaced her, Annemarie Huste, was told to pack her things the minute she announced her intention to write a cookbook.

In truth, anyone who dared write a book without first obtaining her permission was immediately put on notice. Jackie was miffed when Maud Shaw retired to write a book about her time at the White House, and promised legal action unless she was given final approval of the manuscript.

Red Fay's memoir of his twenty-year friendship with JFK, *The Pleasure of His Company*, also annoyed Jackie. Copies of the original manuscript show that both Jackie and Bobby cut large chunks out of Fay's text, and that he grudgingly complied with their wishes. To further mollify Jackie, he donated his first royalty check to the Kennedy Library Fund. She promptly returned it, signaling an end to their friendship.

For all her meddling in the memoirs of former friends and associates, Jackie saved the full force of her anger for two professional writers. Jack had known Jim Bishop, who had scored a major success with *The Day Lincoln Was Shot*, and gave him complete access to the White House so he could write *A Day in the Life of President Kennedy*. Jackie, who considered Bishop a hack, resented the intrusion. Although JFK died before he had a chance to read *A Day in the Life of President Kennedy*, Jackie had read the book and said it was full of "third-rate clichés."

Within a week of the assassination, Jackie learned that Bishop intended to write an account of the assassination along the lines of his Lincoln best-seller. Frantic, she called up Wesleyan University Professor William Manchester, one of JFK's favorite writers and author of the unabashedly sympathetic *Portrait of a President: John F. Kennedy in Profile*. She proposed that he write the full account of what happened that fateful day in Dallas. Then she offered to give Manchester her full cooperation, provided he agreed to submit the manuscript to Jackie and Bobby for final approval.

Not surprisingly, Manchester agreed to Jackie's seemingly generous terms. Within days, Jackie, drinking heavily and still taking the potent combination of uppers and downers prescribed by Max Jacobson and others, began spilling everything to Manchester — in the end, more than thirteen hours' worth of taped conversations. "I know that future historians listening to the tapes of my interviews with her will be puzzled by the clunking sounds," Manchester later recalled. "In order to get through those evenings, Jackie would have a vast bowl of daiquiris mixed with ice and lemon, and we would drink daiquiris."

With Manchester committed to the project, she now focused her efforts on quashing the Bishop book. The first step was to call Bishop's publisher, Bennett Cerf, of Random House. Cerf, known to most Americans as a panelist on the television game show What's My Line?, had long been regarded as a giant in the publishing industry.

Sobbing, Jackie begged Cerf not to publish Bishop's book. "Bennett," she pleaded, "I'm asking you as a personal favor not to publish this book."

Cerf suggested she call Bishop directly to talk him out of it. "I'm sure that if you ask him personally he won't do it."

He was wrong. Bishop saw no reason why there shouldn't be two books on such a momentous event, and told Jackie that if she was so intent on there being only one, she should tell Manchester to drop his.

Before slamming down the phone, Jackie threatened to block his access to all important sources. "I will not talk to you about the events at Dallas," she said bluntly, "and nobody connected with it will talk to you." (Despite Jackie's interference, Bishop published *The Day Kennedy Was Shot* to critical acclaim and commercial success in 1968.)

For Jackie, one of the most effective ways to blow off steam at times like these was to jump on a horse and take off to an open field. She traded in her weekend rental on Long Island for a leased farmhouse in the town of Bernardsville, New Jersey, and joined the Tony Essex Fox Hounds Club. As a toddler, Jackie was a fierce competitor on horseback, and this was no less true in adulthood. While Marilyn Monroe sang "Happy Birthday, Mr. *Pres-i-dent*" to Jack before thousands at Madison Square Garden — "I can now retire from politics after having had 'Happy Birthday' sung to me in such a sweet, wholesome way," Jack remarked — Jackie was in Virginia competing in the Loudoun Hunt horse show. She took home a third-place ribbon.

In New Jersey, Jackie initially impressed the local gentry with her down-to-earth manner. "I was in my late teens when we first rode together in New Jersey," said

Christine Todd Whitman, who nearly thirty years later would be elected Republican Governor of that state. "My horse had an unattractive habit of foaming at the mouth. Jackie was well turned out in white britches. My horse laid his head in her lap and smeared her with green slime from hip to knee. She just smiled and turned her horse around, and my horse did it to her other leg. She never turned a hair. She was an incredibly gracious person."

The other riders were no less impressed with her skills as an equestrienne — and with her fearlessness. After Jackie complained that newspapers had run an "undignified" shot of her catapulting off a horse in 1961, Jack replied, "I'm sorry, Jackie, but when the First Lady falls on her ass, that's news!" Now Secret Service men held their breath to see if Jackie would get up after yet another nasty spill.

As much as she liked the formality of fox hunting, Jackie spent more time hurtling alone through the countryside at breakneck speed — jumping stone fences, darting between the trees, and sending the farm animals scattering. Neighbors grumbled among themselves that she trespassed with impunity, never deigning to ask any of the local landowners for permission. More than that, they were impressed with her vitality. Where did she get the energy?

Where, it turned out, she had been getting it since 1960 — from Dr. Feelgood, Max Jacobson. Now that she lived in New York, Jackie made frequent trips to Jacobson's office — on one occasion arriving tipsy after a liquid lunch with Lee Radziwill. Jackie's sister was no stranger to Dr. Jacobson and his magic elixir; Jacobson had managed to get Prince Stanislas Radziwill hooked on speed even before he was introduced to the Kennedys. "Stas was bright red all the time from the speed he took from Max Jacobson," said Radziwill's friend Taki Theodoracopulos. "It was high blood pressure from whatever on earth it was Jacobson gave to him."

Amphetamines were not the only poison Jacobson dispensed. He had also started giving his patients large doses of Valium to bring them down from their Dexedrine-induced highs. Radziwill became so disoriented and so dependent on these mood-altering drugs that he made frequent trips from London to New York, said their friend Capote, "just to get another fix."

Fueled by Jacobson's potentially deadly potion of amphetamines and steroids, Jackie embarked on a variety of causes, from saving the old Metropolitan Opera House from the wrecker's ball (she lost) to rescuing priceless art treasures threatened by rising flood waters in Florence.

In between, she skied with Bobby and the

children in Sun Valley and the Swiss resort of Gstadd, stopped in Rome to visit with Gianni Agnelli and Pope Paul VI, then skipped down to Argentina so that John-John and Caroline could spend time with some real gauchos.

That May of 1966, Jackie jetted off to catch Seville's famous *feria* — another "vacation" that would rival her official visits as First Lady to Paris and New Delhi. After a brief stopover in Madrid, where she was mobbed by reporters, Jackie flew directly on to Seville. There, the grandest of the Spanish grandees, the Duke and Duchess of Alba, put her up at their breathtaking *palacio*. Befitting her station as the world's most coveted house guest, Jackie slept in the bedroom that had once been reserved for the Duchess's great-great aunt, Napoleon III's Empress Eugenie.

Over the next week, newspapers and magazines were filled with images of Jackie that might have leapt from a canvas by Goya. Off to the *feria* in a horsedrawn carriage, she wore a *peineta,* or high comb, and an elegant white lace mantilla. The next day, Jackie donned the traditional *traje corto* — leather chaps, ruffled shirt, crimson jacket, and broad-brimmed black hat, cocked at a rakish angle over her left eye — and rode the streets on a side-stepping white stallion. The New Jersey–bred Countess of Quintanilla (later the Countess of Romanones) was Jackie's near-constant companion, and even appeared riding alongside Jackie on the cover of *Life*. "The Spaniards adored her," the Countess recalled. "She always looked absolutely stunning, she was obviously very interested in the culture, *and* she spoke the language. It's hard to think of anyone who could have been a more effective goodwill ambassador between the two countries." As for the press: "Jackie knew how to handle them. She obviously got a big kick out of all the attention."

The coverage was by no means completely positive. At Seville's famous bullfights, Jackie upstaged Princess Grace of Monaco when Spain's three greatest matadors Paco Camino, El Viti, and the legendary El Cordobes — all ignored the former Grace Kelly and offered their first kill to Jackie.

Jackie, who did not stick around for the bull's demise, declared that Spain's bloody national pastime was "beautiful." Not surprisingly, animal rights activists wasted no time denouncing her. Unmoved, she returned to the ring.

Relations between Jackie and the royal Grimaldis were also deteriorating rapidly. When young Massachusetts Senator John F. Kennedy was near death, recovering from back surgery in 1953, Jackie had asked Grace Kelly to boost his spirits by paying him a visit. Grace gamely donned a white uniform and popped into his room as the new night nurse.

Now, for reasons that the still-exquisite Princess could not comprehend, Jackie seemed to enjoy humiliating her. Grace and her husband, Prince Rainier, were both conspicuously miffed when at a flamenco demonstration they were ignored while everyone scrambled for a glimpse of Jackie. At the annual International Red Cross Ball, held in the castle of the Duke of Medinaceli, both women pulled out the stops. Wrapped in white mink, hair upswept and diamonds glittering, Grace arrived expecting, as usual, to be the undisputed belle of the ball. Instead, the Raniers were nearly trampled when guests rushed to see Jackie, bare-shouldered in a slinky blue Oleg Cassini gown, arriving nearly an hour late.

The two women took their places at either side of the hapless Duke of Medinaceli. "With relations between the two ladies hovering just above the freezing point," said one reporter at the party, "the Duke, in his role as host, did his diplomatic best to charm them both." Despite his best efforts, Grace, still fuming, stomped off to the ladies' room and did not return for a solid hour.

"I think Jackie's dislike of Grace," Gore Vidal explained, "began when she and Jack were looking at the press coverage of the wedding in Monaco. Jack studied the pictures intently, then frowned and said, '*I could have married her!*' Jackie's face was again tear-stained." As Jack's widow, Jackie was now exacting her revenge.

The "Radiant Conquistador," as she was dubbed by one overwrought journalist, did not enjoy one aspect of the trip — the incessant rumors that she was about to become engaged to Spain's Ambassador to the Vatican, Antonio Garrigues. A handsome, sixty-two-year-old widower and the father of eight, Garrigues did escort Jackie to the bullfights and to Seville's Alcázar, once Spain's royal palace. So intense was the speculation that Jackie asked her old friend Angier Biddle Duke, now U.S. Ambassador to Spain, to call a press conference and officially deny the rumors.

By her own admission, Jackie was drawn to much older men. Adlai Stevenson, then U.S. Ambassador to the United Nations, was only one of several she kept dangling. "Welcome to New York!" he wrote her when she made the move from Washington. "I hope you can find some peace here. I haven't! And I will give you none — until you set aside an evening for me — alone, small group, medium, large — whatever and whomever you wish." The Democratic Party's two-time presidential nominee, another aging Lothario, even asked to accompany her to Seville. "Would you like to be the 'crowning jewel' in an otherwise fantastic *Feria?* If so, your jewel box is at hand, although presently imprisoned by Southeast Asia, the Middle East, Article 19, and sundry alarms. But, after all, how can you see the world save in the tender care of a safe, old chaperone like me!"

Jackie enjoyed the attention from Stevenson and his venerable ilk. "I think men over sixty are often more attractive than younger men," Jackie insisted. "For instance, General Maxwell Taylor was marvelous and lean while classmates of Jack's let themselves go and looked awful. General Taylor's over sixty and plays tennis and is lean."

Lean was an adjective that at the time also applied to Peter Lawford, although at forty-three he was only six years older than Jackie. Less than a month after returning from Spain, Jackie took off again — this time with Lawford, his children, and Caroline and John-John for a vacation in Hawaii.

Relations between Jackie and the rest of the Kennedys had always been strained: They called her "The Deb" and ridiculed her finishing-school demeanor; she considered them a rambunctious "pack of gorillas." Ethel had more reason than the others to be resentful. One day while Eunice and Ethel were getting their hair done at Elizabeth Arden, Eunice said of her brother

Bobby, "He's spending an awful lot of time with The Widder." By this time, tensions between Ethel and Jackie were obvious. Whenever "The Widder" showed up for dinner in Hyannis Port, Ethel would abruptly leave the table.

The Hawaiian vacation with Peter Lawford drove an even wider wedge between Jackie and her sisters-in-law. Although Pat had given Peter permission to take their children to Hawaii, she did not know Jackie was going along until she saw pictures of the two smiling broadly as they got off the plane in Honolulu.

Pat called Peter's manager, Milt Ebbins, and screamed, "How dare he do that?"

"Peter was planning to go there anyway," Ebbins stammered, "and so was Jackie. They decided to go together. So what?"

Ebbins remembered that Pat was "so angry that she just kind of growled." She hung up, and then called back to scream some more. "She was *livid*."

Once she had finished yelling at Peter's friend, she called Lawford directly. "I won't put up with this," she shouted into the receiver. "How dare you go away with this woman!"

He tried to reason with her. "Pat," Peter said, "we've got the children with us."

"How could you go to Hawaii with her? That's where we went on our honeymoon!"

Again, she slammed down the phone.

For the next seven weeks, Jackie and the children stayed in an oceanfront house near the base of Diamond Head, which they rented for $3,000 a month. Just down the beach was Peter's Hideaway Cottage at the Kahala Hilton, with its teak floors and dolphin pools.

Peter and Jackie had been kindred spirits from the moment they met. Like Jackie, Lawford was an aristocrat, and often felt overwhelmed by the loud, rough-and-tumble Kennedy clan. "She and Peter both felt like outsiders in that family," Ebbins said. "That's why they got along so well. They were close all his life. They understood each other." They also had their individual crosses to bear when it came to their marriages. Jackie suffered through Jack's countless infidelities, while Peter confided to a friend that his wife crossed herself before every sexual encounter they had.

There were other similarities. Peter had spent much of his boyhood in France and his first language was French; his mother even called him "Pierrot." It was Jackie who introduced JFK to French cuisine, "and of course Peter loved that," Ebbins said. And whenever Peter and Jackie got together, they whispered to each other conspiratorially in French — much to the consternation of the Kennedys.

Once asked to describe his wife in one word, Jack Kennedy paused for a moment before replying, "fey" — as in "enchanted." Now Lawford told her, "Jackie, you are very fey and you live in a tree. But it's your *own* tree."

In Hawaii, they took the children swimming, walked hand in hand on the beach, and laughed over cocktails in the Hilton piano bar. He lit two cigarettes in his mouth and then handed one to her, à la Paul Henreid in *Now, Voyager*.

Almost the only time they spent apart was when Jackie accepted architect John Carl Warnecke's invitation to take the children on an overnight camping trip. The outing nearly turned to tragedy when John-John fell into a campfire and severely burned his buttocks, hands, and arms. Rescued from the flames by quick-thinking Secret Service agent John Walsh, the boy was treated at a local hospital and released within a few hours.

Not about to let a little accident get in the way of their fun, Jackie returned to Honolulu and to Peter. One evening Lawford threw a garden party for Jackie at the hotel and invited 150 of the island's most influential citizens. Jackie was, as usual, nearly two hours late. When her helicopter finally set down on the hotel grounds, the guests, all decked out in suits and cocktail dresses, were surprised to see Jackie wearing a casual beach skirt and sandals. It was an awkward moment — but not for Jackie, who had recently been inducted into the Best-Dressed Hall of Fame. "The guests felt embarrassed," conceded one, "because *we* were inappropriately dressed." Jackie thanked Peter by reserving every dance that evening for him.

Lawford confided to Patricia Seaton Lawford Stewart, his last wife, that in Hawaii "something went on" between Lawford and the President's widow. "Jackie," Pat said, "was definitely attracted to Peter."

Pat, feeling betrayed by both Peter and Jackie, was not about to take it all lying down. Helicopter pilot Hal Connors had followed the usual procedure and picked up Peter at the Lawfords' Santa Monica Beach house for the trip to the airport. When Connors returned, he was promptly arrested for violating Santa Monica city ordinances against such landings in residential areas.

Connors had been making the takeoffs and landings for years. "Why am I being arrested now?" he wanted to know.

"Because," the officer replied, "Lawford isn't a Kennedy anymore."

No sooner had Jackie returned to the mainland than Bunny and Paul Mellon threw her a thirty-seventh birthday party. Several weeks later she caused a commotion when she attended the wedding of her half-sister Janet Auchincloss, at Hammersmith Farm.

The scene was reminiscent of Jackie's marriage thirteen years earlier, when thousands clogged the streets of Newport to catch a glimpse of the dashing young senator and his regally beautiful wife. The ceremony and the reception were again mobbed, and for the same reason — everyone wanted to catch a glimpse, however fleeting, of Jackie. Janet, all but eclipsed by her big sister on what was to be the most important day of her life, turned to their mother and cried. No one understood better than Lee, who could only offer the stricken bride her handkerchief and words of solace. The tumult should have surprised no one: For the sixth straight year, the Gallup Poll showed once again that Jackie, far and away, was the most admired woman in the world.

Adulation did not come without a price, and sometimes that price was paid by the children. "I'm nerve-wracked about the safety of the children," she confided to a teacher. "There are so many nutcases about."

Walking hand in hand out of New York's St. Thomas More Church on All Saint's Day, Jackie and Caroline were accosted by a woman who grabbed the little girl and began shouting, "Your mother is a wicked woman who has killed three people! And your father is still alive!"

"It was terrible, prying her loose," Jackie recalled. The woman was hustled off to Bellevue Hospital for observation. "I still," she told a friend over lunch at Schrafft's, "haven't gotten over that strange woman."

There was another incident around this time — on the third anniversary of the assassination — that bothered Jackie even more. John-John was now enrolled as a first-grader at St. David's School, just off Fifth Avenue on East 89th Street. Jackie was impressed with her son's strength, and not bothered at all by the fact that he had already gotten into several fights at school. "He surprises me in so many ways," she said. "He seems so much more than one would expect of a child of six. Sometimes it almost seems that he is trying to protect me instead of just the other way around."

St. David's headmaster David Hume thought "Mrs. Kennedy was a sensible, affectionate mom who had a straight relationship with her son. Some people coo over their children. But by the time children are seven or eight, you shouldn't coo. When they reach out a hand, you should hold it. When they want to let go, you should let go. She understood that."

On the afternoon of November 22, 1966, Jackie picked John-John up and noticed a group of his classmates were following them.

Then, without warning, one of the children shouted, "Your father's dead, your father's dead!"

Jackie was shocked, but it wasn't the first time she'd heard those words from the children at her son's school. "You know how children are. They've even said it to me when I've run into them at school, as if . . . Well, this day John listened to them saying it over and over, and he didn't say a word."

Instead, John-John took her hand and squeezed it. "As if," Jackie said, "he were trying to reassure me that things were all right. And so we walked home together, with the children following us."

To be this public is not good for soul.

— *Rudolf Nureyev*
to Jackie

I view every woman as a potential mistress.

— *Aristotle Onassis*

I can't very well marry a dentist
from New Jersey.

— *Jackie*

FIVE

She had spoken to him "in an evening and alone, and it's rather hard to stop when the floodgates open. I just talked about the private things. Then the man went away, and I think he was very upset during the writing of the book. I know that afterwards there were so many things, private things which were mostly expressions of grief of mine and Caroline's."

Jackie's tirade against William Manchester took everyone, especially Manchester himself, by surprise. It was Jackie, after all, who had approached the esteemed author to deliver an account of the assassination, and had until now cooperated fully toward that end. And it was Jackie, knocking back drink after drink and chain-smoking L&Ms (she had switched from Salems) who opened the floodgates.

"Now, in hindsight," Jackie would say years later, "it seems wrong to have ever done that book at that time. Don't forget, these were people in shock. Before we moved out of the White House, Jim Bishop was saying he was going to write a book, *The Day Kennedy Was Shot*. All these people were going to do these things, and you thought maybe to just not have this coming up, coming, getting more and more sensational. Choose one person, ask everybody to just speak to him, maybe that would be the right thing to do. Well, it turned out not to be."

Not that Jackie ever actually *read* Manchester's *The Death of a President* in its entirety. After the author handed in the manuscript to Harper & Row in March of 1966, Jackie turned her copy over to Pam Turnure. Jackie's fondness for her husband's former mistress — she even hosted the wedding reception for Turnure when she married Canadian millionaire Robert Timmins — seemed perfectly logical to Tish Baldridge. "After all," she said, "they had so much in common." Turnure made a few minute editorial suggestions, then sent the manuscript along.

The second-closest person to the story, Bobby Kennedy, also chose not to read the book himself. Instead, he enlisted his savviest political advisors — including Arthur Schlesinger Jr., Richard Goodwin, John Seigenthaler, Ed Guthman, and Frank Mankiewicz — to pore over the manuscript in search of anything that might prove embarrassing to Bobby should he decide to seek national office in 1968.

Predictably, Bobby's advisors found plenty

to be concerned about — particularly sections of the book that showed the Attorney General clashing bitterly with LBJ — and demanded hundreds of deletions. Fortunately for the Kennedys, they were dealing with Cass Canfield and Evan Thomas at Harper & Row. Canfield's stepson Michael had once been married to Jackie's sister, Lee, and the company had published both Jack's Pulitzer Prize–winning *Profiles in Courage* and Bobby's crime-busting saga *The Enemy Within*. Canfield, Thomas, and Manchester somewhat grudgingly agreed to the changes, and the manuscript was put into production.

In November, *Look* magazine snapped up first serial rights for a then-monumental $650,000. Although the contract between the Kennedys and Manchester had called for profits from sales of the book to go toward the Kennedy Library, proceeds from serialization would have gone directly to Manchester.

Enraged at the notion that Manchester would profit personally, Jackie now demanded that *Look* drop its plan to serialize *The Death of a President*. She also took a closer look at what was actually in the book and decided that many of the details she had so freely shared now seemed shockingly personal in print. Unable to convince Manchester to make all the changes she wanted, she threatened a lawsuit blocking the *Look* excerpts, arguing that she had not actually approved the manuscript as stipulated in her contract with Manchester.

Look dug in. Then Bobby, closing ranks with his embattled sister-in-law, filed a lawsuit to stop Manchester from serializing his book. For weeks, the insults flew. Ted Kennedy denounced Manchester for moving ahead with the excerpts "despite the pain he knows it will give Mrs. Kennedy." Cass Canfield blamed Bobby and Jackie for not reading the manuscript in the first place.

Yet it was *Look* that felt the full force of Jackie's anger. The magazine's chairman, Gardner Cowles, had been a longtime Kennedy family friend. *Look*'s editor in chief, William Attwood, had been JFK's Ambassador to Guinea. So when they accepted Jackie's invitation to Hyannis Port, they were surprised at the reception they received.

Jackie quickly became "hysterical and violent," in Attwood's words. She lit into Cowles, calling him a "son of a bitch and a bastard" for forging ahead with plans to serialize the book. Attwood claimed that Jackie was "really out of control" and had become an "embarrassment" to the rest of the Kennedys.

Still, the "Battle of the Book" raged on the front pages for weeks as lawyers for

Jackie and Bobby maneuvered to suppress the *Look* excerpts. Finally, the warring parties reached a settlement. *Look* agreed to make a dozen changes involving only 1,600 words out of 60,000. The passages included scenes of Jackie searching the mirror for signs of wrinkles, of Jack wandering around in his shorts before going to bed, and of doctors using petroleum jelly to remove the wedding ring from Jack's dead hand. Harper & Row made similar minor alterations, and in return Jackie and Bobby dropped their suits against Manchester and the publisher.

For both Jackie and Bobby, it was a Pyrrhic victory at best. "We gave up some slush," *Look*'s Attwood said. "A little gingerbread's off the top, but the structure's intact." In the end, the front-page free-for-all only served to draw attention to the parts of the manuscript Jackie felt most violated her privacy.

Certainly the highly publicized brawl took a heavy toll on all involved. Manchester was hospitalized for nervous exhaustion. Cass Canfield described the dispute as "the most trying and distressing one in a forty-year publishing career." And Jackie called it "the worst thing of my life." Quite a statement, considering.

By the time the dust had settled, polls showed that more than two thirds of the American public — a full 69 percent —

were aware of the Manchester affair, and that 20 percent thought less of Jackie and Bobby for it.

Once again, Jackie dealt with the pressure by fleeing with the children to Bunny Mellon's idyllic Antigua hideaway. Surprised by the strong public reaction against her, Jackie tried to explain to friends what it was like to live her fishbowl existence.

Even the children were affected by the book imbroglio, she claimed. "We didn't talk about it, of course," she said. "But children pick things up. A word here, a word there, and they knew something was happening that involved them. There was no way to keep them from passing newsstands going to and from school. It was natural for them to look at the magazine covers and the headlines. Or be told something at school or on the street. It isn't always easy for the children."

Although she worried that Caroline was too "withdrawn," Jackie seemed fixated on what would become of her son. "I sometimes say to myself, 'He'll never remember his father. He was too young.' But now I think he will. He'll remember his father through associations with people who knew Jack well and the things Jack liked to do. He will be getting to know his father. I tell him little things like, 'Oh, don't worry about your spelling, your father couldn't spell very well, either.' That pleases him, you can bet.

"Then there will always be a Dave Powers to talk sports with him. John seems to know an awful lot about sports. He talks about someone named Bubba Smith, and about Cassius Clay . . . I want to help him go back and find his father. It can be done . . . This coming summer at Hyannis Port, John will sail in his father's favorite boat, with Ted. And that will help, too. And even smaller things that bring him closer to Jack. The school insists that children even as young as John must wear neckties to classes. That was all right with him. It gave him a chance to wear his father's PT-boat tie pin . . .

"I don't want the children to be just two kids living on Fifth Avenue and going to nice schools," she went on. "There's so much else in the world, outside this sanctuary we live in. Bobby has told them about some of those things — the children of Harlem, for instance. He told them about the rats and about terrible living conditions that exist right here in the midst of a rich city. Broken windows letting in the cold . . . John was so touched by that he said he'd go to work and use the money he made to put windows in those houses. The children rounded up their best toys last Christmas and gave them away.

"I want them to know about how the rest

of the world lives, but also I want to be able to give them some kind of sanctuary when they need it, some place to take them to when things happen to them that do not necessarily happen to other children. Caroline was knocked down by a charge of photographers when I took her out to try to teach her how to ski. How do you explain that to a child?

"And the stares and pointing, and the stories . . . the strangest stories that haven't a word of truth in them, great long analytical pieces written by people you never met, never saw. I guess they have to make a living, but what's left of a person's privacy or a child's right to privacy?"

That June, Jackie, Caroline, and John-John made a six-week pilgrimage to Ireland, where they paid a visit to the Kennedy ancestral home in Duganstown. While most of the Irish relatives lived in dilapidated cottages, some without electricity or indoor plumbing, Jackie and the children stayed in Woodstown House, a sixty-room Georgian manor.

After the Irish government, at Jackie's behest, asked the press to leave her family alone, they were free to ride, swim, and tour the countryside. Much of their time was spent in the company of their wealthy New Jersey neighbors the McDonnells, who had eight children of their own.

Their third week in Ireland, Jackie began to slip away in the evenings to swim alone. "With ten children in the house," she later explained, "one needed a bit of solitude. I drove myself, and no one knew where I was going."

For three days, Jackie went to swim alone in a cove along the Irish coast — unaware that Secret Service agent John Walsh had been secretly following her. The spot Jackie had chosen to swim was "dangerous, but I didn't know that, as the tide was fairly low in the evening."

On the fourth day, the Kennedys and the McDonnells were picnicking at high tide when Jackie "escaped from the group, unnoticed I thought," and walked a half mile up the beach behind the dunes to the channel she always swam across and back.

Midway across, she was suddenly caught up in a powerful current. "The tide was rushing in with such force," she recalled, "that if I did not make the end spit of land opposite, I would be swept into a bay twelve miles long." The cold made it impossible for Jackie to hold her fingers together. Her arms and legs were becoming numb. "I am a very good swimmer and can swim for miles and hours, but the combination of current and cold were something I had never known. There was no one in sight to yell to."

Jackie struggled against the tide, but it

was no use. "I was becoming exhausted, swallowing water and slipping past the spit of land," she said. Then, suddenly, Jackie "felt a great porpoise at my side. It was Mr. Walsh. He set his shoulder against mine and together we made the spit. Then I sat on the beach coughing up sea water for half an hour while he found a poor itinerant and borrowed a blanket for me." They then walked a mile until they came to a dirt road. It was there that the McDonnells, who had by now summoned the police, picked them up.

At Jackie's urging, Walsh, who had also pulled John-John from the campfire in Hawaii, was cited for valor by the Secret Service. Later, she succeeded in having him promoted to head up her detail in New York. In less than a year, however, Jackie's relations with the agency assigned to guard her would turn sour.

A year earlier when she visited Spain, gossipmongers linked Jackie with Antonio Garrigues. In Ireland, tongues wagged about Jackie and forty-nine-year-old Lord Harlech. When his wife, Sissie, was killed in a car crash in Wales only two weeks before Jackie's planned trip to Ireland, she rushed to comfort him. (Ironically, Harlech himself would be killed in a 1985 car crash.) As British Ambassador to the United States David Ormsby-Gore, Lord Harlech had been the foreign diplomat closest to President Kennedy. And after Dallas, David and Sissie had been pillars of support for Jackie.

In that sense, then, Jackie had an abiding affection for Lord Harlech. She was not, however, attracted to him romantically. "They were very good friends because of Jack," Charles Bartlett said. "That's all it was. Nothing more."

Still, speculation mounted as they were seen together night after night, at social functions, at the theater, sharing a box at the ballet. Finally, Lord Harlech felt compelled to issue a statement. "Mrs. Kennedy and I have been close friends for thirteen years, but there is no truth to the story of romance between us," he insisted. "I deny it flatly."

His Lordship's heartfelt denial did nothing to stop the rumor mill from working overtime when he accompanied Jackie — as did Charles and Martha Bartlett — on her visit to Cambodia in November of 1967. Jackie had long dreamed of visiting the fabled ruins of Angkor Wat, and when she told Robert McNamara of her plans to make the journey, he, in turn, consulted Averell Harriman. The wily statesman instantly saw the possibilities. In 1965 Cambodia's ruler, Prince Norodom Sihanouk, severed relations with the United States over its conduct of the war in Vietnam. Now, Harriman saw

Jackie's trip as an opportunity to repair relations between the two countries.

"Jackie was on a subtle, probing mission camouflaged as a tourist trip," said television correspondent Marvin Kalb. She had gone to Cambodia, Kalb said, "to pave the way for further diplomatic exchanges between Phnom Penh and Washington."

From the outset, Jackie's trip to Southeast Asia had all the trappings of a state visit. Determined that she be comfortable on her twelve-hour flight from Rome, where she stopped en route, to Bangkok, Alitalia stripped the entire interior of her plane and replaced the first-class section with a special queen-size bed.

Arriving in Phnom Penh in ninety-degree heat, Jackie was met by Prince Sihanouk and two hundred schoolgirls in bright green *sampots*, the traditional Cambodian dress, who sprinkled her path with jasmine and rose petals. To shield the Prince and his famous guest from the broiling sun, Sihanouk's palace guard held a gigantic parasol over their heads.

Wearing a lime green off-the-shoulder gown trimmed in silver to match her shoes, Jackie and Prince Sihanouk chattered away in French during a gala dinner in her honor at Chamcar Mon Palace on the Mekong River. In the royal palace, she stood on a terrace while the Prince's sacred white elephants paid a noontime visit. Leaning over to give them a snack, Jackie asked, "Does one feed them the bananas with the skin?" The answer was yes.

The next day they moved on to Angkor, where Jackie reverted to her role as tourist. At night, the six hundred ancient temples that make up the site were illuminated by candles and spotlights. Jackie doffed her shoes and wandered barefoot from ruin to ruin, running her hands over the ancient carvings and friezes.

They then flew to the port city of Sihanoukville, where on a flag-festooned platform Jackie dedicated a street named in her husband's honor. Jackie had seen an advance copy of Sihanouk's speech, in which he planned to say that if JFK had lived the United States would not have been involved in the Vietnam War. She would not participate in the dedication, she told her host, unless he took out the offending sentence.

At the ceremony, Jackie told the cheering crowd that "President Kennedy would have wished to visit Cambodia. He would have been attracted by the vitality of the Khmer people." Then the Prince led her to the car in which they were to ride together down the new Avenue J. F. Kennedy. As she approached the vehicle, she flinched visibly: It was a black Lincoln convertible nearly identical to the one in Dallas. Gamely, she got in and rode through the streets so the crowd could see her.

At one point during the trip, Sihanouk took Jackie's limousine past a display of an American fighter that had been shot down. When she was told that the two crewmen had been taken prisoner by the Viet Cong, she was visibly upset. On her last day in Cambodia, she asked that her host personally intervene with the Viet Cong to ensure that American POWs not be mistreated. She would not allow him to sidestep the issue.

Sihanouk, who had tried to use Jackie's visit to repeatedly denounce U.S. policy, responded with sarcasm. Jackie, he observed, was "certainly very interested in the destiny" of American prisoners. "I told her that one thing America has to do would be to accept the solution I propose." To withdraw from Vietnam, in other words.

Still, he conceded that Jackie's visit had produced "a lessening of tension between our countries — a very great contribution to a moral and sentimental rapprochement." Kalb agreed that Jackie's "covert mission took the chill out of Cambodian-American relations and by doing so, opened the door to an improvement."

Although she was scrupulously careful not to criticize LBJ's foreign policy publicly, Jackie now shared Bobby's growing frustration over the rapidly escalating war in

Southeast Asia. Sometimes these feelings surfaced unexpectedly. One day Jackie and McNamara were discussing the poetry of Nobel Prize–winner Gabriela Mistral when, he recalled, "she suddenly exploded about Vietnam. She began punching me in the chest and yelling, 'Stop the killing, stop the killing!'"

Jackie was, McNamara believed, "absolutely overwhelmed by the tragedy of Vietnam. She had an acute sensitivity to the tragedy of American deaths and its tearing apart of American society. She had that feeling about the veterans, and the tragedy for American families — and the Vietnamese."

On the home front Kitty Carlisle Hart, who was then on the board of the American Red Cross, asked Jackie if she would join her on a visit to a veterans' hospital in Queens. "I was shocked at the condition of the men when we got there," Hart said. "These young men — most of them couldn't have been more than eighteen, nineteen — had been on the battlefield just thirty-six hours earlier. So some had just had their arms or legs — or both — missing, and others were dying. Some were moaning in pain. It was very traumatic seeing these poor boys, and frankly, given all she'd been through I don't think I would have asked Jackie along if I'd known . . .

"Of course I was wrong to worry about Jackie. Actually, it was *I* who learned from her. She knew instinctively what to say, how to behave. She went from bed to bed, smiling, talking with them, comforting them, never hesitating for a moment no matter how terrible the wounds. No hint of anxiety — she genuinely cared about these fellows and they knew it. You could see it in their eyes. She was . . . cheerful, comforting, and the men really responded to that."

To be sure, Jackie was a superb actress — something, alas, her sister, Lee, was not. Desperately searching for a way out of her sister's looming shadow, Lee tried her hand at an acting career — with predictably catastrophic results. After being blasted by Chicago critics for her stage debut in *The Philadelphia Story*, Lee was cast in the title role of David Susskind's ABC production of *Laura*. That ended her chances of ever having a career in show business once and for all.

"We had to do as many as thirty takes," Susskind said, "and the only way to get it done was to focus the camera on anything but Lee." When the program aired on January 24, 1968, *Time* concluded that Lee "was only slightly less animated than the portrait of herself that hung over the mantel." Even her devoted companion Truman Capote, who had all but shoved her onstage and then in front of the cameras, finally had to concede that he was "slightly demented to think that Lee had even one scintilla of talent."

Still, the night *Laura* aired, the Radziwills threw a party and Jackie showed up to lend moral support. Jamie, meantime, watched the show at 1040 Fifth with Caroline and John-John. "They were so excited," he said, "at seeing their Aunt Lee kissing on the screen." Overnight *Laura* had turned Lee into a laughingstock, although the show itself was a commercial success. Undoubtedly boosted by the public's interest in anything connected with Jackie, *Laura* wound up being one of the network's highest-rated programs that season.

In the first months of 1968, Jackie was once again stuck on her jet-set treadmill, dashing from one social event to another. With the memory of Angkor Wat still fresh in her mind, Jackie decided to visit another famous ruin — this time without a hidden diplomatic agenda. In March of 1968 she flew off to Mexico's Yucatán peninsula to see the Mayan ruins.

For this particular excursion, she picked sixty-two-year-old Roswell Gilpatric, her old flame from the White House years. Gilpatric, unlike Lord Harlech, was a serious prospect. Erudite and polished, with the lean good looks she had already extolled in older men, Gilpatric was a well-known

Washington ladykiller.

Gilpatric had also been one of the most capable men in the Kennedy administration. During the Cuban Missile Crisis in 1962, it was Deputy Secretary of Defense Gilpatric who urged caution when JFK's first impulse was to invade Cuba. By heeding Gilpatric's counsel and ordering a blockade instead of an invasion, Jack avoided the sort of rash action that almost certainly would have led to thermonuclear war. That her husband respected Gilpatric was of utmost importance to Jackie — and one of the reasons she turned to him when she felt the White House walls closing in.

Gilpatric was still two years away from divorcing his wife, Madelin — though it hardly seemed to bother Jackie. On the trip to Mexico, Jackie and her escort climbed the pyramids hand in hand, went on moonlit horseback rides, and kissed each other in full view of Mexican photographers. "It was essential to her nature," Gilpatric said of her behavior on the trip. "When she got interested in a subject, she thoroughly immersed herself." That applied as much to Gilpatric as to the ruins.

Out of deference to the revered wife of JFK, the Mexican press could be counted on to ignore the blossoming romance.

Not so *Women's Wear Daily*, the only paper Jackie reluctantly allowed along on the trip. Jackie had had a long and cordial relationship with *WWD*, and when they proposed doing a series on the Mexican excursion, she thought it might offset the bad aftertaste left by the Manchester affair. She had not anticipated that one of the articles would recount her dalliance with Gilpatric, however.

When the offending article was about to hit the stands, a frantic Jackie asked Rose Kennedy to intervene. The matriarch of the Kennedy clan phoned *Women's Wear* publisher, John Fairchild, and pleaded with him not to run the story "for the sake of the children." Since Jackie and Gilpatric had made no effort to hide their feelings for each other, Fairchild refused and the story ran.

"At that point, we were very much in love, yes," Gilpatric said. "Frankly, we had had these strong feelings for each other for some time, and I was going to divorce my wife and ask her to marry me. The trip to Mexico was very romantic, and Jackie surprised me by being so free and open about us."

Something else surprised him. "Even at the most romantic moments," he said, "she kept mentioning Aristotle Onassis's name — what did I think of him? Was he as rich as they said he was? Was he, as some people said, a 'pirate?' She also said she felt he was very protective toward her, that he cared about the children and their welfare. She was weighing the pros and cons, and it became very clear very fast that Onassis was the man who most intrigued her. Not me, not even Bobby."

It was while traipsing through Chichén Itzá that Jackie first heard of Bobby's decision to seek the Democratic presidential nomination. Two weeks later, LBJ went on television and stunned the nation by saying he would not seek reelection. "Do you know what will happen to Bobby?" she asked Arthur Schlesinger Jr. "The same thing that happened to Jack. There is so much hatred in this country, and more people hate Bobby than hated Jack . . . I've told Bobby this, but he isn't fatalistic, like me."

By this time Jackie, as Gilpatric divined, was involved in a clandestine affair that, if made public, would almost certainly scuttle Bobby's presidential ambitions. Knowing that the Kennedys would never approve of her seeing "The Greek," as Bobby disdainfully called Onassis, Jackie usually made sure that when she was seen together with Aristotle in public — at New York's "21" Club, El Morocco, or the Greek restaurants Mykonos and Dionysos — they were never alone. Onassis's seventeen-year-old daughter, Christina, sometimes tagged along; on other occasions, they were joined by Rudolf Nureyev and Margot Fonteyn. In Paris, he instructed the servants to remain in their rooms and served dinner himself when Jackie visited his apartment on the Avenue Foch.

Onassis, already in the throes of a highly publicized affair with another world-famous woman, had been intrigued with Jackie ever since he first met her with Jack in 1955. "There's something damned willful about her," he said. "There's something provocative about that lady. She's got a carnal soul."

Bobby once described Onassis, who was sixty-eight at the time he was courting thirty-nine-year-old Jackie, as "a complete rogue on the grand scale." That was an understatement. Everything about Onassis was open to question — including the circumstances of his birth. Although his passport listed his birthplace as Salonika, Greece, Onassis was actually born in the Turkish seaport of Smyrna. This fact meant that, in the eyes of most Greeks, he was not Greek at all, but Turkish.

In 1922 Onassis and his family fled as Turkish troops under Kemal Ataturk swept down from the hills and massacred most of Smyrna's Greek population. Many of his relatives were slaughtered and his father was imprisoned, but Onassis escaped with his stepmother and three sisters to the Greek isle of Lesbos.

The following year, he left for Argentina with sixty dollars in his pocket. By the time he was twenty-nine, he had made his first million by importing Turkish tobacco and marketing his own brand of cigarettes under the brand name Bis. Onassis soon expanded into the shipping trade, purchasing six Canadian freighters, which were stranded in the Saint Lawrence Seaway, for a mere twenty thousand dollars apiece. By the end of the 1930s, Onassis's fleet included three of the world's largest oil tankers.

In 1934 Onassis began a torrid decade-long affair with Ingeborg Dedichen, the stunning youngest daughter of Norwegian shipowner Ingevald Martin Bryde. It nearly led to marriage, despite the fact that Onassis routinely beat her. Ari told Dedichen: "Every Greek, *and there are no exceptions,* beats his wife. It's good for them. It keeps them in line."

The onset of World War II nearly dealt a deathblow to Onassis. By possessing a passport from pro-Axis Argentina, registering his ships under neutral Sweden, and sailing them under the flag of Panama, Onassis expected to reap huge wartime profits. Instead, two thirds of his ships were anchored in Sweden and impounded for the duration. What remained of his fleet was forced to zigzag through submarine-infested waters. Nevertheless, in the end, Onassis had lost only two ships — freighters that had been stolen by the Japanese and sunk by American bombers.

It was about this time that Onassis, who had been known as "Aristo" until he was forty, began answering to the nickname "Ari." He joked that the new moniker stemmed from the fact that his American friends thought he was an Irishman — " 'Arry O'Nassis."

Ari might easily have bumped into a real Irish American, Jack Kennedy, in the Hollywood of the 1940s. Like the libidinous young naval officer, Onassis had flings with dozens of aspiring starlets. He numbered among his conquests Paulette Goddard, Veronica Lake, the French sex symbol Simone Simon, Evita Perón, and even Gloria Swanson, who for years had been Joseph Kennedy's mistress.

He very nearly married American sugar heiress Geraldine Spreckles, but she left him standing at the altar. Not long after, the forty-six-year-old Onassis married seventeen-year-old Athina "Tina" Livanos, whose father was at the time the biggest Greek shipping mogul of them all, Stavros Livanos. (Livanos's other daughter, Eugenie, married Onassis archrival Stavros Niarchos.)

In the postwar years, Onassis's connections with fascist dictators, his highly questionable business dealings, and his nearly successful attempt to secure a shipping monopoly on Saudi oil made him a target of the U.S. Justice Department. Ex-FBI Agent Robert Maheu, hired by Niarchos to scuttle Ari's Saudi deal, consulted then-Vice President Richard Nixon. "If you have to kill the son of a bitch," Nixon told him, "don't do it on American shores."

Instead, in October 1953, J. Edgar Hoover obtained a federal warrant for Onassis's arrest. He posed for a mug shot, was fingerprinted and then thrown into a holding cell with male prostitutes, muggers, and a group of Puerto Rican nationalists who had just been accused of shooting up Congress. Charges were dismissed after he paid a fine (he preferred to call it a "ransom") of $7 million.

Onassis was openly contemptuous not just of Washington but of all governments — an attitude plainly evident in the way he conducted another of his enterprises, whaling. Flouting international law, Onassis ignored size limits on whales. An estimated 96 percent of all the sperm whales he slaughtered were undersize. As a direct result of Ari's actions, herds off the Peruvian coast were decimated.

Those who knew him then said Onassis definitely had a violent streak, and that he took pleasure in the carnage. So much so that he invited his guests on whaling "parties," during which the male guests were invited to put down their drinks, grab a grenade harpoon, and join in the slaughter. "It was an amazing spectacle — something out of Melville," said one of those who went along. "There was this great thrashing of tails, and the men at the harpoons shouting in Norwegian and in Greek. Slowly the water would begin to turn red, until it seemed as if the entire sea was crimson."

Around this same time, Ari also bought a 52 percent interest in Monte Carlo's Société des Bains de Mer (Sea Bathing Society, SBM for short). SBM owned Monaco's famed casino, the Hotel de Paris, the Yacht Club, and about 34 percent of Monaco itself. The purchase in effect gave Onassis economic dominion over the tiny principality. For years Onassis, who also maintained ties with organized crime, battled fiercely with Prince Rainier for control of Monaco. By issuing 600,000 new nontransferable shares in the name of the principality — under the Prince's control, in reality — Rainier effectively reduced Onassis's stake to less than a third. Beaten, Onassis sold out and departed Monaco in 1967.

Through it all, Onassis used every conceivable ruse to insinuate himself into international society. It helped that he was conversant in English, French, German, and Spanish, as well as Greek, and made a point of learning as much as he could about topics ranging from ballet and art to British history. A favorite trick was to eat *before* a dinner party, so that he could focus his attention on other guests while others were preoccupied with food. A great believer in maintaining appearances ("You do not stand a chance of becoming rich unless you *look* rich in the first place"), Onassis splurged on penthouse suites, limousines, and helicopters.

None of his other toys could compare to the converted 325-foot frigate he christened *Christina*, after his adored only daughter, in 1954. Onboard were a five-passenger Piaggio seaplane, four motorboats, two kayaks, a small sailboat, three dinghies, a glass-bottomed boat, and a small car. There were gold-plated bathroom fixtures, lapis lazuli balustrades, Baccarat crystal chandeliers, a ballroom, several bars, an Olympic-size swimming pool, an El Greco hanging in Ari's formal study (next to crossed swords in gold scabbards that were gifts from Saudi King Ibn Saud), allegorical friezes of nude nymphs representing the four seasons in the dining room, a private screening room, a grand piano in the glass-walled sitting room, and mosaic floors throughout depicting scenes from Greek mythology.

The children's playroom was decorated by *Madeline* creator Ludwig Bemelmans (who once vied with Jack Kennedy for Olivia de Havilland's affections), and contained a kid-size slot machine from Monte Carlo and dolls dressed by Dior. A jewel-encrusted Buddha that Ari had acquired for $300,000 sat on a bureau in his four-room master suite. Ari's bathtub was of blue Siena marble with mosaic dolphins and flying fish inspired by King Minos's palace at Knossos, and the other eight suites — each named after a Greek island — were no less opulently appointed. Ithaca was the suite most often reserved for Onassis's most honored guests.

At times, it was a toss-up as to who would be assigned the Ithaca suite. From Winston Churchill (Ari's prize catch and one of his most frequent guests) and King Farouk to Richard Burton and Elizabeth Taylor, the great, the notorious, and the merely celebrated clamored for an invitation to cruise aboard the *Christina*. The guest list included, to name just a few: Princess Grace, John Wayne, Clark Gable, Gary Cooper, Aly Khan, Cary Grant, Frank Sinatra, Judy Garland, Humphrey Bogart and Lauren Bacall, Gene Tierney, and the Duke and Duchess of Windsor.

They were not disappointed. With Dom Pérignon flowing freely, there were eight varieties of caviar to choose from (flown in daily by his newest acquisition — Olympic Airways). Ari's parties aboard the *Christina* were, film mogul Darryl F. Zanuck marveled, "as compulsive as Gatsby's." When guests weren't dining on foie gras and lobster or bouncing to bouzouki music on the tiled dance floor, they were waited on by the *Christina*'s black-sweatered crew of sixty, including two chefs, a Swedish masseuse, a band, and two hairdressers.

Ari took special pride in one of the yacht's more curious features — the bar stools with seats covered in the foreskins of white whales. "Madame," he announced to Greta Garbo, "you are sitting on the largest penis in the world!" Garbo would become another regular aboard the *Christina*.

In 1955 the junior senator from Massachusetts and his dazzling wife dined aboard the yacht with Churchill, whom Jack greatly admired. But Churchill, in one of his moods, chose instead to talk to his host and to Jackie. As they walked down the gangplank at the end of the evening, Jack wondered why the Great Man had ignored him. Jackie pointed to his white dinner jacket. "Maybe," she said, "he thought you were the waiter, Jack."

"The Golden Greek," as he was now called, had already passed his fifty-seventh birthday when he first met the love of his life — or at least the woman who came closest to satisfying his needs. She was born Maria Anna Sofia Cecilia Kalogeropoulos in

New York's Lower Fifth Avenue Hospital. By the time she was christened at the Greek Orthodox Cathedral on East 74th Street, three-year-old Maria's pharmacist father had changed the family name to the simpler "Callas."

Pudgy, nearsighted, and unpopular as a child, Maria Callas was nonetheless a gifted singer. She won a number of radio contests in the New York area and used her winnings to pay for singing lessons. At fourteen, she visited Athens and found herself swept up in World War II. She soon joined the Athens Opera Company and, as the world crumbled around her during the closing days of the war, entertained German troops in exchange for food.

After the war, Callas married Giovanni Battista Meneghini, the rotund Italian millionaire who would also serve as her agent, mentor, and personal impresario. Under Meneghini's spell, Callas lost weight, gained confidence, and by 1956 was being touted as the greatest soprano in the world — perhaps the greatest opera singer who ever lived.

But Callas, dubbed "Diva Divana" and "Prima Donna *Assoluta*" by a gushing world press, was as famous for her temper as she was for her talent. Her wild-eyed, window-rattling tantrums — both onstage and off — inspired fear and awe.

Ari and Callas hit it off instantly. Unlike Tina, who had never known anything but great wealth, Callas and Onassis understood all too well what it was to go hungry. Against unimaginable odds, they had clawed their way to the top; in their respective fields they were both without peer.

In early 1959, as their respective spouses — and the world — looked on, Callas and Onassis became lovers. He reminded her "of a gigolo, no longer young, but still predatory, still sexy, still stalking." Late one night in August, Tina, unable to sleep, took a stroll on the deck of the *Christina* and saw her husband and Callas making love in the bar. That November, both Meneghini and Tina Onassis filed for divorce.

Maria was an inch or so taller than Ari, so she was careful to wear flat shoes and to hunker down when they danced. Still, said Aileen Mehle, a close friend of both Callas and Onassis, "they were exquisitely suited to one another. They were both witty, headstrong, very *alive.* Everything they had accomplished, they had done on their own. They had invented themselves, in a sense. Ari hated opera, but he adored the diva.

"There was always this electricity between them — this spark. Whenever they were together, they spoke sort of conspiratorially in Greek. There was this badinage, lots of laughter — they were so absorbed with each other there were times you felt like you were intruding." From Callas's wrist dangled a gold bracelet inscribed TMWL ("To Maria With Love").

"We are the two most famous Greeks in the world!" Onassis liked to boast. In truth, *neither* was. Ari had been an Argentine citizen since the 1930s, and his Turkish roots made him suspect to most Greeks. Callas, New York born and raised, was "more American than anything. Of course she was always doing these marvelous arias in Italian," said writer Doris Lilly, "so when you talked to her you expected this exotic foreign accent. What came out sounded more like a salesgirl at Bloomingdale's. A very bossy salesgirl at Bloomingdale's."

They would have married in 1960, said Onassis's aide Johnny Meyer, had Ari's children not hated her. Alexander, then twelve, referred to her contemptuously as "The Singer." Ten-year-old Christina merely stared at her dolefully. "She had the look," Maria said, "of a child marked for the nunnery."

After she reached forty and her voice began to fade, Maria was subject to belittling by Ari as well. "What are you?" he asked. "Nothing. You just have a whistle in your throat that no longer works." She responded by flying into one of her trademark mad scenes. Occasionally, these confrontations turned violent. "It was a stormy relationship in every sense of the word," Doris Lilly said. "They fought like cats and dogs. Callas was a proud woman. She never said anything about the beatings, no matter how savage, and always wore makeup to conceal the bruises. As I heard Ari say many times, all Greek men beat their wives."

In this manner, the lovers fought, made up, and then battled some more. Most of his peace offerings were eye-popping pieces of jewelry. "Your total understanding of women," Callas quipped, "you got from a Van Cleef & Arpels catalog."

In 1966 Callas became pregnant at the age of forty-two and desperately wanted the child. Ari threatened to end their affair if she went ahead with the pregnancy. She aborted the infant boy as Onassis demanded, but she would spend the rest of her life resenting him for it.

Callas guarded Ari's many secrets, including his penchant for dressing in drag. As early as the mid-1930s, Ingeborg Dedichen remembered Ari donning a skirt, bra, blouse, nylons, earrings, and hat, applying rouge and lipstick, grabbing a purse, and going out on the town as "Arianna" — a character he re-created during parties aboard the *Christina*. "He was an ugly man," Gloria Swanson said, "but as a woman he was, well, unforgettable."

★ ★ ★

When Bobby Kennedy announced his intention to run for the presidency, Ari took it as a clear signal that JFK's little brother could no longer tend to Jackie's personal life. "Now," he told Meyer, "the kid has other fish to fry." The Greek tycoon had his eye on the biggest catch of all.

"For Ari everything was a contest with Niarchos — who had the most money, the biggest yacht, the grandest houses," Lilly said. "Ari was accustomed to winning. Niarchos had a mansion, Ari bought Monaco. Niarchos had a plane, Ari bought an airline. It was no different with women."

There were other, more pragmatic reasons for Ari to pursue Jackie. "Onassis knows that Jackie is an icon," Ari's aide-de-camp, Johnny Meyer, confided to a friend. "And he feels that if he marries her the U.S. government will get off his back." Moreover, Onassis had also hatched a plan to build a "super port" for his tankers at Durham Point, New Hampshire — and, Meyer said, by being married to JFK's widow "he thought he could get that, too."

A few days after Bobby announced his candidacy, at a party in Paris's George V Hotel, Ari described Jackie as "a totally misunderstood woman. Perhaps she even misunderstands herself. She's being held up as a model of propriety, constancy, and so many of those boring American female virtues. She's now utterly devoid of mystery. She needs a small scandal to bring her alive. A peccadillo, an indiscretion. Something should happen to her to win our fresh compassion. The world loves to pity fallen grandeur."

Ari knew the statement would "set the cat among the pigeons at Hickory Hill." When Bobby called and asked what her friend Onassis might have meant by his curious remarks, Jackie confirmed that they had broached the subject of marriage but that she remained undecided. The next day, Ethel and Ted's wife, Joan, paid a call on Jackie in New York. They implored Jackie not to sabotage Bobby's chances of occupying the White House by marrying "The Greek."

The sisters-in-law merely paved the way for Bobby. "For God's sake, Jackie," he said, "this could cost me five states." She then went to Cardinal Cushing, asking what the Vatican's attitude might be toward her marrying a divorced man. Cushing, privately horrified, chimed in with the clan and advised against marriage — at least not now. Reluctantly, Jackie agreed to wait until after the election before making a decision — for Bobby's sake.

To mollify his prospective brother-in-law, Onassis made the sort of gesture he knew

Bobby would appreciate: Ari made a hefty contribution to the Senator's presidential campaign.

Not that Onassis had any illusions about ever winning Bobby's friendship. His prospects for winning over Jackie's side of the family were no better. Back in 1963, Janet Auchincloss was staying at Claridge's Hotel in London and was told that Lee was upstairs in Onassis's suite. Janet stormed upstairs, walked into the suite, and found Ari sitting at his desk, clad only in his bathrobe.

"Where's my daughter?" she demanded.

"And who exactly *is* your daughter, Madame?"

"Princess Radziwill," Janet answered indignantly.

"Ah," Onassis said. "In that case, Madame, you just missed her."

"Mummy stormed out," Jamie Auchincloss said. "She made her mind up right then and there that he was a cretin. I think he may have reminded her a bit too much of Black Jack Bouvier."

On April 4, 1968, the nation reeled at the news that Martin Luther King Jr. had been gunned down outside his motel room in Memphis. Jackie understandably felt that she had seen enough of funerals and intended to pay a private call on the King family once the public grieving was over. Bobby, knowing the political value of having JFK's widow standing alongside the widow of the slain Civil Rights leader, insisted she go to the funeral in Atlanta.

"The Church is at its best only at the time of death," she later told Frank Mankiewicz. "The rest of the time it's often rather silly little men running around in their black suits. But the Catholic Church understands death. I'll tell you who else understands death are the black churches. I remember at the funeral of Martin Luther King. I was looking at those faces, and I realized that they know death. They see it all the time and they're ready for it . . . in the way in which a good Catholic is. We know death . . . As a matter of fact, if it weren't for the children, we'd welcome it."

On a weekend trip to Hyannis Port in April, Bobby picked up the Sunday morning papers after church and read the results of the latest polls. He was, all the reports showed, rapidly overtaking his principal opponent, Vice President Hubert Humphrey.

To whoops of delight from the assembled clan, Bobby proclaimed, "Looks like we're going to make it."

Jackie, who had inherited Jack's house in the compound, walked over to Bobby's to share in the family's joy. They had been so close, and gone through so much, she could not contain her own joy. "Oh, Bobby," she said, "won't it be wonderful when we get back in the White House?"

"What do you mean 'we'?" Ethel snapped. There was dead silence. It was obvious that Ethel, determined to have Jackie out of her husband's life once and for all, was not kidding.

"Jacqueline Kennedy looked as if she'd been struck," recalled Joe Kennedy's nurse, Rita Dallas, who was standing just a few feet away. "She flinched as though a blow had actually stung her cheek. I'll always remember the look of pain in Jackie's eyes."

Jackie stood up and, without a word, walked out. This time, Bobby did not follow. The next day Jackie walked alone on the beach, contemplating her past with Jack and her possible future with a man unlike any she had known. When Jack was alive, she felt emotionally connected to the Kennedys. Bobby had helped her to sustain that sense of belonging. The children would always be Kennedys, but she felt her own ties to Jack's family slipping away.

That night she went to visit the one Kennedy she would always feel close to, Joe. "I've had a lot of thinking to do today," she told him. "You'll always know I love you, won't you Grandpa?"

That Easter, Jackie and her children flew to Palm Beach with Onassis aboard his private plane. Jackie emerged from behind her trademark oversized sunglasses — specially

made to fit her drastically wide-set eyes —
but when Onassis saw photographers waiting
on the tarmac he refused to get off. He
waited in the plane for hours before finally
emerging, telling the one photographer who
remained that he was only Onassis's lookalike "cousin."

The press, still speculating that Jackie
would wed the lanky, dignified Lord Harlech, paid little attention to these furtive outings with Onassis. "It just never occurred to
anybody that they could be *romantically* involved," Lilly said. "It was, well, unthinkable."

Accordingly, no one seemed to notice
when Jackie boarded the *Christina* in May
for a four-day Caribbean cruise — with the
exception of Maria Callas, who, much to
Ari's relief, chose to stay behind. It may
have been bad bouillabaisse or anxiety, but
Jackie spent part of the cruise throwing up
in her cabin.

Onassis's rationale for betraying Callas
was the same he used in all his dealings,
personal and professional. "I am a man of
many passions," he would say with a shrug.
"It is a truth that excuses all of my wicked-
nesses and all of my cruelties."

Now, more than ever, Ari "had to have
her," Aileen Mehle said. "Ari and Stavros
Niarchos were in constant competition.
Jackie was a great big feather in Ari's cap. She

was the widow of the President of the United States, the most famous woman in the world. Jackie was a tremendous trophy for Ari."

Why Jackie would choose Ari over all the other available men in the world was another matter. In the White House, Jack had raged against Jackie's compulsive spending. Since moving to New York, she had tripled her spending on clothes alone. Jackie continued to send the bills, as she had always done, directly to her father-in-law's office in New York.

With Joe's physical condition deteriorating and Ethel's star on the rise, it seemed only a matter of time before the Kennedys stopped bankrolling her expensive tastes. Rose, not nearly so indulgent as her husband, was now warning Janet Auchincloss that Joe's office would cut her off if she continued her reckless spending.

Even a few of her merely wealthy friends were beginning to drop by the wayside. "We spent a great deal of time together in New York during the 1960s, but after a while it became apparent to me that I just couldn't keep up financially. I wasn't *rich* enough to be her friend," said the widow of a famous American composer who collected millions in royalties each year. "She never paid for anything, and it was just understood that when you went anywhere or did anything with her anyone but Jackie was supposed to pick up the bill. Every time she called I found myself sort of tugging at my forelock. She made me feel like her vassal, and frankly, I just couldn't afford to be friends with her anymore.

"I didn't have private jets and a three-hundred-foot yacht. If she wanted to go on a cruise, the best I could do was buy her a first-class ticket and we'd go on the *QEII* with two thousand other people. That was no longer good enough for her. I know I wasn't the only one of her friends who felt this way. We moved heaven and earth for her in the years after the assassination, but she just got to be too expensive for us. The demands she made on our time and on our bank accounts were too great. What she needed was a Bunny Mellon or a Doris Duke — those people had the kind of big money she required. And it wasn't just the money. I didn't like being at somebody's beck and call like that; I started to lose respect for myself. I thought, 'This isn't good for *me*.' So I more or less backed off.

"Jackie was like the Queen of England — actually, she had come to see herself as a sort of American Queen, just like the rest of us came to see her," said the composer's widow, whose own lifestyle could only be described as lavish. "You can't blame her for not wanting to disappoint her subjects by coming down to earth with the rest of us mortals. She needed someone with more or less unlimited funds, and she found him."

The sheer magnitude of Onassis's fortune would certainly be a major factor — *the* major factor — in Jackie's final decision. Worth well in excess of $500 million, Ari consistently ranked not far behind J. Paul Getty and Howard Hughes as one of the world's half dozen richest men.

"Nothing, and I mean *nothing,* mattered more to Jackie than money," Gore Vidal said. "You must realize that this was the one thing Janet Auchincloss pounded into the heads of her daughters. She married Jack for money and she married Ari for money and after them she still went after money. As far as Jackie was concerned, the only thing better than a rich man was an obscenely rich man." Aileen Mehle agreed. "Ari was physically repulsive," Mehle conceded, "but Jackie and women like her don't give a damn about pretty."

Yet it was not just money that lured the world's most desirable women into his bed. "He was short, ugly, but he had far more presence than far-better-looking men," Taki Theodoracopulos said. "He wasn't awed by women. He was extremely generous. And he was a great flatterer. Everything about him was bigger than life. He was a real-life Zorba the Greek."

Ari was also, as George Plimpton pointed out, a pirate, like Black Jack Bouvier, Joe Kennedy, and Jack. "Onassis was a very charming man, and he had that aura of power . . . then there was that element of danger that I think appealed to her."

The Greek had no illusions that Bobby would ever relinquish control of Jackie. "He just sees me as the rich prick moving in on his brother's widow woman," Ari told Johnny Meyer. "Sooner or later it'll come to a test of wills."

Back in New York, Jackie kept up the smokescreen for Bobby's sake, attending several high-profile functions with Ros Gilpatric and Lord Harlech. At 3:45 on the morning of June 6, 1968, she was jolted awake by a call from Stas Radziwill in London. It was the night of the California primary, and she had stayed up until 3:15 A.M. watching the results on TV before finally going to bed.

"Jackie, how's Bobby?" Lee asked.

"He's fine, terrific. You heard that he won California by fifty-three percent, didn't you?"

"But, Jackie, he's been shot. It happened just a few minutes ago."

There was a horrible silence, and then she screamed, "No! It can't have happened. No! It can't have happened!"

Indeed, it had, in the pantry of the Ambassador Hotel on Los Angeles's Wilshire

Boulevard. That is where a young Palestinian named Sirhan Sirhan, presumably angered over the recent defeat of the Arabs in the Six-Day War with U.S.–backed Israel, lay in wait for Bobby. After he spoke to supporters in the hotel ballroom, Bobby and his entourage left out a back door that opened into the pantry. Six shots were fired, and within seconds Bobby, eyes open, was lying on his back in a pool of blood while pro football player Roosevelt Grier and Olympic decathlon champion Rafer Johnson wrestled the gun from Sirhan's hand. Jack's little brother had been hit in the head, neck, and right side. Ethel knelt next to him, whispering, "Ohmygod, ohmygod." A busboy pressed a rosary in his hand and then tried to support his head.

Jackie took the first available flight to Los Angeles and went straight to Good Samaritan Hospital. On the plane, she had taken one of Max Jacobson's pills to help her get through the ordeal. "I was there to meet Jackie at the airport," Chuck Spalding recalled. "She got off the plane wearing those dark glasses, but she seemed very calm, very much in control."

"She asked right away how Bobby was doing — those were the first words out of her mouth," Spalding said. "She said she wanted me to give it to her straight. So I did. I told her, 'He's dying, Jackie. He's dying.' "

George Plimpton, a friend and ardent supporter of Bobby's, had been only a few feet from RFK when the fatal shots were fired. He was at the hospital with Ethel when Jackie arrived. "She came down the corridor and we embraced. We were all taken in two by two to visit him as he lingered for hours. It was a horrifying death watch.

"What I remember most is that Bobby looked *huge*. He was on this very high bed, and he was up at an angle. His head was in this big white bandage. He looked like a medieval knight. It was like visiting a tomb at Westminster Abbey." At 1:44 A.M. Pacific time, with Ethel holding his hand, Bobby died.

Hours later, in a scene eerily reminiscent of the one Jackie had lived through just four and a half years before, those closest to Bobby accompanied his body home on a White House plane sent by LBJ. "We all came back to New York on the plane together," Plimpton said. "It was very emotional. Arthur Schlesinger just dissolved in tears. And there was Ethel going up and down the aisle telling people, 'Cheer up!' But that was her style. Jackie was very quiet. No tears. Just . . . quiet."

Halfway through the flight, the woman who Ethel and the other Kennedys had derisively called "The Widder" reverted to form.

She called ahead to conductor Leonard Bernstein, a friend since the 1960 campaign, and asked what music would be suitable for Bobby's funeral Mass at St. Patrick's Cathedral. Then she dictated Ethel's wishes — that nuns who had taught her at Manhattanville School sing several religious songs from her childhood, and that her friend Andy Williams — then one of the biggest television and recording stars in the country — sing "The Battle Hymn of the Republic."

There were problems. Bernstein reminded her that at the time women were not permitted to sing in the cathedral. He also argued vehemently against Williams's singing "The Battle Hymn of the Republic," purely on grounds of taste. (New York's Terence Cardinal Cooke later weighed in against Williams because the singer's father had been a Protestant minister.)

Jackie brushed these objections aside. Despite their differences, she now staunchly defended Ethel's right to call all the shots when it came to her own husband's funeral. After the plane touched down at La Guardia, Jackie noticed that Ethel suddenly looked lost. Jackie rushed to her side and whispered words of comfort in her ear as a lift lowered Bobby's coffin from the plane.

Jackie then climbed into one of twenty waiting limousines and was driving off when she caught sight of a familiar face. She jumped out of the slowly moving car, ran up to Robert McNamara, and, sobbing, buried her face in his chest. They went to St. Patrick's, and then on to Bobby and Ethel's U.N. Plaza apartment. The mood was resolutely upbeat, with Ethel telling jokes and Rose cheerily greeting her children and grandchildren. "Sometimes you go into a situation like this," said Ethel's doctor, Blake Watson, "and there is nothing but crying. But there was no emotion at all in that apartment." The glaring exception was Jackie, who came undone and nearly collapsed despite McNamara's attempts at small talk.

One person who seemed almost pleased at the tragic turn of events was Aristotle Onassis. Five minutes after Bobby's death was announced, Ari called up his oldest and closest friend, Costa Gratsos. "She's free of the Kennedys, the last link broke," Ari said. Gratsos told journalist Peter Evans that Onassis seemed not at all shocked or upset over the news that Bobby had been gunned down. Instead, Ari was merely pleased that "his biggest headache had been eliminated."

News of Onassis's callous reaction reached FBI Director J. Edgar Hoover, who had been monitoring the Greek shipowner's actions since the early 1940s. Ari had ties to Argentina's fascist dictator Juan Perón, and to so many Nazi war criminals that when his advisors suggested he not invite German armaments king Alfred Krupp to the launching of one of his ships, Ari sighed, "I don't think one more Nazi here or there is going to make much difference to my reputation now." In addition to his attempt to corner the shipping rights to Saudi oil, he now associated with David Karr, a shady left-leaning wheeler-dealer with links to the KGB.

Although Hoover's own reaction to RFK's assassination was comparably cold-blooded, for a short time he considered Aristotle Onassis a possible suspect in the murder of Bobby Kennedy. Those closest to Ari shared Costa Gratsos's belief that Onassis "had always taken what he wanted, and for the first time in his life he had come up against a younger man who was as tough, competitive, and determined as he was. And now that man was dead."

Indeed. Once again — beginning with the earliest all-points bulletin for a "girl in a polka dot dress" who had been running from the scene — serious doubt would be cast on the single-assassin theory. Questions were raised about, among other things, the number of bullet holes in the walls of the pantry and their trajectory.

The Kennedys, in the interest of preserving their collective sanity, reacted the way they always had — by soldiering on and refusing to look back. They had taken the art of denial to new heights. Rather than pressing for answers in the death of her husband, Ethel merely declared that Sirhan Sirhan's name was to never be spoken in her presence again. "Anyone who does," she said, "is not a friend."

It is especially understandable why Ethel Skakel Kennedy could not afford to dwell on the grim circumstances surrounding Bobby's death. Like the Kennedys, the Skakels of Connecticut were a large, rich, and powerful Catholic clan. They also knew more than their share of soul-crushing tragedy. Ethel's parents were killed in a plane crash in October of 1955; her brother George Skakel Jr. in a plane crash in 1966. The following year George Jr.'s teenage daughter, Ethel's niece, hit a bump in the road and sent a small child flying out the window. The child died.

There was another reason why Ethel could not let herself be defeated. She was pregnant with their eleventh child.

Lyndon and Lady Bird Johnson led the two thousand mourners invited to Bobby's funeral service at St. Patrick's on June 8, 1968. Ethel was stoic even as Teddy, delivering the eulogy just a few feet from his brother's flag-draped casket, began to crack.

"My brother need not be idealized," Teddy said, "or enlarged in death beyond what he was in life, to be remembered simply as a good and decent man, who saw wrong and tried to right it, saw suffering and tried to heal it, saw war and tried to stop it . . . As he said many times in many parts of this nation, to those he touched and who sought to touch him, 'Some men see things as they are and say why; I dream of things that never were and say why not?' "

Andy Williams, reading the lyrics from cue cards, delivered an a cappella rendition of "The Battle Hymn of the Republic" that was so stirring even Leonard Bernstein had to admit he had been wrong. It turned out to be, he conceded, "*the* smash of the funeral."

To many present, Jackie, wearing a black lace mantilla and grim-faced in stark contrast to the irrepressibly peppy Ethel, would have made the more convincing widow. "She was in a trance, just completely in shock," said Pierre Salinger. "It just defied belief that she — that we — would be reliving this nightmare." At the funeral, the First Lady tried to comfort Jackie. "I called her name and put out my hand," Lady Bird said. "She looked at me as if from a great distance, as though I were an apparition."

Following the service at St. Patrick's, Bobby's body was carried by funeral train from New York to Washington for burial at Arlington. Two million people lined the 226-mile route as the train slowly made its way to the capital.

On board the train, which was packed with relatives, friends, campaign workers, and press, Ethel continued to play cheerleader. She moved from car to car, patting people on the back, making small talk. "Jacqueline was wandering around with a tray at one point, and looking sort of icy," said a journalist who would one day become Jackie's lover. "It was an interesting contrast."

As if to underscore the growing feeling that the Kennedy family carried with it a terrible curse, a passing train killed two people and injured six others who had come to pay their respects — all in full view of several Kennedy children. Later in Trenton, New Jersey, a teenager watching from atop a freight car was critically burned when he inadvertently touched a power line.

"God gives us no more than we can bear," Rose liked to say. But Jackie could bear no more. "I hate this country," she said bitterly. "I despise America, and I don't want my children to live here anymore. If they are killing Kennedys, my kids are the number one targets. I have the two main targets. I want to get out of this country!"

Ari had been pointedly excluded from the list of those invited to the funeral; Lord Harlech, who was one of the ten pallbearers, explained that it would have been "in very poor taste." That did not stop him, however, from rushing to Jackie's side.

Bobby's sudden, inexplicable, senseless death brought everything into focus. Jackie's first concern was now herself and her children; she could no longer allow her destiny to be charted by the Kennedys. Terrified for her children's safety and craving seclusion, Jackie turned to the one man who could ensure both — on his private island, behind the gates of his guarded homes in Athens and in Paris, and on board the *Christina*.

As for protecting the "number one targets," Jackie had more faith in Ari's private army than she did in the U.S. government. The four-man Secret Service detail assigned to Jackie and the children was dwarfed by Ari's machine gun–toting, seventy-five-member security force, supplemented by trained-to-kill attack dogs.

In Onassis, Jackie also saw an opportunity to escape the public's "oppressive obsession" with her as the widow of the slain President, and to make good her promise not to be used "like a little old widow" the way Mrs. Woodrow Wilson had been.

Marrying Ari would also mean — and this would play a major role in her decision — that Jackie would no longer be treated like a poor relation. "The Kennedy women had always flaunted their money and power," George Smathers said. "This was Jackie's opportunity to say to them, 'Okay, what are you going to say now that I can buy and sell you?' "

"It was definitely a case of 'Ari to the rescue,' " Mehle said. "He showered jewels on her, he *wooed* her. He didn't have much to offer in the looks department — I mean, he was a physically ugly man — but it wasn't just the money. Ari exuded power and strength. He was *so* alive, so vibrant, and so vigorous. He was this life force. It's rather ironic, because this was the image Jack projected the whole time he was battling Addison's disease and crippling back pain. But old Ari was in reality as vital as Jack could only pretend to be. It was impossible not to be bowled over by Ari."

The first weekend after the funeral, Jackie invited Ari to Hammersmith Farm. Onassis brought along his daughter, Christina, who, remembered Jamie Auchincloss, "was just a terrible pain — as rude as her father was charming. Christina obviously was Daddy's Girl and resented Jackie's intrusion into her life. I had to show her around Newport and she was just impossible to please. Basically, she hated all things American. My mother detested both of them."

That summer, Jackie hauled Ari back and forth between Cape Cod and Newport as part of her stepped-up campaign to acquaint both families with her future husband. Caroline and John Jr., who transferred to

Collegiate after teachers at St. David's School felt he should repeat first grade, were not much of a challenge: Onassis emptied out F.A.O. Schwarz, the Manhattan toy store, before every visit to Hyannis Port.

He also spent time actively trying to win the children over — taking long walks with them, swimming with them, and making sure they understood that their mother needed someone to take care of her. Onassis took John Jr. to baseball games, and on fishing trips. "Here," he said, handing the little boy two $100 bills, "go buy some worms."

Onassis also told them that he had great respect for their father, and that he would never try to replace him in their lives.

Before meeting Rose and Joe Kennedy, Ari had dispatched an emissary to the Fifth Avenue apartment of Gloria Swanson with a cashier's check for $100,000 — payment in exchange for her promise never to reveal that Onassis as well as Joe had once been her lover. Swanson, dismissing the offer as an assault on her integrity, nonetheless never spoke a word about her affair with Ari. Joseph P. Kennedy was "someone I never stopped caring for," Swanson said. "He was someone who deserved my respect. I'm afraid I cannot say the same for Mr. Onassis."

Upon meeting Ari for the first time at the compound that summer of 1968, Joe Kennedy could manage only a wan smile and some unintelligible mutterings. Rose later recalled a memory of Onassis "one summer day on our front porch, sitting rather scrunched up in one of our tall, fanback, white wicker chairs. Several of us were in white wicker chairs, too, and others were seated, reclining or sprawled out on cushions which were somewhat the worse from the summer sun and wet and fogs and hard use from grandchildren. The white paint on the wicker was beginning to flake, as it always does.

"Everything," Rose continued, "was pleasant, attractive, practical, but far from elegant. And knowing of Onassis's fabulous wealth and style of life — islands, yachts, and villas with retinues of servants — I wondered if he might find it a bit strange to be in such an informal environment. If so, he showed no sign of it. He was quietly companionable, easy to talk with, intelligent, with a sense of humor and a fund of good anecdotes to tell. I liked him. He was pleasant, interesting, and, to use a word of Greek origin, charismatic."

To Larry Newman, who thirty years later still lived across the street from the Kennedy compound in Hyannis Port, "Jackie and Onassis were a far more romantic couple than Jack and Jackie — at least that's the way it looked early on. Jack lived and breathed politics, and when he wasn't doing that he was chasing women. I used to sit with him at the Monkey Bar in New York and he'd be flirting with every pretty woman in the room. It was automatic. I think he did love Jackie, but it was never in his makeup to be monogamous. . . ."

On election night 1960, according to Newman, Jack "sneaked in the back door, sat in my kitchen . . . and do you know what he talked about the day he was elected President? Girls. He drank beer and talked about women. I don't think it was out of disrespect for Jackie, I really don't. It was just the way he had been raised by Joe. Jack always had women all over him. None of us ever thought he'd get married. We just couldn't imagine it . . . Jack talked about women fifty percent of the time. It was by far his favorite subject."

What struck Newman was the obvious difference in the way Jackie interacted with the two men physically. "Jackie could be very playful, try and give Jack a hug or a kiss, but he'd turn very stiff. He was not a demonstrative person. He didn't like to be touched. I felt sort of sad for Jackie when that happened . . .

"With Onassis things were totally different. They'd have a champagne lunch and then go dancing up the street right in front of my house. I'd see them walking up the hill with their arms around each other, she'd have her head on his shoulder — which was not that easy to do, she was so much taller than he was. They'd hold hands, or they'd have their arms around each other. Sometimes they'd do these cute little dance steps, or they'd be *whistling* . . . And they'd kiss — something you never saw Jack and Jackie do. They seemed to be happy, laughing all the time. She seemed like such a sad and lonely person after the assassination, I thought it was wonderful to see her with someone who obviously made her happy. When people say it was all about money, well, I think they're wrong. But I have to admit — I mean, comparing Onassis to Jack Kennedy — I kept asking myself, 'How in the hell can she love *him?*' "

Wherever Jackie went, she awoke to a bouquet of fresh flowers, and the note J.I.L.Y. — "Jackie I Love You." It was a variation on a familiar theme: Before Jackie it was M.I.L.Y. ("Maria I Love You") and before Callas, T.I.L.Y. ("Tina I Love You").

At Hyannis Port, after a small party in celebration of Jackie's thirty-ninth birthday, the family watched *The Thomas Crown Affair*, a Steve McQueen film about a rich man who is so besotted with money that he cannot stop robbing banks. The movie's Academy Award–winning theme song, "Windmills of

Your Mind," applied perfectly to Jackie.

After the movie, she and Ted sat and talked quietly. Having looked at the marriage issue from every conceivable angle, Jackie told Teddy she had made up her mind. She was going to become the next Mrs. Aristotle Onassis. Teddy saw no point in trying to talk her out of it.

That August, Senator Edward Kennedy was to meet with Aristotle Onassis on Skorpios to hammer out the terms of a prenuptial agreement. Before he arrived, however, Ari had to dispose of a small but potentially explosive problem. He told Maria Callas to leave the *Christina* and return to Paris.

"Wait for me there," he told her.

"Go to Paris in August? Are you mad?"

"You have to go."

"Why? What do you mean?"

"I'm having company and you can't be aboard."

"Who? And why can't I be aboard?"

Ari refused to answer. But Callas was no fool. She knew that Onassis was a collector of famous women, and that now he was after the widow of John F. Kennedy.

"Then, I'm leaving you."

"I'll see you in September after the cruise," Ari said, trying to calm her.

"No, you don't understand. I'm leaving you. You're never going to see me again — ever."

With that Callas departed — not for Paris,

but to the United States, where she announced that she would return to the stage with the Dallas Opera. "Anything to survive," she told her friend John Ardoin. "At my stage of the game, anything to survive."

While Callas tried to contemplate a new life without the man she loved, Ari welcomed Jackie and her brother-in-law to Skorpios, with its five hundred acres of oleanders, fig trees, and cypresses. Determined to appear unconcerned while the men haggled over her worth, Jackie drank vodka and then switched to ouzo as the evening wore on. Teddy, resplendent in pink shirt and matching pink scarf, stuck to ouzo as he dandied a striking blond woman on his knee. A self-proclaimed friend and admirer of Ted's long-suffering wife, Joan, Jackie nonetheless laughed as her drunken brother-in-law, unable to stand up long enough to dance the *surtaki,* settled for fondling the unidentified blond. "Kennedy men are like that," Jackie had once told her distraught sister-in-law when she complained about Ted's philandering. "It doesn't mean anything." Clearly, this was something Jackie still believed.

Nibbling on white grapes, Jackie listened to Ari's favorite ballad:

These are bitter summers
And you have taught me to spend them
with you.

1.

2. LBJ tried to get Jackie to change out of her bloody clothes before he took the oath of office aboard Air Force One. "No!" she protested. "Let them see what they've done."

3. "We're going to say good-bye to Daddy now. . . ." Jackie held on tight to Caroline's and John-John's hands as they left the White House for the Capitol Rotunda where JFK's body lay in state.

4. "My mommy cries *all the time*," Caroline told her teacher. The day after the funeral, Bobby and Jackie visited Jack's grave. From then on, said Ben Bradlee, Bobby was "glued to Jackie's side."

5. & 6. Head held high, Jackie and the children moved into temporary quarters at the home of Averell Harriman just two weeks after Dallas. Later that day, she said good-bye to Bobby and Ethel Kennedy. Consumed by grief, Jackie wept for hours at a time.

7. On February 1, 1964, Jackie's half sister Janet Auchincloss walked Jackie, Caroline, and cocker spaniel Shannon to their new home just down the street from the Harrimans.

8. Their love-hate relationship was legendary. But the Bouvier sisters, Lee and Jackie, drew closer than ever in the days following Dallas. Unbeknownst to the public, Jackie drank heavily and took amphetamines during the yearlong depression that followed.

9. Jackie's brief 1964 affair with Marlon Brando, who had been a supporter of Jack's, came in the midst of her ongoing romance with Bobby Kennedy.

10. Jackie nearly caused a riot when she went with Leonard Bernstein to the Broadway opening of *Leonard Bernstein's Theater Songs* in June 1965.

11. John-John, Jackie, and Caroline celebrated New Year's Day, 1966, on the slopes at Sun Valley, Idaho.

12. As he marched in the 1966 St. Patrick's Day Parade on Fifth Avenue, Senator Bobby Kennedy was surprised when Jackie darted out of the crowd to kiss him.

13. On a trip to Argentina in April 1966, five-year-old John-John proudly showed off his new toy silver dagger to his sister and mother.

14. & 15. Wearing a white lace mantilla, Jackie (flanked by the Countess of Quintanilla, *left*, and the Duchess of Alba) found the bullfights in Seville "thrilling" when she visited Spain in April 1966. That same day, Jackie sipped sherry as she rode through the streets during Seville's annual spring *feria*.

16. Their Spanish host tried to keep the peace at Seville's Red Cross Ball, but Princess Grace fumed at being upstaged by Jackie. Grace later locked herself in the ladies' room for an hour.

17. At Newport News, Virginia, Jackie watched proudly as Caroline christened the $200 million aircraft carrier *John F. Kennedy* in 1967.

18. Always comfortable on horseback, Jackie took her children riding while vacationing in Ireland in the summer of 1967. Several days later, in a harrowing incident that was never reported, Jackie nearly drowned as she swam off the Irish coast.

19. A "tourist" in Cambodia, Jackie had actually been sent by Washington in November 1967 to quell anti-American sentiment over Vietnam. She fed bananas to the white elephants at the palace in Phnom Penh.

20. Rumors of their impending marriage swirled about them as Jackie and her escort, Lord Harlech, toured the ruins at Angkor Wat.

21. Former JFK advisor Roswell Gilpatric accompanied Jackie to Mexico in March 1968. Their on-again, off-again affair, which had begun when she was First Lady, ended his third marriage.

22. Devastated by Bobby's death, Jackie went to St. Patrick's Cathedral the day before the funeral in June 1968 to pray. "We Catholics know death," Jackie said. "If it weren't for the children, we'd welcome it."

23. Jackie was condemned in every corner of the globe for betraying JFK's memory when she married Onassis on his private island, Skorpios, on October 20, 1968.

24. A week after her wedding, Jackie took a dip in the Ionian Sea. Ari was already back at work in Athens, sewing up a half-billion-dollar deal.

25. In November 1968, Lee played host to Jackie and their friend Rudolf Nureyev at Turville Grange, the Radziwills' country estate on the Thames.

26. After a two-month separation, Jackie and Ari stole a passionate kiss aboard the *Christina* off the Canary Islands in March 1969.

27. On a chilly February afternoon in 1969, John and stepdad Ari had a heart-to-heart as they strolled with Mom outside New York's Plaza Hotel.

28. The Onassises leaving the all-night party Ari threw at an Athens nightclub to celebrate Jackie's fortieth birthday. His present: a forty-carat diamond.

29. Jackie and nine-year-old John in November 1972, heading out on one of their frequent bike rides through Central Park. Five years later, he would be mugged in the park and his bicycle stolen.

30. After being stranded for two days in Rome by a freak snowstorm in March 1971, Jackie and Ari commandeered a private jet. He turned one of his Olympic airliners into a flying boudoir.

31. "There was a tenderness between them," said friend Peter Duchin of Jackie and Ari, "that was really very moving."

32. "You'll be so fat," Jackie told seventeen-year-old
Caroline, "nobody will marry you." Jackie's obsession with weight caused her to suffer an eating disorder of her own.

33. & 34. Jackie drew a crowd in Naples just by ordering an ice cream cone, which she ate while pursuing another favorite pastime — shopping for shoes.

35. With a bronze bust of Jack looming in the background, Jackie, escorted by Kennedy Center chairman Roger Stevens, visited the center on June 5, 1972.

36. Jackie, Ari, and John dropped into a small café on Capri during their August 1972 cruise along Sardinia's Emerald Coast aboard the *Christina*.

37. Pursued by photographers, a barefoot Jackie flees down a street in Naples.

38. "I ought to be flattered," Jackie said in November 1972, when photos showing her sunbathing nude on Skorpios wound up in magazines around the world.

39. By the time they visited Egypt in March 1974, Ari had already turned violent toward Jackie and planned to end the marriage.

40. With Ted Kennedy trailing behind, Jackie grabbed Christina's arm as they left the Olympic Airways jet bearing Ari's body back to Greece in March 1975. Ari's only daughter loathed her stepmother.

41. At Ari's funeral on Skorpios, Christina and her Onassis relations literally shoved the widow Jackie and fourteen-year-old JFK Jr. into the background.

42. Both JFK and Ari were jealous of him, but it was not until after Onassis's death that Jackie and Frank Sinatra became involved.

43. Delegates gave Jackie a standing ovation when she appeared at the 1976 Democratic National Convention in Madison Square Garden in New York.

44. An accomplished equestrienne, Jackie nonetheless took several dangerous spills — one of which nearly ended in tragedy.

45. Hollywood's womanizing answer to JFK, Ted Kennedy's pal Warren Beatty had a brief affair with Jackie in 1978.

46. A mutual friend said that "understanding, stability, serenity" were the things Maurice Tempelsman brought to Jackie, here in a rare photograph showing her with a cigarette in its holder.

47. This 1981 photograph of Jackie being pursued by Ron Galella down New York's Eighth Avenue was used as evidence to prove that Galella had violated a court order to keep at least twenty-five feet from her.

48. Clutching two packs of Marlboros, Jackie left New York's La Coupole restaurant after a night out with *Zorba the Greek* director Michael Cacoyannis in 1982.

49. Jackie choked back happy tears as she embraced Ted Kennedy at Caroline's wedding to Ed Schlossberg on July 19, 1986 — the seventeenth anniversary of Chappaquiddick.

50. Jackie and Caroline posed proudly with John at his graduation from NYU Law School in May 1989. Before he went to work for the D.A., he had to clear up $2,300 in unpaid parking tickets.

51. At sixty, "Grand Jackie" still cut a stunning figure when she arrived at a New York theater to give an award to the Dance Theater of Harlem in 1990.

52. "Being a mother has made me the person I am,"
said Jackie, here with John and Caroline at the JFK
Library to present the 1992 Profile in Courage
Award.

53, 54, & 55. Sundays in the park with "Grand Jackie." On one 1992 outing, Rose, four, waited to buy cotton candy while her grandmother kept an eye on Tatiana, two. Later, Jackie and Rose shared a park bench with an interesting-looking character. Another day, Jackie had a heart-to-heart with Rose atop a favorite climbing rock.

56. Like everyone else, Jackie stood in line at the Robert F. Kennedy School to vote in the 1992 presidential elections.

57. Film of a teenage Bill Clinton shaking JFK's hand so impressed Jackie that she invited him to join her aboard the *Relemar* at Martha's Vineyard in August 1993.

58. Mother and daughter sharing a quiet moment. After the births of her three grandchildren, Jackie grew closer than ever to Caroline.

59. On May 12, 1994 — just one week before her death — Maurice took a shockingly frail Jackie on a stroll near her Fifth Avenue apartment.

60. The press gathered outside 1040 Fifth Avenue on May 19, 1994. Jackie died at 10:15 that night.

61. At Arlington National Cemetery, her children kissed Jackie's coffin. Then, in a moving sequel to his famous salute, John reached over and touched his father's gravestone.

62.

Then he asked the band to play "Adiós Compagnia," and Jackie, now visibly tipsy and decidedly off-key, joined in the chorus.

Christina, now eighteen, and her twenty-year-old brother, Alexander, sat sullenly in a corner, whispering conspiratorially. Ari's cherished only son, a skinny version of his father in dark glasses and an Italian shark-skin suit, was meeting Jackie for the first time. Neither he nor his sister made any attempt to disguise their contempt for their father's American guests.

Unlike Christina, who plainly idolized her roguish father, Alexander resented him — with good reason. The children, shown little affection by either parent, had essentially been raised by a succession of nannies and governesses. Now that Alexander had grown to manhood, Ari seemed threatened by him, and took every available opportunity to belittle his heir in public. To anyone who would listen, Onassis complained bitterly that his son had proven to be a disappointment as a student, as a fledgling business-man, and as the designated heir apparent to his far-flung empire. To further complicate matters, Alexander had fallen in love with the beautiful Fiona Campbell-Walter, the Baroness Thyssen-Bornemisza, a onetime international cover girl who was sixteen years his senior. Ari, always the master of manipulation, had pulled every available string to put an end to the affair, but to no avail. What existed between father and son now could best be described as an uneasy truce.

Ari virtually ignored his own children that crucial evening, focusing all his attention on the now not-so-distinguished-looking Senator from Massachusetts. Ted's embarrassing behavior that night on Skorpios was no accident. Seeking leverage in his negotiations — and insurance against any Kennedy opposition to the marriage — Ari had intentionally gotten the Senator drunk. He also sneaked in a Greek reporter, Nicos Mastorakis, disguised as a member of the bouzouki band. Ted was not amused when he discovered that Mastorakis, who was taking notes and snapping pictures, was a journalist. "If you print one word out of place about this, if you hurt me, I'll have your ass," Ted told Mastorakis. Kennedy did not intimidate the Greek reporter, but Ari did. Once Onassis was satisfied that he now had the leverage he desired over Teddy, his henchmen threatened bodily harm to the reporter if he dared print the more lurid details of what went on at the party.

Jackie was dispatched on a shopping trip to Athens while Ted and Ari hammered out an agreement. For his part, Ari had already done his homework over the course of several months and was confident he had the upper hand. "I wasn't looking for a dowry," he told his friend Willi Frischauer. "What did I have to worry about?"

Indeed, at the time he was talking over the terms of his forthcoming marriage, Ari was close to sealing a half-billion-dollar industrial deal with Greece's new military regime, headed by Colonel George Papadopoulos. Ari's Project Omega — he proclaimed it "the biggest deal in the history of Greece" — called for the construction of, among other things, an oil refinery, a power station, an air terminal, shipyards, and an aluminum smelter.

Distracted by Omega, Onassis seemed somewhat less enthusiastic about rushing into marriage with Jackie. According to newspaper publisher Dorothy Schiff, at this point "Jackie wanted to marry Onassis more than Onassis wanted to marry Jackie."

That was not evident in Ted Kennedy's tone when he opened negotiations with Ari. The surviving brother of America's greatest political dynasty — and now the father figure to no fewer than twenty-seven Kennedy cousins — started by reminding Ari that Jackie was like no other woman in the world. She was a beloved American icon, a symbol of all that her late husband had meant to the nation, and any man she chose to marry would come under attack. Onassis did not have to point out that he had survived the Turks, the Nazis, the Allies, and

scores of cutthroat business competitors —
not to mention the FBI, the CIA, and Maria
Callas.

"We love Jackie," Teddy declared.

"So do I," Ari responded without missing
a beat, "and I want her to have a secure life
and a happy one."

Finally, they got down to the real issue at
hand. Once Jackie remarried, Ted pointed
out, she would forfeit the $200,000 a year
she received from her trust and her $10,000
presidential widow's pension. Ari, who was
privately aghast at the Kennedys' penury,
laid out his offer: $3 million for Jackie and
$1 million each for Caroline and John Jr.
Onassis would cover all her expenses —
a provision he would live to regret —
and after his death she would be paid the
$200,000 she would have received from the
Kennedy trusts. When Jackie returned from
Athens, Ari gave her a silver filigree bracelet
stamped — what else? — J.I.L.Y.

No deal, replied financier Andre Meyer
when he was sent a copy of Ari's offer. The
married Meyer, who still harbored a crush
on Jackie despite a thirty-one-year age difference, shot back with a demand for $20 mil-
lion up front. On September 25, 1968,
Onassis commandeered an Olympic Airways
jet and flew to New York to confront
Meyer.

The two haggled for hours, and when it

was over Onassis slunk back to his suite at the Pierre Hotel. "Where's the bottle we keep around here?" he asked his private secretary, Lynn Alpha. She produced the Johnnie Walker Black Label and started pouring. "Make it a double," he said curtly.

Then he dictated a deal memo that made it sound as if he were acquiring another supertanker. From that point on, that was the nickname Alpha and the other Onassis staffers used for Jackie: Supertanker. The memo refers to Jackie only as "the person-in-question":

It is certain that there will be no problem for Mr. A.M. and Mr. A.O. to work out reasonable arrangements to safeguard the person-in-question from inflationary risks.

The most important paragraph dealt with Meyer's demand for $20 million in cash:

The sum of twenty million indicated in the meeting, as a capital, apart from the fact that in the final analysis would be futile, due to gift, income and other taxes that it necessarily would entail, apart from being detrimental to the feelings of either party, it might easily lead to the thought of an acquisition instead of a marriage.

What Ari and Meyer finally agreed to was $3 million for Jackie up front, and the interest on a $1 million trust for both Caroline and John Jr. After Ari's death, or in the event of divorce, Jackie would receive $200,000 annually. There was a catch: Jackie would have to agree to forgo her rights under *nominos mira,* a provision in Greek law that requires a man to bequeath a minimum of 12.5 percent of his estate to his wife and 37.5 percent to his children.

The marital agreement dealt strictly with finances, contrary to reports of a separate "prenuptial contract" that supposedly stipulated where each party would live and how many times a year they would have sex. This colorful document, which purported to contain 170 clauses covering every detail of the Onassises' married life, was strictly fiction — the invention of Christian Cafarakis, a former chief steward on the *Christina.* Onassis, who acknowledged that he owed his fortune to the excitement created by publicity, did nothing to discourage Cafarakis from peddling his story to the British tabloids.

Everyone in both the Kennedy and Onassis camps was so immersed in working out the details of their secret pact, no one noticed another potential crisis in the making. At the weekend house in Bernardsville, New Jersey, the Secret Service detail in charge of guarding Caroline and John Jr. followed a wrong car out of the driveway and lost the children. For two frantic hours, agents radioed back and forth trying to locate Caroline and John. At Secret Service headquarters in Washington, panic set in. After the assassinations of Jack and Robert Kennedy, the disappearance — or worse yet, abduction — of JFK's children was the sort of blow the agency might not survive.

After two hours, Jackie's New Jersey neighbor, Marjorie "Peggy" McDonnell, drove up to Jackie's small farmhouse with Caroline and John-John in the backseat. They had been playing at the McDonnell house, and when no Secret Service agents showed up, Peggy McDonnell decided it was best to deliver them to Jackie personally. In doing so, she left her own eight children unattended — a fact that would particularly rankle Jackie. The incident, which remained hidden from the public, confirmed Jackie's suspicion that she could provide better protection for her young family.

It was only a matter of time before someone realized that Jackie and Ari were more than just friends. Doris Lilly, the *New York Post* columnist and a friend of Ari's, got wind of the unfolding drama. "I went on *The Merv Griffin Show* and said that I thought Jackie and Ari were going to marry any minute," she recalled. "Well, I was booed and heckled, and when I left the studio people in the hallways and out onto the street were shoving me and saying not very nice things. A Greek toad becoming the stepfather of John F. Kennedy's children? How dare I cast such aspersions on *our* St. Jackie?"

"St. Jackie" returned to her old friend Cardinal Cushing in October and told him of her decision. She wanted him to know that, whatever the consequences she might suffer for marrying a divorced man in the Greek Orthodox Church, her children would keep their Kennedy name and their Roman Catholic faith. Pestered by the Kennedys to threaten her with excommunication, Cushing rebelled; although he wouldn't bless the union, he refused to condemn it. What the Vatican would say was quite another matter.

Over dinner in London, Stas Radziwill told Pierre Salinger of Jackie's intentions to wed Onassis. Salinger, who had moved to Paris, kept the secret for weeks before Steve Smith, Jean Kennedy's husband and the unofficial Kennedy family spokesman, called in a panic.

"Something very important is happening," Smith told Salinger. "You've got to come to New York and see me."

"What is it?"

"We've been hearing rumors that Jackie is going to marry Ari Onassis."

"Those aren't rumors," Salinger said, "it's true."

Silence. Then Smith managed to get out two words. "Oh, shit," he said.

Salinger's assignment was to make sure the wedding took place as far away from Kennedy country as possible — preferably in Greece. "I really felt my first allegiance was to Jackie, not to the rest of the family," said Salinger. "I sat down and wrote her a letter in longhand saying she wasn't hurting anyone and she had the right to marry anybody she wanted and to do anything she wanted. But I also knew it would strain relations with the rest of the family if she insisted on having the ceremony in the United States. Of course, the ceremony was on Skorpios, and afterward she wrote me back saying how much my words of encouragement had meant to her. I don't think she was hearing very many of those at the time."

On October 15, 1968, the Boston *Herald-Traveler* broke the story on its front page. Jacqueline Kennedy and Aristotle Onassis, the paper said, were planning to marry — and soon. Quickly, family members were informed of the impending marriage. "I was rather stunned," Rose Kennedy said. "And then perplexed. I thought of the difference in their ages. I thought of the difference in religion, he being Greek Orthodox, and the fact that he had been divorced; and I wondered whether this could be a valid marriage in the eyes of the Church. I thought of

Caroline and John Jr. and whether they could learn to accept Onassis in the role of stepfather so that he could give them the guidance that children need from a man." But she also knew Jackie "was not a person who would jump rashly into anything as important as this, so she must have her own very good reasons." Rose's thoughts were "awhirl" as she anticipated the call from Jack's widow.

Jackie would remember that of all the Kennedys, only Rose offered her unqualified support. "When I married Ari," Jackie recalled, "she of all people was the one who encouraged me. Who said, 'He's a good man.' And, 'Don't worry, dear.' She's been extraordinarily generous. Here I was, I was married to her son and I have his children, but she was the one who was saying, if this is what you think is best, go ahead."

Rose had her reasons. This was the woman who was so cost-conscious that, when it came time to paint the Kennedys' Palm Beach mansion, she ordered workmen to paint only the side facing the street. "I'm sure she did encourage Jackie to marry Onassis," Smathers said. "She was tired of paying all those bills!"

Conversely, Janet Auchincloss reacted to the news with controlled hysteria. Jackie was, she told a friend, "finally getting back at me for divorcing her father. That's what she's doing. I just know it." Once Janet cooled down, she reluctantly agreed to make the wedding announcement.

In New York, Nancy Tuckerman made the announcement to the press. "Mrs. Hugh D. Auchincloss has asked me to tell you that her daughter, Mrs. John F. Kennedy, is planning to marry Aristotle Onassis sometime next week. No place or date has been set for the moment." Jackie saw no reason to start a stampede of reporters by tipping them off to the exact place and time.

Even as Tuckerman was speaking to reporters, Ari had ordered that ninety-three passengers be bounced off Olympic Airways's 8 P.M. flight to Athens. At 5:30 P.M., just two hours after Tuckerman's earth-shattering announcement, Jackie left 1040 Fifth clutching one child in each hand and shadowed by four Secret Service agents. At Kennedy Airport they were joined by Hugh and Janet Auchincloss and, representing the Kennedys, sisters-in-law Pat Kennedy Lawford and Jean Kennedy Smith. The party, which now totaled eleven, then boarded the empty Olympic Airways 707 and flew to Andravida, a Greek military base. There on the tarmac with its engines running was Ari's Piaggio seaplane, waiting to whisk them to Skorpios.

The groom's family and friends, meantime, hardly saw cause for rejoicing. Alexander and Christina, still naively clinging to the hope that their mother and father would someday reconcile, were shattered by the news. "It's a perfect match," Alexander told his sister. "Our father loves names and Jackie loves money." Ari's son then did what he always did at times like these: He jumped behind the wheel of his Ferrari and careened through the narrow, winding streets of Athens.

Lee Radziwill, who had set her sights on Onassis when her sister was still First Lady, called her friend Truman Capote when she heard the news. His friend and sometime collaborator Eleanor Perry was visiting, and though Capote took the call in his bedroom, Perry could still hear Lee's shrill cries coming through the receiver. "How could she do this to me!" Lee screamed. "How could she! HOW COULD THIS HAPPEN?!" Lee's public stance was quite another matter, of course. "I am very happy," she told reporters calmly, "to have been at the origin of this marriage, which will, I am certain, bring my sister the happiness she deserves."

Maria Callas was equally devastated. "First I lost my weight, then I lost my voice, now I've lost Onassis!" she cried. Like Lee, Callas vented her spleen behind closed doors. To the world, she went out of her way to make it clear she harbored no hard feelings. "She did well," the diva said sweetly, "to give a grandfather to her children."

FRIEND: Jackie, you're going to fall
off your pedestal.

JACKIE: That's better than freezing there.

What do I think of the marriage? I can
only give you two words: *highly suitable.*

— *Gore Vidal*

Jackie is like a diamond — cool and
sharp at the edges, fiery and hot beneath the surface.

— *Aristotle Onassis*

SIX

No one — not the bride and certainly not the groom — was prepared for the global firestorm that ensued. "JACK KENNEDY DIES TODAY FOR A SECOND TIME," screamed the headlines in Rome's *Il Messagero*. "AMERICA HAS LOST A SAINT," chimed in West Germany's *Bild-Zeitung*, while Norway's *Verdens Gang* proclaimed, "SHE'S NO LONGER A SAINT." One London paper sniped, "JACKIE WEDS BLANK CHECK." The *Stockholm Express* merely asked, "JACKIE, HOW COULD YOU?"

"The reaction here is anger, shock, and dismay," reported *The New York Times* though, oddly, reaction was even stronger abroad. "Jackie, whose staunch courage during John's funeral made such an impression, now chooses to shock by marrying a man who could be her father," wrote French political commentator Andre Fontaine in *Le Monde*.

"People would come up to me on the streets of Paris," Pierre Salinger said, "and ask, 'How could she betray the memory of President Kennedy like that by marrying a

Greek?' In France and other parts of Europe, there is quite a lot of prejudice against Greeks — they are not seen in a very positive light. The French claimed Jackie as theirs, in a way. It's difficult to believe, but they were even more outraged than the Americans."

Coco Chanel, an idol of Jackie's, echoed the sentiments of her countrymen. "Everyone knew she was not cut out for dignity," the legendary designer said. "You mustn't ask a woman with a touch of vulgarity to spend the rest of her life over a corpse."

Jack's loyal "Murphia," whom Jackie both resented and relied upon, viewed the marriage as something akin to treason. "She's gone from Prince Charming," said one, "to Caliban." Out of deference to JFK's memory, they kept their feelings to themselves. "First, I'll go to Mass and pray for her," Dave Powers said. "Then I'll go home and have a drink for her."

Jackie's old friends from the White House days, all of whom were stunned by Jackie's choice, tried to sound supportive. "Look," Tish Baldridge recalled, "as far as I was concerned it was her decision to make. She was only thirty-nine, and she was terribly concerned for her young children's safety after Bobby's assassination. Obviously Onassis was no Jack Kennedy, but he offered her a sense of security; she felt safe with him."

Besides, she added, "he was a diamond in the rough — he offered her just about anything she could want. That's terrific if you've been through hell."

"People said, 'Oh, God, not *Ari*,' " recalled Aileen Mehle. "But who was she supposed to marry? A doctor from Cleveland? A banker from Connecticut? Jackie would never settle for that sort of thing — a calm, 'normal' life in the suburbs — never. It just wasn't in her makeup. She *craved* excitement. She loved men who were dangerous — for God's sake, look at her first husband! In many ways, Ari was just a sweet teddy bear by comparison."

Her bitter feelings toward Jackie aside, sister Lee insisted the public outcry revealed a not-so-subtle streak of prejudice. "If my sister's new husband had been blond, young, rich, and Anglo-Saxon, most Americans would have been much happier. . . . She loves Onassis. Onassis is rich enough to offer her a good life and powerful enough to protect her privacy." Their half-brother Yusha Auchincloss felt the important thing was that "Onassis made Jackie truly happy — something we really hadn't seen in a long time. She was enjoying life again."

One prominent American felt "strangely freer" because of the marriage. "No shadow walks beside me down the hall of the White House," Lady Bird Johnson wrote in her diary. "I wonder what it would have been like if we had entered this life unaccompanied by that shadow?"

Now Jackie's shadow was being cast in another direction, and one young Greek was powerless to escape it. Alexander Onassis was present at the wedding ceremony, along with Christina (Ari called her *Chryso Mou* — "My Golden One"). Reporters pointed out that both looked more like they were attending a funeral than a wedding. "My father needs a wife," Alexander protested, "but I don't need a stepmother." On the day of the wedding, said Ari's friend Willi Frischauer, both Christina and Alexander "wept bitter tears."

The event itself was mapped out with all the secrecy and precision of a preemptive military strike. According to *Washington Post* columnist Maxine Cheshire, Onassis's influence "extended to his country's naval and air forces. When the press hordes arrived in Athens like war correspondents from all over the world, we found planes grounded and the Greek Navy patrolling the coastal waters, all to keep journalists away from Skorpios. Even worse, reporters were being rounded up and put under what amounted to house arrest at the Grande Bretagne Hotel in Athens."

When she refused to go along peacefully to the hotel, Cheshire was locked in a tiny airport bathroom. "I attacked the lock with a nail file," she said. "In time I escaped and fled from the airport in a rattletrap taxi, government officials in hot pursuit."

It was raining by the time Cheshire joined the dozens of reporters and photographers who had made their way to Lefkas, the tiny village just across a narrow strip of water from Skorpios. Moored alongside the island was the *Christina*, where the bride and groom were preparing for the ceremony. While cruisers and gunboats patrolled the water in front of them, helicopters equipped with bullhorns swooped down to warn journalists to keep off the island.

The editor of a German magazine paid the captain of a motor launch $10,000 to outmaneuver the gunboats and land paparazzi like D-Day commandos on Skorpios's shores. The ploy, though adding to the day's high drama, ended in failure.

At first, Jackie did not want any members of the press present at the wedding. "Please don't bring them here," she pleaded with her fiancé. But Ari, not wishing his moment of triumph to go unrecorded, convinced her to compromise. A small group of reporters would be permitted to cover the wedding party only as it entered and left the whitewashed neoclassic Chapel of *Panayitsa* (the Little Virgin). Jackie also issued a plea to the journalists in hopes of keeping the frenzy to a minimum.

"We know you understand that even though people may be well known," she said, "they still hold in their hearts the emotions of a simple person for the moments that are the most important of those we know on earth — birth, marriage, and death. We wish our wedding to be a private moment in the little chapel among the cypresses of Skorpios with only members of the family present — five of them little children. If you will give us these moments, we will gladly give you all the cooperation possible for you to take the pictures you need."

They were not disappointed when, shortly after 5 P.M. on October 25, the bride appeared on the flagstone walkway leading to the chapel, stunning in a beige chiffon dress by Valentino and a matching ribbon in her shoulder-length bouffant. It was not the first time she had worn the two-piece dress, or even the first wedding she had worn it to. Six months earlier, she had worn the same ensemble to a friend's wedding in Virginia.

Even though she wore flat shoes that matched her dress and he wore lifts, Jackie hovered at least three inches over her five-feet-five-inches-tall intended. Clad in a blue suit and burgundy tie, he looked nattier than usual. (Callas liked to joke that Onassis "has all his suits made in London — unfortunately he is in New York at the time.") They were both wet from the light rain —

viewed by the Greeks as a good omen.

It was not such a good omen, however, that Onassis had turned up drunk at his own wedding. Several guests at the wedding, including one Secret Service agent, confirmed that Onassis was "unmistakably intoxicated."

As they reached the door, Jackie turned to the crush of photographers and said, "No. Not inside." A grim-faced Secret Service agent who barred the press from entering made his own personal statement — he was wearing the PT-109 tie clasp given to White House agents by John F. Kennedy.

Packed into the tiny chapel were twenty-two family members and friends. Among those on Jackie's side were the Auchin-closses; Jean Smith; Pat Lawford; Lee and Stas Radziwill and their two children, Anthony and Christina. Standing with Onassis, who swayed noticeably, were his sister Artemis and half-sister Yerasimos, his niece and her husband, several business associates, and of course his children, Christina and Alexander. Jackie and Ari were already standing at the altar when Onassis's son squeezed through the door at the last minute.

Outside the air was redolent with bougain-villea and jasmine. The interior of the chapel, decorated with small gardenia trees, was heavy with the smell of incense. A solemn-faced Caroline and John Jr. flanked the couple, grasping two slim white candles. As he had done when Black Jack Bouvier was too drunk to give away his daughter in marriage to Jack Kennedy, "Uncle Hughdie" Auchincloss walked his stepdaughter down the narrow aisle.

Greek Orthodox priest Polycarpos Athanassiou, thirty-two and looking, as per Ari's request, "not too much like Rasputin" in spite of his black beard and gold robes, chanted and prayed mostly in Greek. The couple was crowned with wreaths of orange blossoms, which were exchanged to signify unity. Then Ari's brother-in-law slipped gold wedding bands on their ring fingers and, as with the crowns of blossoms, these were exchanged between bride and groom.

Jackie and Ari sipped red wine from the same silver communion chalice. After each drink, the priest recited the same vow: "Do Thou, now, Master, send down Thine hand from Thy holy dwelling place and unite Thy servants, Aristotle and Jacqueline, for by Thee woman is united to man . . ." In the Greek Orthodox ceremony, neither party is asked to say "I do."

Inside the cramped chapel it was becoming more and more difficult to breathe. Even before the ceremony was concluded, Uncle Hughdie slipped outside and nervously lit a cigarette in the rain.

Now man and wife, Ari and Jackie joined hands and walked around the altar three times — the "Dance of Isaiah," during which each tries to step on the other's foot first. According to Greek legend, the winner will be the boss in the marriage. Jackie won.

When they finally emerged in the driving rain, the bride was beaming. A reporter asked Ari how he was feeling at this moment. "I feel very well, my boy," he replied. The same reporter asked little John Jr. if he was happy. The seven-year-old turned away without answering.

As the newlyweds left the church, reporters tossed rice and sugared almonds — the sugared almonds, according to Greek custom, to ensure happiness. With reporters pressing around them, the new Mr. and Mrs. Onassis climbed into a jeep and, with a dazed and unsmiling Caroline sitting in her mother's lap and Ari at the wheel, drove off to the reception aboard the *Christina*.

Sipping pink champagne, Jackie stepped out on deck with Caroline to greet a select few journalists Ari had invited onboard. She shook hands with the reporters, thanked them for their good wishes, and then returned to her guests in the glass-walled sitting room. "When the party grew tired of the attention," said one of the reporters, "the curtains were finally drawn." To calm her nerves, Jackie went for a cigarette — she made sure to lay in a large supply of L&Ms — but before she could open the pack her new husband grabbed it from her hands. Now that they were married, he joked, it was his responsibility as her loving husband to see that she quit.

While everyone dressed for the wedding feast, Ari presented his bride with $1.2 million worth of jewels: a spectacular cabochon ruby ring surrounded by diamonds and a set of heart-shaped ruby-and-diamond earrings to match. He also gave her two gold-and-ruby rams-head Capricorn bracelets — he was a Capricorn, she a Leo — set with diamonds, and two diamond Capricorn rings. Onassis was careful not to forget his guests: Janet was given a diamond-and-platinum pin; Lee and the Kennedy sisters-in-law, gem-encrusted gold rings bearing the signs of the zodiac; and the little girls — Caroline and her cousins Sydney and Tina — sapphire-and-diamond bracelets. Lee's son, Tony, and John Jr. each got elaborate wristwatches.

It was only the beginning of Ari's largesse as far as the children were concerned. To keep them entertained on Skorpios, he purchased a mini-jeep, jukebox, and speedboat for John Jr., a sailboat for Caroline, and Shetland ponies for each. Ari routinely had Coney Island hot dogs — a favorite of Jackie's and the kids — flown from New York to Skorpios, and once John Jr.'s pet rabbit was transported across the Atlantic in the watchful care of a very nervous Olympic Airways pilot.

"Everything, from sugared almonds to the waiting yacht, was ready to celebrate the new life of Mr. and Mrs. Aristotle Onassis," observed *Time*'s cover story. "Everything, that is, except what is known as 'the world,' which seemed unable to comprehend or accept the match."

The strongest rebuke came from the Vatican, which declared that by marrying a divorced man Jackie was now "in a state of spiritual degradation . . . a public sinner. Mrs. Kennedy is not a child," sniffed Vatican spokesman Fausto Valliane, "and therefore she must know perfectly well what are the laws of her Church. Therefore, if she is not a child and not out of her mind, she must have known that she could not legally marry Mr. Onassis."

The Vatican's weekly *L'Osservatore della Domenica* later explained that, while Jackie had not been formally excommunicated, she was banned from the holy sacraments of the Church — including Communion and a Church burial. She was also "not immune from ecclesiastical punishment as well as justified deploration" because what she had done was "in effect a renunciation of her own faith." Jackie was, the paper said, "a prodigal child" existing in "a state of spiritual degradation."

There was a solution to their ecclesiastical quandary. Onassis had already had his mar-

riage to Tina annulled by the Greek Orthodox Church. Now he petitioned the Vatican's Sacred Rota, the board which rules on
marital matters, to grant an annulment of its
own. Once that was done, Jackie would no
longer be considered to have married a divorced man.

Back in Boston, Cardinal Cushing had
had enough of the Jackie-bashing. "The idea
of saying she's excommunicated, she's a
'public sinner.' What a lot of nonsense. Only
God knows who is a sinner, who is not.
Why can't she marry whomever she wants to
marry?" he demanded to know. "And why
should I be condemned and why should she
be condemned? I turn on the radio and all I
hear are people knocking her head off, as it
were, criticizing her and so forth, and they
are so far from the truth . . . Few people
understand Jacqueline Kennedy. I encouraged and helped her in every possible way."

As soon as they heard of the Cardinal's
words of support, Jackie and Ari both called
from the *Christina* to thank him. But Cushing's statements triggered such a flood of
angry telegrams, letters, and phone calls —
"some of which are in the language of the
gutter, if I may characterize them" — that
he threw up his hands. "I've had it," said
the Cardinal, who had been Archbishop of
Boston for twenty-five years. "What the future status of Jacqueline's marriage in the

Catholic Church is is not for me to decide." He added that he had fulfilled his promise "to my dearest friend, John Fitzgerald Kennedy, thirty-fifth President of the United States" to "take care of Jacqueline and the children if anything happened to him." With that, the defeated prelate announced that he was retiring after Christmas 1968 — two full years ahead of schedule.

The next day everyone returned home, leaving Jackie and Ari alone aboard the *Christina* — though not for long. Within days, the newlyweds had reverted to their old ways. On October 24 — four days after the wedding, Onassis and Greek strongman George Papadapoulos were at Papadapoulos's fortresslike villa outside Athens, toasting the announcement of their half-billion-dollar Project Omega with Greek cognac. "Our boss is the only man in the world," joked one of Ari's lieutenants, "who can handle two honeymoons at the same time."

While Ari indulged his consuming passion for making money, Jackie indulged hers for spending it. That would not be difficult, now that Jackie was chatelaine of Skorpios; Ari's opulent pied-à-terre on Paris's Avenue Foch; a mansion in Montevideo, Uruguay; a seaside villa nineteen miles outside Athens at Glyfada; and of course the *Christina* — not to mention her own impressive spread at

1040 Fifth and the farmhouse in New Jersey. Not counting the sixty crew members of the *Christina*, she had now been handed dominion over seventy servants spread across three continents.

Two days after the wedding, Jackie summoned Billy Baldwin, who had provided a shoulder to cry on after Jack's death, to Skorpios. As she welcomed him aboard the *Christina*, she appeared to Baldwin to be almost giddy. "I had never seen her in such high spirits," he said. To him, she had never "seemed so free."

It was more than just the money. Marrying Onassis, Jackie explained, "liberated me from the Kennedys — especially the Kennedy administration. None of them could understand why I'd want that funny, little squiggly name when I used to have the greatest name of all." But, she added mischievously, "I like seeing all these politicians dealing with Ari's squiggly name."

Baldwin had spent nine hours on a plane with the full intention of seeing Onassis's squiggly name — scrawled at the bottom of a large check. First, Jackie insisted on a crash course in the local cuisine. "Billy," she told her guest, "you are about to have your first experience with a Greek lunch. I will kill you if you pretend to like it."

Baldwin, whose assignment was to redecorate the villa nineteen miles outside Athens at the coastal town of Glyfada, the Skorpios house, and the *Christina*, did not pretend to like much of anything. He described the *Christina*'s interior as "the ugliest thing I had ever laid eyes on. Entirely covered with thick wall-to-wall carpeting, and tacky canvas runners . . . the epitome of vulgarity and bad taste." Baldwin deemed both houses similarly "appalling." The only room that genuinely pleased the finicky designer was Ari's paneled, book-filled study aboard the *Christina*. Gazing at the El Greco, Baldwin proclaimed it "one of the greatest rooms I have ever seen."

Jackie's avowed intention to transform Ari's surroundings did not threaten him. "You have to get one thing straight," he told Baldwin when he returned to Skorpios. "This house I want to be a complete surprise. I trust you and Jackie, and I don't want to know anything about it. I have only one request. Can there be a long sofa by the fire so I can lie and read and nap and watch the flames?"

Ari got his long sofa by the fire, but it would cost him dearly. Baldwin's initial consultation fee was $25,000, which he followed up with another bill for $43,855.74. When Onassis discovered that Baldwin had purchased two television sets for the Skorpios house, he was so furious he refused to pay for them. Not only did Skorpios not have any TV reception, but Baldwin had shipped them not on Olympic but aboard a rival airline. As for the bill, records showed that Onassis put through a payment of $27,609.89 on November 28, 1968, and a second $10,000 payment the following February 10. However, he refused to pay the $6,245.85 balance.

The lucrative redecorating job was Jackie's way of thanking Baldwin for standing beside her. In the first few weeks following the wedding, Jackie was left by herself on Skorpios while Ari ricocheted from Athens to Paris and back again on business — time to contemplate the furor that still raged outside the walls of the Onassis compound. No longer the seemingly carefree Jackie who first greeted Baldwin, Jackie now seemed to harbor second thoughts "about the course she had taken."

Feeling "alone and embattled," Jackie sat down and penned a heartfelt letter to Roswell Gilpatric, the one man she felt she could always turn to in times of personal crisis:

Dearest Ros, I would have told you before I left — but then everything happened so much more quickly than I'd planned. I saw somewhere what you had said and I was touched — dear Ros — I hope you know all you were and are and will ever be to me — With my love, Jackie.

Unaware of the letter she had written to her old lover, Ari spent the next three weeks honeymooning with Jackie on Skorpios. They went for long hikes across the island, sunbathed, swam, snorkled, fed the miniature horses Onassis stabled on the island, and sailed the *Christina* to Rhodes. When their idyllic time in the sun was over, Jackie returned to New York to be with her children. Ari planned to join them later, but first he had some business to attend to.

That business was Maria Callas. In truth, neither Mr. nor Mrs. Onassis seemed quite willing to give up old loves entirely. Ari had not even been able to summon the courage to tell Callas of the impending nuptials himself. He left that onerous task up to his chauffeur Jacinto Rosa. "He asked me to tell her nothing would change," Rosa said. "He said to explain it would always be the same between them — that she was still the real lady of the house. When I called Maria on the phone and broke the news, she laughed out loud — but she obviously felt a tremendous bitterness." From that point on, Callas referred to Jackie as "The False Lady" — "a judgment," Rosa said, "the servants came to agree with."

As soon as Jackie boarded Olympic Airways for New York, Ari was on the phone to the diva's Paris apartment. The maid insisted her mistress was not in. He sent her three dozen roses. Again, Callas would not take his call. Six dozen roses arrived at 36 Avenue Georges Mandel. Again, no response. The dance was all too familiar to Ari, although now that he was married to "The False Lady," it would take more than the usual fancy footwork.

Realizing that Callas valued her reputation above all else, Onassis stood under the window of her apartment and began whistling loudly. Nothing. He then began plaintively calling her name. Irate neighbors threw open their windows and hollered for Callas's obnoxious suitor to shut up. Finally, he shouted that he would drive his Mercedes limousine right through the front door.

Finally, she relented. Beginning with quiet dinners, Onassis would slowly rekindle his romance with Callas — an affair that was, according to those who knew them, far more genuine than anything Ari and Jackie had felt for each other. "The two lovers saw each other almost constantly," Rosa said. "Right up until a month before his death — for the truth is that Maria was the only true love of Onassis's life. She was his 'real wife' — even though they weren't officially married."

Still, during that first full year of marriage, the spark of affection between Jackie and Ari that had been so evident to Larry Newman at Hyannis Port was still there. "Of course he provided her with the security she craved after Bobby's assassination," George Plimpton said. "But she really did adore him, and he was devoted to her. People say that it was sort of a financial arrangement from the beginning, but when I was around them they were very warm, very affectionate toward each other. When people are estranged they usually sit in silence, or away from each other. I *never* saw any of that — particularly that first year. They always seemed to enjoy each other's company. *Always*. I can remember Jackie giggling a lot around Ari — but he was an extremely charming fellow."

Plimpton recalled that in restaurants Onassis would "whip off his coat and become the Lord of the Table. The first time he rolled up his sleeves I remember being impressed by how big his forearms were. He was a very earthy, powerful figure with an equally powerful intellect — a very engaging man."

Onassis's encyclopedic knowledge of Greek mythology, which he applied to the modern era, made him even more intriguing. Plimpton, who had become famous writing about his Walter Mitty experiences playing professional sports, was dining with Jackie and Ari in Greenwich Village when Onassis offered a suggestion. "Why knock yourself to pieces playing football?" Ari asked. "Why don't you write about love?"

"So we knocked the idea around a bit and I came up with the idea of replaying the story of Paris — when Zeus rolled the golden apple out onto the floor at Olympus with the words *To the Fairest* on it. Three goddesses fought over the apple: Athena, the goddess of wisdom; Zeus's wife, Hera, the goddess of the home; and Aphrodite, goddess of love. Zeus gave the job of deciding which was the fairest to an honest mortal named Paris. So these three goddesses began to bribe him. Hera offered Paris riches. Athena offered him armies. And Aphrodite offered him Helen of Troy. Well, of course Paris picked Helen and we all know what happened then . . .

"Ari's idea was to do it all with real women of today and publish my account in the *Ladies' Home Journal*. He would put me on the *Christina*, where each of the modern day 'goddesses' would try to bribe me. For the contemporary Hera, who was more or less the goddess of domestic bliss, we picked Betty Furness, who sold refrigerators on TV and later became a big consumer-affairs crusader. Gloria Steinem was our Athena, and for Aphrodite, we had no trouble picking Brigitte Bardot."

And who was the modern era's answer to Helen of Troy? "Why, Jackie, of course." Plimpton shrugged.

In late November, Ari joined Jackie and the children in New Jersey. Before Onassis arrived, his wife had a French photographer arrested for trespassing and put up barricades blocking the road leading to her house.

Once there, Onassis kept to himself. While Caroline and John Jr. joined their mother riding to the hounds — nine-year-old John nearly toppled from his pony when the animal snagged one of its hind legs while jumping a fence — Ari remained inside juggling deals on the phone.

That year, Onassis shared his first Thanksgiving with his new young family at 1040 Fifth. Among the guests was Kitty Carlisle Hart. "We were all trying to explain to this foreigner the history of this purely American ritual," Hart said, "and of course to him it all sounded rather, well, silly. Finally, he smiled and said, 'Oh, *I* get it. First you stuff the turkey, and then you stuff the husband *with* the turkey.' Jackie threw up her hands and laughed."

In front of Hart and the others who socialized with them over the Thanksgiving holiday, Jackie and Ari were openly affectionate. "They seemed, at least in that first year, to be very much in love with each other," Hart said.

Peter Duchin saw them both frequently onboard the *Christina* and in New York:

"There was a tenderness between them that was really very moving," Duchin said. "They really loved each other, and I think in a way that neither had loved anyone before. Each was just terribly concerned about the other. And they had fun! Ari took tremendous pleasure and pride in Jackie, and when she looked at him . . . well, there was obvious passion there."

Onassis called Jackie his "Class A Lady" — a line borrowed from the language on the packs of L&Ms she chain-smoked: "20 Class A Cigarettes."

Jackie also reveled in other people's love stories, and reminded Duchin of the story his then-wife, Cheray, had told him about a low moment in their own sporadic courtship. "Cheray had been in the kitchen about to feed her Yorkshire terrier, when she spotted a photograph of me in the newspaper under the doggie bowl," Duchin said. " 'The moment I saw Peter's face,' she told Jackie, 'I burst into tears. . . . That fall we started dating again.' "

"Ari loved that story," Jackie told Duchin. "He called you 'two wonderful children in love.' When I told him how Cheray had burst into tears, *he* burst into tears."

Displays of affection between Jackie and Ari among groups of friends were one thing. The public still had a difficult time imagining that there could be anything physical between Jackie and her grandfatherly spouse. "Come on. Would you sleep with Onassis?" Joan Rivers cracked. "Do you believe she does? Well, she has to do something — you can't stay in Bergdorf's shopping all day."

Plimpton understood why Jackie might be sexually attracted to Onassis. "True, he was short and dark and no William Holden," Plimpton said. "But there is something about huge wealth — and I mean *huge* wealth — that automatically makes one attractive. Jackie was the first to admit that."

Still, Jackie professed to be "dumbfounded" by the prevailing notion that her motives were strictly mercenary. "Jackie must have said at least ten times to me, 'Isn't it wcird that everybody thinks I married Ari for his money?' I knew Jackie really, really well. She confided in me. If she had married Ari for money, she would have talked about it. Sure, the money was part of Ari's attraction, but only a part. She really loved him."

Ironically, Jackie's marriage to Onassis signaled a kind of sexual renaissance for her. She was twenty when she lost her virginity in Paris to the novelist John Phillips Marquand Jr., son of the Pulitzer Prize–winning author of *The Late George Apley*. Jackie and Marquand were returning to his *pensione* after a night of club-hopping when the lift to his apartment "stalled" between floors, a

357

maneuver Marquand had used before. "Oh!" Jackie said after the encounter. "Is that all there is to it?"

Beginning with Jack and Jackie's furtive fumblings in the back seat of the young congressman's Buick, Jackie may have felt much the same way about her sex life with her first husband. His libido was sent into overdrive by the cortisone he took to combat Addison's disease and Max Jacobson's regular amphetamine injections, but by all accounts JFK's technique left something to be desired.

A cocky Jack, confident that his remark would not be reported, once told newsmen, "I'm never finished with a girl until I've had her three ways." But firsthand accounts belie the notion that he was anything but perfunctory in his approach to sex. "Finesse was not Jack's forte. He definitely sacrificed quality for quantity," said former NBC anchorwoman Nancy Dickerson, who dated Jack before his engagement to Jackie. "He was just so gosh darn physically, animalistically attractive that it was hard to imagine. And of course power is the ultimate aphrodisiac and with that combination he was really something. But to Jack sex *was* just like a cup of coffee — no more or less important than that."

Another lover remembered that sex with Jack was "strictly wham bam, thank you, ma'am. Jack was a very selfish lover. I don't think he really liked women very much. He certainly did not respect them."

George Smathers was "in constant awe" of Jack's prowess with women. "He was like a Roto-Rooter. He'd be with one woman, and before she could realize what had happened, he'd have moved on to another — literally."

Longtime Kennedy advisor and intimate Langdon "Don" Marvin procured women for Kennedy before the televised 1960 Kennedy-Nixon debates and in the White House. "He seldom took longer than twenty minutes," Marvin said. "Not even with Marilyn Monroe."

Jack's sexual recidivism made it highly unlikely that Jack and Jackie approached sex with any sense of adventure. Observed Jacques Lowe, JFK's personal photographer, "They led very separate lives . . . Jack certainly wasn't jumping into bed with her every night." Added to the equation was the traditional Irish Catholic tendency to view women, in the words of one "Murphia" member, as "saints or whores. You had fun with your mistress. Sex within marriage was strictly for making babies."

Certainly neither Jack nor Jackie shared the details of their personal life with others. "They had too much respect for each other," Oleg Cassini said, "to ever discuss such private matters with anyone. They did not bare their souls to anyone, not even their closest friends. They had far too much class for that."

Onassis was another matter. Ari often boasted of his prowess in the bedroom. Within days of marrying Jackie, he was sharing even the most intimate details of their sex life. He bragged to a friend that they made love "five times a night — she surpasses all the women I have ever known." Pierre Salinger remembered that Onassis "was very graphic in the way he described their sexual relationship. Believe me, it was more than any of us wanted to hear. But he would just keep on talking."

Roy Cohn, the cutthroat lawyer who at first gained notoriety as Senator Joe McCarthy's counsel during the televised Army-McCarthy hearings of 1954, knew Onassis and later went to work as his hired gun. Onassis, Cohn said, "was a randy guy who'd had a lot more experience than she had. She felt if she was going to keep him interested, she'd have to perform."

Even Jackie's brief, clandestine trysts with William Holden, Ros Gilpatric, and Marlon Brando offered little opportunity for experimentation. Uncertain how to proceed, Jackie sought advice from Dr. Henry Lax, her New York physician. Lax was surprised at how little Jackie knew about human anatomy, and gave her a crash course on sexual gratification. To illustrate his points he took out a piece of paper and made a detailed drawing of the female sex organs, circling the most highly sensitive areas in red. He gave her the drawing, which Jackie neatly folded and tucked in her purse for future consultation.

Birth control was something she had not practiced during her first marriage. Since neither she nor Onassis wanted more children, Jackie at thirty-nine was put on the pill.

"He was crazy about her," insisted Onassis's personal secretary, Kiki Feroudi Maoutsatsos, "and, despite his appearance, she was just as crazy about him. They shared a great physical love, one they enhanced by taking a variety of drugs Ari got from doctors and other people to increase sexual stamina and desire."

One source was La Prairie, the famous Swiss clinic founded by controversial longevity pioneer Dr. Paul Niehans. Both Jackie and Ari were injected with live sheep cells — a serum Niehans believed both prolonged life and increased virility. In addition, Doris Lilly said, "Jackie brought along her own bag of goodies. She got Ari to start taking shots from Dr. Feelgood" — Max Jacobson's potent amphetamine-steroid concoction. (The unexpected death of Jackie's good friend, *Life* magazine photographer Mark Shaw, on January 26, 1969, at the age of forty-seven should have been a wake-up call for all of Jacobson's patients. The medical examiner determined from the needle tracks on his arms and the amounts of amphetamine in his tissues that Shaw died as a result of drug abuse.)

In addition to the drugs, Jackie and Ari sought to add excitement to their marriage by making love in unconventional places. One *Christina* crew member caught them *en flagrante* aboard the dinghy they kept tethered to the yacht, another time in a lifeboat. They ripped out all the seats in the first-class section of an Olympic airliner and turned it into a flying boudoir. An enormous bulkhead-to-bulkhead bed took up virtually the entire section, and the windows were covered by French tapestries. A steward aboard the plane walked in immediately after takeoff to ask if they needed anything and, like his counterparts aboard the *Christina*, saw Jackie and Ari on the gargantuan bed, nude and "in the throes of energetic and creative lovemaking." Standing paralyzed next to the bed — "I could have reached out and touched them" — the steward soon realized that they were oblivious to his presence. He managed to back out of the room, undetected.

Still, the two spent long stretches of time

apart. Rather than admit that they existed in very different worlds, Onassis tried to portray the arrangement as a kind of child-rearing technique. "Jackie is often at the other end of the world with her children — whom I should say I love very much," Ari tried to explain, "but they need time to get used to me, and I want to give them that time. They need time to understand that their mother has remarried and that I want to be their friend, and not replace their father, whom I admired so much. A father cannot be replaced, especially one like John Kennedy. I only desire that they consider me a best friend. That is another reason why I believe it is a good idea," he added, "that Jackie has time alone with her children."

In December, Jackie hopped a plane alone for Washington as soon as she learned Ethel had given birth to Bobby's eleventh child. Bypassing Ethel's room, she headed straight for the nursery at Georgetown University Hospital to get her first look at her newest niece, Rory Elizabeth Katherine Kennedy. "It's very pretty," she said as they held up the baby girl.

Jackie then went down the hall to a special lounge Ethel had rented for visitors. There she hugged Luella Hennessey, the family nurse who had been present at the birth of all four of Jackie's children — including the stillborn baby girl and little Patrick. Memories of those difficult times suddenly came flooding back, and an emotional Jackie asked everyone else to leave the lounge so she could be alone with Hennessey.

From the hospital, Jackie went straight to Arlington. She asked her Secret Service men to remain in the car while she got out and walked alone up the hillside — first to Bobby's grave, and then to the spot where Jack, the stillborn girl, and Patrick were buried. The only sound was the clicking of tourist cameras as Jackie stood there for a moment, staring at the graves.

From Arlington, she went straight to National Airport, where she refused to take refuge in Eastern Airlines's VIP lounge. "I want to be treated like everyone else," she insisted, and went to a snack bar for lunch. While travelers stared, Jackie stood at the counter, eating a hot dog and drinking coffee from a paper cup. Later, she would join Ari and his children for Christmas on Skorpios.

Maybe it was the shock of seeing Bobby's newborn, of running into Luella Hennessey, or of visiting Jack's grave that suddenly made Jackie want to be "treated just like everyone else." She wanted no less for her children.

On her return to New York, Jackie wrote

a six-page letter to Secret Service Director James J. Rowley complaining that "there are too many agents, and the new ones are not sensitive to the needs of little children." Caroline and John Jr., she said, "must think that they lead normal lives, and not be conscious of a large number of men protecting them from further violence. They must not be made conspicuous among their friends by the presence of numerous agents, or have the households in which they live thrown into turmoil by the intrusion of agents who do not care about them or understand their problems."

She went on to demand that the Secret Service detail be cut in half, from eight to four agents who "should be with the children from the time they leave the house in the morning until they return at 5:30 for supper. I would like to request that the afternoon and night shift of extra agents be terminated. These are the men who are unnecessary and who cause confusion. The children are secure in the apartment in New York at night. In the country, Hyannis, and New Jersey, the local police provide night protection."

What most upset Jackie was the way in which agents disrupted the children's lives during weekends in New Jersey. "Agents tramp outside the children's windows all night, talking into their walkie-talkies," she said. "Cars of each agent pile up in the driveway so that our little country house looks like a used-car lot." At one point, Jackie said, an agent "either went to sleep or was listening to the radio so loudly in his car with the windows steamed up that he did not hear a neighbor's child locked in the car next to him who had been crying hysterically for an hour, and was finally found by her parents. Another time an agent went in and forcibly dragged my children home for supper though I had told his superior that they might stay, etc., etc." She also reminded Rowley of the time the agents had actually lost the children and spent hours frantically hunting for them.

In Greece, Jackie pointed out to the Secret Service Director, Onassis's force of "about seventy-five men" seemed adequate to protect her children. "The children are growing up," she told Rowley. "They must see new things and travel as their father would have wished them to do. They must be as free as possible, not encumbered by a group of men who will be lost in foreign countries, so that one ends up protecting them rather than vice-versa . . . As the person in the world who is the most interested in their security, and who realizes most what threats are in the outside world, I promise you that I have considered and tried every way, and that what I ask you for is what I know is best for the children of President Kennedy and what he would wish for them . . . Thank you so much, dear Mr. Rowley. I hope you have a happy Christmas. Most sincerely, Jacqueline."

Jackie would succeed to a considerable extent in helping her children lead "normal" lives. But, with the exception of the occasional hot dog, normalcy was something she neither required nor actually desired.

Jackie's longtime friend Vivien Crespi remembered sipping wine by the pool at Skorpios in their bikinis. "Do you realize how lucky we are, Vivi?" Jackie asked. "To have gotten out of that world we came from. That narrow world of Newport. All that horrible anti-Semitism and bigotry? Going every day to that club with the same kinds of people. Don't you feel sorry for them? You and I have taken such a big bite out of life."

Ari certainly was trying hard to keep his wife amused. Wherever he was in the world, Onassis made certain that every two weeks a surprise was left on Jackie's silver breakfast tray — usually flowers with a hidden gold or diamond-studded bracelet from Zolotas, Athens's answer to Cartier. "I'm sure Mrs. Onassis must by now have a small museum of the Zolotas firm," store manager Ilias Lalaounius said in early 1969. "She must have at least thirty bracelets" — easily $70,000 worth. When Onassis was on business in Tokyo, Jackie awakened to find a strand of Mikimoto pearls wound around a croissant.

At the White House, Jackie had insisted on separate bedrooms. "Mrs. Kennedy would no more see her husband until she fixed her face," said the children's nanny, Maud Shaw, "than Queen Elizabeth would receive the Prime Minister wearing her bathrobe." She continued the arrangement with Onassis. Even when he was under the same roof, Ari found ways to surprise her. He might leave a poem on her breakfast tray, or a formal invitation that read "Mr. Aristotle Onassis requests the pleasure of your company for deck tennis at 11:30 A.M. aboard the motor ship *Christina.*"

Onassis was proud of his newest acquisition, and eagerly indulged every whim of his guileless child-wife ("the world's oldest sixteen-year-old" is how journalist Midge Decter described her). "Jackie is a little bird that needs its freedom as well as its security," Onassis explained, "and she gets both from me. She can do exactly as she pleases — visit international fashion shows and travel and go out with friends to the theater or any place. And I, of course, will do exactly as I please. I never question her and she never questions me."

"When Jackie married Ari," said Winston's daughter Lady Sarah Spencer-

Churchill, "she wasn't only marrying another man, she was marrying another way of life. From what I've seen, they both agree with her."

To be sure, Jackie was captivated not only by the sheer magnitude of Ari's fortune but by the culture that spawned it. She immersed herself in the Greek myths, soaking up all she could about the gods and heroes that populated them. When her old friend Arthur Schlesinger Jr. likened Jack Kennedy to a noble Roman, Jackie wrote the historian arguing that her late husband was more like a Greek warrior.

"There is a conflict in the hearts and minds of the Greeks," Jackie wrote. "Greeks have esteem and respect for the gods; yet the Greek was the first to write and proclaim that Man was the measure of all things. This conflict with the gods is the essence of the Greek tragedy and a key to the Greek character."

Borrowing from her own love of Eastern mysticism and Asian cultures, she went on to say she believed that "the Greeks are mystics. This mysticism can be traced to the influence of the sea — the boundlessness and mystery of the sea respond to the yearning of the Greeks for a supernatural rapport with divinity. The Greeks are curious and it is this curiosity that inspired a search and a thirst for knowledge and the Socratic contribution to the world that virtue is knowledge."

In an obvious effort to become part of her husband's world, Jackie steeped herself in the history and traditions of his homeland. She learned to make *dolmades,* rice stuffed in grape leaves and soaked in olive oil; donned the flouncy skirts and bangles native to Corfu and Rhodes; and was taught the *surtaki* by crew members aboard the *Christina.*

"Everything she did," the photographer Peter Beard said of Jackie, "was voracious." With Alexis Minotis, director of the Greek National Theater, she attended performances of plays by Euripides and Aristophanes on the twenty-four-hundred-year-old stage at Epidaurus. She investigated the ancient backstreets of Athens, familiarized herself with each plinth and pediment of the Acropolis, and explored every island, from Corfu to Rhodes to Mikonos to Ari's favorite, Itháki.

Jackie was even determined to make at least one small business contribution, hiring Pierre Cardin to design new uniforms for Olympic Airways's stewardesses. The new sleeveless look proved to be an unqualified disaster, however; Jackie had not stopped to consider that, unlike their American counterparts, Greek women seldom shave under their arms.

After spending the 1968 Christmas holidays in the company of Ari and the children on Skorpios, Jackie returned to New York with Caroline and John Jr. in tow. No sooner had she left than Onassis flew to Paris for a dinner with Callas at her apartment. The reunion was arranged by their mutual friend, the Baroness van Zuylen, who made sure friends were invited to make it look more like a dinner party than an illicit tryst. "She was behaving like a nervous teenager," one of the other guests said of Callas, "picking the dogs up, putting the dogs down, opening and closing the windows, arranging and rearranging the flowers. It was as if she wanted to show him that life could go on without him."

Apparently convinced that he could freely continue seeing both women, Ari returned to Jackie in New York before the two went off together on a cruise of the Canary Islands. Jackie, still determined for the children to retain their ties to the Kennedy clan, invited Rose to spend Easter aboard the *Christina.* As a token of his gratitude for standing behind them in the difficult days surrounding the wedding, Ari gave Rose a serpent-shaped 24-karat-gold bracelet glittering with diamonds and rubies.

The dark side of the Kennedy legacy reared its head on July 18, when Ted drove his 1967 Oldsmobile off the Dyke Bridge at

Chappaquiddick, drowning his attractive young passenger, Mary Jo Kopechne. Ted had been among six married men partying late into the night with six single women, the "Boiler Room Girls," who had worked tirelessly on behalf of Bobby's presidential campaign.

Only three months earlier, Ted had gotten drunk on a plane and was overheard by reporters saying over and over, "They're going to shoot my ass off the way they shot Bobby." One reporter then prophetically described Ted as "an accident waiting to happen." Now that it had happened, the way the Senator handled it would speak volumes about his character — or lack of it.

Instead of calling police and summoning help to rescue Kopechne from the submerged car, Kennedy returned to the house where the party was in progress to fetch his cousin Joey Gargan. After diving into the cold water several times and failing to locate the young woman, Kennedy then swam across the narrow inlet to Edgartown, changed his clothes, made an appearance in the lobby of the inn where he was staying, then from his room made seventeen phone calls to friends and political advisors — none to the authorities. Then he went to sleep. It was not until the next day, after he learned that the body had been found, that he reported the accident to police.

Chappaquiddick foreclosed any possibility of the last Kennedy brother reaching the White House. But Jackie, who had grown close to Ted after Bobby's death (although not as close as she had grown to Bobby after Jack's), stood shoulder to shoulder with the rest of the family at Hyannis Port. To underscore the fact that she still respected and admired her embattled brother-in-law, Jackie asked him to take the place of Bobby as Caroline's godfather. "It was a special trust," he later said. "It meant a great deal, and so did the support she gave me at the time."

The tragedy did nothing, however, toward persuading Ted to change his ways. His displays of public drunkenness continued unabated, as did his open pursuit of women.

Not long after the crucible of Chappaquiddick, Jackie agreed to represent the Kennedys at a luncheon given by the editors of *Newsweek* at the magazine's New York headquarters. When someone brought up the issue of sexual discrimination in hiring, Jackie countered that she'd had no difficulty finding a job in journalism as a photographer.

Katharine Graham, who had taken over as publisher at *Newsweek* and *The Washington Post* after her manic-depressive husband Phil killed himself, was dumbfounded by her old friend's comment. "Oh, Jackie, don't you remember," Graham asked, "when we would be at the White House sitting at the feet of Jack and Phil saying nothing, just looking up to them?"

Ten days after Chappaquiddick, Ari gave Jackie the 40.42-carat marquis Lesotho III diamond for her fortieth birthday, along with a matching diamond necklace and bracelet. (The Lesotho III was the third-largest cut from the original 601-carat Lesotho diamond, the eleventh-largest diamond ever found and the biggest discovered by a woman. It sold at auction in 1996 for $2,587,500.) She also received a pair of 18-carat gold-and-ruby *Apollo II* ear clips by Greek jeweler Ilias Lalaounis to commemorate the first lunar landing — the realization of JFK's dream to land a man on the moon by the end of the decade.

Each anchored by a large moon of hammered gold, the textured surface indented with "craters" and studded with rubies, the large globes dangled from lunar capsule-shaped links. At Jackie's birthday party, Greek actress Katina Paxinous sat next to Jackie and complimented her on the new earrings. "Ari was actually apologetic about them," Jackie replied. "He felt they were such trifles. But he promised me that, if I'm good, next year he'll give me the moon itself." Jackie's fortieth birthday "trifles" cost her husband well in excess of $2 million.

The amount equaled — barely — what

Jackie had spent on herself during the first year of their marriage. A compulsive, manic consumer for whom the term *shopaholic* might have been invented, Jackie's spending habit had gotten her into deep trouble with Jack.

Accordingly, her out-of-control spending would ultimately play a major role in destroying her marriage to Onassis. Yet Ari had only himself to blame. "God knows Jackie has had her years of sorrow," he said. "If it makes her happy, she can have anything she wants."

Thus encouraged by Ari to indulge her every impulse — and with no concern for offending the electorate — Jackie splurged shamelessly. Far exceeding her ostensible allowance of only $30,000 a month ("Trying to make Jackie Onassis stick to a budget is like trying to make Jackie Gleason stick to a diet," cracked Lee), Jackie purchased furs, shoes, handbags, stockings, lingerie, antiques, fabrics, compacts, cosmetics, scarves, baubles, and bibelots of every imaginable variety. A regular at the Paris fashion shows, she began scooping up entire collections by her favorite designers. Valentino, Courrèges, Saint Laurent, Madame Grès, Lanvin, Dior, and Givenchy all made up mannequins to Jackie's specific measurements — just so they could fill her orders when she called from New York, Paris, Skorpios, or the

Christina as it plied the waters of the Mediterranean.

Onassis insider Costa Gratsos accurately described her as a "speed shopper," but Jackie was also a "pointer" — a merchant's dream customer, someone who points at the desired merchandise without ever bothering to ask the price. On a typical visit to one Fifth Avenue store, Jackie spent $40,000 in a matter of minutes. "We were all so excited we forgot to make out sales slips," said the store manager, "and we could not remember some of the things Mrs. Onassis bought." One salesman "had to be taken home in a taxi and put to bed with a sedative." On her way home, an Alaskan seal coat caught her eye in the window at Maximilian. She walked out with it *and* a $60,000 sable coat.

In October of 1969, *Women's Wear Daily* proclaimed her "the retailer's best friend. Jackie Onassis continues to fill her bottomless closets. She is making Daddy O's bills bigger than ever with her latest shopping spree. She is buying in carload lots."

She spent a small fortune on less tangible items — massages, facials, manicures (she fought a lifelong habit of biting her nails), pedicures, and cosmetics. When Ari complained about her bedtime attire of flannel nightgowns and cotton underpants, she sent a bra and panties to Halston and asked him to custom-make new lingerie for her.

"She called me from Greece and said, 'Make me something sexy,'" the designer recalled, "and I said, 'Something very Marilyn Monroe.' Remember, at the time none of us knew *anything* about Jack Kennedy and Marilyn Monroe. There was this silence, and then she said, 'She didn't wear any.'" The bill for the satin lingerie and diaphanous silk teddies Halston had custommade for Jackie exceeded $5,000.

Jackie spent more than that at the hairdressers in 1969 alone — a not-inconsiderable sum at the time. "She had been putting chemicals on her hair for so many years that by the time she married Onassis it was severely damaged. Jackie would have been completely gray at forty," said an employee of Kenneth's who saw her routinely, "and her hair was thinning to such an extent that she always wore falls and hairpieces to create the illusion that she had this luxurious mane."

There were other expenditures the public didn't see — $5,000 a year for a messenger just to deliver merchandise to and from stores; $7,500 for drugstore incidentals; $6,000 for the care of her dogs; $15,000 for flowers. Again, when compared to the average income for Americans at the time of under $10,000 per year, these amounts were staggering.

For the most part, Jackie shrugged off

criticism of her spending. She was, after all, married to one of the richest men in the world — *the* richest, according to some accounts — and he had explicitly encouraged her to spend as she pleased. There was no danger of the spigot ever being turned off — Ari labored tirelessly to ensure that the cash would keep flowing. "Ari never stops working," she told a friend. "He dreams in millions."

Mrs. Onassis was bothered, however, by the persistent rumors regarding details of her prenuptial agreement. "It's a lie, a complete lie," she told Truman Capote. "I don't have any money. When I married Ari, my income from the Kennedy estate stopped, and so did my widow's pension from the U.S. government. I didn't make any premarital financial agreement with Ari. I know it's an old Greek custom, but I couldn't do it. I didn't want to barter myself. Except for personal possessions, I have exactly $5,200 in a bank account. Everything else I charge to Olympic Airlines." Capote, like most of her friends, "wasn't fooled by Jackie crying poor — not even one little bit."

The couple's friends also began noticing that Mr. and Mrs. Onassis were being together less. "Jackie loves traveling, sightseeing, long walks, mountain climbing, skiing, and literally hundreds of things that are just not to my liking," Ari tried to explain. "If we were together, she would probably get nervous always seeing me bringing up the rear! I know Jackie would eventually give up her activities to please me and just stay with me, but then, that wouldn't really be Jackie. I don't want that to happen . . . I have found that the longer the separation between us is, the happier we are to meet."

The arrangement suited Jackie just fine — although as she continued to lead her high-profile life in New York, Mrs. Onassis increasingly came to view the press as the enemy. Not that she didn't crave publicity. Jackie actively sought coverage throughout her life, so long as it was strictly on her own terms. "If I had a single issue to get out, and my career and the magazine's future depended on the newsstand sale," said *Women's Wear Daily* publisher James Brady, "I would without any hesitation at all choose Jacqueline Kennedy Onassis as my cover girl . . . there is a continual and enthusiastic, and even perhaps morbid, interest in Jackie, her life and loves."

Yet Brady conceded Jackie's "love-hate relationship with the press . . . There were occasions when her secretary would telephone and say that Mrs. Kennedy would be at such and such a place at lunch that day and she would be wearing so and so. We would thank the secretary, send a photographer to wait outside the restaurant, and have our front-page shot for the next day's paper. At other times she would flee us as from the plague."

That was particularly true of Jackie when dealing with the paparazzi, who shadowed her every move. In early October of 1969, Jackie and Ari went to see the controversial X-rated Swedish film *I Am Curious — Yellow*. Although her husband was intrigued by the movie's explicit sexual content — unprecedented for a general release at the time — and stayed until the end, Jackie got up in the middle and left. Outside the theater on busy 57th Street, two photographers were lying in wait.

Jackie, wearing a leather miniskirt and a brightly colored scarf around her head, went up to the first photographer, who stood well over six feet. "Wait," she said, grabbing his arm. Then she spotted the other photographer, Mel Finkelstein, who at 5 feet 10 and 168 pounds was decidedly less prepossessing. "I thought she was going to say something," Finkelstein said. Instead, she grabbed his right wrist with her right hand, jerked him forward, stuck out her left leg, hitching up her miniskirt, and flipped him over her thigh. The photograph of Finkelstein sprawled on the street with Jackie striding triumphantly away was splashed across front pages the next day.

In a series of harrowing encounters with

the paparazzi that would foreshadow the tragic death of Princess Diana, Jackie narrowly escaped being killed. Several of these dangerous incidents took place in Greece, where the Onassises had a nickname for one of their pursuers: "The Shadow."

Dimitri Koulouris was so intrusive that a Greek judge sentenced him to six months in jail for nearly causing a collision between his speedboat and the Onassises' seaplane as he tried to pull alongside the plane to snap a picture as it took off. According to court testimony, on another occasion Jackie was water-skiing off Skorpios when the paparazzo cut across the stern of the boat that was towing her, severing the line. As Jackie sank beneath the surface, struggling for air, the photographer continued snapping away. John Jr. was another target. According to a witness, Koulouris threw stones at John in hopes that he could catch the boy on film throwing rocks back at him.

Late one night after leaving Maxim's, Onassis's limousine led photographers on a high-speed chase through the streets of Paris that presaged the tragic events of August 1997. Like Princess Diana, neither Jackie nor Ari wore seat belts. Unlike Diana, Jackie told Ari to order his driver to slow down. "A few pictures," she said, "aren't worth getting killed over."

Despite her life-threatening episodes

abroad, it was the indefatigable New York photographer Ron Galella whom Jackie resented above all others. Since a picture of Jackie O was unquestionably more valuable on the open market than that of any other celebrity, she quickly became the freelance photographer's favorite quarry.

Galella stalked her everywhere, popping out from behind shrubs and doorways, weaving and bobbing, snapping hundreds of pictures while taunting her and making strange grunting noises. On Mother's Day, for example, he ambushed her as she got out of a limousine and walked toward her apartment building. Quickly, Jackie put the bouquet her children had given her in front of her face, ruining the picture. Jackie, Ari, architect I. M. Pei, and a few friends were dining at a Chinese restaurant one evening when Galella suddenly materialized and started clicking away. The party quickly broke up. Galella later claimed that the restaurant manager not only tipped him off to Jackie's presence, he fed the photographer and helped conceal him behind a coatrack.

Over the coming years, Galella pursued his prey relentlessly, but with a flair even Jackie acknowledged as unique. On Capri, she would later testify at one of two trials, he dressed up in "a white sailor suit with a little white sailor hat on. He came running alone. He yelled at me, 'Hiya, Jackie. Are you surprised to see me here? How do you like me? I've joined the navy.' "

Nearly all of their encounters, however, were in Manhattan. Coming out of P. J. Clarke's on Third Avenue, a sawdust-on-floor joint popular with celebrities, Jackie and Ari were again accosted by Galella. "He was leaping around, taking pictures, running ahead of us, taking them, running back," Jackie recalled. She and her grim-faced husband took refuge in a record store.

Around Christmas, a man in a Santa suit accosted Jackie as she left her apartment — "pushing, trying to get next to me, pushing, scuffling . . ." — when Galella again materialized, trying to snap a picture. The *National Enquirer* had hired Galella to take a picture of Jackie with Santa to run on the cover of its holiday issue. The photo did not come off as Galella had planned. "She's fast," he said, "and Santa was slow." Later, as Galella tried to catch Jackie sledding with the children in Central Park, Secret Service agents shoved him into a snowbank.

In a number of instances Jackie was able to foil her nemesis. While riding in her limousine, Jackie noticed that she was being followed by Galella. She told her chauffeur to stop at the "21" Club. "I opened the car door as if I was going to get out," she recalled. "That caused Galella to get out of his car . . . Then I leapt back in, slammed the car door and told my driver to go as fast as he could to get away." Galella lost her.

When it came to her children, however, Jackie was in no mood to play games. Once, Caroline's tennis lesson in Central Park was interrupted when Galella jumped onto the court and began taking photographs. "I'm not making you nervous, am I, honey?" he asked.

"Yes, you are," Caroline replied.

"She turned towards me," Jackie recalled, "and there were tears in her eyes." Jackie leaned on a tree next to a glowering Secret Service agent. Then, without warning, Jackie began sprinting across the park, with Galella hot on her heels. Galella kept shooting, and even caught Jackie running past a police car with two officers apparently dozing inside. Jackie, confident that she had lured Galella away from her daughter, made it onto the jogging track that circles the reservoir and put on speed. Galella was literally left behind in Jackie's dust, gasping for air.

By October of 1969, Caroline had transferred from Convent of the Sacred Heart to Brearley, an exclusive girls' school on New York's Upper East Side. She had gone to a carnival at the school when Galella once again materialized out of nowhere and began running around the girl, furiously taking snapshots and humiliating Caroline in front of her friends.

Two weeks later, Jackie and John Jr. were bicycling through Central Park when Galella jumped out of the bushes, frightening her son and causing him to swerve violently. Jackie ordered the Secret Service agent who had been following them on a bicycle to "smash his camera" and arrest Galella for harassment.

The criminal harassment charges against the photographer were dropped for lack of evidence, but Galella sued Jackie for $1.3 million, charging Jackie with false arrest, malicious persecution, assault, and "interference with my livelihood as a photographer." She, in turn, countersued for $6 million, claiming Galella's actions constituted invasion of privacy and caused her mental anguish. She asked the court to issue an injunction keeping him at least 300 feet away from 1040 Fifth Avenue and 150 feet from her and her children at all times.

The case would drag on for years. Ari paid $50,000 to retain legal counsel for his wife, but he also warned Jackie that she would appear spiteful if she pressed the issue. Besides, Ari pointed out, the photographs Galella cleared for publication were among her favorites. Clearly he had gone to considerable lengths to show her only in the most flattering light. One of Galella's favorite Jackie photographs, of a braless Jackie striding purposefully down the street and turning to look into the camera through windswept hair, was also one of her favorites.

Despite Ari's entreaties to drop the suit, Jackie was determined to stop what she called Galella's "reign of terror" once and for all. When the case finally came before U.S. District Court Judge Irving Ben Cooper in 1972, Jackie held the packed courtroom spellbound with her impassioned plea for some small measure of privacy. She claimed to be "an absolute prisoner" of Galella, and that she was, simply, "terrified" of what he might do next.

Judge Cooper gave Jackie even more than she asked for. He tossed out Galella's countersuit ("Not a single event, episode or incident was established in his favor," ruled Cooper) and permanently barred him from coming within 300 feet of her apartment building and the children's schools, within 225 feet of Caroline and John Jr., and within 150 feet of Jackie herself. On appeal, Galella managed to get the distance pared down so that he could come within 30 feet of the children and 25 feet of her. They had not, however, heard the last of Ron Galella.

It would be, at best, a Pyrrhic victory not unlike the one over author William Manchester. During the course of the trial, Jackie had written dozens of warm notes to her attorney, ex-Judge Simon Rifkind of Paul

Weiss Rifkind Wharton and Garrison. "I am so glad," she gushed in one thank-you letter for protecting her on the witness stand, "that chivalry is not dead."

That did not prevent Rifkind from hitting Jackie with a final fee of $400,000 — the largest single bill Jackie would ever submit to her husband. Onassis, who did not want her to proceed with the litigation in the first place, was furious. He simply refused to pay, telling Jackie to cover the bill using her own funds. The law firm sued, and Ari hired Roy Cohn to negotiate a settlement.

"It is absurd, absolutely outrageous!" Ari told Cohn. "There wasn't even a jury — it was open and shut. I just won't pay it!" Onassis eventually agreed to pay another $235,000, which he deposited in Jackie's account. An hour later, Jackie in turn wrote out a check to her lawyer.

By the time of the Galella trial, the marriage was well on the way to unraveling over Jackie's spending. "It was very clear from the way he talked about her," Cohn said, "that he was more or less fed up. The marriage was in deep trouble."

In late 1969 this had not yet become a significant issue between them. Sometimes Jackie even spread a little of her husband's largesse around. While Lee was visiting their friend Truman Capote in Palm Springs, Capote's bulldog, Maggie, chewed up her sable coat. "I could have heard Lee's screams a mile away," Capote said.

When Capote told Jackie what happened, she replied, "Don't worry. We can buy another sable for Lee tomorrow and charge it to Ari. He won't mind." There were times she wished her husband would start spending more on his own wardrobe. "Look at him," Jackie said, shaking her head. "He must have four hundred suits. But he wears the same gray one in New York, the same blue one in Paris, and the same brown one in London."

Jackie's name was fast becoming synonymous with wanton extravagance. Her self-made husband looked at the mountains of shoes (in 1969 alone she purchased 300 pairs) and closets brimming with designer clothes and eventually concluded that she was as shallow as she was avaricious.

There were times, however, when his wife surprised even Ari by revealing the side of herself that had nothing to do with money — the tender, loyal, sentimental side of Jackie. When she was told along with the rest of the clan that Joe Kennedy was very near the end, for example, she rushed to Hyannis Port to be at his bedside.

"Next to my husband, and my own father," Jackie said when she was First Lady, "I love Joe Kennedy more than anybody in the world." She had never stopped loving the old man who had virtually handpicked her to be the future President's bride. When she arrived at the compound on November 15, 1969, Joe was comatose. Jackie went straight to his room, sat down next to the old man, and grasped his hand in hers. She paid no attention to the oxygen tube in his left nostril. "It's Jackie, Grandpa," she said. Then she kissed him on the forehead.

Rose stayed all the next day with him. That night, Jackie stood vigil along with Ted until the early-morning hours when Joe's nurse, Rita Dallas, took over. At 10:30 in the morning, Dallas rang the alarm bell, and everyone knew that it was tolling for the patriarch. Family members came rushing from all corners of the Hyannis Port compound. Jackie bolted from her house and across the lawn to Joe's house without ever bothering to put on a sweater or even shoes. She walked into Joe's room in a flimsy short-sleeved blouse and barefoot.

Jackie and the other in-laws — Steve Smith, Sargent Shriver, Ethel, Joan — stepped back as Eunice, Pat, Jean, Ted, and Rose gathered around the bed. Joe Kennedy was dead at the age of eighty-one. Rose began to shake, her body wracked with sobs. It was a display of emotion the likes of which they had never seen from the matriarch.

Rose placed Joe's crucifix to his lips and began reciting the Lord's Prayer: "Our Father who art in Heaven, hallowed be thy name."

"Thy Kingdom come, Thy will be done," said Ted.

"On earth," continued Jean, "as it is in heaven."

"Give us this day our daily bread," said Pat.

"Forgive us our trespasses," Ethel said.

"As we forgive those," Jackie said, weighing the words carefully, "who trespass against us."

There was a pause before Rose finally spoke, "And deliver us from evil. Amen."

More than ever, Jackie was impressed by the courage of the woman she called *Belle Mere.* Jackie said, "If I ever feel sorry for myself, which is a most fatal thing, I think of her." Not long after Joe's death, Jackie invited Rose to sail with her and Ari aboard the *Christina.* "We were standing on deck at the rail together," Jackie said, "and we were talking about something — just something that reminded her. And her voice began to sort of break and she had to stop. Then she took my hand and squeezed it and said, 'Nobody's ever going to have to feel sorry for me. Nobody's ever going to feel sorry for me,' and she put her chin up. And I thought, 'God, what a thoroughbred.' "

Three months later, a single indiscretion

would set in motion a chain of events leading to the destruction of Jackie's marriage. In February of 1970 five of the highly personal letters she had written to Roswell Gilpatric — four written while she was married to Jack and the note she dashed off during her honeymoon with Ari — fell into the hands of Manhattan autograph dealer Charles Hamilton. Their contents were then leaked to the press. They obviously meant little to Gilpatric; all the correspondence was retrieved from the trash by a staffer working in Gilpatric's New York law firm.

Ari was mortified. Jackie called immediately to explain, but her husband behaved as if his manhood had been dealt a deathblow. He did not particularly mind being characterized as a voracious cretin, a barbarian at the gates, or even a crook. But he could not bear the idea of being publicly cuckolded — not by the woman who was spending his millions with abandon. Aristotle Onassis was convinced that the whole world was laughing at him, and Jackie was to blame. "My God," he said to Costa Gratsos, his voice tinged with remorse. "What a fool I have made of myself."

I think ever since he married Jackie, everything went bad for him. Greeks are very superstitious. Onassis called her "The Widow." We called her "The Black Widow."

— *Stelio Papadimetriou,*
Ari's lawyer and friend

I am a woman above everything else.

— *Jackie*

SEVEN

No sooner had Ari read the text of Jackie's letters to Roswell Gilpatric than he called up an old flame of his own. He went straight to the Paris apartment of Maria Callas and did not leave until the following morning. Then, for three consecutive nights, Ari made sure he was seen on the town with Maria.

The couple was photographed dining at Maxim's on May 21, and the next morning Jackie phoned Ari from New York to say she was headed for Paris. The very next night, Jackie made sure she and Ari were photographed dining out — not only at Maxim's, but at precisely the same corner table where he had dined the previous evening with Callas. "For Jackie it wasn't so much a supper," Ari's aide Johnny Meyer said, "as a sock in the eye for Maria."

Jackie was showing the flag — reclaiming her territory — and Ari went along. Callas, who had allowed herself to believe she had won back the love of her life, was devastated. The next night Callas, clearly afraid of what she might do, begged friends who were visiting her apartment not to leave her alone.

Then, just three days after Jackie's dinner at Maxim's with Ari, Callas took an overdose of barbiturates and was rushed to the American Hospital at Neuilly. Callas survived the suicide attempt, but was too proud to ever admit that she had been driven by Ari and by Jackie to attempt to take her own life. Her emergency trip to the hospital in an ambulance was, she insisted rather unconvincingly, just part of her annual checkup.

The day ambulance personnel worked feverishly to revive Callas, Jackie was back in Athens buying up virtually the entire inventory of a store that sold expensive handwoven rugs. Pausing to sip ouzo at a bistro, she was spotted by reporters and asked if the rumors about Ari and Callas were true. "Oh, my God," she said, smiling her familiar frozen smile, "what will they think of next!"

"All this is complete mythology," Ari lied. "It is unbelievable, absurd. People invent these malicious stories because they have nothing else to do, because it amuses them. It has been obvious there has been nothing behind the stories, but they still persist. We are both ideally happy, and anybody who says that we are not doesn't know what they are talking about. What I want everybody to know is that there is no rift in my marriage to Mrs. Onassis."

None of their friends believed it. "There

seems something not altogether right," said a friend, "about their marriage at the moment." Ari's vehement denials aside, it was a time of emotional upheaval for Onassis. On May 3, 1970, on Niarchos's private island of Spesopoula, Ari's former sister-in-law, Eugenie, also took an overdose of sleeping pills — only this one proved fatal. She was forty-four. Stavros Niarchos told authorities he had desperately tried to revive his wife, and in the process bruised her.

Yet Ari was horrified when he read the coroner's report. It showed, among other injuries, that Eugenie had sustained bruises on the left arm, the left leg and ankle, another on her left eye, a hemorrhage on her neck, a large bruise on her abdomen, internal bleeding in the abdomen and around the fifth vertebra, small abrasions above the collarbone, and swelling on the left temple.

Onassis was convinced that his archrival had had a hand in Eugenie's demise. The body was exhumed and a second autopsy conducted. This time, examiners concluded the injuries, and not the pills, were the cause of death. The prosecutor handed down an indictment for "involuntary homicide" against Niarchos and sought his arrest. Before he could be taken into custody, the charge was tossed out by the Piraeus High Court for lack of evidence.

Less than three weeks after toasting Jackie

in New York on her forty-first birthday, Onassis surprised Callas on her name day, August 15. She was sunning herself on the Aegean island of Tragonisi when Ari helicoptered in, walked up to her, gave her a long kiss under a beach umbrella, planted another kiss on the poodle he had given her, and then presented Maria with a pair of century-old earrings.

The entire touching scene was captured on film. And once again, "like a Dalmatian to the fire bell," as *Time* magazine put it, Jackie raced back to Ari's side "to squelch rumors."

Jackie did have an image to uphold. She was reminded of her status as a former First Lady that fall when she posed at 1040 Fifth Avenue for her official White House portrait. When she was asked if the government should give portraitist Aaron Shikler some guidance, Jackie, herself an amateur painter of long standing, shot back, "Let the artist alone. Don't look over his shoulder."

She had, in fact, selected Shikler herself. In 1968 Jackie had commissioned the artist to paint a portrait of Caroline, then ten, and seven-year-old John. "They look just right to me now," she told Shikler. "I would like to remember them at this age, as they are, just now."

For her White House portrait, Jackie posed in a long black skirt and a prim, high-collared white blouse. Instead, Shikler wound up conjuring an image from his imagination — an ethereal full-length study of Jackie in a shimmering off-white gown — one that evoked the way he and the rest of the world saw her, as "an ethereal woman of almost mythological dimensions."

When it was time for the public unveiling of the painting and another portrait of President Kennedy, the current First Lady called Jackie and asked her if she felt up to it. JFK's widow told Pat Nixon that the notion of returning to the White House she was forced to leave "under such traumatic conditions" was just "too painful." Eventually, she did agree to bring the children along for a private visit followed by dinner with the Nixons on February 3, 1971.

Pat was, to Jackie's surprise, warm, engaging, and particularly at ease with the children as she showed them around the Oval Office where "Daddy used to work." President Nixon seemed genuinely interested in her new life with Onassis, and she was reminded of how Jack had held him in such high esteem when they served together in Congress.

"Nixon is, without question," she admitted to Jamie Auchincloss, "one of the most brilliant, complex men I've ever met — and I think probably one of the smartest ever to occupy the office." According to Jamie,

"Whatever bitterness there had been during the 1960 presidential campaign was completely a thing of the past. In the end, she was very fond of Nixon. Jackie felt sorry for him when he resigned over Watergate. To want something that badly and then lose it the way he did, it just struck her as another Greek tragedy."

A few days after her visit, Jackie wrote to Pat: "Thank you with all my heart. A day I always dreaded turned out to be one of the most precious ones I have spent with my children." (Although it would later be reported that the plaque she left commemorating her time at the White House with Jack was removed by the Nixons, it had in fact been removed by President Johnson, who confided to an aide that he hated to be reminded of Jack Kennedy every time he walked into Lady Bird's bedroom.)

The Nixons made another thoughtful gesture when the President, rather than upstage Jackie at the September 8, 1971, opening of the new John F. Kennedy Center for the Performing Arts, turned over the presidential box to Mrs. Onassis and the Kennedy family. "It should really be her night," Nixon said of the gala event, which featured Leonard Bernstein conducting the National Symphony. It marked Jackie's first public appearance in Washington since her husband's funeral.

Ari, though, was preoccupied with problems on the home front. Fully accustomed to giving orders and having them followed without question, he now watched helplessly as his world spun out of control. He was hosting a small party on Skorpios to celebrate Jackie's forty-second birthday when word came that his adored twenty-year-old daughter, Christina, had been married in Las Vegas to Joseph Bolker, a twice-divorced real estate developer with four daughters of his own. Bolker was twenty-seven years Christina's senior.

No one could remember ever seeing Ari so angry. (He and Jackie had been lobbying to have Christina marry fellow Greek shipping heir Peter Goulandris.) Johnny Meyer told British journalist and novelist Peter Evans that Ari simply "went ape. I'd seen him fly off the handle plenty of times but never like that. He was rampant, he was mad enough to chew nails. That was a day I'd just as soon not have to go through again."

On December 11, her twenty-first birthday, Christina stood to collect the proceeds from her trust fund — $75 million after taxes. Ari cut her off before she could collect a penny. For the next six months, Ari submitted the couple to such "extraordinary pressures," as Bolker put it, that they filed for divorce the following February. "When a billion dollars leans on you," Bolker said, "you feel it."

Another jolt was in store for Ari. While he leaned on Bolker, Onassis's ex-wife (and Eugenie's sister), Tina, secretly married his archenemy Niarchos on October 21, 1971, in Paris. Only sixteen months had passed since Eugenie's mysterious death, and everyone on Skorpios — particularly Ari and the children — was amazed that Tina would marry the man who they felt at the very least had driven her sister to suicide.

Christina — still married to Bolker and living in Beverly Hills at the time — harbored darker thoughts. She knew that Tina had married Niarchos just to spite her father. She was just as convinced that Niarchos had killed Eugenie, and that he would do the same to her mother. "It was a very emotional time," Bolker said. "A lot of yelling and screaming, a really bad scene."

The black moods, the volcanic eruptions — until now Jackie had been spared these Levantine aspects of the Onassis family temperament. Suddenly she found herself caught in the crossfire, and the stress began taking its toll. In addition to the cornucopia of compulsions she had developed over the years — marathon shopping, chain-smoking, nail-biting, and gum-chewing among them — she now added compulsive dieting.

In 1971 Jackie shed so much weight so quickly — twenty-four pounds in ten days — that European newspapers were filled with stories speculating that she was seriously ill. "RIDDLE OF JACKIE'S ILLNESS," read the headline in the British weekly *The People*. "Jackie is ill," stated *France Dimanche*. "Her eyes give the impression of deep suffering." The West German newspaper *Neue Blatt* reported that Jackie was under the care of France's leading cancer specialist, Dr. George Mathe of Paris's Villejuif Clinic. The next day, six Greek newspapers carried the cancer story. "HAS JACKIE GOT CANCER?" screamed the front-page headline in Athens's afternoon newspaper *Ta Nea*. *Akropolis* blared, "JACKIE SAID TO HAVE CANCER."

Using an alias Jackie, also worried about her sudden weight loss and lack of energy, underwent three days of tests at the clinic. The results were negative. What she did suffer from was an eating disorder. Obsessed with becoming as stylishly slim as the woman who was once her husband's lover, Audrey Hepburn, Jackie survived on a half grapefruit, two and a half ounces of meat, three and a half ounces of green vegetables, yogurt, and one apple.

At the time, the diagnoses anorexia nervosa and bulimia had not yet been popularized. Yet, according to several people who knew her, Jackie suffered from both. "Onassis told me she starved herself to stay thin," Roy Cohn said. "Sometimes she would go on a binge and eat everything in sight — hot fudge sundaes, hot dogs, nothing fancy but the things she really liked — then that night before she went to bed she'd stick her finger down her throat and throw it all up. Ari never saw it himself, but one of the maids on the *Christina* accidentally caught her in the act. At first they just assumed she was seasick, but then they figured out what was going on."

"For a while there she seemed terribly thin — almost emaciated — but back in those days nobody ever said anything if you were skinny," said a friend who remains close to the family. "Everybody in that crowd followed the Duchess of Windsor's motto that you can never be too rich or too thin. Besides, you'd see her eating like a horse, so you thought it must be her metabolism." Remembered Doris Lilly, "Here she was the most famous, glamorous woman in the world, married to one of the richest men in the world, and she was *starving* herself. And for what? So she could look as chic as her sister Lee."

Both sisters were so consumed by jealousy of each other that it seems likely Radziwill's rail-thin figure contributed to Jackie's negative self-image. "She's always been the pretty one," Jackie once said, "so I guess I'm the smart one." In 1969 Lee had actually checked into a clinic in Lausanne, Switzerland, to put weight *on*. "I am always trying to gain weight," she said. "It's terribly annoying to be described as 'fashionably gaunt' or 'chic and bony' as if it were on purpose. I have a weight problem in reverse, and I've always had trouble sleeping. I guess I am what one might call high-strung."

As a candy-loving adolescent entering Miss Porter's School, Jackie had been chided by her mother for being "plump" and warned she would never attract "the right kind of fellow" if she didn't exercise some self-control. Now she was subjecting her own daughter to the same pressure. Caroline had inherited her mother's passion for chocolate and as a fourteen-year-old ballooned in weight. The candy was also wreaking havoc with the teenager's complexion.

No amount of scolding seemed to work — Dr. Henry Lax's assistant recalled Jackie screaming at her daughter over the phone at the doctor's office — so Mom took matters into her own hands. Accelerating Jackie's metabolism — and consequently her weight loss — even further were the amphetamine pills she continued to receive from Max Jacobson. Confronted with Caroline's weight gain, she asked Dr. Lax to prescribe diet pills for her daughter. He did — 120 in all.

There was a method to Jackie's madness; she, more than anyone else in the world, never knew when she might be put on display. In November of 1972, ten photographers zipped themselves into wetsuits and lay in wait for Jackie in the waters off Skorpios. The color photographs they took — full-frontal nude shots of the former First Lady sunbathing and walking around — were splashed across the Italian men's magazine *Playmen* under the headline, "THE BILLION DOLLAR BUSH." In the United States, *Screw* was the first to publish the pictures in black and white. But, as was related in the 1996 film *The People vs. Larry Flynt*, the photographs actually put a heretofore unknown porn magazine called *Hustler* on the map. Strictly on the basis of the nude Jackie O photos, *Hustler*'s sales zoomed from a few thousand to more than two million copies.

Within weeks, the nude photos had run in dozens of publications worldwide. Onassis, who was also in some of the pictures, conceded, "I have to take off my pants to put on my bathing suit sometimes. She does too."

Publicly, Jackie laughed it off. "I don't treat it as reality," she said. "It doesn't touch my real life, which is with my children and my husband. That's the world that's real to me." Besides, she conceded, "I suppose I should be flattered."

While they were dining with friends at La Côte Basque, Ari said, "I really don't like to see pictures of my wife's behind in cheap Italian magazines."

"But, Ari," Jackie said, "they're saving yours for the Christmas issue."

Privately, Jackie demanded that Ari sue not only all ten photographers but every publication that had the audacity to publish them. Had she known the truth, it would not have come as a great surprise when he refused. Onassis later confessed to Roy Cohn and others that he personally set the whole thing up — right down to supplying the photographers with a map of Skorpios and the dates they planned to be there. The reason: Onassis figured that once the humiliating nude photos were published, there would be nothing left the press could do to offend her. She would stop complaining and learn to live with the paparazzi — and she would stop threatening costly lawsuits.

In the beginning of the marriage, Jackie was determined to make at least part of her new life on her new husband's turf. "Whither thou goest," she told friends who asked if she didn't feel isolated on Skorpios, "I will go." Yet the photographs of Jackie cavorting in the nude, so meticulously stage-managed by Ari, belied the fact that she constantly complained to her New York friends about being "stuck on Skorpios all summer long." Conversely, Onassis came to view Jackie and her friends as trespassers on his domain.

One of those guests was Peter Beard, the handsome adventurer, photographer, African wildlife conservationist, and party animal. He stayed on Skorpios an entire summer. Beard recorded in huge scrapbooks, which he lugged with him everywhere, everything he saw, thought, or did. Several bulged with information on the Kennedys. "Peter was Jackie's biggest fan," said his friend Porter Bibb. "Hanging out with the Kennedy women was almost a fixation with him. What I saw from Peter when he was around Jackie was that he was coming on to her, and I thought she was amused."

Beard's "ferocious energy," as Bibb described it, his instant rapport with Jackie's children, and his tousle-haired matinee-idol looks ("half Tarzan and half Byron") made him irresistible to Lee Radziwill. Jacqueline's sister, who was four years older than Peter and had just undergone a hysterectomy, would steal into Beard's room. The two carried on their affair under the noses of not only her husband, Stas, and Jackie, but all their children and fellow house guests David Frost and Diahann Carroll.

Beard, not surprisingly, would remember

it as one of the great summers of his life. Jackie, he said, was "like a dormitory room-mate, completely casual. Great meals, fantastic picnics. It was lush — nonstop Dom Pérignon and O.J." They swam and water-skied, and in the afternoons she would vanish for two or three hours at a time to read. "She stacked the library of the *Christina* with the works of new authors — poetry, nonfiction, art books, everything," Beard said. Yet she lacked the confidence to pursue her own talents as an artist and as a photographer "and it frustrated her." At an exhibit of his works, she took Beard aside and said, "I wish I could do what you're doing — but I can't."

Ari was suspicious of Beard, as he was of many of Jackie's friends. One day on Skorpios he bet Beard $2,000 that he could not stay underwater for more than four minutes. While Onassis watched, Jackie was the time-keeper, writing the minutes in black marker on Beard's back so that he could keep track of time. Beard won the bet, and that night Jackie gave him a bonus — a watercolor showing her writing the minutes on his back in realistic detail.

Onassis felt Lee's young lover might have overstayed his welcome. "Do you know why Jackie married me?" he asked Beard, hoping he would take the hint. "For the privacy." Beard did not budge. When Beard cut his

409

own arm, then dipped a quill pen in his blood to make a diary entry, Ari departed Skorpios in disgust.

Still, Ari was genuinely fond of a number of Jackie's friends, notably Peter and Cheray Duchin. The couple went along on three cruises aboard the *Christina* in the 1970s. After boarding the yacht at sunrise in Casablanca, the Duchins found a note on the dresser in their stateroom. "Promise that you will do what you feel like doing today," Jackie had written. She then suggested, Duchin recalled, that they go on a walking tour of Casablanca with one of their escorts, or loll around on the deck of the *Christina*, or simply sleep all day and have their meals sent to their stateroom. "All that matters is that you are happy."

Duchin remembered that during this time Ari was "great, magnetic company." He treated Jackie "with a tenderness bordering on reverence, and she clearly adored him."

Certainly Jackie appreciated Duchin's presence, and never more so than the day he went scuba diving in the Aegean with John Jr. ("then a strapping teenager"). At a depth of forty feet, Duchin looked over to see John Jr. struggling with his oxygen hose. Young Kennedy showed "amazing cool," said Duchin, as the older, more experienced diver shared his mouthpiece and the two swam slowly to the surface. "I kept thinking, my God, I've got the son of the President of the United States here! Jackie was very grateful, as you can imagine."

With few exceptions, Ari was in fact unfailingly generous to his wife's friends and relatives — a characteristic not shared by Jackie or any of the notoriously tightfisted Kennedys, who made a point of underpaying employees and stiffing waiters and waitresses on the tip. When Jackie's aunt Edith Bouvier Beale, Black Jack Bouvier's sister, and her daughter Edie fell on hard times it was Ari — not their world-famous niece — who came to their rescue.

Jackie might never have bothered to tell Onassis about the Beales' predicament at all if it hadn't become what "Little Edie" called a "messy public relations problem" for the former First Lady. Grey Gardens, the ramshackle twenty-eight-room East Hampton mansion in which they lived, was in such a state of disrepair that neighbors asked the county health department to evict the Beales and have the house torn down.

They had a point. Grey Gardens had no heat or running water. The interior was soiled with the excrement of forty flea-infested cats and even a few raccoons. There were gaping holes in the ceiling where the rain poured through, and the once-meticulously landscaped grounds had become a virtually impenetrable jungle of weeds. The fireplace mantels, walls, and tabletops were covered with the Christmas cards they had received over the previous thirty years. At night, they wrapped themselves in newspapers to keep warm. There had been a dispute with the sanitation department and the garbage had gone uncollected for six months. Whole rooms were filled with garbage and abandoned; the stench was overpowering.

Eccentric did not go far enough toward describing the two women. A one-time aspiring soprano who presided over an avantgarde salon in the 1930s, seventy-six-year-old Aunt Edith ("Big Edie") spent most days in bed singing opera to her cats — the same bed the cats used as a litter box. The once-stunning Little Edie — her previously bleached-blonde hair now concealed beneath an ever-present scarf — might have been cast in a touring company production of *What Ever Happened to Baby Jane?* Her makeup slightly askew, Edie fancied herself the keeper of the Bouvier family flame and was prone to delivering lengthy stream-of-consciousness monologues.

Before they raided and condemned Grey Gardens, Suffolk County health officials contacted Edith's son and Jackie's first cousin, Bouvier Beale, and gave him the opportunity to avert a family scandal. If Beale, a wealthy attorney, provided the funds to make Grey Gardens habitable, the house would not be condemned and Edith and Edie would not face eviction.

As it happened, Bouvier Beale had no intention of fixing up Grey Gardens. He had long wanted his mother and sister to move out of the dilapidated house to new, more comfortable quarters on Florida's Gulf Coast. "I'd tried everything to get them out of that dump but Mother wouldn't budge," he said. "When the county threatened eviction, I thought, 'Thank God! Now I can get them into a decent place.'"

It was more than a month before Jackie, stung by allegations in the press that she had shown a callous indifference toward the Beales, took action. Jackie phoned Edith from New York and asked her what *she* wanted. "Grey Gardens is my home," said Jackie's aunt, "and this is where I am staying."

With that, Jackie asked Ari to pay the $50,000 it would take to fix up the place. Bouvier Beale was furious, calling his cousin and telling her that she was sabotaging his efforts to give them a life that was "more normal." Because Jackie wanted to end the negative publicity with a quick fix of the problem, Edith and Edie were now condemned to live out the rest of their lives in "that wretched hole."

Jackie replied that they were obviously not

going to move, that it was their wish to remain there, and that she could no longer bear reading newspaper accounts portraying her as a heartless harridan unwilling to help the poor relations. "They've practically got me saying 'Let them eat cake,'" she told Onassis.

Ari actually had had a warm spot in his heart for the two strange women ever since Edie had written a lengthy and impassioned letter supporting their decision to marry. Not long after the honeymoon, he phoned Edith, and she serenaded him with one of her favorite arias. When she was finished, he sang back to her, a Greek ballad.

Onassis kept a close eye on the repairs — one of the cats on Big Edie's bed had been dead for some time — calling periodically to check up on progress at the house and to chat with "the ladies," as he called them. Jackie and Lee both visited, reliving childhood summers spent at Lasata, the nearby Bouvier family mansion. When Little Edie thanked them for their generosity — Ari had new heating and plumbing installed and paid their utility bills — Jackie replied, "Don't you think I'm lucky to be married to such a splendid person?"

Two years later, the would-be diva and her aging vamp daughter would achieve a stardom of sorts in *Grey Gardens*, the acclaimed documentary by Albert and David

Maysles. The Maysles brothers, whose pre-vious claim to fame was *Gimme Shelter*, their harrowing account of the Rolling Stones's catastrophic 1969 concert at Altamont, Cali-fornia, had actually been hired by Lee and Peter Beard to make a documentary on Lee's childhood. The Maysles interviewed Big Edie and Little Edie as part of their re-search, and when the Lee Radziwill project fell apart over money, they approached the Beales to see if they might be interested.

"At last," Edie said, "we've been discov-ered!" In order to make the film, the Maysles and their crew had to wear flea collars on their ankles. Over time they became accus-tomed to the knee-buckling stench. *Grey Gar-dens* became a cult classic, although most members of the Bouvier clan were plainly horrified to have their kooky relatives put on display as objects of public pity. In one scene, for example, one of Big Edie's shriveled breasts fell out of the top of her bathing suit.

Yet the Beales could not have been more delighted with the attention. "It's the great-est thing that ever happened in my old age," Big Edie said in 1976. "You know, I'll be eighty-one in October. Nobody else wanted to take my picture. I'm thrilled." For her part, Jackie thought the film's depiction of her aunt and cousin was "a hoot. I should think Mr. Fellini might finally offer them a contract!"

When Aunt Edith died in February of 1977, Little Edie realized another one of her dreams, performing her own cabaret act at New York's Reno Sweeney's. The curiosity factor alone was enough to pack the small club during her brief engagement. Opening night, Edie admitted that Jackie had been supporting her for years.

During the renovation of Grey Gardens, Jackie realized that the rambling Victorian mansion was the last tangible link to her Bouvier past. She wanted the Beales to continue living there, and toward that end she sent them $600 a month to cover their living expenses. But it wasn't enough, and soon Grey Gardens had once again turned into a freezing, decrepit hole. Since the Onassis-financed repairs, half the living room floor had caved in, and a stove fell through the kitchen floor into the basement. In a stiff wind, one side of the house would literally begin to sway. "Onassis fixed up Grey Gardens," Edie said not long after her mother's death, "but Jackie did nothing for us. She let my mother starve and freeze."

Not willing to stay in the house alone, Edie put Grey Gardens up for sale to anyone who would meet the $225,000 asking price and agree not to tear the house down. When Ben Bradlee and his new wife, Sally Quinn, agreed to buy Grey Gardens, Jackie was incensed. She regarded his book *Conver-*

sations with Kennedy as an outright betrayal, and the thought of Bradlee occupying a home that had been in the Bouvier family for generations was abhorrent to her.

Bradlee and his first wife, Tony, had been among the two or three couples closest to Jack and Jackie Kennedy during their time in the White House. But once *Conversations with Kennedy* was published, she never spoke to them again. Ben and Sally arrived at a party hosted by Arthur Schlesinger just as she was leaving. "I whispered to Sally that Jackie was coming down the street," Bradlee said. "I stuck out my hand and said, 'Hi, Jackie.' She sailed by without a word." Not long after, the Bradlees had a cabana on the beach in St. Martin that was right next to Jackie's. They spent a week, said Ben Bradlee, "staring at each other" until one night they "almost collided as we left our cabana to go up to the restaurant for dinner. From twelve inches away, she looked straight ahead, without a word, and I never saw her again."

It was classic Jackie, according to Jamie Auchincloss. "No matter how close you were, no matter how long the relationship, once you crossed my sister you were dead," he said. "She kept score on everything and everyone and she could hold a grudge forever."

The Bradlees did buy Grey Gardens, gutted it, bulldozed the grounds, and made it worthy of a spread in *Architectural Digest*. To punish her first cousin, and since Big Edie was no longer around, Jackie cut Little Edie's allowance in half, to $300 a month.

The simplest way to keep Grey Gardens in the family, of course, was for Jackie to buy it herself. Ari would have forced Jackie to dip into her own funds for the purchase, and that she was not prepared to do. When she was told she would have to pay to have her apartment painted, she called the Union Square Painting Company for an estimate. Rather than spend the $3,000, she canceled.

In 1972 she lost $300,000 investing part of her $3 million prenuptial payment in the stock market. Ari, who had warned her to keep her money in tax-free bonds, ignored Jackie's repeated pleas to refill her coffers. Eventually, however, he relented.

"Jackie *always* had her eye," Gore Vidal said, "on the bottom line." Even though Joe Kennedy secretly footed all Jackie's bills during her reign as the most glamorous and expensively attired First Lady in history, Jackie still had ways to earn some extra cash. Back then, Jackie raised cash by selling her clothes to secondhand outlets in New York, primarily Encore on Madison. Those who purchased the hundreds of coats, suits, and dresses that Jackie sold to Encore never knew the true identity of the previous owner.

Mary Gallagher, Jackie's secretary, recalled how Jackie's clothing was "resold under my name and home address. As the various items were sold, Encore's check would come to me and I would deposit it in my personal account. At the same time, I would write out a check for the same amount to be deposited in Jackie's account."

In those days, Jackie tried to recoup whatever she could. In the hectic closing days of the 1960 presidential campaign, Gallagher had been so busy tending to Jackie's needs that she did not have time to buy herself a winter coat. "I remembered that Jackie had a blue double-breasted mohair coat that she no longer wanted. In fact, I had already sent it out to Encore. The blue coat was perfect for me, and since we wore the same size and were the same height, I asked Jackie if she would mind if I asked Encore to return that particular garment — listed at $65. I said I'd be happy to pay her for it. Jackie agreed, and when the coat was returned, I handed her the check. She told me to deposit it in her bank account."

When Jackie was in "a generous mood," Gallagher said, she sometimes gave things away. "You may not ever have any need for this, Mary," Jackie said, handing her a red chiffon dress, "but it's just your color." It was just her color, Gallagher admitted, but it was also a maternity dress — something

Gallagher had no use for and Encore didn't sell.

The arrangement with Encore continued during Jackie's marriage to Onassis, and beyond. When he heard that it took her ten minutes to drop $9,000 (the equivalent of more than $100,000 in 1998) at Valentino's in Rome, Onassis exploded. "What does she do with all the clothes?" he demanded to know. "I never see her in anything but blue jeans."

He eventually discovered the truth: Jackie would purchase an evening gown and, after wearing it once, or not at all, resell it to Encore for up to half the purchase price. Moreover, Jackie expanded her brisk second-hand clothing business to include slacks, blouses, shoes, belts, purses, scarves, gloves, compacts — nearly all bearing prestige labels such as Givenchy, Yves Saint Laurent, Oscar de la Renta, Halston, Oleg Cassini, Chanel, Hermès, Dior, Lanvin, and Gucci (and much later, Christian Lacroix, Calvin Klein, Bill Blass, Perry Ellis, Giorgio Armani, Ralph Lauren, and Gianni Versace).

More than two decades before the historic 1996 Sotheby's sale of items from her estate raised more than $34 million, Jackie was recycling her possessions through auction houses like Sotheby's, Park Bernet, and William Doyle Galleries. She auctioned off everything, from Louis XIV furniture to leather picture frames to John Jr.'s old nursery furniture. Everything was sold anonymously or through a third party, although occasionally word slipped out. A child's chair, battered and worn yet bearing the Choate school crest, given an estimated value of $25, went for $300 when the auctioneer at William Doyle got carried away and mentioned that it had belonged to JFK.

Once again, all the proceeds went directly into other people's accounts, and then into Jackie's. This perfectly legal money-laundering scheme, designed for the sole purpose of duping Ari, may have netted Jackie as much as $1 million a year.

Still, it was not enough. In May of 1972, Jackie and Ari were invited by Iranian oilman Dr. Reza Fallah and his daughter Lilly to spend nine days in Teheran. Lilly and her husband, Bunty Lawrence, were to accompany them from New York, so Ari insisted they fly Olympic. Before leaving, Jackie, acting through Nancy Tuckerman, insisted that they make out a check in the amount of $3,000 to cover their airfare. So Jackie wouldn't deposit it in her account as she planned, an angry Lilly Lawrence made the check payable to the airline. "Imagine," she said. "Jackie wouldn't even give us a free ride on the airline her husband owned — and we were paying for the whole visit in Teheran — hotels, touring, food, everything!"

And pay they did. Each night the Onassises and their entourage went to the most expensive nightclubs and restaurants, racking up stratospheric bills and charging it all to Dr. Fallah. Jackie's daytime hours were spent purchasing anything and everything that struck her fancy: several pounds of golden caviar, earrings, necklaces, bracelets, rings, Persian rugs, sheepskin jackets, antiques, boots, a huge brass trunk just to accommodate her jewelry. When it was all over, Jackie left her hosts with a staggering $650,000 bill — more than $72,000 per day.

While she was in Iran, Jackie admitted to a local reporter, "I do love to live in style." But she also tried to debunk what she felt were common misconceptions about her. As for her being press shy: "I get afraid of reporters when they come to me in a crowd. I don't like crowds because I don't like impersonal masses. They remind me of swarms of locusts.

"The truth of the matter is that I am a very shy person. People take my diffidence for arrogance and my withdrawal from publicity as a sign, supposedly, that I am looking down on the rest of mankind. I am today what I was yesterday, and with luck, what I will be tomorrow."

She also let it be known that she chafed at always being defined by the man she was married to. "Why do people always try to see me through the different names I have had at different times?" she asked. "People often forget that I was Jacqueline Bouvier before being Mrs. Kennedy or Mrs. Onassis. Throughout my life I have always tried to remain true to myself. This I will continue to do as long as I live . . . I love children and I think seeing one's children grow up is the most delightful thing any woman can think about."

Jackie waxed philosophical to Iranian journalist Maryam Khrarazmi about her past. "One must not dwell on only the tragedies that life holds for us all, just as a person must not just think of only the happiness and greatness that they've experienced in life. If you separate the happiness and the sadness from each other, then neither is an accurate account of what life is truly like. Life is made up of both the good and the bad — and they cannot be separated from each other. It is a mistake to try to do that."

Once she returned to the United States, Jackie began selling off her Iranian booty. Even though she raised an estimated $250,000 in cash from this nine-day trip alone, Jackie still complained to Ari that she was running out of funds. Among her unexpected expenses: two hundred pairs of shoes purchased in a single outing for $60,000.

In 1972 Onassis reacted by cutting her

monthly allowance from $30,000 to $20,000, to "teach her the meaning of self-control." He put her, said Costa Gratsos, "on a short leash."

"Jackie went ballistic," said Doris Lilly. Each month, usually no more than fifteen days after Jackie had received her allowance, she dispatched Nancy Tuckerman to beg for more from Creon Broun, Onassis's money manager.

"Things simply can't go on this way at the house any longer!" Tuckerman said to Broun, who in the beginning advanced her the money Jackie so desperately needed. Once Ari realized what was going on, he ordered Broun to stand firm. The hapless Tuckerman, sent to do her friend's bidding, was soon regarded by those on Ari's staff as a "pest." Aware that Jackie, through Tuckerman, could pressure Broun into coughing up more cash, Ari moved Jackie's accounts from New York to his Monte Carlo office, where she had little influence and where he could keep closer tabs on her spending.

Tensions between husband and wife mounted steadily, and it wasn't just the money. Spending, smoking, and excessive dieting were only a few of Jackie's many compulsions. She hired and fired servants so capriciously that staffing their various residences was becoming close to impossible. In the span of just four years, Jackie sacked nearly one hundred employees — six in a matter of two weeks.

Jackie went through nineteen chefs during that short time. One, Carl Jerome, lasted only four days at 1040 Fifth. "You have been asking too many personal questions," she said when Jerome asked why he was being let go. He swore he had asked not a single question of Jackie, personal or otherwise. "I had to spend three days just cleaning up the kitchen. The place was full of cockroaches."

Another chef, Marcel Bodard, was outraged when Jackie gave a dinner party for Rose Kennedy, Leonard Bernstein, and Frank Sinatra, and had it catered by La Côte Basque. When the hostess asked him to help out, Bodard reportedly had a small tantrum. "If anyone is going to lose his temper around here," Jackie replied, "it is *me*." Bodard was history.

The *Christina*'s chief steward, Christian Kararakis, claimed that "what needled the staff was Jackie's terrible untidiness. When she changed her clothes she would try on a dozen dresses and sets of underclothes and leave them on the floor behind her. A maid would always have to be on hand because she would be very cross if she turned around and found any garment lying about on the floor or on furniture, even if she had just discarded it."

425

Jackie fired one maid when she caught the young woman trying on one of her Givenchy gowns. Another maid had been working at the Glyfada villa only a few hours when Jackie told the housekeeper, "That new maid, get rid of her."

"But why, Mrs. Onassis? She seems efficient."

"She has a sad face," Jackie answered. "She depresses me."

While she was going over her correspondence in her cabin aboard the *Christina*, Jackie was disturbed by the sound of someone singing. Costa Argantis, a cheerful twenty-six-year-old crew member, was belting out a spirited rendition of "Jesus Christ Superstar" in Greek as he swabbed down the decks. Jackie told Argantis's superiors that he was to stop at once; the god-awful racket disturbed Mrs. Onassis.

The next day, Argantis forgot himself and was scarcely halfway through the Rolling Stones's "Satisfaction" (again in Greek) when he was given his walking papers. That same day, he was put ashore at Capri.

Unlike Jackie, whose loyalty as an employer extended only to Nancy Tuckerman (and before her to Pam Turnure), Onassis made sure that anyone who worked for him for two years was kept on the payroll but out of Jackie's sight.

The couple's frequent absences led each

to suspect the other of infidelity. Ari became jealous when Frank Sinatra, who had arranged JFK's inaugural gala only to have a major falling out with the Kennedys before Dallas, escorted Jackie to one of his concerts in Providence, Rhode Island. "Ari was convinced Jackie and Sinatra were having an affair," Lilly said. "Onassis said he caught them kissing on board the *Christina* after a party one night, that it all looked a little too cozy and he knew all about how competitive Jack Kennedy and Sinatra were when it came to women." Referring to Sinatra's brief marriage to Mia Farrow, who was twenty-eight years his junior, Onassis quipped, "I'd let him have Jackie, but she's entirely too old for him. He's fifty-six and she's forty-four."

When paparazzi accosted Ari and Elizabeth Taylor — sans husband, Richard Burton — lunching at a café in Rome, Liz dove beneath the table and Onassis tossed a glass of champagne in the intruder's face. The next morning, Jackie blasted her husband over the phone. "I am ashamed of you," she said. "The children read all about your ridiculous behavior in Rome."

Where once she had nothing but fond words for Ari, Jackie now complained to friends about his penury ("Ari is so cheap he won't even pay to sue the vermin who took those horrible pictures"), his lack of taste

("What's *that?*" shrieked Bunny Mellon when she first saw the doorknob-size diamond Ari had given Jackie), and his highly compartmentalized life.

"He is such a loner," Jackie lamented. She thought his friends — mostly oil executives — were as boring as he thought hers were pampered and witless. When the chairman of British Petroleum and his wife visited Skorpios one summer, Jackie refused to even meet them; instead, she sat alone in the Onassises' state-of-the-art screening room watching first-run films imported from the United States until her husband's guests had departed.

She may have grown tired of him, but Ari's attitude had undergone an even more radical change. During the first three years of their marriage, said Gardner Cowles, Onassis "was happy to stay in the background, basking in his wife's social radiance. One had the sense of a man who felt he had accomplished something prodigious and was proud of it."

Ingeborg Dedichen, once Ari's battered mistress, agreed that Onassis "always felt socially unacceptable in the United States. He married her out of pride — to show Americans that 'your First Lady thought I was more than good enough for her.' "

Now Onassis described Jackie to Costa Gratsos and other friends as "cold hearted and shallow." Wherever he happened to be, she found excuses to be somewhere else. If he wished to stay at 1040 Fifth, she invariably told him that Caroline, now a student at Concord Academy in Massachusetts, was in town with friends, or that John Jr. had a cold.

Another favorite gambit for keeping Ari at bay was to keep refurbishing the apartment. "The apartment needs redecorating," she would tell Onassis when he called from Europe. "The workmen are at it right now." It would have been a familiar refrain to Jack Kennedy, who endured Jackie's compulsive need to redecorate before and after they moved into the White House. "Dammit, Jackie," JFK would bellow, "why is it that the rooms in this house are never completely livable all at the same time?"

Ari quickly concluded that it was all designed to keep him from invading her domain. "You'd be surprised," he said, "at how frequently the wallpaper and the paint in my wife's New York apartment get changed!"

Even if he was just down Fifth Avenue in his suite at the Pierre, she seldom included Ari on the guest list for her intimate soirees. "I doubt if he spent more than two or three nights at Jackie's Fifth Avenue apartment in the entire course of their marriage," said Aileen Mehle. "I went up to him once and said, 'Ari, you have to buy a house here in New York.' He sighed and said, 'No, The Widow has her apartment.' " But Mehle thought Onassis was "happy to have it that way. He acted as if they were two completely separate entities with two completely autonomous lives — not at all as if they were man and wife. If he regarded any woman as his wife, it was Callas. Maria was his soulmate, and I think the ink was barely dry on the prenuptial agreement before he regretted what he'd done."

Onassis made little effort to conceal his growing resentment. "After a certain point, I never saw love on his side when it came to Jackie," Mehle said. "When I saw him around Jackie, he *never* held her and he never whispered into her ear, I never heard him say anything nice about her. Now, *she* was sweet and warm and affectionate. He was aloof. He would always say, 'The Widow wants this' and 'The Widow wants that.' She tried to keep up appearances, but he was obviously mad at her. And I mean all the time."

Over the years Onassis had taken obvious pleasure in lavishing expensive gifts on his wife; now he made it clear that he no longer intended to indulge her. "Jackie had a charming little rule," Costa Gratsos told columnist Jack Anderson, "that Ari had to bring back a present from every part of the world he visited. Once, all he brought her was a simple apron from Africa. She was livid. I suppose she expected a shoebox of raw diamonds."

Whatever was going on behind the scenes, Jackie did do her best to at least maintain the façade of a viable, if flawed, marriage. For their fourth wedding anniversary, in October of 1972, for example, she threw a surprise party at New York's El Morocco. Salinger, one of many New Frontiersmen invited, entertained the other sixty-five guests with an impromptu piano solo. Jackie had made out the guest list, which included her sister Lee, Rose Kennedy, and such social friends as William F. Buckley and his wife, Pat, Oleg Cassini, and Doris Duke. Conspicuously absent were any of Ari's Greek pals or business associates.

Described diplomatically by columnist Earl Wilson as "extremely slender," Jackie was showing the obvious signs of her off-again, on-again eating disorder. She was still receiving amphetamine "treatments" from Dr. Feelgood, Max Jacobson — which obviated the need for the diet stimulants she had obtained for Caroline — and chain-smoking more than ever. Wearing a long white skirt and blouse with a jeweled belt, she looked, said one guest, "like the world's most stylish skeleton. They had everything there — caviar, salmon, filet mignon with truffles, Dom

Pérignon — and I did not see Jackie so much as nibble at anything."

Ari came to eighty-two-year-old Rose's rescue when she was suddenly confronted by a pack of photographers. "Those lights blind me!" she screamed. Onassis led her out another exit and into a waiting limousine. Was he surprised by the party Jackie had gone to all the trouble to throw him? someone asked.

"When you're married four years," he replied, "what surprises you?"

In December of 1972, Ari met with Roy Cohn at Cohn's town house on New York's East 68th Street just off Madison Avenue and told him the marriage was over. He had already instructed his attorneys in Greece to lay the groundwork for divorce proceedings there. Now he wanted the notoriously ruthless Cohn to handle the American end of things. "He was fed up with Jackie's spending," Cohn recalled. "She was completely out of control, and yet she felt she owed him nothing. Wherever he wanted her to be, whatever he wanted her to do, Jackie did the opposite. He kept saying that he didn't like being taken for a sucker, that she was taking him for all he was worth, that the free ride she was getting from him was over."

According to Cohn, Onassis knew that the Greek Orthodox Church would allow him to end the marriage strictly on the grounds of incompatibility. "That was not the problem," Cohn said. "Money was the problem. He knew Jackie wasn't going to sit back and just accept the $3 million he'd given her as part of their prenuptial pact, and he was willing to work something out. But he had found out about how she'd been selling her clothes to raise cash, and he knew how greedy she was. Onassis was really worried that Jackie would try and hold him up for a huge amount — $100 million or more, and that scared him shitless."

In addition to unleashing his legal bloodhounds, Onassis asked his Mr. Fixit, Johnny Meyer, to tap Jackie's phone and bug her apartment. On the slightest pretext, he was ready to accuse her of infidelity. "Meyer hired a couple of wiretap experts to do the job — the same guys he used when he worked for Howard Hughes — but they couldn't get past the Secret Service agents," Cohn said. "It was too risky, so Ari called them off."

At one point, when the *Christina* was docked in Haiti, Ari actually suggested to Jackie that — to quell persistent rumors she was in the marriage only for money — they obtain a divorce in which she received no alimony or settlement at all. Then, Onassis promised, they would secretly remarry the very next day. The public, he said, "would be no more the wiser." He had had the divorce agreement ready for her to sign, but Jackie declined. Ari figured, he told Cohn, "it was worth a try."

Onassis flew to Paris in January 1973 and met Alexander for dinner. His son had undergone rhinoplasty to rid himself of the prominent Onassis nose, and his new look took Ari by surprise. To Alexander's unalloyed delight, Ari announced that he was divorcing "The Widow." He intended to pay her an additional $1 million — no more. Alexander shared the good news with his sister, who, having been continually pestered by Jackie to lose weight, shared in his joy. Alexander also called Fiona Campbell-Walter (Baroness Thyssen-Bornemisza), the woman Ari had long been urging his son to dump.

There was another reason for Alexander to be happy. After months of his warning his father that their Piaggio amphibious plane was a "death trap," Ari belatedly agreed to replace it with a helicopter. They would eventually sell the amphibian, but first Onassis wanted Alexander to check out a new pilot at the Piaggio's controls.

Less than three weeks after that dinner in Paris, at 3:12 P.M. on January 22, Alexander was taxiing into position at Athens International Airport with the new pilot at the controls. Fifteen seconds after takeoff, the plane veered to the right and plummeted to earth.

Jackie and Ari were in New York when they were told the news. According to the earliest reports, the pilot and a passenger had been seriously hurt but only Alexander's injuries were critical. He had been rushed into surgery so doctors could remove blood clots that had formed on his brain.

Onassis swung into action, arranging for a 149-passenger British Airways Trident to fly the noted British neurosurgeon Alan Richardson to Athens. Another top neuro-surgeon, this one from Boston, was also flown to Athens. The superstitious Onassis, who shared Maria Callas's belief in witch-craft, also ordered one of his men to go to a Greek village and find an icon that suppos-edly had healing powers. The icon, a Greek Orthodox crucifix, was rushed to the hospi-tal.

Jackie, meantime, phoned Caroline at the Concord Academy. She told her daughter, who had been training for her pilot's license at nearby Hanscomb Airfield, that there would be no more flying lessons. JFK's only daughter was grounded — literally.

Alexander was on life support, Fiona Thyssen at his side, when Ari and Jackie ar-rived at the hospital. Onassis's sisters Artemis, Merope, and Calirrhoe were in the adjacent waiting room, their sobs audible halfway down the hall. Contrary to later re-ports that he was identifiable only by his monogrammed handkerchief, his face was unmarked. That made the diagnosis — irreversible brain damage — all the more impossible to believe.

Onassis asked that nothing be done until Christina arrived from Brazil, where she had heard the news on her car radio. As they waited, Jackie went to comfort Fiona, the love of Alexander's life. After a few consoling words, Jackie asked the grieving woman if Alexander had mentioned anything to her about the size of the divorce settlement Ari had in mind.

Fiona was "amazed" that Jackie, who had lost so many loved ones, would be so callous as to ask such a question while her husband's only son lay dying. Alexander had mentioned the $1 million figure to her, in fact, but she was too dazed to answer the question. "I really think that is a question for you to ask your husband, don't you?" Fiona said.

Once Christina arrived to say good-bye to her brother, Ari ordered that life support be turned off. Was he sure? doctors asked. "I won't have anything of him!" exploded Onassis, trying to summon the courage to end his son's life. "He *must die!*"

As soon as his son was pronounced dead, Ari was gripped by denial. At first he even refused to bury Alexander. Instead, he instructed Johnny Meyer to get in touch with the Life Extension Society in Washington and arrange to have Alexander's body frozen. His right temporal lobe had been reduced to pulp, but through the promise of cryonics, Alexander could be frozen until science found a way to repair his brain.

Eventually, Ari was convinced by friends that he could not keep his son's soul in limbo, and agreed to have him buried on Skorpios. At the grave site, Ari turned to Christina. "You are my future now," he told his only surviving child.

Onassis would never recover from his son's death — not because he had been a loving father, but because he was consumed with guilt over having *not* been one. Moreover, Onassis's vast empire represented his bid for immortality; as his sole male heir, Alexander was the embodiment of that future. Now he would have to groom Christina for power — she would, in fact, prove herself a formidable businesswoman — but it would never be the same.

Indeed, Alexander's death sent Ari into an emotional tailspin. "He became moody, short with people, and impossible to live with," Duchin said. Whether Jackie actually felt compassion for Ari, feared he would react to Alexander's death by cutting her off without a cent, or — most probably — a little of both, she tried to ease his pain. "She was always very kind and very sweet to him," Mehle said. "She was always trying to think of ways to entertain him, to bring him out of his blue funk. She would ask, 'Who should I invite to dinner? Who would make him laugh?' "

Two days after Alexander's funeral, the phone rang late one night at Pierre Salinger's apartment. "Pierre, I have a very big favor to ask of you," Jackie said. "I hope so much you'll say yes."

"Of course. What is it?"

"Ari is in very low spirits. Alexander's death has just devastated him. I've convinced him to take some time off, for a cruise, but he needs someone else to be with him, another man." Jackie asked Salinger and his wife, Nicole, to set aside ten days right away to spend with Onassis. "Ari has always liked you, and I think it could be very good for him to have you there." She asked the Salingers to meet them at Orly Airport in forty-eight hours.

Two days later, both couples were aboard an Olympic Airways jet bound for Dakar, Senegal. There they were to board the *Christina*. While Jackie read, Salinger and Ari spent endless hours debating history and politics. "He loved Pierre," Nicole Salinger said. "They always argued about Franklin Roosevelt — Ari hated FDR — and all sorts of subjects from American history, present and near past. They went on for hours and

438

hours, pacing up and down the deck, talking and arguing."

During the cruise, Jackie took Pierre aside and asked him to tell fourteen-year-old Caroline and John Jr., eleven, about their father. "I made certain to stress their father's wonderful sense of humor and his love of life — and especially of them. Without going into detail about his injuries and bouts of illness, I pointed out that even though he often had reason to be sad, he was the person who cheered up all the others in the room." The image of "those two innocent, beguiling faces turned up to me and listening with rapt attention" would stay with Salinger forever.

JFK's friend and press secretary also credited Jackie with making sure her children knew their father was, as Salinger put it, "a human being, not a myth. I wasn't sure at first if Jackie would approve, but I thought it was important that they not be spoon-fed all the Camelot stuff — that would just give them a warped, unrealistic view of President Kennedy. But I think she knew exactly what I was trying to do, and she agreed. In the end, Caroline and John had a healthy perspective on their father. All the credit goes to Jackie."

Salinger departed the *Christina* thinking the cruise "did seem to help" Ari's state of mind. He was wrong. Over the next year,

Jackie kept trying to distract Ari with trips to Spain, the Caribbean, Mexico, and Egypt. Nothing seemed to work. "Not long after Alexander's death, I was staying with Gloria and Loel Guinness down at their place in Lantana, Florida, when Ari and Jackie showed up," Mehle recalled. "I went down to the beach and there was Ari, curled up on the sand in a fetal position. Onassis was a mortally wounded man."

Grief soon turned to anger, as Ari concocted several conspiracy theories to explain his son's senseless death. He was convinced the CIA, at the urging of his old business ally Colonel George Papadopolous, had sabotaged Alexander's plane. Onassis, meantime, ordered that tapes and documents of Alexander's be burned or shredded. "Ari was driving us all bananas," Meyer told Peter Evans. "His paranoia didn't exempt anyone."

Onassis offered a $1 million reward to anyone who could prove that his son's plane had been sabotaged. He hired the world's top crash investigators to conduct a separate investigation. He could uncover no proof that Alexander had been murdered, but Ari remained a man possessed. Evenings, he listened to the cockpit tapes of doomed pilots as they tried to regain control of their aircraft.

There was little Jackie could do about her

husband's mental disintegration. In the spring of 1973, she suddenly found herself confronted with a new and wholly unexpected crisis. When the highly questionable practices of her old friend, Dr. Max Jacobson, were exposed in a *New York Times* article, the Kennedy camp went on full alert. Federal drug enforcement officials launched their own investigation of Dr. Feelgood after one of his patients, Kennedy photographer Mark Shaw, died of long-term methamphetamine abuse at the age of forty-seven. Not long after, the New York State Attorney General's office joined in, threatening the revocation of Jacobson's license to practice medicine.

Jack Kennedy was named as one of Jacobson's patients, but the full extent to which both President Kennedy and his wife were dependent on speed was unknown. "Everyone was scared," JFK's old friend Chuck Spalding said, "about what would happen if people knew just how often the President and the First Lady were getting these regular amphetamine shots inside the White House. They were afraid it would tarnish the Kennedys' image."

Fear turned to panic when a license revocation hearing was scheduled and Jacobson was called to testify. Jackie turned to Spalding for help. On May 28, 1973 — two days before the hearings were to begin in New

York — Spalding phoned Jacobson. His wife, Ruth, took the call. Spalding asked to see Dr. Max, but Ruth explained that her husband needed to rest before the hearings.

Spalding insisted that it was vitally important that he see Jacobson immediately. He would pick the doctor up at his apartment early the next afternoon.

The next day at noon, Spalding called to apologize. He would not be able to pick Jacobson up, but would it be possible for the doctor to drop by Spalding's apartment? Jacobson arrived there around 3 P.M. and rang the bell. Spalding greeted him at the door.

"Here is somebody who wants to see you," Spalding said.

"All of a sudden," Jacobson would write in his diary, "I found myself embraced and kissed by that 'somebody' who was Jackie. Chuck ushered us into a room and then excused himself."

Alone with Jacobson, Jackie said she was sorry about the "unfair" publicity he had been receiving in the press. "I asked whether she had any idea as to who instigated the vicious attack on the late President," Jacobson recalled, referring to articles that had questioned the extent of JFK's dependence on the discredited doctor and his injections. "I said, 'You know better than anyone what I did for Jack.'" He then reminded Jackie of the time she came to him, upset over the vial of Demerol she had found among the President's things. A Secret Service agent had supplied JFK with the illegal drug, which Jacobson demanded Kennedy stop taking immediately. Noting that Demerol was highly addictive and "would interfere with the President's function," Jacobson had threatened to stop treating the Kennedys with his magic elixir if he ever caught Jack sneaking the Demerol again. Of course, the speed Jacobson was injecting into the veins of the President and the First Lady was also highly addictive — although in the early 1960s that had yet to be scientifically established.

Jacobson was miffed that Jackie "seemed to have forgotten all about" the Demerol incident. "I also reminded her about when I accompanied them on the Paris-Vienna-London trip [in 1961], and how well JFK functioned in spite of the enormous pressures of the meetings, and countless other occasions at the U.N., the Carlyle, in Washington, Hyannis Port, Glen Ora [the Kennedys' country home in Virginia], and West Palm Beach." He also reminded Jackie that during all those years, he "never charged a penny."

Jacobson continued, "In that Chuck had called the meeting under the pretense of its extreme importance, I soon found out to whom it was important. Jackie asked what I would say if the White House came up during the hearings. I reassured her that there was no reason for concern. Medical ethics and discretion had been a part of me for the past fifty years. I had no intention of changing now. I said that my conscience was clear and that I had nothing to hide."

To defend himself against allegations of wrongdoing, Jacobson had hired famed attorney Louis Nizer and had already run up legal fees of $35,000 — and this would likely amount to less than 10 percent of his total bill.

On top of those expenses, the Constructive Research Foundation, which had been set up to fund Jacobson's multiple sclerosis research, now owed him $12,000. "Money had never been my concern and I had accumulated none," he said. But now he was in trouble, and Jack had promised to come to his financial aid if ever he needed it. "I repeated the discussion with Jack . . . now that I needed him, Jack was no longer available. She replied, 'Don't worry, all will be taken care of.'

"After we said our good-byes, Chuck escorted me downstairs in the elevator. He said that help was forthcoming. He suggested that the Foundation write to Jackie, addressed to his attention, requesting a contribution . . . I was relieved after the long two-hour meeting, and arrived home elated.

The forthcoming assistance, however, never arrived."

Jacobson's medical license was revoked on April 25, 1975. He died five years later. During the entire lengthy process, Jacobson kept his word and refused to discuss the White House. Jackie, on the other hand, provided no support whatsoever. However misguided, even dangerous, Jacobson was, the fact remained that John F. Kennedy depended on his "treatments" to help him get through some of the greatest crises of his administration, including the Cuban Missile Crisis. The man her husband once defended as his medical savior ("I don't care if it's panther piss. It works," he told Jacobson's critics in the White House) was completely ignored by the President's widow. He had become the one thing Jackie was congenitally incapable of tolerating: an embarrassment.

For the first time since Alexander's death, Onassis returned to Skorpios in August of 1973. He drank his Johnnie Walker Black Label Scotch and sang his favorite Greek ballads, but the spark was gone. After everyone had gone to bed, he would walk outside and sit on his haunches beside Alexander's tomb, rocking back and forth as he held his head in his hands. To share his sorrow, Ari invited Alexander's mother, Tina, and her husband, Stavros Niarchos, to Skorpios. Jackie, knowing how much pain they had both caused Ari, was aghast.

For someone who had experienced so much tragedy in her own life, Jackie was surprisingly ineffectual when it came to consoling Ari. Not knowing where to turn, Jackie even confided in her cousin Edie Beale during one of her periodic calls to Grey Gardens. Jackie told Edie that "everything went wrong" after the crash. "Mr. Onassis really lost his mind when his son died . . . It wasn't anything to do with her, it was that tragedy . . . Onassis was no longer interested in life. He became a perfect horror to live with."

Peter Duchin agreed that "Alexander's death knocked him out of the box. It completely changed Ari's personality. He related very much to ancient Greece in a curious way — Ari was a Sophist — and he felt that fate had turned against him. He became morose, snapping, nitpicking, critical — just extremely difficult to even be in the same room with. All the spark he had was gone. Jackie got the worst of it."

It was not long before Jackie began to fight back. "I saw the biggest fights between them you could ever imagine," Peter Beard said. "He would blow up all the time — tantrums about everything. Yelling and screaming at her."

Ari's headaches worsened, and his rages became more terrifying. Onassis later confessed to Roy Cohn that during this period he struck Jackie — and more than once. "They were having one of their screaming matches when Onassis lost his temper and hit Jackie across the face," Cohn said. "She had a black eye, but since she wore those dark glasses all the time anyway nobody suspected a thing. He thought that was terribly funny — that he could get away with hitting her because she liked to play movie star behind the glasses. He was more or less bragging about striking Jackie, saying all Greek men beat their wives and that it was good for her. His son's death had really pushed him off the deep end . . . I think from then on Jackie knew it was over. They spent very little time together after that."

Onassis's depression, for which he refused to seek psychiatric help, seemed to manifest itself in other ways as well. For all his womanizing, Ari had, according to those who knew and worked for him, also carried on several short-term relationships with young men. In the wake of Alexander's death, these too turned violent."

"During the time I was in Rome there were two Italian boys," said Frank Monte, who worked as Onassis's bodyguard in 1973. "One lived in Ari's apartment and the other was always on call when Ari wanted him. One was dark, the other was blond-haired but deeply tan. They were handsome, in their early twenties. Ari would play around with them, making lewd jokes in front of me and other bodyguards."

Onassis, according to Monte, turned his violent rage on these and other young men. "He mistreated them," Monte said, "even beat them for pleasure."

Onassis had always been outspokenly open-minded on the subject. He readily acknowledged the role of homosexuals in ancient Greek history, and often reminded guests — particularly prim heterosexual American guests — that Alexander the Great was homosexual. And Onassis, whose long-time penchant for cross-dressing proved that his masculinity was not easily threatened, often stated that he had experimented "with anything you can think of" sexually. "I got the impression," said Cohn, "that he was a very macho guy, but that he had probably tried just about everything."

Onassis, said Monte, "would talk quite openly about his two regular boys and other occasional boys. He'd say, 'There's nothing wrong with it, I just like to do it with boys.' " Onassis's employees became alarmed, however, when these young men were subjected to violence. "He'd often take one or the other to his bedroom and after a while, there'd be the sounds of punches and screams," Monte said. "Then we'd get a call from Ari to fetch the poor kid and throw him out. Sometimes a boy would be yelling, 'No, no, I love you.'"

Ari's precarious mental state was no less alarming than his failing health. In addition to the headaches, he was losing weight and complained of constant fatigue. His right eyelid drooped. Onassis was in no shape to face one of the biggest crises of his career. In October of 1973, the Arab states embargoed oil in an effort to discourage the United States and other Western nations from supporting Israel in its ongoing conflict with its Middle Eastern neighbors. In a matter of months, it was reported that Ari's worth had plummeted from nearly $1 billion to $600 million.

That November of 1973, Jackie was involved in various ceremonies marking the tenth anniversary of the assassination, and all but oblivious to Ari's rapidly deteriorating physical condition. An added distraction was the marriage on November 17, 1973, of Bobby's daughter Kathleen to David Townsend at Holy Trinity Church in Georgetown. Ted gave the bride away, and Ethel's boyfriend Andy Williams sang "Ave Maria."

"At one point before the ceremony, Jackie swept into the church, trailed by a small entourage," Ted's aide Richard Burke recalled. "Every head, except a few in the family, turned. The famous face, the famous smile, added the extra touch to the wedding that immediately stamped it a full-blown Kennedy affair." On the way out, she shot an icy glare in the direction of one of the guests: the actress Angie Dickinson, who had slipped away with JFK the night of his Inauguration.

In December, Ari checked into Lenox Hill Hospital on Manhattan's Upper East Side under the name of Philipps. Christina, as deeply concerned about her father as Jackie was blasé, rushed to New York from Athens to be by his side. Ari's wife, meantime, never visited "Mr. Philipps," even though he was only a few blocks away. Not surprisingly, such seemingly callous indifference did not sit well with Christina. Alexander had detested The Widow even more intensely than she did; now it was left for Christina to hate for both of them.

At first, doctors suspected Onassis may have suffered a stroke, but after a week of tests the verdict was clear: Onassis suffered from myasthenia gravis, a relatively rare, incurable muscular disease. "This is God punishing you for all your sins," Christina joked.

"I never think about sin," he replied wryly. "It's my nature."

With the exception of his family and a few of his closest aides, Ari kept the diagnosis to himself. But when he appeared in public with one eye shut, it was widely rumored that he had indeed suffered a stroke. To keep his right eye open, Christina took white adhesive strips and literally taped the lid to his forehead. The bizarre result was soon captured on film and splashed across the front pages of newspapers around the world.

Strangely, Jackie did not seem very concerned about her husband's medical state. She behaved, as one Onassis staffer put it, "as if he had a bad head cold." Ostensibly to get his mind off his problems, Jackie convinced Ari to fly to Acapulco to celebrate the New Year. In fact, she had an ulterior motive — to convince Ari to buy her a hacienda there.

For years, Onassis had put up with Jackie's constant references to her first husband. "Even when she and Ari were dining intimately by candlelight on the yacht," said Ari's friend Willi Frischauer, "she kept making references to Jack." And it was not enough that she still owned Jack's house in the Kennedy compound at Hyannis Port; Jackie also pressed Ari to buy a larger house nearby, one that would "completely dwarf" the Kennedy estate. Onassis refused.

Ari knew all too well that Acapulco was where Jackie spent her honeymoon with Jack, in a fairy-tale pink villa that clung to the side of a cliff. When Jackie announced in Acapulco that she wanted to buy a home near that very spot, Onassis saw it as the final insult.

On the flight from Mexico back to New York, the couple argued so bitterly and so openly that the crew worried things might turn violent. "Onassis was in the middle of what amounted to a nervous breakdown. There was no way for the marriage to work under those circumstances," Tish Baldridge said. "Jackie could be understanding only up to a point, I think. She knew how to stand up for herself."

This time, as they returned to New York, Jackie took the offensive, repaying him for the months and years of abuse she felt he had heaped on her. "She had a very sharp tongue indeed," Gore Vidal said, "and knew when to go for the jugular." Concurred Jamie Auchincloss: "My sister could be ferocious; it wouldn't surprise me at all if she gave as good as she got with Onassis."

And on that fateful return flight from Acapulco, she did. Meyer told Peter Evans that Jackie reminded Ari of "every lapse of taste and style he was ever guilty of in their five years together; she could be cutting about the faults of others . . . she obviously knew how to wound a man as well as how to flatter him." Among other things, Jackie chastised him for his "horrendous" table manners — "slurping soup, making animal noises while you chew, it's disgusting." She accused him of passing along his same boorish manners to Christina. "No man finds a fat girl with food on her chin attractive," Jackie said, "no matter how rich she is." According to Costa Gratsos, she made it clear she would no longer eat with either of them.

When the onslaught was over, Onassis said nothing. Physically as well as emotionally drained, he slunk back to a quiet spot in the cabin and began scrawling on an unlined white pad. With Jackie stewing at the other end of the plane, Onassis was writing his will.

I don't dislike her, you know.
I hate her.

— *Christina Onassis*

I thought I was buying a prize cow when I married Jackie. How could I know the cow would cost me $50 million?

— *Aristotle Onassis*

I am happiest when I am alone.

— *Jackie*

EIGHT

"To My Dear Daughter," Ari began, filling page after page as his private jet wended its way from the Pacific coast of Mexico to New York. When the plane made a refueling stop in West Palm Beach, Mr. and Mrs. Onassis got off the plane and put on a show strictly for public consumption, dropping into the terminal coffee shop to wolf down two BLTs.

Once back on board, they resumed their positions at opposite ends of the plane. In his new will, Onassis left Jackie a yearly income of $200,000, plus $25,000 annually each for Caroline and John until they turned twenty-one. If she contested the will, neither she nor the children would get anything.

He also set up "The Alexander Onassis Foundation, its purpose, among others, to operate, maintain, and promote the Nursing, Educational, Literary Works, Religious, Scientific Research, Journalistic and Artistic endeavors, proclaiming International and National Contests, prize awarded in money, similar to the plan of the Nobel Institution in Sweden, I entrust and command the undersigned executors of my will to establish such a Cultural foundation."

The rest of the will, scribbled in longhand in accordance with Greek law, spelled out a scheme whereby the intricate tangle of interlocking corporations that only Onassis could fathom was boiled down to two companies — Alpha and Beta. All of Ari's assets were put into Alpha, with his principal heir, Christina, getting everything in Alpha — as well as a $250,000 yearly allowance and another $50,000 for her husband when she remarried. Beta, which would run the assets in Alpha, was to be owned by the new Alexander Onassis Foundation. Ari's cousin and trusted lieutenant Costa Konialidis would pick the directors of the foundation, who then would help Christina manage her far-flung empire.

Ari then made generous bequests to relatives and loyal friends: $60,000 a year each to all his sisters and to Konialidis; $30,000 annually to Gratsos; Nicolas Cokkinis, his New York–based managing director; and to his longtime attorney Stelios Papadimitriou; the head of Ari's Monte Carlo operation, Costa Vlassapoulos, was to receive $20,000 yearly. Housekeepers, maids, chauffeurs, cooks, and butlers who had spent any significant amount of time in his employ were also mentioned by Ari in his will.

Onassis then jotted down the terms governing the disposition of his two most cherished possessions. "My yacht, the *Christina*, if my daughter and wife so wish, they can keep for their personal use," he wrote, giving Jackie a 25 percent interest in both the ship and Skorpios. The remaining 75 percent went to Christina. Since annual operating costs for the *Christina* were running at around $600,000, he realized that they might decide the vessel was too expensive to maintain. Under those circumstances, they were to hand it over to the Greek government. The same was to be done with Skorpios if they decided they did not wish to keep it — but only with the understanding that Alexander's tomb and some thirty acres around it were to be left undisturbed in perpetuity.

Instead of naming his wife as executor, he chose "Athina née Livanos-Onassis-Blandford-Niarchos, the mother of my son, Alexander." Next to naming Maria Callas as executrix of his will, Onassis could not have taken a more direct swipe at Jackie. Apparently Ari was more interested in punishing Jackie than in making sure his will was properly executed. Tina's husband, Stavros Niarchos, was obviously a constant threat to the Onassis fortune, and Tina herself had become addicted to sleeping pills, tranquilizers, and painkillers since Alexander's death.

As he stepped off the plane in New York, it was clear that Ari's condition had worsened dramatically just over their brief holiday in Acapulco. His speech was slurred, he had trouble holding his head up, and his swarthy complexion was now slightly green.

A month later, Christina moved from Paris to New York, where she would learn the ropes of the family business working in her father's office. Ari, aware that his strength was waning, approached the task of grooming her to succeed him with a new urgency.

From her new vantage point, Christina got a closer look at the frisson existing between her father and his wife. "Why does he put up with that horrible woman?" she asked a friend over lunch at P. J. Clarke's. "She is so awful to him. Can't she tell that he is sick? Doesn't she care?"

Christina was so incensed about "The Black Widow" and her cold-blooded behavior that she was actually becoming fond of the other woman in Daddy's life — the woman Christina and Alexander had always referred to disdainfully as "The Singer."

Making an appearance on the *Today* show in April of 1974, Maria Callas told Barbara Walters that Onassis had been "the big love of my life." She went on to observe with some conviction that "love is so much better when you are not married." Walters asked if she harbored any ill will toward Jackie. "Why should I?" she answered with a shrug.

"Of course, if she treats Mr. Onassis very badly, I might be very angry." Christina was seeing her father's old lover in an entirely new light.

That spring, Ari and Christina sailed the Mediterranean aboard the *Christina*. Jackie, as was now her custom, chose to remain behind, partying in New York, but promised to join them in Spain. Stopping in Monaco, they entertained Prince Rainier and Princess Grace, who were shocked by the toll Ari's myasthenia gravis had already taken. "It was all very sad," Rainier later recalled, "to have come so far just to end up heartbroken and ill onboard his vast yacht with only your daughter for company seemed almost unfair."

Depressed, Ari began drinking heavily. Nights, he went out on the town, sometimes in the company of the same young men he had, according to his bodyguards, sado-masochistic relations with. At the Crazy Horse Saloon, one of Paris's most famous strip clubs, an obviously drunk Onassis invited photographer Roger Picard to capture "the secret of my success" on film. After leading Picard to the men's room, Onassis unzipped his pants, grabbed the plate on which customers left their tips, and placed it under his exposed penis. "There it is," he roared. "That says it all. Sex and money — that is my secret."

Back in New York, Jackie was confronted by an abrupt reminder of her own vulnerability — and that of her children. While riding his expensive Italian ten-speed through Central Park, thirteen-year-old John Jr. was accosted by a man who leaped out of the bushes, shouted, "Get the hell off of the bike," grabbed the bike and John's tennis racket, and pedaled away. The mugger, who had not recognized John, was later caught. But Jackie, fearing that any trial would inevitably turn into a media circus, declined to press charges.

She had always been philosophical about the dangers lurking in Central Park. As a regular on the jogging path that circled the reservoir, she had to be. "Whenever she'd set out for the park at dusk on a winter's evening," Tuckerman said, "I'd warn her of all the terrible things that could happen to her, and true to form, she never paid any attention. By nature she was fearless, and I think experience had taught her to trust her fate."

Oddly, Jackie did not seem entirely displeased by her son's mugging. She had told friends that she worried John would become a "fruit" without the toughening influence of a father figure. Try as he did to endear himself to Jackie's children — Ari told John they were *filaracos* ("buddies" in Greek) — Onassis was never really around them enough to have a lasting impact on their young lives.

To compensate, at age eleven John joined his cousin Tony Radziwill at the Drake Island Adventure Center in England to spend a week canoeing, camping, and climbing.

As for the Central Park mugging: "She was pleased that this had happened to John," Secret Service agent John Walsh reported in a confidential memo to his superiors in Washington, "in that he must be allowed to experience life. He is oversheltered now with all the agents and unless he is allowed freedom he'll be a vegetable at the age of sixteen when we leave him."

"I don't want you on his heels," Jackie said. "Secret Service agents are told to follow counterfeiters all over the place without them knowing they're being followed. Why can't you do it with John?"

She had no interest in making the agents' jobs easier for them. "She does not want us to inquire of the governess when John is going," Walsh reported, "or how he is getting there. We should be prepared for him to go any one of a number of ways."

Walsh went on to say that Jackie "is glad John had this experience but she is displeased about all the publicity it is receiving because people will think he isn't being accompanied by anyone and there is a danger in that."

"So can we tighten up security?" Walsh asked Jackie.

"No," she answered. "No agent is to be in

John's pocket. John is not to get in an agent's car and the agents are not to walk with him. They must follow him, hiding behind cars and bushes — whatever they need to do so he never sees them. I want him followed, but I don't want him to feel like he's constantly being guarded. It's not healthy."

Yet Jackie made it clear she would tolerate no more slipups. "If anything happens to John," she said, referring to the kind words she had for agents after Dallas, "I will not be as easy with the Secret Service as I was the first time."

Meanwhile, as part of her continuing campaign to keep John from becoming a "fruit," Jackie signed him up that summer of 1977 for the Outward Bound program — a full month of survival training on Maine's rocky Hurricane Island. Two years later, John and a half dozen others would trek through the wilds of Kenya as part of a ten-week course run by the National Outdoor Leadership School. At one point John's party disappeared, and it would be forty-eight tense hours before he and his fellow survivalists were finally located.

Reassured that her children would be safe, Jackie left them behind to meet up with Ari in Madrid. To the amazement of those present, she dragged her ailing husband out onto the dance floor while she played the castanets.

In Madrid, Jackie needled Ari about his daughter's aimless pursuit of gigolos and playboys. Christina had rekindled her relationship with Peter Goulandris, the shipping scion Ari and Jackie felt she should marry, but Goulandris's mother, Maria, a foe of Onassis, stood in the way of any union.

Christina bounced from Arnaud de Rosnay, a wealthy young baron, to Brigitte Bardot's former lover Patrick Gillis, to French pharmaceuticals heir Thierry Roussel. She quickly became fixated on Mick Flick, the fast-living Daimler Benz heir. Flick, who had declined to go to bed with her, said he preferred long-legged blondes. Christina obligingly dyed her hair, but there was nothing she could do about her thighs.

Rebuffed once again, a despondent Christina holed up in her house in London. On August 16, she took an overdose of sleeping pills and was rushed to Middlesex Hospital where she registered under the name of "C. Danai." The first to learn of the suicide attempt was Tina, who immediately flew from the Côte d'Azur on the Niarchos jet. With the exception of one or two catnaps in a waiting room armchair, she never left her daughter's side. No one, not even Ari, knew at the time. Wanting to spare the fragile Onassis any unnecessary strain, Tina waited until Christina was off the critical list to tell him.

Less than two months later, on the morning of October 10, 1974, Tina was found dead in her room at the Niarchoses' mansion in Paris. She was forty-five. Initially, death was attributed to a blood clot in her leg that had traveled to her lung. Another spokesman for Niarchos said she had suffered a heart attack. The suspicious nature of her aunt Eugenie's death still fresh in her mind, Christina was convinced Niarchos was behind her mother's death. Less than four hours after the body had been discovered, Christina had obtained a court order for an autopsy. If it turned out that he had killed Tina, Christina vowed to have Niarchos assassinated.

Medical examiners found no marks on the body, and concluded that Tina had died of edema of the lung. At the funeral, Christina broke down. "My aunt, my brother, now my mother, what is happening to us?" Niarchos, meantime, bristled at Christina's suggestion that he might have contributed to his wife's death. He put out a statement revealing that Christina had tried to kill herself. This incident, coupled with Alexander's tragic death, the statement concluded, simply proved too much for Tina.

Christina did not blame herself. She did not even blame Niarchos. She blamed "my father's unhappy compulsion," the woman who had brought heartache to her family the moment she walked into their lives. She blamed The Black Widow. She blamed Jackie. "John Kennedy. Bobby Kennedy. Now Eugenie, Alexander, Tina. It seemed wherever she went Jackie brought death. To Christina, Jackie was a curse, a jinx," Costa Gratsos said.

For her part, Jackie was too preoccupied with a project of her own to pay much attention to what her stepdaughter thought of her. For years now she had been toying with the idea of returning to work in some capacity. But when NBC television producer Lucy Jarvis asked her to work on an NBC documentary on Angkor Wat in 1973, Ari objected. "Grace Kelly was a working girl when she married a prince and became a princess," he told Jarvis. "You want to take my wife, whom I consider a princess, who was the wife of a head of state, and turn her into a working girl?"

With some prodding, Ari agreed to let Jackie write the afterword to Peter Beard's book *Longing for Darkness: Kamante's Tales from Out of Africa*. The book had been inspired by the writings of Isak Dinesen. "She was one of the first white people to feel that 'black is beautiful,' " Jackie wrote. "She was the first to see how all the dark forces of time, evolution, nature were being disrupted in Africa."

On January 13, 1975, *The New Yorker*

published Jackie's first piece in twenty-two years, an article on the opening of the International Center of Photography and its founder, Cornell Capa. "Downstairs, in the entrance hall, the long-haired young girl was still simultaneously talking on the telephone and filling envelopes," Jackie wrote. "A bearded young man was squatting on the floor beside her with another telephone and an open book . . ."

At the same time, she joined the Municipal Art Society in its battle to prevent Grand Central Station from being torn down and replaced by a skyscraper. "She was very gutsy and determined — a real fighter," said then-Congressman Ed Koch. "Even though it was Grand Central Station, Jackie gave the battle a visibility and a legitimacy it might not have had otherwise. Grand Central would probably be a dim memory if it weren't for Jackie Onassis."

While his wife pursued her new interests, Ari checked himself back into Lenox Hill Hospital for more tests and treatment. Ironically, Ari's adrenal function was now seriously impaired, just as Addison's disease had destroyed Jack's adrenal glands. Like Jack, now Ari was forced to take heavy doses of cortisone. The side effects were also the same. Just as the cortisone caused Jack's normally gaunt face to flesh out, giving him a robust, handsome appearance, the medicine caused Ari's already jowly face to blow up to twice its size.

The cortisone also had an effect on Ari's temper. While her husband battled the wasting-muscle disease alone, Jackie spent tens of thousands of his dollars at Bloomingdale's, Bergdorf Goodman, and Saks Fifth Avenue, as well as several pricey boutiques. When she finally did pay him a visit, he threw her out of his hospital room.

As soon as he left the hospital, Onassis arranged a secret meeting with Washington columnist Jack Anderson. "My colleague Les Whitten and I flew up on the shuttle to New York and were met by a limousine," Anderson remembered. "It was rather ironic, but Larry O'Brien, who had been one of Jack Kennedy's closest advisors, was on the same plane so I offered him a ride into town."

Anderson was taken to La Caravelle, which, incidentally, had been a favorite hangout of both Jack Kennedy and his father, Joe. "Ari was sitting there in his dark glasses, looking very gnomelike," Anderson said. "Over lunch Onassis accused Jackie of embezzling millions from him. He explained the whole scheme in detail — how she paid thousands of dollars, *hundreds of thousands of dollars*, on clothes that she then secretly resold to used-clothing stores in New York. He took us back to the fifty-one-story Olympic Towers, which he had just finished building across from St. Patrick's Cathedral, and he showed us the proof — stacks and stacks of bills, ledgers, memos, receipts, canceled checks. Then Onassis's henchmen gave us the numbers of several people who could confirm Jackie's spending habits."

The proof of Jackie's frenzied extravagance was overwhelming. "I was shocked," Anderson claimed. "Here was a woman with an enormous monthly allowance — we're talking $360,000 a year just for personal expenses, not rent or food or basics. That was all paid for by Onassis separately. Every person we talked to confirmed what we'd been told — that Jackie would just waltz through Paris and New York and Rome charging up a storm, reselling the merchandise and, without ever telling her husband or for that matter anyone, pocketing the cash."

Ari did not merely wish to sever his ties to Jackie, he wished to humiliate her. He told Anderson he wanted the columnist to unmask his wife's profligate spending habits. "Onassis made it perfectly clear he was going to divorce Jackie. Once he had exposed her as this very greedy, voracious person, he felt she'd be in no position to demand more millions in a divorce settlement. But there was something else that bothered him: 'Find out,' he barked, 'what in the hell she has done with all that money!' "

His marriage to Jackie was not the only

thing that was falling apart. After a protracted struggle, Onassis had failed to maintain control of Olympic Airways. It was announced on January 15, 1975, that the state airline that he had controlled for nearly two decades would be handed back to the government.

Less than three weeks later, on February 3, 1975 — before any divorce papers could be filed and before Anderson could publish his exposé — Jackie received a call saying Ari had collapsed in Athens with severe stomach pains. Dr. Jacques Caroli, the French liver specialist who had been Ari's personal physician for twenty-five years, insisted that Onassis be flown immediately to Paris for surgery at the American Hospital to remove his gallbladder. Dr. Isidore Rosenfeld, the noted American heart specialist, thought Ari, wasted by his disease (Onassis even found it difficult to chew), was too weak to withstand a major operation.

Jackie flew to Athens immediately, where she was joined at Ari's bedside in Glyfada by Christina and Onassis's sisters. The cultural clash was evident to even the most casual observer. In contrast to the over-emotional Greeks, Jackie, whose quiet dignity under the most trying circumstances had earned the world's respect, affected an air of detachment. Christina, Levantine to the core and by now nearly hysterical, had never hated her stepmother more.

When Dr. Caroli first told Onassis he required surgery, Onassis replied, "I am a fatalist."

The statement was made, said Caroli, "in such a resigned way that I knew he wanted to die.

"He said he wanted to die in the United States — but by that time he was too weak to travel that far," Caroli said. "His daughter and sisters were determined to keep him alive and insisted he be hospitalized."

Ultimately it was Ari himself who made the decision to fly to Paris and have the operation. His physicians wanted him to go directly to the hospital, but he insisted on spending the night before the operation at his apartment at 88 Avenue Foch. On the limousine ride from the airport, Ari, forty pounds underweight and ashen-faced, slumped between his wife and his daughter. Spotting the small army of paparazzi waiting outside his building, he insisted on walking unaided from the car to the entrance. "I don't want those sons of bitches," he said, "to see me being held up by a couple of women."

Rather than stay with Jackie at the Onassis apartment, Christina took a suite at the Plaza Athénée. That evening Onassis, brooding over the loss of Alexander and Tina, told Johnny Meyer that he would rather die than go on living with ghosts.

At noon the next day, Onassis was spirited through a side door of the American Hospital while photographers clamored for pictures of Jackie and Christina entering through the front. The one thing he took with him into the hospital was a red cashmere Hermès blanket that Callas had given him for his birthday.

Doctors determined there was an added complication: Onassis was admitted "shaken by very heavy influenza." Said Dr. Maurice Mercadier, "I examined Onassis and gave him only a five percent chance of surviving." In addition to the myasthenia gravis, Ari "had developed an infection of the bile tract and had an incredible number of gallstones. Then came a further problem — bronchial pneumonia. He also had an infected lung and irregular heartbeats."

Once her husband was admitted to the hospital, Jackie went to the salon of designer Emanuel Ungaro and spent several thousand dollars. She then shipped the clothes back to New York for immediate resale.

Onassis's gallbladder was removed on Sunday, February 9. For the next five weeks, he remained comatose in Room 217 — a first-floor suite in the hospital's Eisenhower Wing. Christina and Ari's sister Artemis camped in a room next door, taking turns at his bedside. Jackie dined out with friends nearly every evening; when she dropped in each day to check on Ari's progress, Christina and Artemis pointedly ignored her.

Over the next several days, Jackie visited the Louvre three times, the Orangerie once, and the hairdresser twice. On February 22, Jackie was assured by doctors that her husband's condition was stable, and that it would be fine for her to return to New York to spend time with her children. But when she called her trusted physician Dr. Lax in New York, he cautioned her to remain in Paris for the time being. Borrowing an anti-war slogan from the Vietnam era, Lax reminded Jackie that "the whole world is watching." Jackie, bored and eager to see her family and New York friends, went anyway.

One of the reasons Jackie gave for wanting to return to New York was to catch a program that was airing on public television. Caroline had spent six weeks working on the documentary about coal miners in east Tennessee, "interviewing miners, miners' wives and widows, many with black lung disease, children, mine operators, and officials."

Meanwhile, praying that it might give her father a reason to live, Christina convinced Peter Goulandris to propose to her. Ari had wanted nothing more than to unite the Onassis and Goulandris fortunes through marriage. Christina and her intended came to Ari's bedside with the happy news. But it was too little, too late.

Jackie was skiing in New Hampshire when Ari's condition suddenly took a nosedive the first week in March. Told by doctors that his condition was now grave, Jackie seemed unconcerned.

Nevertheless, she returned to Paris on February 28. Again, she spent her days shopping and visiting museums, her nights dining with friends. On March 7, she dined at Lucas Carton, an exclusive restaurant on the Place de la Madeleine. Her date was the president of Air France. Jackie, a talented mimic whose uncannily accurate imitations of every world leader from Churchill to De Gaulle used to have JFK doubled over with laughter, entertained everyone with her dead-on impression of Ari. "Given the grave circumstances," said one Parisian who witnessed Jackie's performance, "I think we were all quite shocked." Three days later, Jackie went to a cinema on the Champs Élysées to see *The Towering Inferno*. Ignoring warnings that Ari could die at any moment, she returned to New York.

Onassis slipped into a coma on Wednesday, March 12, "and when this happened," said Dr. Mercadier, "it was inevitable he would die." Jackie was informed, and still chose to remain in New York. On Friday, an abscess in his lung ruptured. The following day — March 15, 1975 — Onassis, who never completely regained consciousness after his gallbladder surgery, was given a dose of morphine. Within moments, he died with Christina at his side. He was seventy-five.

"All of a sudden I am a widow!" cried Maria Callas, who was in Palm Beach when she heard the news. With Ari's help, she had amassed a personal fortune of more than $10 million, but now had little will to spend it. Heartbroken over the loss of her "one big love," Callas remained a virtual recluse for two years. Then in the spring of 1977, she visited Ari's tomb on Skorpios. Five months later, on September 16, Callas suffered a heart attack and died at the age of fifty-three.

Ari's real widow reacted quite differently to the news of his death. Jackie had just returned to 1040 Fifth from an appointment at Kenneth's hair salon when Johnny Meyer called to tell her she was once again a widow. She seemed, he later recalled, almost cheerful. The first call Jackie then made was to Teddy Kennedy. She would need a sturdy ally in the inevitable battle over her share of Onassis's estate. The second call she made was to Valentino. Jackie needed a new black dress to wear to the funeral.

Jackie arrived at Orly Airport with her mother (Caroline, John, and Ted would meet up with them in Paris and fly on to Greece). Hordes of reporters and photographers — and no one from the Onassis family — was there to meet her. Wearing a black leather coat and her huge sunglasses, Jackie flashed an incongruous smile. That and a statement she had dictated on the plane were all she shared with the waiting press. "Aristotle Onassis rescued me at a moment when my life was engulfed with shadows," Jackie wrote. "He meant a lot to me. He brought me into a world where one could find both happiness and love. We lived through many beautiful experiences together which cannot be forgotten, and for which I will be eternally grateful."

Christina had not taken her father's death nearly so well. The day he died, the unstable Christina tried to commit suicide yet again, this time by slitting her wrist. Reporters who spotted the bandages on her wrist as she left the hospital were told it was "an accident, a bathroom slip," nothing more.

Inside the hospital chapel, Ari, his tan restored by mortuary cosmeticians, lay in state, clutching a large Greek Orthodox crucifix. Jackie arrived at the hospital to see her husband for the last time, beaming for photographers. She visited him for seven minutes, then attempted to speak to members of her husband's inner circle.

Heavily sedated, Christina was in no condition to see anyone — least of all Jackie. She, and for that matter all of Onassis's family, friends, and advisors, were outraged that Jackie chose not to be there when her husband died — despite the fact that she had had ample warning that the end was near.

Asked why Jackie was not at her husband's side when he died, Nancy Tuckerman explained that "there was an agreement that she had with Ari that she should spend part of the time with him and part of the time with her children. He wanted it that way. And at the time she just felt she should be with John and Caroline." She failed to mention that Caroline was away at boarding school, and that while fourteen-year-old John spent his evenings at the New York apartment, his mother was out on the town virtually every night.

Still, when the Olympic Airways 727 carrying the body and thirty-four family and friends touched down in Greece, Jackie and Christina seemed to cling to each other as they were confronted by the waiting press. "Hang on, take it easy," said Jackie, who had run this particular gauntlet countless times before. "It'll soon be over."

Jackie's ear-to-ear grin, again captured by photographers, contrasted sharply with the grief clearly etched on Christina's face. Still, the two women looked, for the moment at least, as if they had enough in common to forge some sort of understanding. The funeral cortege was to wend its way through the countryside toward the fishing village of Nidri, where Onassis's body was to be placed on a launch bound for Skorpios. Jackie, Christina, and Ted sat together in the back of the second car, behind the limousine carrying Onassis's three sisters.

The motorcade had traveled less than a mile when Ted Kennedy, amply briefed by Jackie on Ari's intentions to limit her inheritance, leaned over to Christina. "Now," he said, "it's time to take care of Jackie."

"Stop the car!" Christina ordered the chauffeur, and with that the motorcade came to a screeching halt. Horrified not only by the patently avaricious nature of the remark but also by its timing, Christina leapt from the car and ran ahead to join her aunts in their limousine.

On Skorpios, Ari's sisters Artemis and Mirope complained that Jackie acted "as if she was going to a movie premiere, not a funeral." Father Apostolos Zavitsianos, the village priest who conducted the simple half-hour funeral service, admitted that "the smile on the face of the widow Jackie before, during, and after the funeral has caused a lot of gossip. In all the hundreds of funeral services I've conducted, this smile was a new experience for me."

A half dozen pallbearers carried the casket up the meandering footpath to the chapel, followed by the funeral party. But when Jackie began to take her place immediately behind the casket, Christina and Onassis's sisters literally elbowed Jackie out of the front of the procession, forcing her far to the rear.

"To me it was obvious," Johnny Meyer said, "that Christina and Onassis's sisters were acting according to plan when they moved up to the coffin. It was a deliberate move to block Jackie off — to isolate her."

As soon as Jackie had set foot in Greece, not a single member of the family or of Onassis's inner circle offered Jackie words of condolence, or for that matter even acknowledged her presence. "In all my years in the Church," said Greek Orthodox Archdeacon Sylianos Prounakis, "I don't recall another funeral where the widow was pushed into the background this way. Mrs. Onassis was made to feel as if she did not really belong to the family. I find this extremely tragic."

Onassis was buried just a few steps from Alexander's tomb. Her face contorted with grief, Christina wept inconsolably as her father was laid to rest. Jackie, looking over her shoulder, appeared, as one dumbfounded observer noted, "radiant."

"ONLY CHRISTINA CRIED. JACKIE WAS COLD" blared the Athens *Acropolis*.

The state-run television station was deluged with calls and letters angrily denouncing Jackie's seemingly carefree demeanor. "As a government official," said the station's Director-General Byron Stamatopoulos, "I have to admit Mrs. Onassis's manner at her husband's funeral has caused a wave of public indignation in Greece."

The rest of the world was preoccupied not with Jackie's enigmatic smile, but with the size of her inheritance. So was Jackie, though she gave no sign of her concern. The day after her husband's funeral she was photographed laughing as she had her hair done at one of Paris's most exclusive salons.

At his death, Onassis was once again worth close to $1 billion. His vast holdings included a fleet of more than fifty oil tankers ("each a corporation unto itself," Gratsos said), a bank, and a half share in Olympic Towers — not to mention Skorpios, the *Christina*, fleets of automobiles, private planes, and a half dozen homes and apartments.

Unaware of the prenuptial agreement and the new will Onassis had angrily drafted on a flight from Acapulco to New York, the press speculated wildly about Jackie's likely windfall. *Time* was fairly typical: "The best guess seems to be that Jackie will end up with about $100 million, and her children, John and Caroline Kennedy, with $15 million each. She is also expected to get the prime pickings of Ari's $20 million art collection, part of which already adorns her fifteen-room apartment."

With the battle lines drawn at Ari's graveside, Jackie and Christina fought fiercely during the next year and a half over just what Ari's widow was actually entitled to. Using a loophole in Greek law that requires that a will be made in "a single sitting in a single location," Jackie's attorneys challenged the will on the grounds that the plane in which Ari sat was in fact moving. Besides, a number of witnesses could attest to the fact that Onassis took a break from his writing to get off the plane and wolf down a BLT in an airport coffee shop while the plane was being refueled. If she could succeed in convincing the courts that Ari had died without a valid will, she could then lawfully lay claim to 12.5 percent of Onassis's estate — or roughly $125 million.

As much as she loathed her stepmother, Christina did not want to go through a drawn-out war in the courts. She would, however, never forgive Jackie or the Kennedys. Christina told Aileen Mehle about a visit from Jackie's brother-in-law, the Senator. "Teddy Kennedy came over to Skorpios to say, 'Look, you have to do right by Jackie,'" Christina said. "I didn't need that big walrus sloshing around in my pool and telling me to do right by Jackie. Of course I was going to do right by Jackie — but in my own good time."

On May 8, Christina met with British bankers and oil executives in London to make it abundantly clear that she would be personally running her father's empire. "Everyone knows," Ari's longtime spokesman Nigel Neilson said, "that Christina is now definitely the boss."

Seeing an opportunity to corner her, Jackie flew coach to London under the name of "Mrs. Wyberg" and went straight to Ari's permanently reserved suite only to find that Christina had canceled the suite and cleared out all of Jackie's clothes.

Determined to sit down with Christina and hammer out a financial settlement, Jackie called her stepdaughter's house but was told she wasn't in. She called the next morning only to be rebuffed again. Her characteristic unflappability gone, a fuming Jackie demanded that Christina meet with her.

Finally, Christina agreed to negotiate — but only on her terms and not face-to-face. At 2 P.M. the following day, the two women arrived at law offices in London's IBM tower. According to Neilson, "The two women didn't actually meet. They sat in separate rooms and legal papers were shuttled back and forth between them by the firm's clerks."

Throughout the bizarre nonmeeting, Ari's daughter rejected Jackie's demands for more money. "If you want it," she told Jackie through the intermediaries, "then come get it."

Jackie cut short her meeting and flew to Skorpios. The *Christina*'s longtime captain, Costas Athanassiades, said Jackie spent a week on the island "rubbing more salt into the Onassis family's wounds. Frankly, I hadn't expected her to even come back to Skorpios after the memorial service. But she went about giving orders to everyone on the island. She acted as an absolute mistress. At one point she sent all the house servants off the island and onto the *Christina*. I don't know why . . . it was very puzzling."

Athanassiades concluded that Jackie was "putting on the 'I'm the boss' act for everyone to see. She'd never put her foot down on the island like this before."

Ari and Jackie had had several arguments over the landscaping of Skorpios. Jackie had wanted scores of trees and shrubs replaced and huge tracts of the island replanted with her favorite flowers. In front of the staff, Onassis had angrily shouted at her to not touch anything. Not long before Ari's final illness, *Christina*'s Chief Engineer Dmitri Skoula witnessed one of these battles. "I heard him tell her," Skoula said, "to leave his garden alone." Gratsos explained that

"Onassis had personally selected all the trees and plantings and each meant a great deal to him. He was a very emotional, sentimental man and he loved his beautiful island just the way it was."

Yet on this visit back to Skorpios, Jackie brought a botanist to look things over. The changes she wanted, said Skoula, were precisely the ones she and Ari had bickered over.

Eventually, Christina agreed to pay Jackie $26 million in cash — a $20 million lump-sum settlement and the additional $6 million to cover taxes. In return, Jackie waived any future claims on the estate. "There is not," Nigel Neilson sighed, "a lot of love lost between them."

The six-year marriage and its contentious aftermath left a bitter taste in everyone's mouth. Jackie's children, once so fond of their stepfather, now sided with their mother against the Greeks. On the other side, the Greeks felt only contempt for the woman they still called The Black Widow. "Please don't talk to me about that woman," said Gratsos, who effectively ran the day-to-day operations of the Onassis empire after Ari's death. "She's despicable. I can't bring myself to even think about her." Nor could Christina. "She can't bear the thought of that woman," Gratsos added. "She never wants to see her again, or hear her name."

The emotionally shattered Christina took little comfort in her newfound status as perhaps the world's richest woman. After her father's death, there was no need to continue the sham engagement with Peter Goulandris. Her aimless, club-hopping, pill-popping life now allowed room for numerous lovers, several more suicide attempts, and three more failed marriages — to Greek banking scion Alexander Andreadis, to suspected KGB agent Sergei Danyelovich Kauzov, and to Thierry Roussel. The pharmaceuticals heir fathered her only child — and Ari's only grandchild — Athina, who was born in 1985.

Unfortunately, at about the same time "Tina" was born, a stunning Swedish model named Marianne "Gaby" Landhage was also giving birth to a Roussel child. Christina paid Roussel, a multimillionaire in his own right, $50 million to end the marriage.

Christina was staying with friends in Buenos Aires when, on the morning of November 19, 1988, her body was found naked in a half-filled bath. She had succumbed to pulmonary edema three weeks short of her thirty-eighth birthday — the inevitable result of a lifetime spent abusing prescription drugs.

Jackie was not about to make the same tragic mistakes with her children that Ari had made with his. Now that she was $26 million richer, she could relax, and focus more of her attention on Caroline and John.

They did not always appreciate it. Dissatisfied with John's mediocre grades at Collegiate, she sent him to a psychiatrist, Dr. Ted Becker, to see if he couldn't help the boy overcome whatever blocks stood in the way of his getting good grades.

Caroline, however, was too plump for Mother's taste. One weekend she picked the seventeen-year-old up at Concord and took her to lunch at Boston's Ritz-Carlton Hotel. Caroline asked to see the dessert menu. "You're not going to have dessert," Jackie said flatly. "You'll be so fat nobody will marry you." Grandmother Rose Kennedy chimed in, telling her to stand with arms away from her sides so she would "always look thin."

The Kennedy women's obsessive body consciousness — the pressure was felt even more by Caroline's cousin Maria Shriver — left JFK's adolescent daughter unsure of herself. The comparisons to her svelte mother were inevitable, with the predictable results. Caroline's self-esteem plummeted, leading her to shave off one of her own eyebrows in a fit of pique.

"Larry, do you have the same problems with your girls as I have with Caroline?" Jackie asked her Hyannis Port neighbor

Larry Newman. "She knows everything and I don't know anything. I can't do anything with her."

"Jackie, you know it isn't going to be any different; it isn't going to get better," Newman replied. "What you've got to do is let her grow up alone. Keep your distance. I'll tell you what I do with my girls — we have wonderful conversations."

"I can't talk to her," Jackie said, shaking her head.

"Maybe you don't talk about the things *she* wants to talk about."

Jacqueline was a strict parent; she had firm ideas about what was right for Jack's children and brooked little in the way of adolescent rebellion. Tiffany's Design Director John Loring recalled how if she did not approve of something, she said firmly, "Well, I wouldn't want Caroline to do a thing like that."

She had already nipped her daughter's career as a photographer in the bud. When it was learned that Caroline, who was given her first pointers on operating a camera by Peter Beard, had accumulated a portfolio of her own, agents clamored to represent her. For a time it appeared as if Caroline would have her own exhibition, with photos selling for $10,000 apiece, at Manhattan's Lexington Gallery.

Once the intrepid Inquiring Camera Girl

for the Washington *Times-Herald*, Jackie might not have been entirely averse to Caroline following in her mother's footsteps. But Jackie realized that it was Caroline's Kennedy name and not her talent that was being exploited.

Instead, Jackie encouraged her daughter to spend that summer visiting drug rehabilitation centers in Hong Kong and working in her uncle Ted's Washington office. The following year, her vacations were spent working for NBC on documentaries about Scandinavia and tensions in the Middle East.

It was not easy for Caroline, whose natural diffidence made people think she was distant and aloof. "Everyone hates me!" she blurted out to a friend. "They all think I'm a snob." On the contrary. Despite the fact that Jackie had once been Debutante of the Year and was now insisting her daughter go through the customary social coming-out ritual, Caroline refused to attend a deb ball.

Above all else, Jackie did not want Caroline, and most of all John, to fall under the influence of their out-of-control Kennedy cousins. Ethel, whose own manic mood swings made it virtually impossible for her to exert any steady control over her brood, watched as her sons wreaked havoc wherever they went. At Hyannis Port, they threw lit firecrackers into people's homes, vandalized boats tied up at the pier, threw water balloons and fired BB guns at passing motorists. At a children's birthday party witnessed by the Kennedys' Hyannis Port neighbor Larry Newman, they pulled out a knife and robbed a young girl of her presents.

As they grew older in the psychedelic sixties and seventies, things got even more out of hand. Bobby Kennedy Jr. and Bobby Shriver were arrested for marijuana possession. Young Shriver learned his lesson, but Bobby Jr., with his brother David and cousin Chris Lawford, began dabbling in heroin. RFK's eldest son, Joe Kennedy II, was also no stranger to drugs, and he sought help from a series of psychiatrists as he drifted aimlessly from one college campus to the next on the strength of his name.

One weekend on Nantucket, Joe got behind the wheel of a friend's Jeep and careened wildly along the narrow roads with David and David's girlfriend, Pam Kelley. Swerving to avoid an oncoming car, he plowed into a ditch — hurling all three passengers out of the vehicle. The Kennedy boys, as usual, walked away. Pam Kelley, paralyzed from the neck down, would spend the rest of her life in a wheelchair while Joe II went on to become a Massachusetts congressman.

As it turned out, Jackie did keep her children away from the gravitational pull of their cousins. But that would not stop them from getting into trouble anyway. At twelve, John was caught drinking with a friend at Madison Square Garden. Three years later, while at Skorpios attending his stepfather's funeral, he swigged Ari's favorite Johnnie Walker Black Label Scotch straight from the bottle.

For years John was also a frequent marijuana smoker. He was still in his early teens at Collegiate when he began smoking pot, and was disciplined numerous times by school administrators. "We were always getting caught," said John's classmate Wilson McCray, "for getting stoned." McCray also revealed that he and John smoked pot several times in the bathroom at Jackie's Fifth Avenue apartment and on the roof of the building.

Caroline was no less adventurous during this period, reportedly going so far as to grow marijuana plants in Jackie's vegetable garden at Hyannis Port. Together, brother and sister sampled the homegrown stash.

After John enrolled at Phillips Academy in Andover, Massachusetts, in 1976, the pot smoking continued. Caught with a joint by campus security, he did not deny that he had been smoking marijuana. The Secret Service, which was still guarding John at the time, knew all about the drug abuse. Fearing a confrontation with Jackie, they chose to look the other way.

Much of this time Jackie had been preoccupied by her legal wrangling with Christina. Even if she had known about her children's drug use, it would all have been put in perspective by what happened one crisp October morning in 1975.

Following her graduation from Concord Academy, Caroline spent a year studying art at Sotheby's auction house in London. She was staying at the home of Conservative Member of Parliament Hugh Fraser, a longtime friend of JFK's and an ardent foe of the IRA. Each weekday, Sir Hugh drove his young houseguest to her work-study program at Sotheby's. Caroline and Fraser were about to leave the house and get into the car when there was a huge explosion in the street outside. A bomb had gone off under Fraser's red Jaguar sedan prematurely, killing a neighbor who was taking his dog for a morning walk. A shaken Jackie called and asked her daughter if she wanted to return home. Caroline remained in London.

Caroline returned to the United States to follow in the footsteps of both parents. She enrolled at Radcliffe-Harvard College, and after her freshman year tried journalism, just as her mother had, working as a summer intern at the New York *Daily News*. (Her mother's new friend at the time, writer Pete

Hamill, helped her get the job. Hamill happened to be visiting Hyannis Port the day Elvis Presley died, and took Caroline along with him to Memphis to cover the story.) Unfortunately, Caroline's own celebrity usually got in the way of her reporting. Sources and subjects she approached usually wound up interrogating *her*. Soon, she would be forced to explore other career options.

Caroline's interest in journalism did, however, reawaken something in Jackie. As she turned forty-six in 1975, the world's most famous woman — perhaps the world's most famous *person* — was growing restless. In New York, she had settled into a familiar routine: up around 9 A.M., late morning speed walks around the Central Park reservoir in her torn blue jogging suit and worn white running shoes, afternoon bike rides through the park, and thrice-weekly workouts at the Vertical Club. Four times a week she visited her psychoanalyst, Dr. Nadine Eisman; then there were regular sessions with her shiatsu-acupuncturist, Lillian Biko; and weekly pilgrimages to Kenneth to have her hair colored, cut, and styled.

Jackie turned to electrolysis to solve a persistent problem of unwanted facial hair. When they met in 1976, singer Tina Turner was surprised that "Jackie's got peach fuzz. It's all along her chin and jawline. And her face is enormous. She also has a lot of hair.

Too much. But she has a nice smile, a firm handshake, and is a good dresser. I liked her overall look."

On a typical day, Jackie might shop at Bloomingdale's, browse through the Madison Avenue Book Shop, or sit alone at the counter at Leo's coffee shop and, with all eyes upon her, devour a hamburger with unself-conscious glee. She still favored P. J. Clarke's and Serendipity, where Jackie now always ordered the same thing — an omelet with caviar and sour cream, followed by a hot fudge sundae. For John, who usually went with her, the order never varied: a foot-long hot dog with chili and onions, washed down with a frozen apricot slush.

"Everyone thinks that I'm living it up all the time, but nothing could be further from the truth," Jackie said of the months following Ari's death. "I'm just trying to lead the normal life of any other American mother and be with my children. I never intended to let John and Caroline be subjected to the glare of publicity. I want them to lead the life of normal youngsters. After all, those poor children have been through so much over the past few years. I just want to be like any other mother with two children and lead an uncomplicated life."

On one of Jackie's jogs through the park in mid-June 1975, a reporter stopped her and asked for an interview. Seizing an opportunity to counter the adverse publicity surrounding Ari's death, she sat down on the lawn and, while chewing on a blade of grass, tried to convince the young journalist that all the stories about her were exaggerated. "My life is very dull right now," she insisted. "I'm doing just very ordinary everyday things. Really, my life at the moment would make very uninteresting reading. Do you think it would be of much interest for anyone to know that I go shopping at the local A&P?

"I'm sure I'm going to be watched closely for the next year or so. Maybe people will find out what Jackie is really like and write something different for a change. I sure wish people," she added wistfully, "would write something nice about me sometime."

Her popularity was, in fact, the lowest it had been since her marriage to Onassis. "Most people here just don't like her," said Muriel Harris, one of Jackie's New Jersey neighbors. Joseph Badger, the local veterinarian, obviously didn't. "She goes around with the attitude that she's a tremendous celebrity," he sniffed. "People don't do that here. This is a high-class area. They are all celebrities — they've got it made, too! She likes to be the whole show, but people just ignore her."

The locals also complained about Jackie's notorious stinginess — most residents donated $200 or $300 to the local community chest, compared to Jackie's $25 — and what appeared to them to be poor grooming habits. According to her neighbors, Jackie often appeared unkempt in public, with mussed hair and dirty fingernails. Once, to the astonishment of the local gentry, she arrived at an equestrian competition with cold cream on her face. "I guess," said another horsewoman, "she didn't think we country folk were worth being presentable for."

That summer, Jackie visited Rose Kennedy at Hyannis Port. Jackie's thoughts were on her late husband — but not Ari, dead less than six months. "Sometimes I think that time heals things," Jackie said then, "and you forget certain things. I mean, I can't remember Jack's voice exactly anymore but I still can't stand to look at pictures of him."

A dozen years had passed, and yet Jackie had still not fully come to terms with Jack's death. Returning to Hyannis Port, her memories still haunted her. "When I came back, everything just hit me, because this was the only house where we really lived, where we had our children, where every pickle jar I had found in some little country lane on the Cape was placed, and nothing's changed since we were in it and all of the memories came before my eyes.

"After I had looked around and unpacked," she said of that first visit to Hyannis Port after burying her second husband, "the first thing I did was walk over to see Rose. And we were sitting and talking about a lot of things, and I said, 'It really hits, doesn't it?'" Later that evening, Rose called and asked Jackie to go for a walk around 9:30 "because I don't want you to be here and be alone and sad."

A certain ennui was setting in. Until now, her life had been one great adventure. But what now? With money no longer an issue, and with Caroline college-bound and John about to leave for boarding school, Jackie was at loose ends.

"Bored and restless" was the way friends began to describe Jackie. "When she telephoned friends to chat," said social chronicler Stephen Birmingham, "she seemed to have little to chat about."

One of these friends, Tish Baldridge, suggested she get a job. "Who, me — *work?*" was her first dumbfounded reaction. Vast segments of the public had never forgiven her for marrying Onassis, and she was routinely depicted in the press as a golddigger with a mad passion for spending. Gradually, Jackie came to realize that employment might be one avenue toward rehabilitating her image.

Baldridge had other reasons for urging her old friend to go to work. "Jackie was not a feminist," she said. "Now, she may have had feminist leanings without really knowing it. But she was never challenged by men. She was never forced to be competitive. Jackie always saw men as protectors, the suppliers of money. She never had to fight for anything in a man's world. It would never have occurred to her to question why there wasn't a woman on a board of directors."

First and foremost, Baldridge argued that Jackie needed to work for her own mental health. "I really felt she needed something to get out in the world and meet people who are doing interesting things, to use that energy and that good brain of hers. I suggested publishing."

The Viking Press was Baldridge's publisher at the time. "I said to her, 'Look, you know Tom Guinzburg — why don't you talk to him?' "

Guinzburg, Viking's publisher and an acquaintance of Jackie's for nearly twenty years, was "thunderstruck" when Jackie mentioned the idea over lunch at Manhattan's Le Périgord Park restaurant. Jackie's presence would, of course, add an undeniable cachet to the house. It was also difficult to imagine anyone in the New York publishing world with more connections, more access, or more clout. What author could not be lured to Viking by the promise of having Jacqueline Bouvier Kennedy Onassis as his or her editor? What newspaper or magazine would ignore a book that Jackie had edited, or fail to cover a publishing party for one of her books. And although no mention was ever made of Jackie actually writing a book herself, it would be a major coup for Viking if she did. "I was not unmindful," conceded Guinzburg, "of all these things."

For the moment, it was sufficient to merely announce to the world that Jackie had been hired as a "consulting editor" at Viking at an annual salary of $10,000 — her first job since she quit being the *Times-Herald* $42-a-week Inquiring Camera Girl to marry Senator John F. Kennedy. The Viking staff, Guinzburg conceded, was "stunned by the news. Everybody wondered, 'What's this giant celebrity doing in our midst?' " The immediate problem was "how to get her started working here with the least amount of turmoil and public furor."

What, exactly, was she going to be doing as a junior editor at a major publishing house? she was asked. "Learning the ropes at first," Jackie replied. "You sit in at editorial conferences, you discuss general things, maybe you're assigned to a special project of your own. Really, I expect to be doing what my employer tells me to do."

On September 16, 1975, Jackie was to report to work at Viking's offices at 625 Madison Avenue. Instead, she spent most of her first week on the Viking payroll trying on Valentino's couture line. When she finally did start coming to work toward the end of September, Jackie and the rest of Viking's 250 employees ran the gauntlet of television crews, photographers, and garden-variety groupies. The crank phone calls and fan mail continued unabated, but after a time the press and public stopped keeping vigil.

Four days a week, Jackie would arrive at the office by taxi between 9:30 and 10:00 in the morning. Once while taking her to work a cabdriver asked Jackie, "Lady, you work and you don't *have* to?"

"Yes," she answered.

The cabbie studied her in the rearview mirror for a few seconds. "I think that's great!" he boomed.

Once deposited in front of Viking, Jackie made her way to her spartan office with its small desk, typewriter, filing cabinets, and two chairs. Her working attire varied little: slacks, sweater, no jewelry. In other words, said her twenty-six-year-old assistant, Rebecca Singleton, "she dressed just like the rest of us, except somehow she managed to do it a little better."

Jackie handled her own files, placed her phone calls, did her own typing, made her own instant coffee, and, again like everybody else, stood in line at the Xerox machine. She told everyone to call her "Jackie," and insisted she was there "to work, not to play." Gradually, she learned the nuts and bolts of the job — how to write introductions and jacket copy, supply captions, and edit text.

The legendary *Life* photographer Alfred Eisenstaedt, who had taken JFK's official presidential portrait and had shot Jackie on several previous occasions, was hired to shoot Jackie at her new job. She wore dark pants, a beige top, and a cashmere scarf tied loosely around her neck. "She was forty-seven but might as well have been twenty-two," Eisenstaedt said. "Jackie was more beautiful — softer, more relaxed, more *natural* than I had ever seen her. It was very strange, but it seemed to me that somehow hard work — and I think she took her job more seriously than people realized — had made her look younger. Not just a few years younger, but younger than before Kennedy was elected President. Politicians' wives have that hard look — you know, the helmet hairstyles, with faces like they've been sprayed with varnish. In that little office at Viking, with all her books and papers piled up around her, she looked like a kid straight out of college, all excited about her first job."

As for those who persisted in dismissing her as a rank amateur, Jackie could only throw up her hands. "It's not as if I've never done anything interesting," she said. "I've been a reporter myself and I've lived through important parts of American history. I'm not the worst choice for this position."

Still, there was no way she could pretend to be your average working girl. After what was supposed to be her first day on the job, Jackie attended Frank Sinatra's concert with Ella Fitzgerald and Count Basie at the Uris Theater, and afterward was taken by Sinatra to the "21" Club for a midnight supper.

Jackie attended staff meetings and conferences, but it was an uphill battle convincing Viking's foot soldiers that she should be taken seriously. "In the beginning everyone saw her as a dilettante — Marie Antoinette playing milkmaid," one Viking editor said. "She seldom spoke up, and most of the time it looked as if nothing was sinking in. She had those huge eyes, that fixed smile, the vacant look. But then you'd bump into her in the hallway and she'd let out this huge laugh and you'd be completely blown away. There were little things — she would hold the elevator door open for you, and once I saw her help a man on crutches into a taxi in front of the building. There was nothing imperious about her, nothing at all. But never in a million years could you ever forget who this was."

"She doesn't expect things to be done for her," Becky Singleton said. "There's no standing on ceremony with her. She's out to prove herself an independent working person. It's amazing. She gets coffee for everybody. We have authors' conferences and I've volunteered to go for coffee, but Jackie's beaten me to it — jumping up and saying, 'Oh, no. I'll go!' " Several editors coined a nickname for her based on the footwear she favored in the office: "Earth Shoes."

The most famous editor in the history of book publishing had only been on the job a few days when Muffie Brandon, wife of the *Sunday Times* of London's Washington Bureau Chief Henry Brandon, walked in to Viking's offices with a book proposal. "My appointment was with Tom Guinzburg, and when I walked in to the meeting I was quite surprised to see Jackie there . . . As I explained the idea, I saw her eyes begin to light up. She sat forward in her chair. She caught the idea immediately, and for the next two hours she asked the most penetrating questions."

Brandon, who was active in the bicentennial effort to restore homes in Plymouth, Massachusetts, was pitching *Remember the Ladies: Women in America, 1775–1815* by her historian friends Linda Grant De Pauw and Conover Hunt. Finally, Guinzburg turned to Jackie and said, "What do you think?"

"Oh, let's do it!" she answered.

Then, Jackie took Brandon on a tour of

Viking. "She showed me the art department, the marketing department, the paperback division. She was so proud, so professional," Brandon recalled. "It's obvious she'd made her peace, that she was born for this."

Jackie likened her job as an editor to childbirth. "For her," said Singleton, "it's like being there for the delivery. She's pushing and pulling and tugging." In putting together *Remember the Ladies*, Brandon and Jackie spent eight hours at a stretch, sometimes crawling around on the floor arranging and rearranging the more than two hundred pictures in the layout. At one point, they dissolved with laughter trying to figure out how to illustrate an eighteenth-century sex manual that was part of the book. When they came upon information about a root women chewed to induce abortions, Jackie insisted, "Put that in the book."

Brandon searched Jackie for some reaction when they got to the part about First Ladies of the period, but "there wasn't a flicker." Jackie might have had more in common with Martha Washington than she ever imagined. "I lead a dull life — a state prisoner," Martha said. Jackie laughed at the remark. They also found a letter in which Martha described Georgetown as "a dirty hole." Jackie chuckled for a moment and said, "It still is."

At Viking, Jackie gravitated to the Studio

Books division, focusing her attention on editing lavishly illustrated coffee-table books. One of the projects she was most excited about was a book on fireworks by her friend George Plimpton. The author warned her that her colleagues would probably not think the book commercial enough. "They'll never let you do it," he said.

"Oh, just you watch me," Jackie replied.

"Of course, she was right," Plimpton said. "She was a wonderful editor — *very* meticulous. In the end the book was truly splendid — and it wouldn't have happened at all if it hadn't been for her."

When fashion doyenne Diana Vreeland came up with the idea for a book called *In the Russian Style*, Jackie latched on to the project immediately. The lush volume was to coincide with Vreeland's exhibit of Russian Imperial Court dress at the Costume Institute of New York's Metropolitan Museum.

In the Russian Style provided Jackie with all the expenses-paid, tax-deductible reasons she needed to make her first trip to the Soviet Union. "When she got into something, she was inexorable," said then–Metropolitan Director Thomas Hoving, who accompanied her on the trip. She pleaded with officials of the Soviet Ministry of Culture ("Communist Party stooges" she called them behind their backs) to let her return to the United States with the costumes actually worn by Czar Nicholas and the Czarina Alexandra. "She absolutely hammered them," Hoving said, "or stepped back and then nudged."

The Soviets refused to let Jackie return with the Imperial clothes for the book and the exhibit, but she was allowed to try on Alexandra's hooded white fur coat. Once the book was published, Jackie attended a carefully orchestrated press luncheon for five handpicked reporters in the Versailles Room of the Carlyle Hotel.

Writer Joyce Maynard remembered that the woman who had survived so much "offered a handshake so fragile it seemed almost as if the fingers would melt." How did her children view her book? "Rapidly," she laughed, reaching for a cigarette. Asked if she didn't long for the opulent clothes and lifestyle of the period, "You love to see it, the way you love to see *Gone With the Wind*," she observed, taking a bite of shortbread cookie. "But wouldn't you rather wear your blue jeans than wander around in a hoop skirt?"

Between the nervous giggles and frozen smiles — any inquiry not directly about the business at hand was met with silence — she mused about her path to publishing. "I always wanted to be some kind of writer or newspaper reporter," Jackie said. "But after college, I did . . . other things."

In January of 1976, Jackie gave one of her dinner parties at the apartment — four round tables with six people at each table. Mr. and Mrs. Arthur Schlesinger were there. So were the George Plimptons, the Roger Mudds, Peter and Cheray Duchin, Barbara Walters, and Candice Bergen, among others. A dozen or more of the guests stood to toast Jackie on leaving the ranks of the unemployed. Jackie beamed.

To those who knew her well, Jackie had undergone a transformation. "She was much more like the girl I first knew who had a great sense of fun and enthusiasm," George Plimpton said. "It must have been an extraordinary thing for her to be on her own. She was always somewhat diminishcd by the men around her."

The woman who told her to go back to work in the first place agreed. "She has pulled herself together lately," Tish Baldridge said at the time. "She's become more independent. Now she realizes she doesn't need a dominating man to lean on. Jackie is looking radiant. Work is good therapy for anybody."

Outward appearances aside, Jackie would grow increasingly dissatisfied with her working life at Viking, and vice versa. After two years, the woman whose connections were supposed to lure some big names to Viking had failed to produce a single major title.

Within a few months of joining the company, Jackie tried and failed to land two authors who would have instantly put her on the publishing map: Britain's Queen Elizabeth and the Duchess of Windsor. Prior to the Queen's state visit to Washington in July of 1976, Jackie had written to Buckingham Palace offering to be her guide in the nation's capital. Once she had Her Majesty's ear, Jackie planned to coax her into authorizing a glossy coffee-table volume on the Royal Family.

Instead, Jackie received a terse reply — not from the Queen herself, but from one of her many anonymous secretaries. Her Majesty had received Jackie's request, but it had been determined that "the possibility of employing a private individual in the capacity Mrs. Onassis suggested was quite unacceptable."

The publishing neophyte did not fare any better with the American divorcée who caused Edward VIII's abdication. Jackie had written the Duke of Windsor's elderly widow imploring her to write her memoirs for Viking. She proposed flying to Paris, where the Duchess lived in a mansion in the Bois de Boulogne, and discussing the project over tea.

Again, Jackie was rudely rebuffed. "Such a meeting is not possible at this time," replied a member of the Duchess's staff. The letter went on to assert that the Duchess was not about "to discuss her life story or anything else with any publisher or publisher's assistant."

The "publisher's assistant" later tried to convince Princess Margaret's ex-husband, the photographer Lord Snowden, as well as her old friend Frank Sinatra to pen their memoirs for Viking. But at a lunch Jackie set up with Viking executives, Snowden was, she later confided to a friend, "treated very rudely." And Sinatra, whose interest in Jackie was strictly of a personal nature, told her he had no intention of baring his soul in print. Like Jackie, he understood well the importance of maintaining one's mystique.

Jackie would switch employers, but over reasons that would have nothing to do with the working environment at Viking. In late 1976, Doubleday Editor Lisa Drew turned down a novel by British Conservative MP and suspense writer Jeffrey Archer (later Lord Archer). The novel, titled *Shall We Tell the President?*, dealt with an imaginary assassination attempt on the life of Ted Kennedy after Ted took office as President in 1981. Drew said she was "appalled" and told the British agent who brought her the book that it was "totally tasteless and that I wouldn't have anything to do with it."

When Viking bought the book in February of 1977, Drew was "dumbfounded." Over lunch, she mentioned it to Jackie in passing, and was surprised that Viking's most celebrated staffer knew nothing about the book. When Jackie got back to the office, she was assured by Guinzburg not to worry — that the book would in no way be associated with her.

Jackie had no reason to doubt Guinzburg. Besides, she suddenly had her hands full trying to debunk rumors that President Jimmy Carter was about to appoint her Ambassador to Great Britain. "Every time someone is hard up for news," she complained, "they throw in my name as ambassador to some place or other. And then my phone rings all day." To handle unwanted calls, she merely answered in a Spanish accent and insisted that "Mee-sess Onassis *no está aquí.*" She explained to Barbara Gibson, Rose Kennedy's personal secretary, "I have to do that to get rid of people."

Six months later, Viking published *Shall We Tell the President?* The book was blasted by the critics, including *The New York Times*'s John Leonard, who accused the author of "mainlining on the cesspool of the American mind" and concluded his review with the memorable line: "Anyone associated with the publication of this book should be ashamed of herself."

Jackie was "extremely upset" over the subsequent furor and that night called Drew to tell her so. For his part, Guinzburg claimed only Stephen Smith had objected to the book's publication as "an act of venal commerce." Jackie, Guinzburg insisted, expressed distress but didn't shout "stop the presses" when he told her Viking had bought the book in England several months earlier. Instead, he claimed she expressed "a feeling of resignation that people will go on using this bleak material." Jackie's boss conceded that the book was "going to bring out more crazies. But if we hadn't published it, someone else would have." Besides, he claimed that the American edition was toned down from the British original "so that the Kennedys would not be upset."

But one Kennedy, or ex-Kennedy, was upset — enough to quit her job. "Now here he [Guinzburg] is on the front page of *The New York Times* saying that I knew all about exactly what happens in this book, and I didn't know about it at all!" Two hours after talking to Drew, Jackie sent her handwritten resignation to Guinzburg by messenger.

Even her loyal assistant, Becky Singleton, thought "quitting the way she did wasn't a particularly classy thing to do. She never said anything about the book. From the time she came, Tom was so consistently protective of her special situation. She didn't tell Tom herself she was going to quit. There was no personal discussion of the incident itself. You do have the right as an employee to leave. But there are ways and ways to do it."

A few days later, Jackie again lunched with Drew, and gently broached the subject of employment at Doubleday. Nancy Tuckerman already worked in Doubleday's publicity department, and the courtly head of the company, John Sargent, had been a friend since the early 1950s.

It was the urbane, bearded Sargent who made the first formal overture to Jackie. "After she left Viking and Tom Guinzburg," Sargent recalled, "I made the initial call to Jackie. We had been personal friends and we had been social friends. I saw no reason why we could not be professional friends as well."

This time, Jackie worked a somewhat sweeter deal with her new employer. She would join Doubleday as an associate editor in February of 1978, and be paid a salary in the neighborhood of $20,000 to work only three days a week.

"She was so low-key," one associate editor remembered. "She was given a ridiculously small windowless office, which she brightened by taping a ballet poster on the wall. She made it perfectly clear she wanted to be treated like everyone else." As for the lack of natural light, it was John Sargent who broke the news to her that she would not be getting a window. "Oh, that's all right, John," she replied. "I've lots of windows in my home."

"She did everything she could to put people at ease," Sargent concurred. "She knew people were afraid to talk to her, that they were awestruck in her presence, but she did everything she could to get past that. She always *downplayed* her celebrity, as if she didn't feel she deserved any special attention."

Still, Jackie would find the initial reception at Doubleday to be even chillier than it had been at Viking. "Everyone was twittering and fluttering about," remarked one of Doubleday's authors. "Some people thought she was out of her depth at the beginning," Doubleday Art Director Alex Gotfryd said, "but she was really just shy." Editor in Chief Sandy Richardson remembered that, when it was time for her to present her titles to the assembled group of editors for the first time, "she turned to the person next to her and in that famous little-girl whisper asked what she was supposed to do. It did strike me as odd, because she'd presumably been doing pretty much the same thing at Viking for years." Another Doubleday editor was markedly less charitable. "For the first six months she was there, she went around like a scared rabbit," she said. "The woman didn't have a clue."

The object of all the water-cooler gossip

took it in stride. "No, I don't get questioned about my salary or why I work," she said. "At least I've never felt that kind of resentment. Perhaps it's just that the people who resent my working say it to everyone else — but not to me."

The simple fact remained that, no matter how self-effacing she tried to be, Jackie was too much a part of everyone's collective consciousness ever to be treated like a mere mortal, much less a peer. Paul Bresnick, who was then an editor at Doubleday, recalled the day Jackie materialized at his door with a cigarette and asked if he had a light. He fished a matchbook out of his desk drawer and handed it to her. At that moment, he realized ("to my horror") that John F. Kennedy's face was on the matchbook cover. "There was the tiniest flicker of recognition on her face as she looked down at the matchbook, but nothing more than that. I just thought, God, this must happen to her *all the time*. Even the most quotidian human interaction is necessarily *fraught*."

One Doubleday author was standing with Alex Gotfryd going over the cover design for his biography of the actress Susan Hayward when Jackie suddenly appeared dressed head to toe in black — black turtleneck, black sweater, black pants, black shoes. The author thought this must be what it's like for Doubleday employees: "You're totally absorbed in what you're doing, and suddenly there's Mount Rushmore standing in the doorway."

Jackie leaned over and studied the sexy photograph of Hayward on the book jacket for a moment. "My," she said, "she was really something, wasn't she?"

Once, after a visiting author beat a hasty retreat, Jackie asked Gotfryd, "Why do they all run like scared bunnies?" Without waiting for him to answer, she continued, "I can't blame them. When I think of my life, *I* have a hard time believing it. It seems like it all happened to someone else."

John Sargent conceded that "at first there was some resentment — a feeling that perhaps Jackie wasn't all that serious. She was not full-time, and she had *everything* in the world, so naturally there was that perception among the troops that this was just a diversion for her. But she was so relaxed and so unaffected — not at all the wildly extravagant, ultra-glamorous figure she was made out to be — that her co-workers couldn't help but be charmed. They developed a very warm regard for her as a person. In the end, I think everyone also had a very high *professional* regard for Jackie. I wished I had five more editors just like her."

Sargent was biased. Ever since Ari's death, he had been one of a dozen or more men who had been squiring Jackie to public

events in Manhattan. "Once we were pic-
tured on the cover of an Italian magazine,
under the headline 'JACKIE'S NEW BOY-
FRIEND!' " Sargent said. "We both got a
big laugh out of that."

To be sure, no one was subject to more
scrutiny or speculation than the woman now
known the world over simply as Jackie O —
not even the future President of the United
States. Out of loyalty to the Kennedys, she
donated $25,000 to the presidential candi-
dacy of her former brother-in-law Sargent
Shriver, knowing full well he did not stand a
chance of winning the Democratic nomination. At the same time, she was secretly de-
briefing the Democrats' 1972 nominee,
George McGovern, on the man who had the
nomination sewn up — Georgia Governor
Jimmy Carter. "She asked a lot of precise,
intelligent, highly sophisticated questions,"
McGovern said. "She just wasn't sure if he
was strong enough or good enough to be
President."

On June 27, 1976, after a night of cards
at a friend's country house, Stas Radziwill
collapsed and died of a heart attack while
undressing for bed. His ex-wife Lee seemed
less upset than Jackie, who along with
Caroline attended the funeral in England.
"Jackie loved Stas," said his niece Isabelle,
Countess d'Ornano. "He and Lee were so

different, they had nothing in common. Jackie had much more in common with him than Lee did. She understood him. Jackie always missed Stas. He counted in her life." At Stas Radziwill's funeral — unlike Ari's — grief, not elation, was etched on Jackie's face.

A few weeks later, the Democratic Convention was held at New York's Madison Square Garden, and Jackie triggered a stampede when she made the first of several appearances in support of Shriver. As she took her place with Ted Kennedy in the VIP box just above the Garden floor, hundreds of delegates surged toward her, waving placards and cheering wildly. Her expression changed from terror to delight and back again.

After Jimmy Carter made his acceptance speech, Jackie whispered to her brother-in-law, "They're right. Jimmy Carter *does* look like Howdy Doody." Neither did Jackie spare the future First Lady Roslyn Carter, who would soon be described as the White House's resident "Steel Magnolia." Batting her eyelashes and slipping effortlessly into a plantation drawl, Jackie said, "Why, I do declare, Lady Bird is just gonna *luv* her."

One of Jackie's escorts to the convention was Felix Rohatyn. A powerful figure in Manhattan's financial community, Rohatyn had been living with photographer Helene Gaillet. "I thought she was my friend," Gaillet said of Jackie at the time. "I'd even been her house guest on Skorpios. But men get bowled over by her. Felix and I had been together for years until he started taking her out and they were seen together on national television. Felix kept saying to me it was nothing, just a casual date, that it didn't change anything between us. It changed everything . . . everything was destroyed between Felix and me."

Had Sargent Shriver been picked as Carter's running mate, Jackie would have felt compelled out of loyalty to campaign. But since Carter selected Minnesota Senator Walter Mondale instead, JFK's widow felt free to sit this campaign out as she had every campaign since Bobby's assassination in 1968.

The night Carter was elected president, Jackie and author David Halberstam were both guests at the home of writer Michael Arlen. "A couple of years earlier, a friend of mine had asked Lee Radziwill what her sister thought of my book about the Kennedy administration, *The Best and the Brightest*," Halberstam said. "She said 'Jackie loved it, absolutely loved it.' So I sent Jackie a signed copy of the book, and she wrote back a very nice letter."

Still, that night at Michael Arlen's "everyone was in total awe of her," Halberstam remembered. "It was hard not to be. She was such a part of history. Nobody dared approach her. Later on in the evening, I walked into this study and there she was sitting absolutely by herself in front of the television, watching them declare Jimmy Carter the winner over Gerald Ford."

"So," Halberstam asked Jackie, "what was it like the night you got the news in Hyannis Port?"

She looked up and smiled. "We were all so *young*," Jackie replied.

The rest of their encounter consisted mostly of small talk, though it left Halberstam with "an abiding sense of Jackie's innate political intelligence. The Kennedy Machine had annexed her for her beauty, and she understood implicitly the tremendous political leverage that gave her. The more they needed her, the more power she had. If she always stayed slightly out of reach, they had to pay attention to her. Jackie was a very supple political animal. She played the game exquisitely."

She took the same approach to raising her children. "Jackie didn't want Caroline and John *inhaled* into that frenzied macho world of the Kennedys," Halberstam said. "She wanted them to be a part of their father's legacy, but she wanted them to develop the kind of self-control that many of their Kennedy cousins lacked. Jackie accomplished this very, very shrewdly, bringing them up in New York but letting them show the flag at Kennedy functions. She didn't want her children sucked in, and they weren't."

The woman herself seemed to Halberstam to be "not at all nervous or ill at ease, but completely secure in herself. Hers was an uncommon life, and you got the sense that she would not have had it any other way." It was Jackie, after all, who made clear her intentions when she graduated from Miss Porter's School in 1947. Next to "Ambition in Life" she wrote, *"Not to be a housewife."*

That same month Jackie's stepfather, Hugh Auchincloss, died. Ironically, the man Janet had married to rescue herself from Black Jack Bouvier's financial irresponsibility had himself nearly gone broke. The downhill slide began with the 1969–1970 recession, and worsened as Hugh was forced to sell off Merrywood, the family's palatial Virginia estate, to pay off mounting debts. Finally, Hammersmith Farm in Newport was also sold to a group of investors who turned it into a museum. Under the terms of sale, Jackie's mother was allowed to stay in the yellow farmhouse that had served as the servants' quarters near the entrance to the estate. To ensure that Janet Auchincloss would always live comfortably, if perhaps not in the lavish style she had become accustomed to, Jackie set up a $1 million trust in her name.

The dissipation of the once-great Auchin-closs fortune merely strengthened Jackie's resolve to remain independent. Peter Beard claimed that after Ari's death, Jackie had consciously "decided her next move was to prove herself on her own without a man" — hence her new career in publishing. As a signal that she was trying to carve out an identity for herself apart from the powerful men she had been married to, she signed her name "Jacqueline Bouvier Onassis" (not "Jacqueline Kennedy Onassis"), and used the initials JBO.

"Yes, it's correct form, you know," explained Nancy Tuckerman. But according to Emily Post's rules of etiquette, "If she was married for a long time and if she has children, a widow will undoubtedly prefer to keep the name of a man with whom she spent many years and which identifies her with her children." There was little she could do about the Onassis name — he was her last husband. But for Jackie, replacing the Kennedy name with Bouvier was an act of self-assertion.

Not that Jackie was spending very many of her evenings alone. Her list of escorts and suitors was, in the late 1970s and well into the 1980s, longer than it had ever been. One of Jackie's earliest dates after Ari's death was with a man virtually unknown to the American public. On August 20, 1975, Jackie had her first known date with wealthy diamond merchant Maurice Tempelsman. One month younger than Jackie, Tempelsman was born into an Orthodox Jewish family in Antwerp, Belgium. In 1940 the Yiddish-speaking Tempelsmans fled the Nazis for New York, where they settled with other Orthodox Jews on the Upper West Side.

It was in this tight community that Tempelsman met and in 1949 married another refugee from Belgium who was two years his senior, Lily Bucholz. Forgoing college, Maurice joined his father's diamond importing business, Leon Tempelsman & Son, Inc. At the height of the Cold War, Maurice was supplying the U.S. government with diamonds for military and industrial use — making him a vital link between Washington and the diamond suppliers of Africa. In the mid-1950s, he used his attorney Adlai Stevenson to help pave the way, forging important links with the powerful Oppenheimer diamond-mining family as well as a half dozen African heads of state. He soon became a "sightholder" — one of only 160 people in the world allowed to purchase diamonds directly from the De Beers cartel ten times a year.

Casting his lot with the Democrats, Tempelsman contributed heavily to the party. In 1958 one Democrat with his eye on the White House, Jack Kennedy, asked Tempelsman to set up a meeting with those South Africans who virtually controlled the world's diamond supply. It was then that Maurice and Lily Tempelsman became casual friends of the Kennedys, and both would later be frequent guests at the Kennedy White House. They were even invited to the very first state dinner hosted by the Kennedys — the spectacular 1961 candlelit event for Pakistan's President Mohammed Ayub Khan on the lawn at Mount Vernon, overlooking the Potomac.

Maurice was still very much married to Lily when he began taking Jackie out in 1975. The Tempelsmans had three children: Rena, then twenty-one; Leon, nineteen; and Marcy, fourteen. Yet from the beginning Jackie made no attempt to conceal her new-found affection for Tempelsman. For their first date, they went to see the new musical *Chicago*, then lingered over an after-theater supper until 3 A.M. Over the next several months at such high-visibility establishments as La Côte Basque and Lutèce, the two sat close to each other and shared whispered intimacies in French.

"He seems to do most of the talking while Jackie listens and gazes fondly into his eyes," said a witness to several of their cozy tête-à-têtes. "He obviously makes her happy. She's constantly laughing and smiling." One photographer spotted her getting out of his car in front of Lee Radziwill's apartment building when she suddenly turned and kissed Tempelsman — "passionately."

Meantime, Lily held down the fort at the couple's Riverside Drive apartment. When asked what she thought of her husband dating Jackie, Mrs. Tempelsman replied, "We don't comment on our personal friends." But then she said, her voice tinged with sarcasm, "Why don't you ask her?"

Jackie was not eager to remarry, but Tempelsman's status as a married man with children made her somewhat uneasy. Lily was more devoutly Orthodox than her husband, and as such she refused to give him a divorce. As fond as Jackie and Tempelsman were of one another, the relationship cooled — for a time.

As she entered her late forties, Jackie was surprised to discover that the once-antagonistic press had become a willing co-conspirator in her calculated effort to project a new image — that of working woman and single mom. But it soon became clear that the demands of part-time employment, in Vidal's words, "did not exactly cramp her style."

There was the usual number of galas, parties, and openings, and the faces of many of Jackie's escorts were familiar: Peter Duchin, Rohatyn, Tom Hoving, and Karl Katz, the

Metropolitan Museum's Special Project Director alternately described as a "confirmed bachelor" and Jackie's "intellectual boyfriend." After she showed up at one or two functions with George McGovern, there was speculation that he might leave his wife, Eleanor, for Jackie.

Then there was the night Jackie glided onto the dance floor at a Kennedy Center bicentennial ball with Alejandro Orfila, the dashing former Argentine Ambassador to the United States and General Secretary of the Organization of American States. As President Gerald R. Ford, Vice President Nelson Rockefeller, Henry Kissinger, Ted and Rose Kennedy, and half of Washington officialdom looked on, "Jackie swept into the Kennedy Center on Orfila's arm," as one columnist gushed, "in the manner of a beloved queen returning from exile."

The highly touted relationship with Orfila, if there ever really was one, fizzled. In subsequent months, Jackie was linked with heart transplant pioneer Christiaan Barnard, Saudi tycoon Adnan Khashoggi, and NBC executive Karl Killingsworth. No one noticed that, largely away from the prying lens of the paparazzi, Jackie was carrying on a romance with one of the towering entertainment figures of the century.

In 1976 the myth of Camelot remained relatively intact. Details of John F. Kennedy's affair with Marilyn Monroe, of his rampant womanizing, and his ties to the Mafia were yet to shock the American people. It would not be known for at least a year that Frank Sinatra had introduced Mafia moll Judith Campbell (later Judith Campbell Exner) to JFK, and that while Exner was sleeping with the President in the White House she was also the mistress of Chicago crime boss Sam Giancana.

All the public knew then was that Sinatra had mobilized his notorious Rat Pack (consisting of Dean Martin, Sammy Davis Jr., Kennedy brother-in-law Peter Lawford, Joey Bishop, and ex-officio member Shirley MacLaine) and half of Hollywood to get JFK elected President. They also remembered that Frank had produced the 1960 Inauguration Gala (his rendition of the patriotic ballad "The House I Live In" reduced Jackie to tears). Most people had forgotten, if they ever knew, that at Bobby's urging Jack had distanced himself from the Mob-connected singer, causing a permanent rupture in their relationship.

From the beginning, JFK admired Sinatra's success with the opposite sex. "Even though he had his hands full with Marilyn Monroe and all the others," George Smathers said, "Jack still asked about Sinatra and his women. He wanted to know all the details."

Significantly, just as Ari had suspected that Jackie and Sinatra were having an affair in 1972, Jack Kennedy was wary of Old Blue Eyes's intentions. Kennedy, in fact, was always highly suspicious of his wife. "Believe it or not," said Chuck Spalding's wife, Betty, "Jack was jealous of Jackie seeing any other man . . . because he was convinced she was doing the same things he was doing." Oleg Cassini agreed that "Jack was jealous of her," but added that "if she had slept with somebody other than him, it would have been disaster for her."

Yet as First Lady, Jackie had not given the slightest indication that she was interested in Sinatra. On the contrary, Jack told Peter Lawford that Sinatra was welcome at the White House only when Mrs. Kennedy was out of town. "Jackie hates Frank," he told his brother-in-law, "and won't have him in the house."

Still, JFK remained vigilant when it came to Sinatra. "Jack was a jealous guy," Smathers said, "and he didn't like it when Jackie showed too much interest in another man — especially not another man whose interests, shall we say, were so similar to his."

After Onassis's death, Sinatra took Jackie out on a few low-key dates, only to be ambushed by waiting paparazzi. Subsequently, they devised a plan to keep their budding relationship a secret. Jackie and Sinatra met in the early-morning hours at various watering holes around New York — Jimmy Weston's, P. J. Clarke's, and "21" among them. Occasionally, Jackie would go to the theater or the ballet on the arm of one decoy escort only to "bump into" Sinatra at a pre-arranged restaurant or nightclub.

The ploy worked. While newspapers speculated about the nature of her relationships with Katz, Barnard, and even McGovern, Jackie and Sinatra quietly pursued their behind-the-scenes courtship. But among those who knew them, rumors flew. "I remember seeing them go into her apartment quite late at night," Doris Lilly said, "but it didn't really surprise me. Everybody was talking about it."

There is little doubt that Sinatra persisted in his hatred of the Kennedys, but that in Jackie he recognized someone who had also endured much at their hands and managed to survive. "I suppose they reminded each other of happier times, and they were both single at the time," Nancy Dickerson said. "A dalliance, if you will, seemed logical."

In 1976 Frank married Zeppo Marx's widow, Barbara. Years later, while sitting at the bar of a private men's club in Manhattan, Sinatra became emotional as he discussed his feelings for Jackie. "The lady is one class act," he said. "Look at all the crap she has had to put up with in life, and still she can laugh . . . I was in love with her once."

Whatever feelings Sinatra and Jackie may have shared for each other at the time, she had reached a crossroads in her life. "She was simply no longer willing," Baldridge said, "to be dependent on an older man." Jack had been twelve years older than Jackie; Ari twenty-nine years older. Nearly all the other men she had leaned on to varying degrees over the years — Andre Meyer, Roswell Gilpatric, Lord Harlech — were also many years her senior. Sinatra, born the same year as Jack, was simply too old for her now.

By this point in her life, Truman Capote said, "Jackie had lost her taste for domineering older men. She didn't need any more sugar daddies in her life telling her what to do. She wanted to be the one to call the shots for a change, and so she started looking around for some young stuff."

The manner in which Jackie selected her escorts was rather Byzantine. "People would get a signal," Halberstam said, "that she might be interested in going out with a particular person, and then word was relayed to you by her friends and you'd call her up and you'd go out."

One of the most highly publicized of these relationships was with New York *Daily News* columnist Pete Hamill, who at forty-two was five years younger than Jackie. When they began going out in mid-December 1976, the news came as a shock to the woman Hamill had been living with for seven years, Shirley MacLaine. Just seven months earlier, Jackie, escorted by Peter Duchin, had been all smiles at the star-studded opening of MacLaine's one-woman show at Broadway's Palace Theater.

Hamill and MacLaine were apparently on the verge of splitting before Jackie came on the scene. He had wanted to marry the sole female member of Sinatra's Rat Pack, and she preferred the status quo. She saw no reason to end her trans-Pacific open marriage to Tokyo-based producer Steve Parker, her husband since 1954 and the father of her daughter, Sachi.

At first, Hamill was careful to date Jackie only when MacLaine was out of town. "I like Jackie and she likes me," he conceded. "There's nothing clandestine about it. It doesn't alter my relationship with Shirley — things are still the same between us. She knows I'm taking Jackie out."

But as the dates became more and more frequent and the intimate nature of their "friendship" became more and more evident, it became obvious that the Hamill-MacLaine arrangement was in peril. Rohatyn's ex-girlfriend Helene Gaillet said Jackie "runs through men like she runs through clothes . . . She did the same thing to Shirley MacLaine with Pete Hamill. Pete keeps saying that nothing has changed between him and Shirley. Ha! They should ask Shirley how she feels."

For the next several months, Jackie and the journalist were virtually inseparable, popping up at such high-visibility spots as Elaine's, P. J. Clarke's, and the Top of the Tower, where a waiter described her as "terribly engrossed and fascinated" by Hamill. "They never seemed to stop laughing and talking together." At a private screening of the film *Welcome to L.A.* at Manhattan's MGM building, writer Lindsey Van Gelder watched as Jackie talked "in a teeny-tiny whisper, breathlessly asking her date all about the newspaper biz and the big stories of the day." She was "very flirty, all fluttering eyelashes," said another guest seated next to the couple. "You know, playing up to him and making him feel manly."

In addition to his youth and energy, Hamill was Jackie's pipeline to a number of exciting young writers who might be persuaded to write a book. Hamill's own proven talents as a writer added to the attraction, although, in an odd twist of fate, they would prove to be his undoing.

Hamill had been working for the *Daily News*'s chief competitor, the *New York Post*, back when Jackie wed Aristotle Onassis. He had written a piece about the marriage, but decided it was perhaps too caustic and wrote something else instead. The column was filed away. Now that Hamill and Jackie were having a very public affair, however, the *Post*'s publisher, Rupert Murdoch, decided it was the perfect time to run excerpts of the column on Page Six, its widely read gossip section. The excerpts ran for four days under the headline "WHO WROTE THIS?"

"If it were possible to see the Aristotle Onassis–Jackie Kennedy story as a novel, instead of a rather tedious serial, we could understand Onassis's motives," Hamill had written. "But understanding Jackie Kennedy is a more complicated matter. She spent part of her adult life hidden behind the Kennedy publicity machine; she spent another crucial part, after the murder of her husband, enshrined as some national object of veneration.

"She was not, of course, the victim of that veneration; she encouraged it, indulged it, created the desire for more knowledge by cultivating the image of aloofness . . . In a world where men have most of the power and money, many women must use guile, intelligence or feigned submission to exist.

"It is outrageous to think," Hamill continued to rail, "that someone will spend $120,000 a year on clothing in a world where so few people have more than the clothes on their backs. It is obscene that a woman would have more money in a month to use on applying paste to her face and spray to her hair than the average citizen of Latin America could earn in 100 years."

The *Post* ran a photograph of Jackie and Hamill on the fifth day, and pointed out that it was Jackie's new boyfriend — rumored soon to be Mr. Jackie Number 3 — who wrote of her that "no courtesan ever sold herself for more."

The moment the first installment hit the stands, Hamill was on the phone to Jackie with apologies and explanations. She told him she understood, and instead focused her considerable wrath on "that loathsome Rupert Murdoch."

Jackie's reassurances to the contrary, her romance with Hamill began cooling almost immediately. Months later, on November 17, 1977, she caused the customary chaos when she showed up at O'Neal's Balloon restaurant across from Lincoln Center to help celebrate the publication of Hamill's novel *Flesh and Blood*. Both at O'Neal's and later at a private gathering at P. J. Clarke's, Jackie and Hamill barely spoke to each other.

Two days later, Jackie arrived *sans* date at the premiere of the film *The Turning Point*. Along with her social guru Bunny Mellon, Jackie chaired the event, which benefited the

American Ballet Theater. "Farrah Fawcett-Majors was in the TV series *Charlie's Angels* at the time and was a *huge* star — on magazine covers everywhere," Aileen Mehle said. "When she came out of the theater the waiting pack of photographers just went crazy, tripping all over themselves to snap her picture. Then Jackie came out and all of a sudden it was as if poor Farrah didn't exist. Farrah just looked daggers at her. But that's the way it was. Jackie just smiled and smiled while celebrities all around her bit the dust." Another celebrity at the premiere smiling through gritted teeth was one of *The Turning Point*'s principal stars: Hamill's old girlfriend, Shirley MacLaine.

Over the holidays, Jackie maintained her feverish schedule, reverting to old standbys like Brendan Gill, John Sargent, and New York City Commissioner of Cultural Affairs Henry Geldzahler as she ricocheted from one party to another. Andy Warhol was one of those ubiquitous characters she often encountered on her travels through New York's demimonde.

The Pop Art patriarch had his first "really nice talk" with Jackie at a party thrown for author Jean Stein at the Dakota, the legendary neo-Gothic apartment building on Central Park West. CBS founder William S. Paley and his wife, Babe; Norman Mailer;

photographer Richard Avedon; U.N. Ambassador Andrew Young; and Dennis Hopper were among the guests.

Like so many others, Warhol was so awestruck at having his first extended conversation with Jackie that he could not recall much of what was said — "The magic of people in the movies, or something." Warhol did recall Hollywood agent Sue Menger's "running around bragging the same thing that she always brags — that she could offer President Carter a three-picture deal at $3 million a picture and that he'd take it, because *everybody* wants to be in the movies. So I pointed at Jackie and told Sue to go prove it, but she was afraid."

Warhol and his friend Bob Colacello, the journalist, accompanied Jackie and her sister Lee on a daylight excursion to an exhibit of Egyptian artifacts at the Brooklyn Museum. As they walked through the museum corridors, stopping to look at each sarcophagus and hieroglyph, all eyes were on Jackie. "You could hear her name in the air: Jackie . . . Jackie . . . Jackie."

Warhol was amazed at how Jackie "completely ignored all the stares — just screened them out. She existed in her own little vacuum. I guess she had to or she'd go crazy." On this increasingly rare public outing with her sister, Jackie seemed to defer to Lee.

"Lee seemed to know everything there was

to know about the exhibition," Colacello remembered. " 'Oh, look, Jackie,' she would say, 'that bowl is just like the one we saw in the Cairo Museum.' She could list the pharaohs and the dates they ruled. She seemed to have the mind of a curator and the taste of an esthete. Jackie looked at her the way a pupil looks at a teacher, intently, taking it all in. Lee talked. Jackie listened. Lee led and Jackie followed."

Warhol learned on the ride back to Manhattan that Jackie's interests were more in synch with his own. In keeping with Gore Vidal's theory that "celebrities are invariably celebrity-mad," Jackie shared Warhol's well-known passion for gossip.

During the debut of the Austrian Ballet at Lincoln Center a few months earlier, Jackie and Elizabeth Taylor had bumped into each other in the VIP lounge. "The ladies just stared at each other," public relations executive James Mitchell recalled, "so I introduced them. Taylor seemed curious, but neither of them said anything. Superstars rarely do."

In fact, Jackie was the curious one. She knew Warhol had made a cameo appearance in the film *The Driver's Seat* with Elizabeth Taylor. "So, Andy," she asked in her breathless voice, "what's Liz really like?"

Glenn Bernbaum, owner of Mortimer's, another tony Upper East Side hangout, remembered the day Claudette Colbert left the restaurant. Jackie got up from her table and went to Bernbaum. "Was that Claudette Colbert?" she asked, sounding remarkably starstruck. When Bernbaum told her it was, Jackie bounded out onto the sidewalk and introduced herself. "Miss Colbert," she gushed, "my name is Jacqueline Onassis, and I just wanted to say I am a tremendous fan of your work." Even at ninety, Colbert was impressed.

Greta Garbo was another of Jackie's celebrity obsessions. "I saw her today again!" she would tell Nancy Tuckerman. "Just walking by herself. She's so mysterious! This time I followed her for ten blocks before she finally lost me."

Once again Jackie was first among equals at a party held in February of 1978 at the fortresslike Seventh Regiment Armory on Park Avenue to honor the posthumous publication of James Jones's novel *Whistle*. Lauren Bacall and Woody Allen were there. So were Walter Cronkite, Teddy White, superagent Swifty Lazar, William Styron, Art Buchwald, Irwin Shaw, and of course Warhol, to name only a few. Lee Radziwill arrived with her new lover, high-powered lawyer Peter Tufo. Shirley MacLaine, alone, nibbled on canapés and talked about her Academy Award nomination for *The Turning Point*.

The chatter was deafening — until Jackie walked into the room and all talking ceased. MacLaine, hovering over the buffet table, pretended not to notice. "God, I'm starved," she said, reaching for a plate. Lee, no longer a center of attention, slunk behind a potted palm and made her getaway in the elevator — never coming eye to eye with her sister.

Everyone else just froze, too intimidated to approach the icon who had landed among them. For an awkward minute no one, no matter how revered and celebrated in his or her own field, had the temerity to invade the six feet of personal space that separated Jackie from all the other guests. So Jackie simply stood there, alone in the center of the room, until a couple she did not know merely walked up and introduced themselves. There was a fleeting moment of relief on Jackie's face. Now that the ice was broken, the rest of the celebrities began to flock to her.

"Jackie was fully aware of the power she had over people," Kitty Carlisle Hart said, "and she was savvy enough to use it to promote the causes she really believed in." Chief among these continued to be landmark preservation. Jackie had, for example, joined forces with one of the world's wealthiest women, Doris Duke, to protect the historic homes of Newport. But she remained most passionate about preventing a skyscraper from being built over Grand Central station — an act she described as "architectural mutilation."

On April 16, 1978, Jackie led a whistle-stop train expedition to Washington to lobby on behalf of Grand Central. "It's easy to get the impression," said Municipal Art Society Trustee Fred Papert, "that what she brought to the cause was just her celebrity. But before that she was in on the strategy meetings. Showing up at rallies, concerts, train trips was the least of it. She had a very, very clear picture of how things would work. She was a good commanding general."

Years later, a seven-foot aluminum plaque went up in a restored waiting room at Grand Central. The inscription:

> Jacqueline Kennedy Onassis led the fight to save this beautiful terminal. The victory won in the United States Supreme Court in 1978 established the public's right to protect landmarks in cities and towns all over America.

From her historic restoration of the White House to her victory over real estate developers in Manhattan, Jackie had done as much as any individual of her generation to preserve America's architectural heritage. "When Jackie truly believed in something," Salinger said, "she could be fierce." But as she approached her forty-ninth birthday, she was far less certain about the direction her private life should take.

In the wake of her disastrous affair with Hamill, Jackie became enamored of Peter Davis, a forty-one-year-old writer and documentary film producer. The boyish Davis had also known his share of tragedy. Davis had been married to *Time* magazine writer and novelist Johanna "Josie" Mankiewicz, daughter of *Citizen Kane* screenwriter Herman Mankiewicz and niece of the legendary Hollywood producer Joseph Mankiewicz.

In 1974 Davis's wife was walking with their twelve-year-old son through their New York City neighborhood when a taxi jumped the curb. Pushing her son to safety, Josie Davis was struck by the cab and pinned against a mailbox. She died of head injuries.

Not only did Peter Davis bear more than a passing resemblance to Bobby Kennedy, but his brother-in-law, Frank Mankiewicz, had been Bobby's press secretary. Moreover, Davis had won an Academy Award for his controversial Vietnam War documentary *Hearts and Minds*. On their first date, appropriately enough, they had ringside seats at the Robert F. Kennedy Pro Celebrity Tennis Tournament in Forest Hills. "They were sitting close to one another," Jackie-watcher Ron Galella observed, "and she kept whispering into his ear. There was obvious warmth between them."

The following week, they chartered a plane and flew to Hyannis Port. There they holed up alone in the house she had shared with Jack. Four days later, the front gates to the compound swung open and out zoomed Caroline's red BMW with Davis behind the wheel and Jackie in the passenger seat. As she had done a hundred times with JFK, Jackie dropped Davis off at the airport with a kiss, then returned to the compound.

Over the next several months, Jackie and her handsome younger man were inseparable. Davis spent nights on the town and weekends in the country with Jackie, slipping in and out of 1040 Fifth at all hours of the day and night. Ultimately, this, too, ran its course. "I think," said his friend Richard Merryman, "Peter was just grateful for having known her."

If nothing else, the affairs with Hamill and Davis "clearly whetted Jackie's appetite for younger men," Swifty Lazar said. "And why not? She was a very stunning, youthful-looking woman. I never bought that idea that she was not interested in sex. I know for a fact that she had, shall we say, an active personal life."

Not remotely as active, it would turn out, as that of her next lover. In light of the Hamill saga, this new romance would take on an almost incestuous quality.

Before she took her mother's maiden name and shot to movie stardom, Shirley MacLaine was Shirley Beaty, the high-school principal's daughter from Richmond, Virginia. Shirley had a brother who was three years younger, and when he invaded Hollywood he changed his name as well. Little Brother simply added a *t,* to become Warren Beatty.

"No actor of his generation, not Redford or Nicholson, has been a star half as long as Beatty has. Few in the film industry make as much money. No one can do so many of the jobs required to create a successful film as he. In the most visible function, acting, Beatty, unlike Travolta or De Niro, began at the top. He has been a sensation ever since he first appeared on the screen in *Splendor in the Grass* seventeen years ago." Thus, at around the time he began secretly seeing Jackie, *Time* launched its July 3, 1978, cover story on Beatty and the incredible success of his romantic comedy *Heaven Can Wait.*

Notorious as a womanizer even before his first film's release — he carried on simultaneous affairs with Joan Collins, Natalie Wood, and Leslie Caron during the shooting of *Splendor in the Grass* — Beatty went on to some memorable films (*Bonnie and Clyde, McCabe and Mrs. Miller*) and more famous ladies: Julie Christie (Beatty's star in his hugely successful 1975 comeback film

Shampoo), Michelle Phillips of the Mamas and the Papas, Carly Simon, Joni Mitchell, Diane Keaton, and scores of others.

Given his track record, the libidinous star's pursuit of the world's most famous — not to mention most glamorous *and* mysterious — woman came as no surprise to those who knew him. One wag, parodying a then-popular commercial, said, "Warren suffers from the heartbreak of satyriasis."

Even before he became involved with Jackie, Beatty, who had turned down roles in such films as *The Godfather* and *The Sting* to do fund-raising for George McGovern's disastrous presidential bid, was familiar to the Kennedys. While Ted was still married to the long-suffering, alcoholic Joan, he and Beatty shared the same nubile young women sexually — some of whom also enjoyed snorting cocaine with the Senator.

In at least one instance, a Secret Service agent and Ted Kennedy's aide watched as the Senator frolicked nude with one of their mutual girlfriends in Beatty's hot tub. In the tub with them were Beatty, Jack Nicholson, and two *other* women. The aide and the Secret Service men tried not to appear shocked as the three couples leaped out of the water and hastily departed to a back bedroom to make love. When he emerged twenty-five minutes later, wearing a fresh suit and trailed by the girl who divided her time between him and Beatty, Senator Kennedy bellowed, "She's a wild one!"

Once again, Beatty escorted Jackie to a couple of events, and she was spotted whispering into his ear at parties. But the press, aware that Beatty had just ended a long-term relationship with Julie Christie and was now romancing Woody Allen's ex-girlfriend Diane Keaton, dismissed rumors of a Jackie-Warren affair.

Among Hollywood leading men, Beatty was famous for jealously guarding his privacy. Given the level of his self-confessed promiscuity, he had reason to be discreet. But around friends, according to Warhol, Bianca Jagger, and others, Beatty was forthcoming about his conquests. Jackie was no exception. Studio 54 co-owner Steve Rubell put it bluntly. Warren told him and others, Rubell said, "that he fucked Jackie O."

On December 20, Jackie threw a Christmas party at 1040 Fifth and invited loves past and present. Pete Hamill and Beatty, who was there with Keaton, eyed each other warily. At one point Jackie and Beatty were overheard arguing, presumably over what he had divulged about their more intimate moments together. What he had done, she said, was "disgusting."

The other guests at Jackie's Christmas party were charmed — particularly Bob Colacello, whom Warhol brought along. When the butler forgot to bring Colacello his glass of Perrier, she shared hers with him — "it's *ours*," she said.

The next day, Jackie badgered Warhol with phone calls. Finally she reached him at home. Gone was the whispery baby-doll voice. "She sounded so tough," Warhol said.

"Now, Andy, when I invited you, I invited *you* — I didn't invite Bob Colacello," Jackie said, adding that she was upset because "he writes things." Caroline, Warhol then remembered, had made a similar remark at the party. If Jackie had been kind to Colacello at the party, it was merely to mask her distrust.

Warhol reassured her that Colacello would not write anything, but as he hung up it was obvious from the tone of her voice that Jackie was still concerned. "So something," Warhol determined, "must have happened there she doesn't want written about." That something, close friends later confirmed, was Jackie's bitter confrontation with Beatty.

Initially, Jackie reacted by plunging into her work at Doubleday. Mornings she would take a cab or walk to Doubleday's Park Avenue headquarters three blocks north of Grand Central, bringing along carrots and celery sticks neatly wrapped in tinfoil to nibble at the desk in her windowless office. "It was strictly all business when she went to

Doubleday," Tuckerman said. "There were no frills, no preferential treatment."

Jackie had fun with the notion that she was no different than any other worker. "Like everybody else," she said with mock seriousness, "I have to work my way up to an office with a window."

In February of 1979, Jackie appeared on the cover of *Ms.* magazine. As a favor to her friend Gloria Steinem, Jackie wrote the cover story defending working mothers. "What has been so sad for many women of my generation," Jackie wrote, "is that they weren't supposed to work if they had families. There they were, with the highest education, and what were they to do when the children were grown — watch the raindrops coming down the windowpane? Leave their fine minds unexercised? Of course women should work if they want to."

It was journalism that first appealed to Jackie — "being a reporter seems a ticket out to the world" — but now, she said, she would not choose it as a career. "Journalism," she explained, "has variety, but doesn't allow you to enter different worlds in depth, as book publishing does."

Sister Lee Radziwill was still searching for her place in the world. After her abortive attempt at acting, she launched her own interior design business. After she was commissioned to redecorate the elegant

Huntington Hotel atop San Francisco's Nob Hill, Lee became engaged to the hotel's dashing owner, Newton Cope.

The last week in April, Jackie invited Lee and Newton to a dinner party at 1040 Fifth. Before he left San Francisco, Cope, who was worth about $10 million, was pressured by friends not to go through with the wedding. "How can you go with that woman?" they asked. "She and her sister are the two worst piranhas in the United States." Cope said, "They told me Lee would chew me up and spit me out."

At Jackie's, Lee, according to Cope, was terrified of her sister. "Her reaction every time Jackie spoke," Cope said, "was like her mother was about to spank her. It was as if Jackie controlled her. I could feel the tension, the vibes going between them — it was Lee, not Jackie. It was quite obvious that Jackie intimidated her."

That evening, Jackie told them she would not be able to attend their wedding in San Francisco because of a previous engagement. Her dear friend, the philanthropist Brooke Astor, was throwing a party at the River Club. But she did wish the happy couple the best.

According to Cope, Jackie's lawyer Alexander Folger called the following day and tried to pressure him into signing a prenuptial agreement. Cope agreed to a flat $1 million payment in the event he died or they divorced, but that was not enough. Jackie also wanted her sister to get at least $15,000 a month during the marriage.

"I'm not buying a cow or a celebrity the way Onassis did!" Cope shouted at the lawyer. "I am in love with this woman." Cope was convinced Jackie was behind the last-minute demands for money. "She had just gone through that whole deal with Onassis, and she thought, 'What the hell, I'll get my little sister taken care of too.' . . . Lee wasn't as money-hungry as Jackie."

As it turned out, Lee had independently sought Jackie's advice in coming up with an appropriate figure. *People* magazine went to press reporting that Lee Radziwill had married Newton Cope in San Francisco on May 3. Unfortunately for the magazine's editors, the wedding was called off one hour before the ceremony.

Hours later, Aileen Mehle walked into Brooke Astor's party at the River Club. "The first person I saw was Jackie," Mehle said. "I went straight up to her and said, 'Look what Sister has done!' "

"What?" Jackie asked.

"She has called off her wedding to Newton Cope."

"Oh, my God!" Jackie gasped. "*That* takes guts."

In truth, Cope, not Lee, called the wedding off. That did not stop them, however, from going ahead with their planned two-week Caribbean honeymoon at La Samanna on St. Martin, where Jackie had vacationed with John and Caroline only two weeks earlier. "We had," Lee told Jackie, "a *marvelous* time."

Over a period of sixteen years at Doubleday, Jackie would edit seventy-four books — and not just the elegant, eye-popping coffee-table pictorials that marked her tenure at Viking. Her Doubleday titles ranged from children's books by her friend Carly Simon to memoirs (Martha Graham, Gelsey Kirkland) and biographies (Napoleon, Marie Antoinette, Jean Harlow, Chicago Mayor Richard Dalcy, Czar Nicholas II), to critically acclaimed fiction (*The Cairo Trilogy*, *Call the Darkness Light*), to best-selling nonfiction (*The Power of Myth*, *Healing and the Mind*).

While her salary never topped $50,000, Jackie's three-day-per-week job did have its perks. Unlike overworked editors who seldom had the time or energy to leave their offices — much less the country — Jackie viewed her job as a passport to the world. At company expense, she traveled to such exotic locales as Russia, China, the Middle East, India, and Eastern Europe — all trips ostensibly to gather information or confer with authors, and all either tax-deductible or charged to the company as a business expense.

Just as Jack Kennedy and Jackie had carefully compartmentalized their lives so that one category of friends would never cross paths with another, Jackie kept her working and social lives separate. Co-workers who encountered Jackie at a party could not expect to be introduced to her socially superior friends. In the evenings, she sometimes pointedly ignored those she labored shoulder to shoulder with during daylight hours.

Yet there was an undeniable camaraderie between Jackie and her co-workers. At the office she was relaxed and casual, again sitting cross-legged on the floor as she rearranged photos like so many jigsaw pieces. Once the puzzle was finished, she would blow into her large hands, rub them together with obvious glee, and incongruously shout, "Hot spit!"

She worked with her office door opened, cribbed cigarettes, sat in the stairwell during fire drills, stood in line at the coffee wagon, and brought sliced ham and potato salad to company picnics. She had not lost her mischievous streak. "If she had someone into her office who was haughty and arrogant," Doubleday Deputy Publisher Bill Barry said, "Jackie was capable of doing a pretty fair imitation after the meeting."

Jackie came to consider a chosen few —

notably Steve Rubin, Lisa Drew, Nancy Tuckerman, Shaye Areheart, and later her editorial assistants Scott Moyers and Bruce Tracy — as members of her tight "little family."

When Tracy had the opportunity to go to Europe for the first time, he went to Jackie and asked if she minded his missing the publication party for the book they were working on, *The Last Tsar*. "She looked at me like I had two heads," Tracy recalled. " 'Of course you go,' she said. 'Life comes first.' "

"For someone with her finishing-school background," Teddy White once remarked, "there's an awful lot of Jewish mother in Jackie." More than once, Jackie scolded her co-workers for coming to work in the dead of winter without wearing a hat ("You'll catch your death of cold" were her actual words, according to Tuckerman). No one had the courage to point out that JFK had almost single-handedly killed the men's hat industry by refusing to wear one even in subfreezing temperatures. Or that, as she nervously chain-smoked in her office, she was doing more damage to her lungs and those of the people around her than anyone who chose to go bare-headed.

During flu season, she walked around the office with a bottle of TheraFlu, dispensing it freely. Other times, she referred co-workers to her doctor. Describing Jackie as "a sort of mother figure to us all," Moyers recalled that when he was struck by a drunk driver and "shredded" his knee, Jackie said to him gently, "Now listen, Scott, if you need to borrow a few bucks . . . Your family isn't in New York . . ." Moyers was touched, but politely declined his friend's offer.

As she approached her half-century mark, Jackie had never looked more fit or more radiantly beautiful. Yet when she studied herself in the mirror, she was not satisfied. She asked Dr. Lax if he would refer her to a plastic surgeon for a face-lift and Lax refused. With the exception of a few crow's-feet and perhaps an almost imperceptible puffiness in the eyes, she had somehow managed to hold the aging process in check.

Lax did refer his patient to New York plastic surgeon Dr. John Conley for a minor "eye job" — in this case a minimal procedure that involved removing excess fat and skin from the upper and lower eyelids. Jackie underwent the surgery at St. Vincent's Hospital in downtown New York, where she registered under the name of "Mrs. Lancaster."

The effect was so subtle that no one made note of the change. Jackie, whose eyes were invariably hidden behind those custom-made dark glasses anyway, merely looked "refreshed," the overall impression Dr. Conley had promised.

A few days before she turned fifty, Jackie smiled and gamely posed for photographs at the publication party for Nancy Zaroulis's *Call the Darkness Light.* Zaroulis's moving tale of nineteenth-century women working in the textile mills of Lowell, Massachusetts, was the first work of fiction acquired by Jackie for Doubleday. Not surprisingly, Zaroulis was practically knocked to the floor as reporters tried to get past the author to get their picture taken with her editor. Zaroulis did not mind: Because of the attention Jackie drew to the book, she earned close to $1 million in foreign sales and paperback rights alone. Until the party, the two women had never met.

Earlier, Jackie had walked into Doubleday's store at 53rd Street and Fifth Avenue and gone straight up to the suite on the fourth floor. "Oh, it's sooooo hot," she said as she came into the air-conditioned room, fanning herself with a press release. Only the hands — "slightly gnarled," as one guest ungallantly put it — gave any indication of Jackie's true age.

When Zaroulis arrived, Jackie took her hand. "Are you excited?" Jackie gushed. Before her author could say a word, Jackie said, "You're so pretty."

"May I say — so are you," Zaroulis answered.

Jackie posed for more pictures, waved to

agents and editors with a friendly "Hi!" She embraced a chosen few. Then Jackie lit up a cigarette in a long holder and began chatting with a delegation from *Publishers Weekly*. A dazed waiter brought her a gin and tonic. When it was all over, author and editor literally linked arms to get past the paparazzi to a taxi. They were "shoved and pushed around, but Jackie just remained perfectly calm, looking straight ahead, not reacting at all." Later, someone suggested Zaroulis might use Jackie's life as the basis for her next novel. "It would take a genius," Zaroulis said, "to make anyone believe it."

On October 20, 1979 — nearly sixteen years after Dallas — Jackie journeyed to the Boston suburb of Dorchester for the dedication of the John F. Kennedy Library. I. M. Pei's stark white futuristic structure with its high glass walls looking out over the sparkling waters of Dorchester Bay reflected JFK's eternally youthful, forward-looking appeal.

It also reflected Jackie's exquisite taste. She had been so involved from the beginning that contractors, landscapers, electricians, and others working on the building scattered whenever she paid a surprise visit. At one point, Jackie decided that polished stones that had been placed along the water's edge looked "cheesy" and ordered them removed. When she came back the next day and found them still there, one subcontractor recalled that she "really chewed us out. She threw tantrums about one thing or another all the time. It got so when one of the guys spotted her, everybody hid."

Yet Jackie's vision prevailed. Rather than overwhelm the visitor with musty minutiae, she sought to re-create the Kennedy White House with scaled-down replicas of the Oval Office and other rooms in the Executive Mansion. The library was also ahead of its time in the use of both audio and video to conjure up the Camelot mood.

The library also offered vast resources for researchers: virtually everything written, said, and photographed about Kennedy and his administration — provided, of course, that it met with the approval of the Kennedys themselves. A small part of the library was also dedicated to preserving Bobby's memory — too small a part, his offspring would bitterly complain.

The dedication ceremony that autumn was more than just a chance to pay homage to Jack and gather together survivors of the New Frontier for a reunion. It was an opportunity for Ted, who had his eye on wresting the Democratic Party nomination away from President Carter in 1980, to declare himself as the rightful heir to Jack's legacy.

Rose was home recovering from a hernia operation, but twenty-eight of her twenty-nine grandchildren attended the dedication. Jackie and Ethel sat squinting in the brilliant sunshine with the siblings — Ted, Eunice, Pat, and Jean.

Jimmy Carter was also on hand to speak, and as he approached the podium he shook hands with members of the Kennedy family and survivors of both Jack's New Frontier and Bobby's Impossible Dream, who had gathered to honor their fallen leaders. As he approached Jackie, Carter, whom she had never met, leaned over and kissed her on the cheek. "The former First Lady," said Ted's aide Richard Burke, who was sitting only a few feet away, "recoiled as if bitten by a snake. My eyes met the Senator's. I heard someone behind me whisper, 'I can't believe he just did that.' " Added ABC's Sam Donaldson, "I swear to God, I thought she was going to deck him."

After the ceremony, Jackie remarked to Arthur Schlesinger Jr., "Isn't that strange the way we hardly know each other, and the President kissed me? I suppose he thought it was *droit du seigneur.*" Explained Schlesinger: "That was an old feudal right of the lord of the manor to have his way with the serfs' wives! She was *very* angry that Carter had been so presumptuous as to kiss her."

Caroline, now twenty-two, sat next to her brother. Thanks to her mother's unrelenting pressure to lose weight, she was now an exercise and diet fanatic. The results were plainly evident. When she stood up, the assembled crowd was surprised to see that she had turned into, in Andy Warhol's words, "a raving beauty" — all teeth and cheekbones and windblown chestnut tresses.

She was also painfully shy. The press had not bothered Caroline at Radcliffe, and it was all she could do now to muster up the courage to stand up in front of all these dignitaries and introduce her younger brother. Not yet nineteen and already standing a broad-shouldered six feet one inch tall, John was a strikingly handsome cross between the Kennedys and the Bouviers. As he stepped to the podium, he also seemed to inherit the natural poise of both parents. As a tribute to his father, he read Stephen Spender's poem "I Think Continually of Those Who Were Truly Great."

As JFK's widow and their children left the library that day, the wind ripped at the sails of Jack's boat the *Victura*, which would remain on display outside the library. They stopped next to the boat for a moment, and John whispered to his mother. "You know," he said, "I don't even remember him. Sometimes I think I might, but . . . I don't."

Jackie put her hand on John's shoulder. Then, slowly, she led him toward their waiting car.

If you bungle raising your children, I don't think whatever else you do well matters very much.

— *Jackie*

NINE

Jackie had never been happier. For the first time in her life, she had a sense of her own worth as an individual; she was no longer defined by the man at her side. By the same token, she was beginning to enjoy her own fame. Over lunch, the conductor André Previn asked if it bothered her that she was being stared at. "That's why I always wear my dark glasses," she explained. "It may be that they're looking at me, but none of them can ever tell which ones I'm looking back at. That way I can have fun with it!" (Accordingly, a Doubleday editor in desperate need of a pencil opened her desk drawer and found it filled with sunglasses.)

Another time, Jackie and Doubleday executive Bill Barry rushed to catch the shuttle to Washington and managed to board at the last minute. The plane was full, and as they made their way to their seats in the back, people began to crane their necks and peer over their headrests. They turned to see all eyes on them, as Jackie said to her traveling companion, "Oh, Bill, they all know you!"

She was not always so easygoing. Robin

Leach, host of television's *Lifestyles of the Rich and Famous*, remembered getting ready to board the same shuttle and spotting Jackie. It was the week phone calls went from a dime to a quarter, and "Jackie was trying to make a call to her psychiatrist on East 63rd Street. We were running late — she wanted the psychiatrist to hold her appointment. She kept putting in dimes. She tried two other phones. Finally, I gave her a quarter. Then I managed to wangle a seat beside her on the plane."

Leach tried to strike up a conversation. "I've learned," she said, looking him in the eye, "that every Englishman in America is a reporter. Therefore, I will not enter into a conversation."

As the wife of two powerful men, she had been drawn mothlike to the flame of celebrity as a way of validating her own existence. For Jack, she had won votes and dazzled heads of state. For Ari, at least in the early years of their marriage, she had fulfilled her duties as the ultimate trophy wife.

Not long after her marriage to Onassis, Jackie told Aileen Mehle, "Once I read that I stood on the deck of the *Christina*, laughing as I tossed jewelry overboard! After that article, I stopped reading anything about me."

The novelist Louis Auchincloss, a distant

cousin by marriage, thought "Jackie showed an ambivalent attitude towards the press, which had brought her both fame and pain." Now Jackie seemed to be enjoying her celebrity on her own terms. She voraciously devoured every syllable written about her, going so far as to instruct her maid to purchase tabloids like the *National Enquirer* and the *Star* so that she could peruse them. All references to Jackie were methodically circled in red. At times, she scrawled her own editorial comments in the margins — most often "HA!," "REALLY?," or a bold exclamation point.

"You should see that woman!" Lee said of her sister. "She wakes up in the morning and goes through all the newspapers looking for her name, and if she doesn't find it, she just throws them all away, and when she sees her name, she cuts it out immediately!"

Yet Jackie did worry about her children. She felt an obligation to their father to make sure that they found their place in the world. "If Jack turned out to be the greatest President of the century and his children turned out badly," she said, "it would be a tragedy."

At the dawn of the 1980s, Jackie and Caroline carefully nurtured their memories of John F. Kennedy. Like her mother, Caroline, who gradually came to see herself as a defender of her father's legacy, still collected JFK memorabilia: stamps, coins, statues, plaques, banners, flags, books — knick-knacks and mementos of every conceivable variety. She also continued to cut pictures of her father out of newspapers and magazines, just as she had done when she was a little girl back in Sister Joanne Frey's religion class.

John did none of these things. Caroline could look at the famous photographs of the two children crawling beneath Daddy's desk, or dancing as JFK clapped in the Oval Office, or waving good-bye as he took off from the White House lawn in his helicopter, and the memories flooded back. John, who was barely three when his father was killed, looked at the same images and felt oddly detached. For years, he would say publicly that he remembered these things, and at times a memory did surface. One day Chuck Spalding walked in the room when John was taping one of his father's recordings — a tribute to Eleanor Roosevelt — for school. "Listen! Right in here is where I crawl under the desk and Dad kicks me," he told Spalding. "It's coming up now. Here it is. He was talking on the radio and I crawled under the desk and grabbed him."

Such epiphanies were few and far between. As he grew to manhood John ultimately conceded that he viewed his father "through the color of others and the perception of others and through photographs and what we've read." Even the heart-tugging photo of John-John saluting his father's coffin — one of the most famous of all time — evoked no memories.

Jackie had backed John's decision to go to Brown University instead of Harvard; she realized that at Harvard her son would be totally submerged in the Kennedy myth. At Brown, John studied his father and his administration like any other student, taking a seminar course on the Vietnam War. He prevailed on his mother, who had always encouraged her children to find out as much as they could about their father from as many sources as possible, to have Peter Davis bring his film *Hearts and Minds* to class.

It was the theater, not world affairs or politics, that most intrigued young John. Beginning with his first appearance at age eleven as Fagin in a Collegiate production of the musical *Oliver!*, John, in the words of his cousin David, was "badly bitten by the acting bug."

At Phillips Academy, it was obvious *Petticoats and Union Suits* was not just another student production when it was reviewed by *The New York Times*. The venerable newspaper's theater critic wrote that "one can't help be aware of the fifteen-year-old John Kennedy in his role, although like the others in his celebrated family, he seems to be trying painfully to avoid special attention." Two years later, he co-starred with his first serious girlfriend, Jenny Christian, in *Comings and Goings* at Phillips, and then in a 1978 production of *A Comedy of Errors*.

John was nineteen when he played the Jack Nicholson role in Ken Kesey's *One Flew over the Cuckoo's Nest*. He did such a convincing job that in the scene where John's character is suffocated, Jackie, who was sitting in the audience, became visibly distressed. "She had sort of a hard time with it," said a student who was watching her. "She was gasping."

At Brown, the critic for the school newspaper gave twenty-year-old John a glowing review for his role in Ben Jonson's *Volpone*, but later retracted it because he had been unduly influenced by Jackie's presence in the audience. As an undergraduate, John would have major roles in plays ranging from *The Tempest* and David Rabe's *In the Boom Boom Room* (where his new crew cut caused a bigger stir than the student actress who went topless to play his go-go-dancer girlfriend) to J. M. Synge's classic *Playboy of the Western World*, to Miguel Piñero's *Short Eyes*, in which John played a child molester.

Although Jackie had dutifully attended most of his college productions, she made it clear that she did not approve. "His mother laid down the law," said a Brown classmate. "She told John in no uncertain terms that acting was beneath him, that he was his father's son and that he had a tradition of public service to uphold." Mother and son "really had terrible fights over this. John is pretty good at controlling his temper, but there were times when he talked about his mother when he just lost it. What he wanted from her was respect, and for a while there he just didn't feel as if he had it."

When *Saturday Night Fever* producer Robert Stigwood offered him the chance to play his father in a feature film based on JFK's early years, John badly wanted to accept. He begged his mother to let him take the role, but Jackie put her foot down. She wanted him to finish college. "And then can I do anything I want?" he asked.

"Anything," she answered, "but act."

It remained to be seen whether JFK Jr. ever got over his love of acting. After he graduated from Brown, he and his then-girlfriend Christina Haag played doomed lovers in *Winners* by Brian Friel, a production of Manhattan's Irish Arts Center. Jackie and Caroline, both adamant that he not pursue a show-business career, pointedly refused to attend. Moreover, Jackie insisted that there be no reviews or reviewers.

"John is an extraordinary and very talented young actor," said the Irish Arts Center's Sandy Boyen. John, said Boyen, "could have a very successful stage and film career if he wanted it." Added Boyen's associate Nye Heron, "Evidently, that's not going to happen." (Years later, John would make his film debut delivering two lines as a "guitar-playing Romeo" in *A Matter of Degrees*.)

At Brown, John chafed under his mother's iron-fisted authority. "His mother would come up and visit and it was obvious they had a very warm relationship," said another classmate who became a well-known journalist. "It was also obvious that she ran the show and he was not always happy about that. There was a lot of friction under the surface that people just don't know about. He wanted her to take him seriously, to treat him like an adult, the way she treated Caroline. But she didn't. Jackie was a stern taskmaster."

During this time, John, like so many of his classmates, sampled drugs. No sooner had Jackie left his eighteenth birthday party at New York's Le Club than John and his friends from Phillips Academy lit up joints. They remained at the club smoking and drinking tequila until dawn. A *National Enquirer* photographer accosted them as they tried to leave undetected and a scuffle ensued. John ended up sprawled on the pavement.

Pot was his drug of choice, but John did

experiment for a time with stronger substances. At one party, John was present when his friends allegedly passed around a tiny silver straw and an ashtray filled with cocaine. Each time someone took a hit, a little more of the design on the bottom of the ashtray was revealed. As it was finally handed to John, everyone shuddered at what they saw on the bottom of the ashtray — the face of John Fitzgerald Kennedy staring up at them, with the years 1917–1963 printed below. There was a pause reminiscent of the moment Jackie looked at JFK's face on the matchbook cover. Then John, according to one witness, "saw what was on the ashtray and took it anyway."

"Despite those expcricncces and the reckless seam that ran deep through the Kennedy nature," said Kennedy biographer Wendy Leigh, "he had a powerful inner compass that ultimately steered him away from excess."

Certainly both JFK Jr. and Caroline were model citizens compared to their wild cousins. This was no accident. Jackie had been careful to keep them away from the Kennedys who seemed to be constantly getting busted for one transgression or another. When Ethel called to invite Caroline and John to spend two weeks at Hickory Hill, Jackie declined. "Jackie said, 'No way,' " Richard Burke said. "With all that stuff going on at Hickory Hill — especially with the problems the boys were having — Jackie just didn't want Caroline and John there."

Burke soon learned that Jackie wasn't the only family member who forbade her children to visit Hickory Hill. One day when he was chauffeuring Caroline, Maria Shriver, and Sydney Lawford to the Shrivers' Maryland estate, Burke heard the girls "saying what a mess [Bobby's kids] all were and how their mothers wouldn't let them go near Hickory Hill. There was definitely a hands-off attitude on the part of those three mothers — Eunice, Jackie, and Pat." (Still, when Ethel was supposedly running "short of funds" and the rain was pouring through holes in the roof at Hickory Hill, Jackie was the only family member who offered to help. "I will buy Ethel a new roof," she told Rose Kennedy's nephew Joe Gargan. "This is ridiculous." So, said Rose's secretary Barbara Gibson, "Ethel got a new roof courtesy of Jackie.")

Oddly, it was the solid, dependable Caroline who came closest to becoming embroiled in the dangerous antics of Bobby's tribe. Bobby and Ethel's son David, a twenty-eight-year-old Harvard dropout, made regular trips to Harlem to feed his heroin addiction. On August 25, 1984, his body was found in Palm Beach's Brazilian Court Hotel. He had died after injecting himself with cocaine, the tranquilizer Mellaril, and the painkiller Demerol (which he had stolen from his grandmother Rose, who was prescribed the medication for a heart condition).

But no illegal drugs were found at the death scene, and tests indicated that the other drugs had been flushed down the toilet. After examining all the evidence, Palm Beach investigators concluded that someone may have tried to clean up the death scene.

The morning his body was found, Caroline, who had been close to David, arrived at the Brazilian Court and went looking for him. Later, someone identifying herself only as "Mrs. Kennedy from Boston" called and asked the front desk to have someone check up on David. When Bell Captain Douglas Moschiano went to the room, he found David's clothed body.

Caroline and Sydney Lawford, Peter and Pat's daughter, then arrived. When they were told David was dead, Sydney broke down but Caroline did not react at all. The family closed ranks immediately. Authorities were frustrated by the young women's reluctance to answer questions.

In depositions, the bell captain was asked if anyone could have gotten into David's room before he discovered the body.

"Could have been Caroline Kennedy," he said. "She called the room; there was no answer. She walked back toward the room, knocked on the door; this is what I heard. This is when I saw her coming out from the south wing area."

Caroline insisted that she was never in the vicinity of David's room, much less inside it. Local law enforcement decided not to pursue the issue, and Caroline returned to New York. The episode marked the one and only time she came close to being dragged into a Kennedy scandal.

Had it turned out that Caroline had cleaned up the crime scene in some ill-conceived effort to protect David's name, Jackie would have blamed herself. She had carefully orchestrated the Kennedys' involvement in her children's lives, taking the good but scrupulously avoiding the tawdry.

"One of the big decisions Jackie made in her life was to get her children the hell out of Hyannis Port and away from the Kennedys," Peter Duchin said. "The cousins were left to their own devices, and she knew it could only spell trouble. It was something she worried about all the time. I remember one summer Jackie sent John on a diving expedition to Micronesia just to keep him away from the Kennedy kids. She said to me, 'Do you think that's far enough away?' "

She also tried to manipulate her children's love lives — especially John's. To begin with, Jackie made a point of screening all her son's calls. Whenever someone telephoned the apartment asking for him, the routine was the same.

"Who's calling? What is this for?" And, in the nine out of ten instances when she did not approve, "He's not available."

Jackie approved of Jenny Christian, who met John when he was sixteen and remained his steady girlfriend for four years. She went off to major in psychology at Harvard, and gradually they drifted apart. "If he had fallen out of a pickup truck, he still would have been irresistible to me," she later said. "He was extremely handsome, nice, and sweet. It was a great romance."

Jenny was replaced by Caroline lookalike Sally Munroe, who also received Jackie's stamp of approval. After an on-again, off-again romance that stretched over several years, Munroe was replaced by another Jackie favorite, Christina Haag. The daughter of a wealthy marketing executive and a graduate of Manhattan's exclusive Brearly School, the lushly beautiful Haag had known John since they were both fifteen, but their romance took off at Brown. Their tumultuous romance would last until a willowy blond movie star stole him away in 1988.

Meantime, Caroline proved less of a challenge for Jackie. Her one serious relationship — with Yale-educated aspiring screenwriter

Tom Carney — broke up shortly before Caroline graduated from Radcliffe in 1980. His ego, he confessed, would not survive his being labeled "Mr. Caroline Kennedy." Moving back to New York, she went to work in the Metropolitan Museum's Film and Television Department. Although her mother's massive apartment was located across the street from the museum — only steps from her office — Caroline preferred to set up housekeeping in a small West Side apartment with two roommates and take the bus.

It was at the museum where Caroline met Edwin Arthur Schlossberg, a self-styled cultural historian–artist–author, an acolyte of Buckminster Fuller's, and founder of a small company that produced multimedia video projects for museums and businesses. The son of a wealthy Manhattan-based textile manufacturer, the prematurely gray Schlossberg was also Jewish and thirteen years Caroline's senior.

Schlossberg earned a Ph.D. at Columbia in science and literature; his doctoral thesis consisted of an imaginary chat between Samuel Beckett and Albert Einstein. Gibberish, it nonetheless impressed some of Schlossberg's admirers on the faculty as academically daring.

Schlossberg's veneer of erudition masked what appeared to be a checkered career. After a brief stint writing novelty books and doggerel, he tried designing T-shirts before embarking on a career as a conceptual artist. When that didn't work, he started his multimedia business — an enterprise that was still struggling to get off the ground when he met Caroline.

Given the size of his father's fortune, it hardly mattered. Jackie's daughter was smitten. "Caroline likes funny people," Andy Warhol mused after she told him they were a couple. "He probably was babbling intellectually and she got fascinated. He was probably saying strange peculiar quotations or something." After a party in Aspen in December of 1981, Warhol noted in his diary, "Saw Caroline and the Schlossberg boy. They're madly in love."

Before long, Caroline was spending most nights at Schlossberg's million-dollar loft in SoHo. Ed had even taken to redesigning Caroline's look. She surprised the guests at her twenty-seventh birthday party by showing up in uncharacteristically slinky yellow-and-black silk pajamas. "Ed picked that out for her," a friend said. "He buys most of her clothes."

Janet Auchincloss was mortified at Caroline's choice. Three years after Hugh's death, Janet had married her childhood friend Bingham Morris, a rich (of course) investment banker. Now she learned that, as her daughter became increasingly enamored of Maurice Tempelsman, her granddaughter was involved with Ed Schlossberg. The trouble was, her devoutly Catholic offspring had both fallen in love with men from Orthodox Jewish families.

"Hugh Auchincloss was an old-fashioned Republican Club anti-Semite," said his stepson Gore Vidal. "The first question he'd always ask when he met someone was, 'Do you know what Kirk Douglas's real name is?' But Hughdie was an anti-Semite of the reflex variety. He told stories about Jews the same way he told stories about Blacks and so on."

It is doubtful that the Scottish-American Hugh Auchincloss could have held a candle in that department to the Kennedy family patriarch. While serving as the United States Ambassador to the Court of St. James prior to World War II, the famously anti-Semitic Joe Kennedy was openly sympathetic toward Hitler and the Nazis — a position that turned the British people against the entire Kennedy family and forced an infuriated FDR to recall him. "Mr. Kennedy is a very foul specimen of double-crosser and defeatist," Lord Halifax cabled the new Prime Minister, Winston Churchill. "He thinks of nothing but his own pocket. I hope this war will at least see the elimination of his type."

Bobby, Jackie's soulmate and lover after

Dallas, inherited his father's anti-Semitic streak. A Civil Rights champion in the 1968 presidential campaign, Bobby nonetheless had been heard to scream such stinging epithets as "Jew bastard!" at those who crossed him.

Joe and Bobby had been the most important men in Jackie's life next to Jack and her own father. Surely she must have heard their ethnic slurs periodically, if not on a more or less routine basis. There is no account of her offering a word of protest. Between the "restricted" country clubs of East Hampton and riding to the hounds with Virginia bluebloods, she lived in a world that was as gentile as it was genteel.

Yet Jackie's marriage to Onassis had, as she told her friend Vivian Crespi, freed her from the narrow mental confines of the world she had known and opened her eyes to new horizons, new possibilities. At her Christmas party in 1981, Jackie welcomed Ed warmly and led him around the room. "I want to introduce you to somebody," she said in her little-girl whisper. "I want you all to meet my daughter's new friend, Ed Schlossberg." She now was not only capable of giving her blessing to Caroline's dating an Orthodox Jew, she encouraged the relationship. She had, after all, come at long last to the realization that she was deeply in love with one herself.

Maurice Tempelsman was not Jewish enough, however, for his wife, Lily. Whereas Maurice no longer regularly went to temple, Lily attended Synagogue weekly and strictly adhered to a Kosher diet. Despite the fact that his affair with Jackie had become highly public, Maurice still technically resided with Lily at their Riverside Drive apartment. Perhaps to gain some insight into her own strange predicament, Lily returned to graduate school. As it became painfully clear that she had lost her husband to Jackie, Lily, apparently oblivious to the sad irony, went to work as a marriage counselor at the Jewish Board of Family and Children's Services.

Up until 1980, there had been a reluctance on the part of the press to acknowledge the possibility of a romance between Jackie and the pudgy, balding, Jewish, and married Tempelsman. Coming on the heels of her highly publicized romances with the significantly younger Hamill and Davis (not to mention her secret liaisons with Sinatra and Beatty), it was easier to believe that the diamond merchant was merely a friend who offered her valuable financial advice.

Years earlier, when New York City teetered on the brink of default, Jackie went to Tempelsman in a panic. If the city did go broke, she stood to lose millions. After the crisis passed, Tempelsman continued to oversee her financial affairs, and would wind up parlaying Jackie's $26 million settlement from Onassis into a $100-million-plus fortune (some published estimates put Jackie's fortune as high as $200 million). On the side, he quietly arranged for John Jr. to spend the summer of 1980 in South Africa learning the ropes of the diamond business — just in case he might someday be interested in entering the Tempelsman family trade.

With the exception of a few close friends, no one picked up on Jackie's new romance as she campaigned for Ted Kennedy. Believing that Carter was too unpopular to ever defeat likely Republican challenger Ronald Reagan, Ted pursued his bid to trounce Carter in the primaries. "We knew that Jackie, Caroline, and John Jr. would be available for only a handful of occasions," Kennedy's aide Rick Burke said, "so we determined to play these trump cards when the stakes were high. Jackie, in particular, was our greatest draw at important fund-raisers." Comparing Jackie with Ted's wife, Joan, who was battling alcoholism: "With Joan, they come to make sure she's sober. With Jackie, it's different. She comes in like visiting royalty, looking elegant and beautiful, has a drink, and goes. People are thrilled just to get a glance at her."

Typical was her appearance before a group of fifteen hundred Greek Americans in the ballroom of a Queens Hotel. "Oh, I'm so homesick," Jackie said, alluding to her life on Skorpios. "I'm just so happy to be among Greek Americans." At most of the dozen or so fund-raisers she attended in the entire course of the campaign, Jackie did not even say this much. Unlike First Lady Roslyn Carter, who spoke on behalf of her husband wherever she went, Jackie stuck to smiling, sipping champagne, shaking hands, and, if the spirit moved her, signing autographs. "Jackie's presence," said a Kennedy insider, "*is* her statement."

Not even Jackie, however, could convince Democratic voters to abandon Carter for Ted. Carter went on to win the nomination but lose the general election to Reagan. When Reagan was shot and seriously wounded by John Hinckley on March 30, 1981, Jackie was horrified — and relieved that Teddy was not now occupying the White House. "She was very kind to me when my husband was shot, and we didn't know whether he was going to live," Nancy Reagan said. "She wrote a very sweet, sensitive note and called me. She couldn't have been nicer at a time when I really needed it."

Nancy Reagan made no secret of the fact that, in her role as First Lady, she saw herself as the logical successor to Jackie Kennedy. She started by consulting Tish

Baldridge on whom to appoint as White House social secretary and then taking her advice and hiring another friend of Jackie's, Muffie Brandon, for the job.

"Nancy wanted to get Jackie to the White House in the worst way possible, but Jackie would never come," said a member of Nancy Reagan's senior staff. "She invited her to tea, dinner, lunch, anything. She wanted to rub against that. Bad."

Jackie called White House Aide Jim Rosebush in 1983 and asked if President Reagan would intercede to allow the late White House Usher, J. Bernard West, to be buried at Arlington, an honor usually reserved for career military people and medal winners. When Nancy heard this, she seized the chance to phone Jackie. "We called each other Jackie and Nancy, even though we've never met," Mrs. Reagan gushed. "We feel like we know each other."

It would be another year before Nancy and Jackie actually did meet, at a fund-raiser for the Kennedy Library held at Ted Kennedy's home in McLean, Virginia. After Ronald Reagan delivered a rousing speech likening Jack to a blazing comet, Jackie went up to him in tears. "Mr. President, nobody ever captured him like that," Jackie said. "That was Jack."

Having proven her loyalty to the folks at Hyannis Port by campaigning for Ted in

1980, Jackie set out to build a seaside compound of her own. In January of 1978, she had quietly paid the Hornblower family of Martha's Vineyard $1.15 million for 356 acres (later expanded to 474 acres) along Squibnocket Pond in the Vineyard's Gay Head section. The undeveloped tract was covered with Scotch pines, sand dunes, scrub oaks, marshes, and ponds. It also included 4,620 feet of oceanfront.

As soon as word got out that Jackie was building an estate on Martha's Vineyard there was an uproar among the locals. Although the island was known for its celebrity inhabitants — including Walter Cronkite, James Taylor, Carly Simon, Art Buchwald, Mike Wallace, and William Styron — Jackie raised the ante considerably.

"Everybody was scared shitless," said longtime summer resident Cranston Jones, "that Jackie was going to build this Newport-sized mega-estate out there in the dunes — something stately and probably tasteful but totally inappropriate for the rural nature of the island. And they didn't like the idea of hundreds of paparazzi suddenly swarming all over the place to get a picture of her skinny-dipping. The tourists that came to pose next to John Belushi's headstone were bad enough," Jones added, referring to the gravesite of the comedian who died of a drug overdose, another onetime Vineyard resident.

Washington architect Hugh Newell Jacobsen was hired to design nothing more daring than a nineteen-room saltbox — more like a connecting series of saltboxes — and a separate barnlike two-bedroom guest house. Even before construction began, Jackie had taken the architect's plans to the site and drawn the entire thing on the beach "so she could walk from room to room and visualize the spaces," Jacobsen said. "More than any other client I've ever had, she wanted to participate, rather than just trust in blind faith."

On any given morning Jackie and Bunny Mellon would appear, styrofoam coffee cups in hand, to assay the contractor's progress. There were a few hurdles to clear: Neighbors at first objected that the thirty-four-foot central chimney on the grounds was taller than local zoning laws permitted. Planners gave Jackie a variance when she promised to conceal the chimney from public view. She was not so lucky when the same objections were raised to the silolike portion of the guest house being built expressly for John. To comply with the code, the building was shortened by three feet.

Jackie dubbed the estate Red Gate Farm, and moved in in the summer of 1981. The house and guest house boasted white oak floors. The rooms, all decorated in pastels and lined with books, looked out over the ocean through multipaned windows made the old-fashioned way, with wooden pegs instead of nails. The kitchen boasted a sixteen-burner Vulcan stove capable of cooking four turkeys at a time, and breathtaking views of both the Atlantic and Squibnocket Pond. Not only were there heated towel racks in the bathrooms, but the toilets all flushed with hot water to prevent condensation. Behind the house were a vegetable garden and sun decks of imported Southeast Asian teak.

The main house had eight fireplaces, and Jackie insisted on having the one in her bedroom lit by her butler every morning — even at the sweltering height of summer. The total price tag for what Jackie called "my wonderful little house": more than $3 million.

William Styron's wife, Rose, a resident of Martha's Vineyard and a friend of Jackie's, figured that in addition to the magnificent terrain and the ocean, what most appealed to Jackie was that "the Vineyard did not have a history for her."

Every Memorial Day Jackie would move in and stay there until September. Those enchanted months were spent running along the beach, swimming in the ocean, rowing or kayaking in the pond, bird-watching at the edge of the marshes, hiking across the dunes. Friends who were lucky enough to be invited cherished their time there. "Once, I had forgotten my sunglasses at her beach house," the designer Valentino said. "She returned them to me in an envelope with a few grains of sand and a shell."

"It was a dream place," George Plimpton said. "A sunlit place. It's hard to explain the effect it all had on you — all the variations in color, water sparkling like diamonds everywhere you looked."

The mistress of Red Gate Farm awoke every day precisely at 7 A.M. and ate breakfast — half a bowl of All-Bran with skim milk; a banana, peach, or plum; and Folger's coffee — on a tray in bed. When she was finished eating, Jackie slathered her face with Ponds cold cream and swam for two hours in Squibnocket Pond. She'd return famished, but all she allowed herself for lunch was a few tomato slices, shredded carrots, cottage cheese, one slice of plain toast, and two glasses of herbal iced tea.

Compulsively, she struck out again in the afternoon, rowing, biking, running, or swimming for several more hours. At dinnertime, she ate broiled chicken or fish with vegetables and maybe a baked potato. Red meat and sweets of any kind were *verboten*.

"She didn't eat enough to keep a sparrow alive," said Mary Ronan, who worked as a maid at Red Gate Farm. "Yet she exercised morning, noon, and night." She wanted desperately to eat, but it was more important for her to be "pencil thin. There wasn't an ounce of fat on her body."

Jackie did, however, satisfy her appetite for gossip. Although she insisted the household staff call her "Madam," Jackie treated them "more like family members than servants." She spent part of each day sitting in the "little kitchen" next to the main kitchen in her bathing suit, her hair up in curlers, kibitzing with the help over a steaming cup of strong coffee. Occasionally, she would glance over at the bulletin board covered with snapshots of Jack, John, Caroline, and Jackie taken over the years.

Nothing delighted Jackie more than a juicy piece of gossip. The first time Jackie read about Woody Allen's scandalous affair with Mia Farrow's adopted daughter Soon-Yi Previn, said Ronan, "She put her hand to her mouth to try and stifle her laughter." Later, she would bombard Farrow with letters and phone calls in an attempt to get her to tell her side of the story in a Doubleday book.

Ronan confirmed that Jackie also monitored everything that was written about herself — from *Vanity Fair* and *The New York Times* to the *National Enquirer* and *The Star*.

Although she cherished the solitude, Jackie welcomed visits from Maurice. The year before, they had taken Maurice's seventy-foot yacht, the *Relemar* (named for his children, Rena, Leon, and Marcy), up the Georgia–South Carolina coast. At the Vineyard, he took the controls of her thirty-foot SeaCraft powerboat while she water-skied. In the evenings, like any married couple, they ate dinner off trays in the living room while watching rented videos.

Red Gate Farm was a haven for Jackie, the only home she had ever had where she could claim near-total privacy. The Gay Head region was secluded enough for a nude beach, and for some islanders to cultivate marijuana in the backwoods. "Those farms," said one of Jackie's neighbors, "are probably the only places around with tighter security than she's got."

Whenever Jackie could add to her privacy by snapping up additional property, she did. Even before she built her dream house, Jackie paid only $1,000 for a one-sixth interest in a 1.5-acre oceanfront parcel from a Wompanoag Indian family. Not long after, she moved to acquire the remaining five sixths by forcing a public auction; she was confident she would be the highest bidder.

That infuriated the other Wompanoag owners, who claimed that the beach property Jackie was attempting to snatch from them was actually sacred ground. According to Wompanoag lore, Chief Moshup and his wife, Squant, are buried on the disputed ground. Moshup, the legend goes, hurled his children into the sea when he saw the white men coming.

"I'm in a state of wonderment why she feels she must have a little strip of land when she has hundreds of other acres," said Thelma Weissberg, one of Jackie's Wampanoag foes. "She doesn't care about us. She just wants everything she can get."

The bitter legal warfare would drag on for ten years until a settlement was reached in 1990. The agreement called for Jackie to sign over a two-acre parcel and $120,000 in cash for the sacred beachfront.

It was not the only courtroom battle in which Jackie found herself embroiled. Even with all her property — enough to make her one of the two or three largest landowners on Martha's Vineyard — Jackie was still under attack from the paparazzi. Once, while she was swimming with her friend Carly Simon, a squadron of helicopters hovered overhead. Jackie looked at the singer and shouted over the din of surf and chopper blades, "They must know you're here!"

Not every intrusive episode could be defused with humor. Over the years, photographer Ron Galella did not always heed the 1975 court order instructing him to stay at least twenty-five feet from Jackie at all times. Around noon on July 21, 1981, the manager of a revival house in one of the sleazier parts of New York tipped off Galella to the fact that Jackie was inside his theater watching *Death in Venice.*

"When we got there ten minutes later, Jackie was just coming out," said photographer David McGough, who accompanied Galella on the hunt. "She was totally shocked to see Ron." Jackie later claimed that the manager tried to hold her in the doorway so that Galella could take his pictures.

Then, as she left the theater, Jackie later testified in court, "Galella was blocking my path. He was as close as a foot. I wanted to get away from those people and get a taxi, but he was jumping all around in front and in back of me, so no taxi could see me."

She said she was "frightened and confused. I was frightened on two accounts. One was being hit by a car coming from one direction or another; the other was a lot of rather weird people were coming out of the buildings along Eighth Avenue."

These "weird people" began pointing and yelling, "Oh, look, it's Jackie O. Hey, Jackie!"

"So there is Jackie on Eighth Avenue in the middle of the sex district at high noon," McGough said. "She finally gets in a cab, but then the cab dies! Now Jackie is standing in the middle of Eighth Avenue, there are no cabs to be seen anywhere, and there is this very strange crowd. She is completely stranded. There are hookers everywhere, and Ron is shooting and jumping around her and shouting, 'Jackie! Jackie! Hey, Jackie, it's Ron!' "

"You get away from me!" Jackie yelled. "Get away!"

"Oh, come on, Jackie," Galella replied.

"I'll see you in court!" Jackie yelled back as she kept trying to hail a taxi.

"You will take me to court, will you, Jackie?" he taunted her.

"It was funny," McGough said, "but when Jackie yelled at Ron she didn't sound like Jackie at all. She sounded *exactly* like a Kennedy."

By now several hookers, drug addicts, and assorted street people were teasing Jackie. They began to follow her down the street. By the time she finally found a taxi and sped off, Jackie said, she felt a mixture of "confusion and fright and desperation."

Incredibly, this encounter alone was not enough to prompt Jackie to make good on her threat. Six weeks later, over Labor Day weekend, Jackie and Maurice were trying to board Jackie's powerboat moored at Menemsha Pond when suddenly Galella and several other photographers "came zooming by, making a wake, frightening us. The engine of our boat stalled. We couldn't start it."

Back in New York on September 23,

Jackie and Maurice were leaving a performance of Twyla Tharp's dance company at the Winter Garden Theater when again they were accosted by Galella.

"Ron and his wife, Betty, literally jumped on the hood of their limousine," said McGough, who again was on hand to witness the encounter. "They were bending over, shooting in through the windshield. I couldn't believe it. Jackie freaked out." As their limousine pulled away, Galella piled into a car and tailed them. Tempelsman told his driver to pull over at a police station on East 69th Street, and went in to file a formal complaint.

At the trial in December, Galella faced Judge Irving Ben Cooper, the very same judge who had found in Jackie's favor nearly a decade earlier. If convicted of violating the judge's order, Galella faced up to seven years in jail. There was little Galella's attorney, famed lawyer Marvin Mitchelson, could do to offset Jackie's tearful testimony — or the preponderance of evidence against his client.

David McGough, whose pictures of Galella snapping Jackie on Eighth Avenue would be used to bolster Jackie's case, found Jackie's performance on the stand disillusioning. "Jackie would bring in a big picnic basket full of food and have lunch with the judge in his chambers," said McGough, who was called to testify. "It was a complete sham — a despicable case." As for her testimony: "I used to really respect Jackie," McGough said. "But she testified that Ron circled her on Eighth Avenue making ape noises, and that was completely false. I was sitting just a few feet from her in the courtroom and she looked right at me and lied through her teeth."

Not that anyone — including Ron — denied that he had violated the 1975 court order. "Yes, I may have broken this distance," Galella admitted. "But it was not intentionally . . . My favorite, and to me the biggest celebrity in the world, is Jacqueline Onassis." Not surprisingly, Judge Cooper found in the plaintiff's favor and ordered Galella never to take another picture of Jackie and to pay her $10,000 in damages. "That's justice," Galella smirked, "*me* giving Jackie Onassis money."

Lending credence to Aristotle Onassis's belief that his wife was perhaps unnecessarily litigious, Jackie filed another suit several months later. This time she charged that the fashion house of Christian Dior was using a Jackie lookalike to hawk its sportswear line. In addition to Dior, Jackie named the Lansdowne Advertising Agency, photographer Richard Avedon, Ron Smith Celebrity Look-Alikes, and model Barbara Reynolds in her suit.

The ad in question, which ran in publications ranging from *The New Yorker* to *Harper's Bazaar*, purportedly showed "notables" at a wedding reception. Sprinkled among the fakes were a few real celebrities: actress Ruth Gordon and Shari Belafonte, the *Today* show's Gene Shalit. Even though Barbara Reynolds's "Jackie" is wearing her 1960s pillbox hat and standing next to "Charles De Gaulle," Jackie claimed the presence of the real celebrities implied this was also the real Jackie.

In her sworn affidavit, Jackie claimed the ad "is embarrassing to me. It makes it appear that I am acting as a photographer's model for Christian Dior, endorsing its product, and participating in a Dior publicity campaign. I have never permitted the public value of my name, likeness or picture to be used in connection with any commercial products. I have authorized such use only in connection with certain public service, civic, art and educational projects which I have expressly supported."

Again, Jackie won. The ads were yanked, and Dior was permanently enjoined from doing anything that used the same are-they-or-aren't-they-the-real-McCoy? approach.

To be sure, Jackie was not afraid of a fight. Over the years, Jackie remained an active soldier in landmark preservation. In addition to Grand Central Station, she played

593

a pivotal role in saving Lever House, one of the first glass-walled skyscrapers. "It would be too bad," she said, "if we treated our buildings as disposable and threw them away every thirty years." She also blocked developers from building a skyscraper over St. Bartholomew's Church on Park Avenue, and from throwing up two office towers at Columbus Circle that would have cast a looming shadow over the southern end of Central Park. "They're stealing our sky!" she protested at a packed news conference. "It's time to stop the overbuilding in New York City by drawing the line at Columbus Circle."

Yet when it came to her private life, Jackie eschewed the courts. She did not pressure Maurice to get a divorce from Lily, for example, although there was little doubt she would have married him if the path had been cleared. "Maurice's wife was not about to just roll over and give him a divorce," Mehle said, "and the very last thing Jackie wanted was a nasty fight in the courts. She and Maurice were both adults, they loved each other deeply, they liked the arrangement they had — so why put themselves through all that misery?"

In 1982 Tempelsman, who had made a habit of leaving Jackie's apartment in the predawn hours wearing an overcoat covering his pajamas, finally left Lily after thirty-one years of marriage. He moved out of their apartment in the Normandy on West 84th Street into the Stanhope Hotel across from the Metropolitan Museum — and just down the street from 1040 Fifth.

"Of course Lily was very, very bitter about it," a friend of the family said. "How would you like to open the paper every day and see your husband and another woman laughing it up at the opera or strolling down the street arm in arm? How would you like to have people whispering behind your back at the office? Lily and Maurice were happy until Jackie came along and stole her husband — it's as simple as that. It was no secret that Jackie liked married men, and that she obviously never thought about what pain she caused the wives. I guess she figured all is fair in love and war. But Lily never forgave Jackie. Never. Why should she? Jackie broke her heart."

Lily Tempelsman apparently did not blame Maurice, however. According to a friend of Maurice's, they continued to maintain a relationship that was "extremely friendly and harmonious." Lily and Maurice were not legally divorced, but after he moved out she did grant him a "get," an Orthodox Jewish divorce. In 1985 Maurice moved into Jackie's apartment. He had his own nickname for Jackie. Maurice called Jackie "Jack."

"They were natural together," Maurice's longtime friend Tony Coelho said of Jackie and her new man. "Most people put her on a pedestal, but with Maurice it was different. He didn't regard her as a trophy." "Maurice is a curious choice for Jackie," her friend Slim Keith observed, "but one that works for her."

Jackie was no longer defined by the man at her side but, as with Jack and Ari, she deferred to him. Even when they were hosting a dinner party at her apartment, he led the conversation and supervised the serving staff. Gently, she would prod him with barely audible lines like, "Maurice, should we have coffee here or in the living room?" And he would respond by commanding, "We'll have coffee here."

Aileen Mehle was one of those who felt Maurice was "perfect for Jackie. A teddy bear. A very smart teddy bear. He was warm, caring, attentive, totally without ego when it came to her. Maurice was just crazy about Jackie in a way that I don't think any of the others were. And she loved him for it."

"Husbands did not always treat her the way she deserved," added Vivian Crespi. "Maurice, however, worshiped the ground she walked on. He did not dominate her, she did not dominate him. They were equals." Said another friend, "It's probably the happiest relationship she's ever had in her life. She looks to him for support and companionship. She looks to him to make decisions."

As a couple, they were happiest on Martha's Vineyard. "They had an intimate, loving relationship," Marian Ronan said. "Maurice had his own bedroom next door to Jackie's — but he slept with her . . . There was a big hallway door that could be closed and locked, cutting them off from the rest of the house and giving them complete privacy."

As she entered her mid-fifties, Jackie faced what many eldest daughters face at this time of life — the precipitous physical decline of a parent. Since the early 1960s when she gave her oral history for the archives of the Kennedy Library, Jackie's mother complained of problems with her failing memory. Now that she was seventy-six, Janet's memory lapses had become alarming. In 1983 she was diagnosed with Alzheimer's disease.

As with most Alzheimer's sufferers, it was Janet's short-term memory that went first. Midway through a conversation she would forget what she was saying, or even who she was talking to. Gradually, she became more disoriented and confused. At times, tourists who had come to see the home where Jackie spent her adolescence and where Mr. and Mrs. John F. Kennedy held their wedding reception were instead treated to the sight of Jackie's mother wandering through the rooms tidying up as if she still lived there. At other times, she drifted across the lawns like an apparition.

Toward the onset of the disease, there were times when she asked the maid to get the White House on the phone. "I want to speak to my daughter, the First Lady," she commanded. Over time, even those memories faded. A reporter managed to get Janet on the phone and asked her a question about John F. Kennedy. "Who," she asked, "is John F. Kennedy?"

Jackie paid for her mother's round-the-clock nursing care, and as time went on tried to spend weekends with her at Newport. Eventually, Janet would lose the ability even to feed herself. Jackie, according to her brother, then fed her mother "just as if she were an infant."

The family managed to keep Janet's Alzheimer's secret for three years. Quietly, Jackie consulted with Princess Yasmin Khan, vice president of the Alzheimer's Disease and Related Disorders Association. Yasmin's mother, Rita Hayworth, was also a victim of Alzheimer's. Later, Jackie would quietly donate more than $250,000 to Alzheimer's research.

Over the next several years, Jackie would become increasingly concerned that she, too, would fall victim to Alzheimer's. After Janet's younger sister, Winifred d'Olier, was also diagnosed with the disease, Jackie was, in the words of one family member, "panic-stricken that she might lose her mind. This was something she thought about a lot. Sometimes if she misplaced her car keys or picked up the phone and forgot who it was she was going to call, she'd say 'Oh my God, I think I've got it.' You'd tell her it was silly, that these things happen to everybody, but she still worried."

Enough so that she repeated her concerns to her psychiatrist, Dr. Nadine Eisman. On one occasion, she recalled walking down the street and forgetting where she was going; on another, she got dressed up and waited for a limousine to take her to a party — only to realize that the function was the next day.

Another time, after her customary jog around the Central Park reservoir, she stopped at an ice cream shop and ordered a cone from a waitress behind the counter. A few minutes later, another waitress came by, so Jackie ordered again. When the waitresses returned with the two identical orders, Jackie became flustered. According to her brother, she was "terrified" that these might be the first symptoms of Alzheimer's. After several studies linked Alzheimer's with a buildup of aluminum in the brain, Jackie threw out the few aluminum pots and pans she had — just to play it safe.

Most of Jackie's twice-weekly sessions with her analyst dwelt on her children and on the one event in her life that friends insist she never got over — Jack's murder. "Twenty-five years after Dallas," said an intimate who remains close to Caroline and John, "Jackie told me she was *still* having nightmares about the assassination."

Jackie's close friend Peter Duchin doubted that "anyone could have completely gotten over the kind of horror she went through. She recovered from the loss of Jack, but the assassination itself was such a *searing* experience that I think Jackie was always haunted by it to a certain extent. Part of it had to do with the fact that it was all so public. People have tragedy in their lives, but they're not reminded of it on a more or less constant basis the way Jackie was."

Alzheimer's was another main topic of conversation, along with another disease Jackie feared she stood a chance of inheriting. Her father, Black Jack Bouvier, had been an alcoholic, and several of her Irish relatives on her mother's side of the family were heavy drinkers. "Jackie was knowledgeable about the strong genetic factors in both alcoholism and Alzheimer's," Yusha Auchincloss conceded, "and she was very worried she might inherit one or both diseases."

Jackie, who drank heavily during the year immediately following Jack's murder and then again during her carefree early days with Ari, did not have to look far for proof that she was genetically predisposed to alcoholism.

In 1981 Jackie forced Lee to seek help for her severe drinking problem. One summer evening, Jackie physically escorted her sister to a meeting of Alcoholics Anonymous at Saint Luke's Episcopal Church in East Hampton. While the AA rank and file stared in disbelief, Jackie sat Lee in the back of the meeting room and walked back to her car. She waited there, parked outside the open door of the church, just to make sure that her sister stayed. Jackie watched with pride as her sister stood up and proclaimed, "My name is Lee and I am an alcoholic."

Lee's battle with alcohol was severe enough for Jackie to help out with the children, Tony and Tina Radziwill. "Tina and I talked about the time in her life when her mother was drunk all the time and she had to take care of her," a friend of Tina's told Diana DuBois. "But it's great her children at least had Jackie."

Jackie was also there for her half-sister, Janet Auchincloss Rutherford. Janet lived with her husband, international financier Lewis Polk Rutherford, and their children —

Lewis, Andrew, and Alexandra — in Hong Kong. It was while staying with Jackie on a visit to New York in the fall of 1984 that Janet complained of a dull, persistent pain in her back. It turned out to be lung cancer.

For the next six months, Janet went through bone marrow treatments and chemotherapy in Boston and New York. Jackie was among those relatives who donated bone marrow in the vain attempt to save her. "Jackie really came through for our sister," Jamie Auchincloss said. "When you add up all the Auchincloss children, I was seventh out of seven. Janet was sixth. Jackie was our eldest sister — so much older that we always thought of her more as an aunt than a sister, really. She was a better aunt, in fact, than our aunts were. She was the only one who always remembered to send us a card and a present for Christmas.

"When Janet got sick, my brother, Yusha, would drive her up to Boston for her treatments. Jackie pushed aside everything else to be there for Janet. I think that was one of Jackie's finest moments, really." Yusha choked back tears as he agreed with his younger brother. "The strength and concern and love she showed for Janet was inspiring. It was hard for me to respect Jackie any more than I already did. But it shouldn't have come as a surprise. When the chips were down, Jackie was that kind of person.

Totally loyal to her friends and to her family."

Jackie was holding her sister Janet's hand in March of 1985 when Janet died at Boston's Beth Israel Hospital. She was thirty-nine. "It was a terrible blow. I think it drew everyone in the family a little closer together."

Jamie was equally impressed with the way Jackie swung into action after Janet's death. "Jackie was so acquainted with death, she was an incredible person to have around at a time like that. She handled everything. When it came to funerals, she understood ritual better than anyone. She was like a priest." At their sister's memorial service in Newport, "everyone reverted to form. Jackie was afraid the press might turn the whole thing into a media circus, so she allowed only a select few people to attend. Even some of Janet's best friends were barred from the service. Jackie and Lee wouldn't sing any of the hymns — or talk to each other for that matter. They had been told that the only photographs that looked good were the ones that showed them with their mouths closed or smiling. They did not under any circumstances want to be shot with their mouths open."

Emotionally drained, Jackie went to the place she came to regard as her spiritual wellspring: India. Her fascination with all things Eastern — particularly Buddhism, Hinduism, and the mystics — by all accounts bordered on the obsessive. She now made pilgrimages there on an annual basis. Jackie's 1985 voyage to India was her favorite kind: an expense-accountable business trip. Jackie had edited Doubleday's *A Second Paradise: Indian Courtly Life 1590–1947*, also in conjunction with an exhibit at the Costume Institute of the Metropolitan Museum. Presumably by way of research — she did return with nineteen pages of annotated notes for the author, Naveen Patnaik — Jackie stayed in the glittering palaces of Jaipur, Hyderabad, Delhi, and Jodhpur. It was not difficult to understand why Jackie kept returning to the region. "The people of India," John Kenneth Galbraith said, "revered her."

Her spirits restored by her Indian interlude, Jackie returned to New York and the endless stream of galas, openings, and $1,000-a-plate fund-raising dinners. Grudgingly, she continued to host publishing parties for her authors.

At one of these cocktail parties, she looked out over the crowd of editors, lawyers, photographers, brokers, and social movers and shakers and turned to two close friends from her White House days. "They don't do anything, do they?" she asked.

Nonplussed, her friends said nothing.

"But they really don't do anything," she persisted.

"They do things," one of her friends assured her, and proceeded to point out who was who and what each did.

"But," she sighed as someone lit her cigarette (by now she had switched to Marlboros), "they're so *dull*."

In a few rare instances, the feeling was mutual. "I sat across from her at several dinner parties," said the wife of a powerful New York publishing executive, "and she really had nothing of interest to say. If she was anyone else, you would have described her as vacuous. But of course people, especially the men, were drooling all over her."

The women spent more time ogling her wardrobe, hair, and jewelry — and trying to figure out just how much plastic surgery she had undergone. She now favored the sleek designs of her friend Carolina Herrera, and had left Kenneth for colorist Thomas Morrissey when Morrissey left Kenneth to open his own salon on Madison Avenue. In a private room Morrissey reserved for Jackie, he attended to her hair while Margaret the manicurist painted her fingernails pale and her toenails fuchsia.

At this point, Jackie was not above wearing costume jewelry — including knockoffs of some of her more expensive pieces. With Jackie's blessing, Kenneth Jay Lane copied a spectacular Van Cleef ruby-emerald-sapphire-diamond necklace Ari had given her and included it in his collection. "One day Jackie said to me in her wonderful whisper, 'Kenny, I saw our necklace again on *Dynasty*.'"

With all eyes constantly riveted on Jackie, nothing she did or said went unnoticed. At a gala dinner honoring Isamu Noguchi, one of her giant earrings fell off and shattered on the floor. Several waiters rushed to her aid while the male guests dove under the table. Philip Johnson retrieved the earring and handed it in pieces to Jackie. "Somebody would think," said the architect, "you dropped it to spice up the party."

Having spent her entire life surrounded by servants, Jackie never noticed that over the course of a year one waiter or waitress might serve her a half dozen times. One stole her used dessert spoons and framed them, unwashed. Another stuffed a tiny camera down the front of his pants to take photos of Mrs. Onassis through his fly.

Caroline had no illusions about ever upstaging her mother — not even at her own wedding to Ed Schlossberg. More than 2,500 spectators — hundreds of them members of the press — clogged the streets of Hyannis Port and nearby Centerville, where the ceremony was conducted at the Church of Our Lady of Victory on July 19, 1986. In insisting on the wedding date — it was the seventeenth anniversary of Chappaquiddick — the bride and groom showed little regard for the sensitivities of others or the possible political fallout.

Nor did the feelings of the groom's family appear to be taken into consideration. Before marrying, Schlossberg not only had to consent to a Catholic ceremony with no rabbi present, but he had to agree that any children born to the marriage would be raised in the Catholic faith. The objections of Ed's parents were ignored.

The mother of the bride, meanwhile, chose to remain unobtrusive. Jackie's friend Carolina Herrera, who designed Caroline's dress, said that "unlike most mothers, Mrs. Onassis did not interfere with Caroline's wedding-dress design. In fact, she did not see the dress until it was finished. She said, 'I am not going to get involved because Caroline is the one who will wear it. I want her to be the happiest girl in the world.' "

At the bridal dinner the night before the wedding, John stood up and gave a toast in which he talked about how close he, his sister, and mother had been. "All our lives, it's just been the three of us," he said. "Now," he said, turning to Ed Schlossberg, "there are four."

Later, author Doris Kearns Goodwin

talked to Jackie about that touching moment. "I want that kind of closeness for my sons," Goodwin said.

"It's the best thing," Jackie said, looking Goodwin straight in the eye, "I've ever done."

John was best man, and his cousin Maria Shriver was maid of honor. From her stunning white satin gown with its twenty-five-foot train to the bridal party's lavender-and-white outfits by Willi Smith, Ed's favorite designer, the event was a Technicolor spectacle. White limousines transported the wedding party to the Kennedy compound, where the 425 guests (404 of them Caroline's) dined by the light from Japanese lanterns under huge tents. Carly Simon sang (one of her biggest hits, "You're So Vain," was reputed to be about Jackie and Carly's mutual lover Warren Beatty), and for the grand finale there was a fireworks display orchestrated by Caroline's old friend George Plimpton.

"Earlier I had wanted to beat this fog that was rolling in so I asked if Carly Simon couldn't sing after the fireworks," Plimpton recalls. "Her manager said, 'Carly Simon doesn't *follow* fireworks.' So she sang and by the time she was finished, this huge fog bank that looked like the white cliffs of Dover was almost there.

"We managed to shoot off fifteen displays

in honor of the guests that were there — bow tie for Arthur Schlesinger, a rose for Rose Kennedy, and so on. I was narrating each as we went along. But the bank was right over us for the second half of the show, so while you heard the booming as the fireworks went off, you couldn't see anything. 'And this,' I announced, 'is what Ed Schlossberg does for a living.' Jackie *loved* it. She got a huge kick out of it, because it was totally appropriate. We were all in the dark when it came to what Schlossberg actually *does*."

There was no such confusion where the disciplined, self-directed Mrs. Schlossberg was concerned. After the couple honeymooned in Hawaii and Japan and settled into an East Side apartment, Caroline enrolled at Columbia Law School.

For John, the road to success — both personal and professional — would be considerably more circuitous. After graduating from Brown with a bachelor's degree in history, John spent nine months in India taking courses in public health and education at the University of New Delhi.

"It was great gallantry on Jackie's part to send him to India for nine months during the twentieth anniversary of his father's assassination," Jackie's friend, the writer Gita Mehta, told Ed Klein. "I mean, he could have grown up terrified, with a state-of-siege mentality, but she has given him the courage to address a place as alien as India without any sense of fear. This is an example of how subtle and intelligent a parent she has been."

It was precisely because it was the twentieth anniversary of the assassination that she wanted her son out of the country. Ever since millions of Indians jammed the streets to cheer her as First Lady, Jackie had felt a spiritual bond with the subcontinent. She felt, oddly enough, that he would be safer there.

On his return to New York, John went to work for a group his mother founded: the nonprofit 42nd Street Development Corporation. His salary was $20,000 a year. Much to Jackie's chagrin, he still wanted to pursue an acting career — something by all accounts he had a natural talent for — but she leaned on him to follow Caroline's example. Only Rudolf Nureyev, who was closer to Lee than to Jackie, showed the courage to stand up to the intimidating Mrs. Onassis. "Show some balls!" Nureyev told John. "Do what *you* want."

While weighing the possibilities, he indulged his love of sports — biking, hiking, rowing, sailing, water-skiing, roller skating (later in-line skating), swimming, tennis, running, playing touch football in the park. He also regularly attended Knicks games at

Madison Square Garden, and spent Monday nights at sports bars watching football games with his friends.

He developed other interests as well. Wearing shorts and a backpack as he strolled through Times Square unnoticed in the middle of the day, John would closely study the graphic photos of nude women posted outside sex clubs. Then, having decided which women most appealed to him, went inside to spend hours watching "LIVE SEX LIVE." He also developed a taste for pornography. At one point, a video store owner accused him of running up more than $1,000 in fines for dozens of X-rated videos he had failed to return.

At the same time, John, now routinely described as "pectorially perfect" by the press, was himself garnering a reputation as something of an exhibitionist. Like his father, who swam naked in the White House pool and sunbathed nude in Palm Beach, John Jr. had no qualms about displaying his body in public.

At Edgartown on Martha's Vineyard, locals accused him of walking around town wearing only a towel around his waist and coyly letting it slip. "He loves to walk around in the nude," said Couri Hay, who worked out at the Aspen Club in Colorado when John was there. "He walks around in the gym with his bathrobe open, and when he takes a shower he leaves the curtain open." According to Hay, John skinny-dipped at a Hyannis Port pool party, then strolled around nude while waiters served guests drinks. Hay wound up thinking JFK Jr. "could have been a porno star."

This exhibitionist streak would persist. Not long after his thirtieth birthday in 1990, John vacationed on St. Barth's in the French West Indies. Once again, he swam and walked around on the beach nude — only this time he was captured on film by New York travel agent Shelley Shusteroff. The photographs, for which Shusteroff was allegedly offered a six-figure sum, were not published.

In the fall of 1986, John delighted his mother by enrolling in New York University Law School. With both of her children taking their first tentative steps toward respectable careers in the legal profession, Jackie felt she had fulfilled her unspoken promise to Jack. Caroline and John were launched. "Now," Jackie joked, "I can die a happy woman."

Just as her children were embracing the sort of occupation she felt was worthy of their illustrious name, Jackie was busy chasing down celebrities for Doubleday. In 1982 she had been promoted to Senior Editor and moved into an office with a window. When Doubleday was bought by the German conglomerate Bertelsmann and eventually moved to new headquarters at Broadway and 45th Street, Jackie relocated to comparably modest quarters there. Her salary was $50,000 — barely enough to cover the taxes on her Martha's Vineyard property alone.

By now she had come into her own as an editor. "Did you know that Jackie Onassis is the *best* editor?" Theodore White asked a friend rhetorically, as if undone by the realization. "She does the work of ten editors, and she has such a fertile imagination." Plimpton proclaimed her one of the best line editors in publishing. "She was a tough editor," said author Jonathan Cott, four of whose books, including *The Search for Omm Sety*, were edited by Jackie. "She was rigorous about correcting usage. Typical sidenotes were 'Omit' and 'Do something!' " But when she got enthusiastic, Cott added, "you thought she was going to burst into song."

Another of Jackie's authors, the novelist Gita Mehta, described her as "an extraordinary, nineteenth-century sort of editor." The novelist Louis Auchincloss, one of Jackie's cousins by marriage, shared that view. When they worked together on *Maverick in Mauve*, an inside look at New York's Gilded Age, she hit him with a blizzard of queries: "Could you describe what was going on in the world then, to set the reader in historical time?" she asked in one memo. "Who was president, king? What were national issues, scandals, headlines for the day, what was being written, what was being read? Who were popular and avant-garde artists? Did they have electric lights yet, cars or horses and carriages? What were wages, hours of work, size of household staffs, various economic levels, etc.?"

Auchincloss and his editor clashed over the book's illustrations — she wanted simply to use the most interesting photos, he wanted the pictures to coincide precisely with what was being said in the text. "Oh, Louis," she groaned, "don't be such a Ph.D."

A later memo, this one outlining her thoughts on Auchincloss's *False Dawn*: "This is what I have decided I feel; it is a little too concentrated in spots, more for an English audience than an American one. Could you get a little more air flowing through it in places where information is more tightly packed? Could we have some lovely stories, some waspish stories?" Several pages later, she concludes, "I do look forward to our lunch and am prepared to be told that I am an utter dolt." Auchincloss viewed Jackie as nothing less than "a writer's dream as an editor."

She did not always tinker with manuscripts; in many instances she asked for no changes at all. Sometimes, the one comment she offered made all the difference. Auchincloss had written an introduction to a book commemorating the 150th anniversary of Tiffany's, devoting a paragraph to Tiffany descendant Harry Platt's biennial ball "for the most beautiful and best-dressed ladies in society." Jackie pointed out one sentence in which Auchincloss referred to "the photographs of Harry's balls."

From the cover art to jacket copy to typeface to illustrations and layout, every book that Jackie edited bore her unfailing sense of style. "She infused everything she touched," Scott Moyers said. "You can't learn that. You've either got it or you ain't."

For Jackie, it was hard to imagine anything more rewarding. "I love books," she explained. "I've known writers all my life . . . I'm drawn to books that are out of our regular experience. Books of other cultures, ancient histories. I'm interested in the arts in general, especially the creative process. I'm fascinated by hearing artists talk about their craft. To me, a wonderful book is one that takes me on a journey into something I didn't know before."

She still prided herself in the eclectic range of the books she edited — from Carly Simon's *Amy, the Dancing Bear* to Larry Gonick's *The Cartoon History of the Universe* to *Ten Men and History* by Don Cook. "I learned never to second-guess what she'd be interested in," said Doubleday Editor Bruce Tracy, "because she was interested in just about everything."

There was one subject, however, Jackie claimed didn't interest her in the slightest. When Mimi Kazon met her at a Doubleday party, Jackie asked to see Kazon's columns to determine if they might not make a book. Kazon sent the columns off, and a few weeks later was sitting in her kitchen when the phone rang.

"It's quick and witty," Jackie said of Kazon's writing, "but it's all about power, and I'm not into power."

As much as she enjoyed being "taken on a journey" by the writers she did edit, her job had its frustrations — not the least of which was the fact that the impossibly well-connected Jackie had found it nearly impossible to lure any major celebrities to Doubleday. Jackie was not surprised when one of her books, Gelsey Kirkland's *Dancing on My Grave*, turned out to be a bestseller. "Young girls are always fascinated by ballet or horses," Jackie said with a shrug. "I was fascinated by both."

But she was ill-prepared for the stone wall of resistance she encountered every time she tried to sign up a megastar. It was not for lack of trying. Over time, she was turned down by, among others, Greta Garbo, Elizabeth Taylor, Brigitte Bardot, Katharine Hepburn, Bette Davis, Barbara Walters, Prince, Ted Turner, and even her old friend Nureyev.

"You'd think that nobody could impress Jacqueline Kennedy Onassis," John Sargent said. "On the contrary, she was *fascinated* by people." Observed her friend John Russell, chief art critic for *The New York Times*, "It was a fantasy of hers that everybody else's life was much more interesting than her own. 'Think of the plots that are being hatched down there!' she would say, looking down from the balcony of the Four Seasons restaurant, with her Schlumberger bracelets dangling over the edge." Yet Jackie did not appear to see the irony in the world's most private famous person trying to convince other celebrities to, as she quipped more than once, "spill their guts." Even George Hamilton, whom Jackie spotted on *The Merv Griffin Show*, in the end refused to take the bait.

She persisted, watching television talk shows, quizzing her children on the new crop of stars she had never heard of, perusing the gossip columns in search of leads. Yet she did not lose perspective. When it was reported that Dolly Parton was writing her first tell-all book for someone else, Jackie smirked, "Sounds like another cultural watershed."

In the fall of 1983, Jackie set out to snag what was then the biggest celebrity of them all. Along with fellow Doubleday Editor Shaye Areheart, she flew to Los Angeles to meet with Michael Jackson.

Next to Elizabeth Taylor and his mother, the woman Michael most admired was Jackie. This was apparent back in 1977, when he visited the apartment of New York *Daily News* reporter Bob Weiner. While Weiner prepared a promised home-cooked meal for Jackson, Michael made himself right at home, plowing into the books, photographs, tapes, and knickknacks that cluttered Weiner's apartment.

Suddenly, Michael let out a horrified gasp, and his host came running from the kitchen. Michael was staring at a calendar that featured one of the nude snapshots of Jackie taken on Skorpios. "Oh," said Michael, stricken at the sight of a topless Jackie, "why did she pose for these pictures?"

"Since it's not every day that I encounter an eighteen-year-old millionaire with innocence intact," Weiner recalled, "I broke it to him gently that the photographs were taken without Mrs. Onassis's knowledge. He breathed easier."

By the time of their scheduled lunch in L.A., the mercurial Michael was a lot richer — and a lot less innocent. Still riding high on the phenomenal success of his all-time best-selling *Thriller* album, he actually stood Jackie up at the restaurant where they were to have their first meeting. The next day, Michael invited Jackie and Areheart to Hayvenhurst, the Jackson family compound in Encino.

After months of delicate negotiations, it was announced that Doubleday had paid the Gloved One $300,000 for his memoirs. Michael celebrated by escorting Jackie on a guided tour of Disneyland. Just weeks after the announcement, Michael was severely burned when fireworks ignited his hair during the taping of a Pepsi commercial. Jackie was among the first to call him at the hospital.

Shortly before the publication of *Moonwalk* in the spring of 1988, Michael kicked off the U.S. portion of his world tour in Kansas City. He invited Jackie and Caroline to be in the opening night audience. When illness kept them both home in New York, Michael arranged for a special phone hookup so they could listen to the concert live. Whenever there was a break, he would dash into the wings and shout, "How'm I doing?" into the phone.

More than 300,000 copies of *Moonwalk* hit bookstores in April. Michael's memoirs featured a brief introduction by Jackie ("What can one say about Michael Jackson?") and were dedicated to Fred Astaire.

In the end, Jackie was as curious as everyone else when it came to Michael's peculiar habits (masks, a single glove, makeup, plastic surgery, bizarre getups, a strange fondness for chimpanzees). More particularly, she wondered aloud about his sexual preferences. Book designer J. C. Suares, who worked on *Moonwalk* and accompanied Jackie to meetings with Michael at Hayvenhurst, claimed Jackie "couldn't figure out what made him tick. His house was kitschily furnished with paintings of clowns, kind of a La-La Land. She kept asking me if he was gay." Indeed, they would "get in the car and she'd say, 'Well, do you think he likes girls?' She was really fascinated by his sexual orientation. She never quite figured it out."

Dealing with the chimerical Mr. Jackson, Jackie confided to a colleague, left her feeling like a "wreck." Nevertheless, she was game to do it again. "Is there anybody else you'd like me to try and get?" she asked Lisa Drew. "Because people do sometimes take my phone calls."

"Barbra Streisand," Drew answered without skipping beat.

Once again Jackie, who reportedly found Streisand's voice "grating," nevertheless flew out to Los Angeles to seduce the famously temperamental star over lunch.

It would be a year before Streisand called Jackie back to say she was not interested in doing a book. What she wanted, Jackie later said, was "the name of a good libel lawyer. I told her I didn't have one because I don't sue for libel."

Moonwalk reached number one on the *New York Times* best-seller list. It marked Jackie's biggest commercial success to date — and the beginning of a bizarre friendship between the former First Lady and the self-styled King of Pop. Soon, Michael was imitating Jackie's little-girl whisper and wearing sunglasses at night.

Just how highly Michael thought of Jackie was evident right after the publication of *Moonwalk*. He confided to friends that he was ready to become a single father, and by 1991 was saying he was willing to pay up to $2 million for a surrogate mother to bear his child — by means of artificial insemination. The woman would have to, he stated at the time, combine the physical and intellectual traits of the three women he admired most besides his mother: Diana Ross, Elizabeth Taylor, and Jacqueline Onassis.

In July of 1992, Doubleday published Jackson's *Dancing the Dream*, a slim coffee-table book of poetry, photographs, and "reflections." As with *Moonwalk*, Jackie oversaw the project, although the actual editing was done by Shaye Areheart.

"When I hear the name *Michael Jackson*," Elizabeth Taylor wrote in the book's introduction, "I think of brilliance, of dazzling stars, lasers, and deep emotions . . . one of the most gifted music makers the world has ever known . . . intense caring and love . . . alarmingly bright . . . unearthly, special, innocent, childlike . . . a wise man, one of the sharpest wits, so giving . . . an incredible force of incredible energy . . . one of the finest people to hit this planet."

But a poet? In "Quantum Leap," Michael wrote, "I looked for you on hill and dale / I sought for you beyond the pale." Then there was "Planet Earth": "Cold as rock without a hue / held together with a bit of glue . . ." More interesting were the photographs, which he and Jackie selected together. These included full-page color portraits of Michael as Napoleon, Henry VIII, and Julius Caesar.

By this time Jackie, who now religiously practiced yoga and meditated between 7:00 and 7:30 each evening, was sharing health tips with her emotionally fragile author. She introduced Michael to Deepak Chopra, author of *Quantum Healing: Exploring the Frontiers of the Mind*, and in August 1992 Jackson brought Chopra along on the European leg of his 1992 world tour — along with one or two "special friends," the prepubescent boys of whom Jackson had grown especially fond.

The air of wide-eyed, breathless innocence Jackson and Jackie shared served as their armor against an ever-intrusive world. The childlike persona also masked a dimension of Michael's psyche that Jackie found troubling.

At Hayvenhurst and later at Jackson's spectacular Neverland Ranch in the mist-shrouded foothills east of Santa Barbara, Jackie had commented on the young boys who always surrounded Michael. "Doesn't it strike you as, well, *odd?*" she asked a colleague.

Dancing the Dream was one of the first gifts Michael gave the twelve-year-old boy the superstar would later be accused of molesting. These explosive charges, which came to light when police raided Neverland in August of 1993, made lurid headlines around the world for more than a year. During that time, his career in shambles, Jackson teetered on the brink of a nervous breakdown.

Despite her own precarious health, Elizabeth Taylor rushed to Michael's side in Singapore. She was practically the only one of Michael's many famous "friends" to stand up and be counted in his defense. Diana Ross, Liza Minnelli, David Geffen, and hundreds more who once clamored to be photographed beside him now remained stonily silent.

Most conspicuously absent of all was Jackie. Facing criminal prosecution and a possible prison sentence, a frantic Michael placed several calls from Neverland to Jackie's Doubleday offices. Mrs. Onassis, conveniently, was never there to take his calls.

Eventually, Jackson agreed to buy his accuser's silence. Without the victim's testimony, prosecutors in Los Angeles and Santa Barbara felt they no longer had a case. Coincidentally, the amount Michael agreed on with the boy's litigators was identical to the settlement Christina Onassis paid Jackie: $26 million.

Of course, when it came to celebrities and their memoirs, Jackie was far and away the biggest prize of all. Yet even as she ran other celebrities to ground, Jackie would not consent to an interview, much less agree to put her own life story on paper. When Mehle asked to interview her longtime friend for her "Suzy" column, Jackie became "completely flustered."

"I couldn't," she said, "I just *couldn't*. I'd feel like such a jackass, like such a fool. My answers are always so asinine."

Then, deftly turning the tables, Jackie tried to cajole Mehle into writing a novel. "She loved gossip and she read all my columns," Mehle said. "She would say, 'You're so *wise*. Why don't you write a novel about the women you know who seem to hold the world in their hands and beneath the façade are so desperately unhappy? The terribly rich ladies who live the glamorous life but are actually very sad women.'

"I just looked at her," Mehle recalled, "and thought, '*Et tu,* Jackie?' "

There was an unspoken understanding at Doubleday, said one editor, "that if Jackie ever did decide to write her memoirs, she would do it for us. She was offered $5 million, but she could have named her price." Some of the most fervent pleas came from those closest to her. "She witnessed so much history, and she was such a marvelous writer," George Plimpton said. "I felt it would be a terrible shame if she didn't get it down on paper, if only for posterity."

It was while Jackie was spending one of her idyllic summers on Martha's Vineyard that Plimpton decided to make his pitch. "I knew Red Gate Farm was the kind of place where one could be inspired," he said. "I sat down and wrote Jackie a letter — the best letter I ever wrote — offering to come up and work with her on her memoirs. She would tell me whatever she wanted to tell me, we would walk along the beach and talk it through in that marvelous setting, and then I would go away and type it up and give it to her. No one would need to know it ever existed. She could just put it away, and when they needed to, her children could refer to it, and her children's children."

Jackie thought over Plimpton's proposal,

and when he visited her at Red Gate Farm she gave him her answer. "Well, you know," she told him, "I don't really want to sit at a window looking out at a field and feel that life is going by."

Even her own family tried to get Jackie to relent. "My mother was almost as private as Jackie," Jamie Auchincloss recalled, "but even she thought Jackie should write about her life."

In the late 1980s, Janet asked Jackie, "You are going to work on your memoirs at some point, aren't you?"

"Why," Jackie asked, "would I do that?"

As she approached her fifty-ninth birthday, Jackie faced more reminders of her own mortality — and of how sweet life could be in her later years. In early 1988, Jackie began telling friends, "I'm going to be a grandmother — imagine that!" On June 25, Jackie cheered when Caroline gave birth to a seven-pound twelve-ounce girl at New York Hospital. They named the baby Rose, after the ninety-seven-year-old Kennedy family matriarch.

Three months later, Lee, now working as special events coordinator for Giorgio Armani, married Hollywood director Herb Ross (*The Turning Point*, *The Goodbye Girl*, *Steel Magnolias*) in a brief civil ceremony at her Manhattan apartment. She had already alerted the paparazzi to be on hand when she arrived at Jackie's for her wedding dinner. Among the guests were Steve Martin and Bernadette Peters, producers Ray Stark and Doug Cramer, and Rudolf Nureyev, who in the course of conversation felt compelled to mention that "Yeltsin has a large dick, which he is eager to share." Also on hand was one of the stars of the *Steel Magnolias* ensemble cast, Daryl Hannah.

"Isn't it wonderful that Lee's happy?" another guest, Karen Lerner, asked the hostess.

Jackie had only met Ross the previous day and answered with a question of her own: "But isn't he homosexual?"

"Well," said Lerner, "I never heard he wasn't!"

With Lee's marriage, all three Bouvier women had something else in common: To-the-manner-born Catholics, Jackie, Lee, and Caroline were all happily involved with wealthy, devoted, intelligent Jewish men. As one Jewish friend of Ross observed, "Little Herbie Ross from Brooklyn . . . got the quintessential *shiksa*."

The nation observed the twenty-fifth anniversary of Jack's assassination with all manner of essays, retrospectives, and ceremonies. Jackie avoided them all, preferring to join Caroline and John for a private morning Mass not far from her apartment at modest St. Thomas More Church.

Less than two weeks later, Jackie thought for a moment that she might have lost the current man in her life. On December 8, Jackie rushed to the coronary care unit of Lenox Hill Hospital to be with Maurice after he suffered a heart attack. Over the next several days, she was a frequent visitor at his bedside.

Maurice's recovery was as swift as the coronary had been unexpected. Soon they were both looking ahead to a full schedule that included the launching of the new John F. Kennedy Profile in Courage Award and a $1,000-a-plate fund-raising dinner at the Kennedy Library. Jackie, knowing that she would be scrutinized even more closely than usual, decided she needed a lift.

In March of 1989, she checked into the Manhattan Eye, Ear, and Throat Hospital under an assumed name and got one — a full face-lift — at the hands of noted plastic surgeon Dr. Michael Hogan. Jackie took time off to recuperate with Maurice, first at her country place in New Jersey and then in the Bahamas. When she appeared with her new, cosmetically enhanced visage at the Kennedy Library dinner, the crowd buzzed that "Granny O," as she was now being called, never looked more striking. The only giveaway: Jackie's hands, which one guest described as "talons that showed every day of her sixty years."

★ ★ ★

On July 22, 1989, six years after her Alzheimer's had been diagnosed, Janet Lee Bouvier Auchincloss Morris died at Hammersmith Farm at age eighty-one. Lee wept quietly and Jackie registered no emotion as her mother's ashes were placed alongside Uncle Hughdie's after a brief funeral service at Newport's Trinity Church.

Two weeks later, Jackie was in Paris for the bicentennial of the French Revolution. She celebrated by shopping in the Faubourg-Saint-Honoré and stopping in at Porthault (purveyors of "The Linen of Queens") to buy scallop-edged white cotton sheets festooned with pink bunnies for Baby Rose. Then, with the architect himself as her guide, she checked out I. M. Pei's controversial glass pyramid at the entrance to the Louvre. More than ever, Jackie was determined not to waste a single moment.

At about this time, yet another friend of Jackie's begged her to write her autobiography. Again, she said she would rather spend her time "feeling a galloping horse, or the mist of the ocean up at Martha's Vineyard." Whether or not she sensed that there might not be all that much time left, Jackie clearly took nothing for granted. "Life is too precious," she said. "I want to savor it."

What she is, is poetic.

— *I. M. Pei*

She was tougher than anyone I've ever met.

— *Jamie Auchincloss,* Jackie's brother

It's the best thing I've ever done. Being a mother is what I think has made me the person I am.

— *Jackie*

TEN

"Oh no!" the rider yelled as her horse, Toby, jolted to a stop. A collective gasp went up from the crowd at the Essex Fox Hounds Hunter Trials in New Jersey as Jackie hurtled through the air and hit the ground. Dazed, she managed to get up on all fours and then get back on her feet, even before help arrived.

It was not Jackie's first tumble at the club, and it would not be her last. No matter. Jackie, her fellow riders agreed, appeared to thrive on danger. By the early 1990s, Jackie had become so addicted to the thrill of jumping horses that when she wasn't riding in New Jersey she was competing at horse shows in Virginia. So frequent were her trips to Middleburg that she rented a white clapboard cottage less than a mile from Wexford, the house she had shared with Jack.

At the Piedmont Hunt Club in Upperville, Virginia, Jackie was riding when the horse next to her stepped in a hole and stumbled, pitching his rider headfirst into the ground only feet from Jackie. The man was instantly paralyzed from the neck down.

"That made the danger vivid for her,"

said fellow rider Charles Whitehouse, a former ambassador to Thailand and Laos and an old friend of Jackie's. "She also had falls from time to time. But that added to the zest of it, too."

Jacqueline had long ago decided that she could not allow herself to succumb to fear — though she had more than ample reason to be concerned for her own safety. At Doubleday, Jackie's private extension was 9747. Whenever someone called the company's main number asking to speak to Jackie, they were put through to one of her assistants on 9728 — "the kook line," as Scott Moyers called it. "You had to steel yourself for anything when it rang — UFO reports, conspiracy theorists, troubled people spewing out surrealism. And you'd get weird things in the mail — adult videos, women from Brazil proposing marriage to her son."

The first week in March 1985, Jackie's secretary at Doubleday opened a package addressed to Mrs. Onassis. Inside were a loaded .38-caliber Smith & Wesson snub-nosed revolver, forty rounds of ammunition, and a one-and-a-half-page handwritten note that, among other things, asked Jackie to support the note's author in a 1988 presidential bid. "Let's just say," an FBI agent commented when they apprehended the suspect in California, "the guy was off the straight line."

Doubleday's most high-profile employee was not about to let a little thing like a snub-nosed .38 upset her. Jackie, Nancy Tuckerman explained, "tends to be philosophical about such matters — she has to be."

From earliest childhood, when Janet and Black Jack Bouvier were locked in a bitter contest for their daughters' allegiance, Jackie learned to conceal her true feelings behind a perpetual look of wide-eyed wonder. "At her core," Gore Vidal said, "was a will of pure steel."

Pierre Salinger and Jackie harbored a genuine affection for each other before, during, and after the White House years. Yet even Salinger admitted that "Jackie had a formidable temper. I was on the receiving end of it a number of times as President Kennedy's press secretary. Jack had an even bigger temper, but he would blow up and then forget about it. Jackie did not forget. You did not want to cross her."

A few of Jackie's infrequent rages appear justified. One morning, she awoke to discover that a dozen miniature paintings she had brought back from India had been thrown in the garbage. Tuckerman hit the phones and everyone breathed a sigh of relief when a garbage man with an eye for art told them he was holding the valuable paintings for their rightful owner. They had less luck with the new Christian Lacroix evening gown the maid had tossed into a pile of old jeans and sweatshirts bound for the local thrift shop. By the time Tuckerman got through to the thrift shop, the $10,000 dress had already been sold — for $100.

At this stage in Jackie's life, mistakes — apparently even $10,000 mistakes — could be forgiven. But when loyalty was the issue, Jackie was unbending. If Jackie felt her trust had in any way been betrayed, even dear friends like Ben and Tony Bradlee suddenly dropped off the face of the planet as far as she was concerned.

In this respect, she was perhaps hardest on members of her own extended family. After her first cousin John Davis wrote books about the Bouviers and the Kennedys, Jackie cut him off. She also severed all ties with Black Jack's devoted twin sisters, Michelle Putnam and Davis's mother, Maud. Jackie did not even bother to R.S.V.P. when she was invited to the sisters' joint birthday party, and pointedly excluded all three from all her own family functions — most notably Caroline's wedding, to which hundreds of nonfamily members were invited.

Never one to miss a funeral, Jackie did show up for her aunt Michelle's in 1987. Even there she made a point of letting John Davis know that he was strictly persona non grata. And when Rose Kennedy Schlossberg was christened at St. Thomas More Church just blocks from where the Davises lived, John Davis professed not to care. But Maud Davis, who had watched Jackie play as a child at Lasata, the Bouvier mansion in East Hampton, was "crushed."

Her own half-brother, Jamie, also got the silent treatment after he talked freely to a reporter, sharing such explosive revelations as where her wedding dress and the pink suit she had worn in Dallas were stored (in cardboard boxes in Janet Auchincloss's closet).

"She was one of the most emotionally self-sufficient people ever," Jamie said. "You'd be in her life one moment, and out the next. Gone. And it really didn't seem to bother her one bit.

"With my sister you always got the feeling you were on borrowed time — that she could jettison you at any moment for the tiniest infraction. That's why people were always tiptoeing around her. You'd get a call from Nancy Tuckerman saying, 'Don't you think you should . . .' It would scare the hell out of a lot of people.

"She was my sister, but she was also Queen Jackie to the world. Everybody knew it. *She* certainly knew it. Even with the people she liked most, there was never any pretense that you were her equal. She called you up when she felt like it — usually after ten or eleven P.M. — and it didn't matter at all if you were in bed. No matter how famous or powerful or rich you were, you went along because it was such a *privilege* just to be talking with her."

Jackie could indeed be fickle, and that left even her brother wondering where he stood. "Jackie could be absolutely giddy and enchanting one moment," Jamie said, "and then you'd turn around, and for no apparent reason, she'd just turn off as if somebody had flipped a switch.

"Louis Auchincloss would come to her apartment, and she would focus her laserlike attention on him as if she was a schoolgirl. Staring at him open-mouthed, hanging on his every word. Then she would turn away to someone else and from then on look right through him as if he didn't exist. It was as if she was saying, 'Hey, I'm finished with you now — your fifteen minutes of fame are over.' "

Presumably her favorite surviving Auchincloss relatives were her elder half-brother Yusha and Louis. But Jackie never invited Louis to the White House or Yusha to Martha's Vineyard. "I know that hurt Yusha," his half-brother Jamie said.

Louis also admitted that he was "disappointed" at Jackie's inattention, but he offered his own explanation for her seemingly capricious behavior. "I have some reason to suspect that Jackie was a person of peculiar visual memory," he said. "With her it was a case of out of sight being literally out of mind. If she had chanced upon me in Washington, she might well have exclaimed, 'Where have you been? Why don't you come around?'" I have heard other people complain of being forgotten or dropped by Jackie, and I think this may well have been the reason."

Even Louis conceded, however, that even as a teenager "Jackie was very strong, even willful. She had no public persona then, but when she developed one, it amused me that it was so soft and gentle."

She came close to meeting her match when, in 1988, John became involved with a young woman no less known for her *chutzpah*. Her name was Madonna. The Material Girl's interest was piqued by John's own meteoric rise as an American sex symbol.

That July, John made his political debut when he introduced his uncle Ted at the Democratic National Convention in Atlanta. When JFK's strikingly handsome son stepped up to the podium, a collective gasp went up from the delegates. *Time* magazine's Walter Isaacson worried that the roof of the Omni Auditorium might collapse "from the sudden drop in air pressure caused by the simultaneous sharp intake of so many thousands of breaths."

"Over a quarter of a century ago," John

intoned, "my father stood before you to accept the nomination for the presidency of the United States. So many of you came into public service because of him and in a very real sense it is because of you that he is with us today."

Watching her son's polished performance on television, Jackie was overjoyed. She had waged a war of attrition to force him to abandon his dream of becoming an actor, and now it looked as if he was about to enter the family business — politics. The remarkably poised twenty-seven-year-old was finishing his last year at New York University Law School. The timing, Jackie confided in friends, could not have been better.

Things took a sudden and unexpected turn when, on the cover of its September 12, 1988, issue, *People* magazine proclaimed John "The Sexiest Man Alive" (two years earlier the magazine had dubbed him "America's Most Eligible Bachelor"). The "Sexiest Man" story began:

Okay, ladies, this one's for you — but first some ground rules. GET YOUR EYES OFF THAT MAN'S CHEST! He's a serious fellow. Third-year law student. Active with charities. Scion of the most charismatic family in American politics and heir to its most famous name.

"Listen," John would later tell Barbara Walters, "people can say a lot worse things about you than you are attractive and you look good in a bathing suit." As flattering as the *People* cover story was, however, it effectively defused any immediate political aspirations John might have entertained. Overnight, he was transformed from Camelot's last best hope to the power elite's equivalent of Hollywood hunk.

The Sexiest Man Alive endured the merciless teasing from his friends graciously. But Jackie, seeing the story as a crass commercial attempt to cash in on the Kennedy name, fretted over the damage it had done to her son's nascent public-service career.

Ever since the stories about Jack's White House affairs with Marilyn Monroe, Judith Campbell Exner, and dozens of others had begun to surface in the late 1970s, Jackie had managed to convince the children that they — along with all conspiracy theories and reports of links to organized crime — were to be discounted as fiction. It wasn't hard. Blind allegiance to the family was mother's milk to all Kennedy offspring. And, as Jackie learned early on from Rose Kennedy, it was only through chronic denial that Jackie would be able to preserve some semblance of sanity.

To even her closest friends, Jackie appeared unaffected by the ever-flowing "river of sludge," as she called it. "There would be headlines all over the place about Jack's affair with Marilyn Monroe or some other bombshell about JFK and the Mafia," said veteran celebrity-watcher Earl Blackwell, "and you'd see Jackie at a party laughing up a storm. At times like those, she got out a lot more than usual, just to prove to people that she wasn't bothered by all the stories. She was a *superb* actress, and if she was feeling any pain or embarrassment at all there was no way she was going to let you see it."

She was indeed a superb actress. "She apparently had tremendous self-control and never threw things or broke down crying or anything," said one of John's classmates at Brown. "She never even spoke about Marilyn Monroe or any of the other stuff directly — not even with her kids. But it bothered her that John and Caroline might be teased about all the stories that kept coming out about sex in the White House. Whenever there was a new revelation about JFK's other women, she'd just call and see how John was doing."

An unwelcome reminder of Jack's affair with Marilyn Monroe manifested itself in the person of Madonna, Louise Ciccone. "I'm tough, ambitious, and I know exactly what I want," Madonna liked to tell her many critics. "If that makes me a bitch, okay." Already a global pop icon, she was best known at the time for her video homage to Marilyn's "Diamonds Are a Girl's Best Friend" number from the 1953 film *Gentlemen Prefer Blondes*. As a result, she was constantly being compared to the other blond bombshell. To a large extent, that comparison, which Madonna encouraged, seemed valid — with one significant caveat. Unlike Monroe, Madonna was nobody's victim.

The Material Girl and John Kennedy Jr. met briefly at a party in 1985. By 1988, following the breakup of her violent marriage to Sean Penn, she made the conscious decision to pursue the Sexiest Man Alive. Beyond the obvious reasons — her own voracious sexual appetites were legendary — Madonna described her motivation for wanting to hook up with John as "cosmic."

Madonna had read every Monroe biography ever written, knew all the details of Marilyn's star-crossed affair with the late President. As undisputed heiress to Monroe's persona, she confided to friends she felt fated to consummate a relationship with Kennedy's only son. For his part, John was dazzled by the notion of "dating" Madonna, the most glamorous, celebrated, and, by all accounts, exciting woman of her generation.

They decided to keep their relationship as private as possible. Since they both worked out religiously at the same health club, it provided a convenient locale for their initial rendezvous. They jogged together in Central Park, and later Kennedy took Madonna to meet his mother.

At 1040 Fifth, Madonna was greeted somewhat frostily by Jackie, who wondered what designs the unpredictable superstar might have on her son. Madonna, whose divorce had not yet come through, coyly signed the guest register "Mrs. Sean Penn."

Jackie was not amused, according to a friend of John's. Kennedy told him that after meeting Madonna, his mother "hit the roof. She warned him to stay away from Madonna. She felt Madonna would exploit the Kennedy name for publicity, and basically, that she was a crass social climber, a tramp — and still married to Sean Penn." (This last point seemed disingenuous, considering Jackie's own relationship with Tempelsman.) The single most important thing in Madonna's favor: "John didn't have to worry that she was after him for his fame or his money. She was twice as famous as him and ten times as rich."

The fact that Madonna was technically a Roman Catholic might otherwise have been a major plus for her in Jackie's eyes, if it hadn't been for her habit of publicly thumbing her nose at Catholic rituals and symbols. "Jackie thought Madonna's use of crucifixes and other Catholic imagery was incredibly sacrilegious," another family acquaintance said. "Jackie didn't want her son involved with a woman who was being widely condemned as a heretic."

Jackie's objection to Madonna's presence in John's life, suggested John's friend, had as much to do with the woman who Madonna sought to emulate. "Jackie was shocked when she picked up *Life* magazine and saw Madonna looking exactly like Marilyn. It must have been like Marilyn coming back from the grave, this time to steal her son instead of her husband. It was a nightmare for her."

Had Madonna not ridden to fame on a shock wave, Jackie would have found her less onerous. The exponent of blond ambition was well read, articulate, and knowledgeable about dance, fashion, and art. She also boasted a genius-level IQ and was by all accounts a brilliant businesswoman. According to no less an authority than *Forbes*, which put her on its cover, Madonna was worth in the neighborhood of $39 million.

Yet Madonna knew, as she herself confessed, "how to push people's buttons" — including Jackie's. And the star who begot a generation of wannabes made no apologies. "If I weren't as talented as I am ambitious, I'd be a gross monstrosity," she conceded. "I've been called a tramp, a harlot, a slut, and the kind of girl who always winds up in the backseat of a car. If people can't get past that superficial level of what I'm about, fine."

Madonna and John managed to conceal their relationship from the press in New York, going to such lengths as attending plays and parties separately — only to get together in private afterward. They let their guard down on Cape Cod, where, bundled in sweaters and jackets, they jogged along the beach near the Kennedy compound in Hyannis Port.

John's affair with Madonna had not gone unnoticed by her husband. After a tribute to Robert De Niro by New York's Museum of the Moving Image, John joined Jeremy Irons, Matt Dillon, Penny Marshall, Liza Minnelli, Sean Penn, and other celebrities at a party in De Niro's honor at the Tribeca Grill.

John spotted the ex–Mr. Madonna chatting with a friend. He went up to Penn, extended his hand, and introduced himself.

"I know who you are," Penn replied stonily. "You owe me an apology." Kennedy said nothing, and walked away. Apparently, Penn was still seething over reports linking Kennedy to Madonna during their marriage. The next morning, John received a funeral wreath of white roses with a black-and-gold ribbon bearing the inscription "MY DEEPEST SYMPATHY." The card read simply, "Johnny, I heard about last night." It was signed "m."

The Penn–JFK Jr. incident coincided with yet another *Vanity Fair* Madonna cover story. Again, Madonna conjured up the ghost of Jack's legendary paramour. To illustrate a story titled "The Misfit," Madonna struck two nude poses as part of her "Homage to Norma Jean" pinup portfolio.

Eventually, John made it known that he was not at all squeamish about the stories linking his father to Marilyn Monroe. On the cover of the September 1996 issue of *George*, the political magazine John founded and publishes, Drew Barrymore posed as Marilyn singing "Happy Birthday, Mr. Pres-i-dent."

The Kennedys were aghast. "I don't see what possible taste questions could be involved," John shrugged. "If I don't find it tasteless, I don't know why anyone would. It's part of the iconography of American politics. It's an enduring image."

By way of symmetry, Madonna went on after John to have a very public affair with Jackie's former lover Warren Beatty. "A perfect match," Jackie commented without a trace of sarcasm.

There was an audible sigh of relief at 1040 Fifth when John took a $29,900-a-year job as an Assistant District Attorney in the office of Manhattan D.A. (and old Bobby Kennedy ally) Robert Morgenthau. And Jackie got on the phone to congratulate her son when, after two humiliating failures to pass the New York bar exam (spawning the *New York Post*'s famous "THE HUNK FLUNKS" headline) he passed on his third try.

By contrast, Caroline passed the first time out and was already writing a book with her Columbia classmate Ellen Alderman when she gave birth to Jackie's second grandchild, Tatiana Celia Kennedy Schlossberg, on May 5, 1990. Less than a year later, William Morrow and Company marked the bicentennial of the Bill of Rights by publishing the Alderman-Kennedy co-authored *In Our Defense: The Bill of Rights in Action*. The book, an anthology like *Profiles in Courage*, examined a variety of legal cases. It was critically well received and, largely on the strength of the Kennedy name (Caroline did not add the "Schlossberg"), became a *New York Times* bestseller.

With Madonna fresh in her mind, Jackie was less than pleased to learn that her son had become involved with another dazzling blond star — albeit one better known for her onscreen performances than her private shenanigans.

John and Daryl Hannah had actually met when they were both eighteen and vacationing with their families at La Samanna on St. Martin. At the time he could not help but be impressed by her. Daryl, whose stepfather

648

was Chicago financier Jerry Wexler, carried a teddy bear with her wherever she went.

By the time they met again at Aunt Lee's wedding to Herb Ross, Daryl had already rocketed to stardom in such films as *Splash*, *Roxanne*, and Ross's *Steel Magnolias*. She was living with rocker Jackson Browne in California, and John had returned to Jackie's favorite potential daughter-in-law, Christina Haag. Nevertheless, John and Daryl had a brief fling until the summer of 1989, when she made her choice and returned to Browne.

Jackie harbored strong opinions about her children's lives and the direction they should take. But her own life, as her spiritual advisor Deepak Chopra stated, remained the proverbial quest "for inner peace."

Despite years of therapy, Jackie still smoked two packs or more a day; the fingers of her right hand were stained with nicotine. She continued her yoga and the weekly treatments from her acupuncturist Lillian Biko. Increasingly, Jackie leaned on her chiropractor, Dr. Stephen R. Hoody ("my guru"), for advice. Among other things, he reportedly put her on a plum diet to "cleanse" her system.

Jackie's continuing fascination with Buddhism and Eastern mysticism led her to delve more into the realm of alternative medicine. She approached Bill Moyers, who had done a popular series of television interviews exploring the link between the mind and illness, and suggested a book. He resisted, but Jackie was personally so engrossed in the subject that she convinced him *Healing and the Mind* would become a major bestseller.

What had fascinated her most was Moyers's interview with Jon Kabat-Zinn, founder of the Stress Reduction Clinic at the University of Massachusetts Medical Center, on reducing stress through meditation. Similarly, she edited Naveen Patnaik's *The Garden of Life*, which delved into the healing properties of plants.

In February of 1991, Louis Auchincloss's wife, Adele, died after a long battle with cancer. Jackie personally delivered a note to his building the next morning.

> I just heard this afternoon. I still can't believe it. My heart goes out to you and to your wonderful sons . . . . All I can think of is the gallantry of her long and final battle — and yours, who accompanied her through it. You will know the beautiful words: "Nothing became her life so as her manner of leaving it" . . . It seems to me that all Adele did in her life was to give — to her family, to things that mattered to the community,

to the world. She should not have had to suffer so. There are not many people who are obviously so profoundly good as she was. Everyone whose life her spirit touched will remember, will acknowledge, will miss her forever.

Said Auchincloss, "I could have written the same of Jackie, alas, only three years later."

Family loyalty was tested once again when Jackie's nephew William Kennedy Smith, Jean Smith's son and a fourth-year medical student at Georgetown University, was charged with raping Patricia Bowman, twenty-nine, on the lawn of the Kennedy estate in Palm Beach. The incident, which occurred in the early-morning hours of March 30, 1991, followed a night of drunken revelry with Uncle Ted Kennedy and Ted's son Patrick at Palm Beach's trendy Au Bar.

Like much of the nation, Jackie was shocked not only by the charges leveled against Willie Smith but by the reports of a wanton Ted careening about town with his own son and nephew trying to pick up women. A particularly disturbing image was one of the Kennedy patriarch, clad only in the top half of his pajamas, behaving lewdly in front of Patrick's date.

Jackie had stood up for Ted after Chappaquiddick, but enough was enough. Out of loyalty to Jean, who had always been the closest to her of all the Kennedy sisters, Jackie did bring her children to play touch football with all the Kennedy cousins — including Willie — at the clan's annual Labor Day picnic on the Cape. Jean was grateful for the photo opportunity, but that was as far as Jackie was willing to go.

That December the rest of the family — Eunice and Sargent Shriver, Ethel, Pat, and their respective broods — put up a unified front, appearing at Willie Smith's trial and declaring their unshakable belief in his innocence to any reporter who would listen.

While Caroline followed her mother's lead and resisted family pressure to attend, John yielded to incessant pleas from his cousins and spent five days in the courtroom. He was also spotted having lunch with Willie Smith's high-powered defense team. Asked by reporters why he had risked besmirching his own reputation by standing by Smith, John replied, "He's helped me out in the past and I was glad to come and be of assistance. Willie is my cousin. We grew up together. I thought I could at least be with him during this difficult time." Ultimately, Smith was acquitted.

In September of 1992, Daryl Hannah decided to leave Jackson Browne for John and told Browne so. A fight ensued, and she ended up in the hospital. John rushed to

Daryl's side, brought her to New York, and nursed her back to health.

As far as Jackie would know, Daryl was the last serious woman in John's life. He moved into her West Side apartment, and until August of 1994, they would appear to be inseparable. Like everyone else, Jackie read newspaper story after newspaper story chronicling the Kennedy-Hannah romance. They were photographed necking on a stoop, in the park, and against a parked car; in-line skating down Fifth Avenue, and vacationing everywhere from Switzerland and Hong Kong to Vietnam and the Philippines.

"Daryl really liked him," said her friend Sugar Rautbord. "She was *desperate* to marry him." Her purchase of an antique wedding dress at a flea market fueled speculation that nuptials were imminent.

There was a problem. Jackie was fond of Daryl, and certainly appreciated the fact that her family had money — "*big* money," as Gore Vidal once recalled her saying. Daryl told friends Jackie was "very warm and supportive" in light of her alleged battering at the hands of Browne. But Jackie made it clear to her son that a movie star — particularly a sexy blond movie star — was not an appropriate choice for the only son of John Fitzgerald Kennedy.

In her own life, Jackie dramatically scaled back her social schedule. She still attended the occasional Doubleday book party and hosted several black-tie affairs for her favorite organization, the Municipal Arts Society — including the society's gala centennial celebration for six hundred guests held, appropriately, at Grand Central Station.

Yet the role she most savored at this time was that of Granny O — or, as Rose and Tatiana called her, "Grand Jackie." Frequently Jackie would walk the ten blocks to the Schlossbergs' $3 million co-op at East 78th Street and Park Avenue, pick up Rose and Tatiana, and head out for Central Park. Like any other parent or grandparent in Manhattan, she became expert at maneuvering strollers over curbs and through crowds and revolving doors, at hailing cabs while never letting go of her charges' hands, and at keeping a watchful eye on mean-looking dogs and suspicious-looking characters. The task became even more daunting when Caroline gave birth to John Bouvier Kennedy Schlossberg on January 19, 1993.

Two or three times a week, Jackie could be spotted pushing Tatiana on the swings at the 72nd Street playground, or sitting sharing an ice cream on a park bench with Rose. Each week they also dropped in to Grand Jackie's apartment, where, said Nancy Tuckerman, "with her flagrant imagination, she was able to hold their attention for hours on end. There was this enormous red wooden chest in which she kept all sorts of hidden treasures for them: pirate loot, Gypsy trinkets, beaded necklaces, rings with colored stones.

"As soon as they arrived, everything from the chest was dumped out on the bedroom floor and the children would dig in. They'd deck themselves out with jewelry, and put on costumes they'd made from old scarves and odd bits of material. Jackie would then take them on a so-called 'fantasy adventure.' She'd weave a spellbinding tale while leading them through the darkened apartment, opening closet doors in search of ghosts and mysterious creatures. Once they were finished playing, they'd have their traditional afternoon tea party sitting on the livingroom floor."

"She was so wonderful with them," said Rose Styron. "She got such a kick out of watching them tumble and play together." At Martha's Vineyard, Jackie planted vegetables with her grandchildren, and spent entire days boating and swimming with them. They were given free rein in the house, where Jackie would sit on the floor for hours coloring and playing with them. When Rose and Tatiana spilled paint on one of the antique rugs she had brought back from India, Jackie laughed it off. "It doesn't matter," she told the housekeeper. "It's only an old rug."

As she settled with surprising ease into the

role of matriarch, Jackie craved anonymity more than ever. She was such a fixture on the streets of Manhattan, that with the exception of an occasional "Hiya, Jackie" from a passing cabbie, she was usually left alone. But Jackie was still careful to keep her eyes hidden behind the famous sunglasses and her smile resolutely fixed.

In the summer of 1992, Jamie Auchincloss was sitting in New York's Plaza Theater watching the film *Howard's End* when he "felt her presence in the room. We were always on the same wavelength. When the movie was over and the lights in the theater went on, she stood up a few rows ahead of me. No one recognized her. She turned and saw me and there was the strangest look in her eyes. She was looking at me as if to say, 'Don't say "Hi, Jackie," *do not* draw attention to me.' She was obviously terrified at the thought of the crowd in the theater mobbing her. Then she walked out of the theater and up the street and never looked back. We never spoke."

Incredibly, the more Jackie withdrew into her own comfortable cocoon, the more determined she became to reel in the memoirs of a major celebrity for Doubleday. There was only one way to top the success of Michael Jackson's *Moonwalk*, and that was to land the only woman who could claim to be as famous as she was: Diana, Princess of Wales.

Even before Di's storybook wedding to Prince Charles in July of 1981, Jackie had been bombarding all her contacts in London with requests for a meeting. It was not easy for Jackie, who had been so rudely rebuffed by both Queen Elizabeth and the Duchess of Windsor when she approached them on behalf of Viking in 1976.

But Jackie was intrigued by the shy nineteen-year-old from the moment she became engaged to Charles. "Jackie admired Diana at first. She saw something of her younger self in the Princess," Jamie said. "There were many parallels between the lives of Jackie and Diana. Both women were very young when they were thrust center stage, and despite difficult marriages grew into their roles. But there were also major differences. Jackie was much brighter than Diana — more intellectual, certainly better educated."

Once again, Jackie's request was summarily rejected by Diana's faceless, nameless handlers at Buckingham Palace. It is doubtful the Princess was ever shown the correspondence from Jackie. As time passed and the soap opera that was Diana's marriage unfolded, Jackie's opinion of the Princess underwent a gradual change from admiration to sympathy to disapproval.

In June of 1992, Andrew Morton's biography *Diana: Her True Story* hit bookstores, exposing the Prince and Princess's marriage as a sham. With Diana as his principal source (although that fact would not be known until after the Princess's death), Morton portrayed Charles as a cynical adulterer and Diana as the bulimic, suicidal victim of the Prince's infidelity.

Early on "Jackie respected Diana for rising to the occasion after her marriage," a publishing colleague said. "She thought Di was beautiful, elegant, charming, very stylish, and a wonderful mother. She did not feel the same way about Fergie [Sarah Ferguson, Duchess of York]. Diana and Jackie also shared the problem of having to cope with powerful, philandering husbands. In their approach to this they differed greatly."

Diana's dissatisfaction had been written on her face for years before she took the unprecedented action of airing her marital woes in the press. In contrast, Jackie felt her marriage to Jack was sacrosanct. "She wore a mask," Tish Baldridge said.

The Kennedys' longtime friend Oleg Cassini believed Jackie's "natural dignity" prevented her from taking her personal problems outside the family. "She was a woman of great pride. If she and Jack had had a fight ten minutes before she *never* would have shown it."

Cassini said Jackie was turned off by the spectacle of Diana "disemboweling herself in public — Mrs. Kennedy would never have done that. Jackie was of sterner stuff made." Aileen Mehle agreed that Jackie "loved gossip but hated it when people whined about their problems. She just didn't think it was very classy. I never once heard Jackie complain, not even after all that had happened to her!"

Following Diana's ritual "disemboweling," Jackie tried a different angle. Instead of beating her head against Buckingham Palace walls, she turned her attention to Charles's longtime mistress, Camilla Parker Bowles. As Diana marshaled more and more public sympathy, Jackie wondered what story Camilla had to tell. In part because Camilla had maintained a dignified silence — and also because she herself had been "the other woman" in Maurice's life for more than fourteen years — Jackie began courting Di's nemesis. In March of 1993, Camilla, still the soul of discretion, turned down Jackie's $2 million book offer.

For her part, Diana later told *The New Yorker*'s Editor-in-Chief Tina Brown that she admired the job Jackie had done raising her children in the harsh glare of publicity. She wanted her sons, William and Harry, to grow up to be just as media savvy. "I try to din into him all the time about the media — the dangers, and how he must understand and handle it," Di said of the heir to the throne, William. "I think it's too late for the rest of the family. But William — I think he has it. I think he understands. I'm hoping he'll grow up to be as smart about it as John Kennedy Jr. I want William to be able to handle things as well as John does."

Notwithstanding her words of praise, Diana did not admire Jackie half as much as the newest occupants of the White House did. Over the decades, Jackie had steadfastly refused overtures from literally every President and First Lady to occupy the Executive Mansion since she left it. Lyndon and Lady Bird Johnson, Richard and Pat Nixon, Gerald and Betty Ford, Jimmy and Roslyn Carter, Ronald and Nancy Reagan, George and Barbara Bush had all tried and failed to establish some sort of social rapport with JFK's widow.

Bill Clinton was different — not only the first Baby Boomer elected President, but the first President inspired by JFK's example to enter politics. Moreover, his youth (at forty-six he was only three years older than JFK when Kennedy was elected President) and easy charm evoked memories of Camelot. "You know," she told Ted, "in some ways he reminds me of Jack."

So much so that Jackie preferred Clinton over Massachusetts's favorite son, Paul Tsongas, in the primaries. Jackie and John both contributed to Clinton's campaign, as did Maurice, who remained a heavy hitter among Democratic Party contributors.

In 1992 the Democratic National Convention was again held in New York, and this time Jackie showed up at Madison Square Garden to watch the famous film clip of a starry-eyed, sixteen-year-old Bill Clinton shaking hands with John F. Kennedy in the rose garden Jackie had created. "I think," Ted Kennedy said, "that established an emotional link for her."

Both Bill and Hillary Clinton made no secret of the fact that they idolized Jack and Jackie Kennedy — "they worshiped at the Kennedy altar," as one White House staffer put it — and that was just fine with Mrs. Onassis. A month before the convention, Jackie invited Hillary to lunch at 1040 Fifth Avenue. Topic A: How best to protect First Daughter Chelsea Clinton from the voracious Washington press corps.

Once again Jackie declined an invitation to attend the Inauguration, though in May of 1993 she did make one of her increasingly rare public appearances — this time at an American Ballet Theater Gala. Wearing a stunning floor-length white satin sheath and white gloves, she looked, said one guest, "as if she were heading for the East Room of the White House for a state dinner. If Maurice Tempelsman hadn't been standing beside her instead of Jack Kennedy, I would have thought it was 1961 all over again."

After a brief interlude in Provence, Jackie and Maurice returned to Martha's Vineyard to discover that John and Daryl had thrown a Memorial Day party for their friends there and had left the house a shambles. It was not the first time. When his mother wasn't there, John would invite as many as sixteen people at a time to spend the weekend drinking beer and, apparently, smoking pot.

Jackie's housekeeper, Marta, scolded John. "You should have more respect for your mother's house!" she told him. A convincingly contrite John promised that it would never happen again — and went right ahead and did it anyway.

When she walked in the house, Marian Ronan told reporter David Duffy, "I couldn't believe my eyes. The house was strewn all over with wet towels and empty champagne, beer, and wine bottles. The carpets were stained, there were half-eaten plates of food discarded in every room, and food had even been splashed onto the walls."

Ronan also claimed she found marijuana buds and half-smoked joints in the bedrooms and bathrooms. An enraged Jackie exiled John permanently to the "Barn," the guest house he shared with Daryl.

As obsessive as she was about her diet, Jackie was actually not very persnickety when it came to housekeeping at Red Gate Farm. Except, that is, when it came to her sanctum sanctorum — her bedroom. Here her hairbrush had to be placed on the dresser in precisely the same spot each day — cleaned so that not a single strand of hair remained on it. A different freshly cleaned nightgown had to be laid out on her bed each night. Jackie's Irish-linen sheets — four sets of white and two sets of pink — had to be hand-laundered and ironed and changed every day.

In August Jackie invited the Clintons to Martha's Vineyard for a cruise with the Kennedys aboard the *Relemar*. She regretted the prospect of having her peaceful domain overrun with the press and Secret Service agents almost as soon as the Clintons accepted. "Oh, Marian, I wish they weren't coming," she confessed to Ronan. "I'd rather be canoeing!"

The President and First Lady were overjoyed. This was, after all, quite possibly the most coveted invitation in Democratic politics. Jackie did not overlook the political possibilities for her family, either. When the Clintons arrived, Jackie, who had been waiting on the upper deck of the *Relemar* with the rest of the family, ordered Teddy to go down and greet the President.

"But Maurice is already there," Ted replied.

"Teddy, you do it," said Jackie, her political instincts still very much intact. "Maurice isn't running for reelection."

That day they dropped anchor off the coast of a tiny deserted island and went for a swim. Caroline and Chelsea jumped fifty feet off the *Relemar*'s highest diving board, and then the President goaded Hillary into following them. Hillary was terrified when she reached the top and looked down. With her husband and the others yelling at her to jump, Jackie shouted, "Don't do it, Hillary! Don't do it! Just because they're daring you, you don't have to." Grateful for Jackie's words of wisdom, she retreated to a less-harrowing height before taking the plunge.

After the Clintons departed, Maurice went to Russia on business. Jackie's behavior the day he was set to return spoke volumes about their feelings for each other. "Jackie was like an excited kid on Christmas eve," Ronan recalled. Or more like a teenage girl waiting for her date to arrive. She pulled on white jeans and a T-shirt and paced until "she heard his car approaching long before anyone else in the house . . . Jackie ran to the front door with a huge smile on her face . . . She kissed him tenderly . . . It was a very touching sight."

Jackie and Maurice said farewell to the summer with their annual Labor Day beach picnic for family and friends. While Caroline looked on, an off-key Grand Jackie sat with Carly Simon on the beach teaching little Jack Schlossberg how to sing the "Eeensie Weensie Spider." "They make my spirits soar!" Jackie said of her grandchildren.

At the picnic, Rose Styron told Jackie she wished she had taken her up on an offer to take her kayaking. "Don't worry," Jackie replied. "We'll do it first thing when I arrive next spring."

For Jackie, the arrival of fall signaled a return to the riding circuit. This year, Maurice made clear his reservations about a woman Jackie's age bounding over fences and hedges on horseback. He worried she might someday wind up paralyzed — or worse.

As might have been expected, these objections fell on deaf ears. Not much frightened Jackie, and certainly not the prospect of another spill. On November 22, 1993 — the thirtieth anniversary of her husband's assassination — Jackie was competing in the jumping horses at Virginia's Piedmont Club when the horse ahead of her knocked some stones off the top of one of the fences. Jackie's gelding, Clown, cleared the fence but stumbled on the stones, hurling his rider to the muddy ground.

This time, Jackie did not get up right away. "Oh my god, she must have broken her neck!" screamed one spectator. "She landed very, very hard and looked like a broken doll," said another eyewitness. "We expected the worst. Jackie was totally lifeless. Her head was twisted to one side and her protective riding hat had been ripped from her head. Her eyes were closed, her mouth was wide open, and she didn't look like she was breathing."

Jackie was out for thirty minutes while the crowd that had gathered anxiously waited for an ambulance to arrive. "Mrs. Onassis was unconscious for some time," Middleburg Police Chief Dave Simpson said. "She gave us quite a scare." By the time the paramedics finally did arrive, Jackie had come to and was trying to get up. "I'm perfectly fine," she protested, and apologized for the "false alarm."

The ambulance took her to Loudon Hospital Center, near Middleburg, where she remained under observation for the next day. "She was in some pain," said Jerry Embrey, Captain of the Middleburg Rescue Squad, "but I think she was in shock more than anything else. For a lady of her years to have taken such a fall and come through pretty much unscathed is almost a miracle."

In the hospital, doctors noticed a slight swelling in Jackie's abdomen — possibly an injury that had become slightly infected. Antibiotics were administered, and the problem seemed to subside.

Jackie's tumble was not the only close call

she experienced that day. While she narrowly escaped death in Virginia, an unemployed Indiana man was arrested as he drove through New Jersey asking directions to Jackie's country house. In his 1982 Dodge pickup, police found a one-hundred-page manuscript in which the man described himself as a "special agent" in a "paramilitary unit" — and, concealed beneath a blue pillow, a .44-caliber handgun and a box of bullets.

LIFE BEGINS AT 64 FOR JACKIE O
GRANDMA JACKIE . . . LOOKIN' GOOD
WOW! LOOK AT JACKIE NOW!
SHE'S 64 AND FIT AS A FIDDLE

The headlines and the stories that followed them all conveyed the same breathless message: Thirty years after Camelot, Jackie had changed remarkably little. She was still svelte, vibrant, and, well, sexy. To illustrate the point, most of the pieces were accompanied by photos of Jackie in a swimsuit on the beach at Martha's Vineyard, jogging in Central Park, sailing down the street behind a stroller, or outsparkling everyone in a dazzling haute couture confection. She seemed, as one writer phrased it, "the very picture of radiant health."

Appearances were deceiving. That Christmas, Jackie was sailing in the Caribbean with Tempelsman when she noticed her lymph nodes had swollen. She began to feel stabbing pains in her stomach, and she could not seem to get over a persistent cough. They returned to New York over the Christmas holidays, where a biopsy of her lymph nodes revealed Jackie was suffering from a form of cancer called non-Hodgkin's lymphoma. Doctors also told Jackie that hers was a particularly aggressive form of lymphatic cancer, and that it was highly likely to metastasize to other organs. If she had any chance to beat it, she would have to begin chemotherapy immediately.

Her first reaction was one of stunned disbelief. "I don't get it," she told Arthur Schlesinger. "I did everything right to take care of myself and look what happened. Why in the world did I do all those push-ups?" Amazingly, only now did she give up — grudgingly — the three-pack-a-day smoking habit she had so masterfully concealed from public view.

The memory of her half-sister Janet's painful death was still fresh in her mind as she began receiving chemotherapy and steroid drugs. Jackie had once been the young woman who fought to keep her husband alive. Now she was locked in a life-and-death struggle of her own. She conspired with Maurice and her children to keep her illness a secret, but it soon became obvious that this would not be possible. The side effects — bloating, nausea, blotchy skin, hair loss — could not be hidden for long under floppy coats, wigs, and scarves.

After Christmas, she went to the Doubleday offices as usual and dropped the bombshell of her diagnosis on Scott Moyers. "Well," Jackie said, "I have to make the best of the situation, and I'm going to do that." She was, Moyers said, "very upbeat about it, said she felt great, and there was a good chance she was going to beat it."

Moyers and a handful of others kept her secret. Between chemotherapy treatments, Jackie even managed to fly to Hyannis Port in January for a brief visit with Rose Kennedy, now 103. Rose could not speak any longer; she had not uttered a single word in months. It didn't matter. The two women sat together in the living room of the house Rose had shared for nearly a half century with Joe and, in total silence, stared out at the choppy waters of Nantucket Sound.

It became progressively harder to conceal Jackie's swollen, blotchy face and hair loss. When a photographer tried to take a closeup of her as she left on a walk, the ever-protective Maurice charged at him. The paparazzo, taken by surprise, backed off.

As rumors of illness proliferated, Jackie instructed Nancy Tuckerman to talk to Robert

D. McFadden of *The New York Times*. On February 11, 1994, Tuckerman confirmed that Jackie was being treated for non-Hodgkin's lymphoma, and added that "there is an excellent prognosis. You can never be absolutely sure, but the doctors are very, very optimistic."

Predictably, the shocking news made headlines around the world. The announcement caught even family members by surprise. "I feel so badly that this has happened," said Joan Kennedy, who during her marriage to Ted had grown close to Jackie. "I didn't know until I heard it on the radio. I suspect that is how a lot of family members heard about it." Added Ted: "All of us are very hopeful. We love her very much."

One source of inspiration came from Paul Tsongas, the former Massachusetts Senator Jackie had opposed in favor of Clinton during the 1992 presidential race. Tsongas had already survived almost eleven years with the same disease. "Most of the devastation is psychological," Tsongas said. But when it came to Jackie, he added, "I don't think the issue of mental toughness is at all in question."

In the face of everything, no one was more resolutely upbeat than Jackie herself. John and Caroline cried when she told them about the diagnosis, but she promised them she intended to beat it. She would not allow herself to be defeated even by the distinct possibility that she would not triumph over cancer. "But even if I have only five years," she told a friend, "so what, I've had a great run."

Jackie joked with Arthur Schlesinger about her disease being "a kind of hubris." She had always been, she said with mock indignation, "proud at being so fit. I swim, and I jog . . . and walk around the reservoir — and now this suddenly happens."

"She was laughing when she said it," Schlesinger recalled. "She seemed cheery and hopeful, perhaps to keep up the spirits of her friends, and her own. Chemotherapy, she added, wasn't too bad; she could read a book while it was administered."

As frightened as she was of falling victim to alcoholism or Alzheimer's, Jackie never considered cancer. There were several reasons why she should have. The steroids that were part of "Dr. Feelgood" Max Jacobson's amphetamine cocktails have been linked to a number of cancers. So, too, was Jackie's forty-five-year smoking habit, which at the very least may have compromised her body's immune system.

Even the dark hair dye Jackie used had been linked to lymphoma. Dr. Sheila Zahm of the National Cancer Institute pointed to hair coloring agents and herbicides as "the two possible culprits we are looking at in connection with non-Hodgkin's lymphoma." The American Cancer Society's Dr. Michael Thun pointed out that "women who used black hair dye for twenty years or more had a four-times-greater risk for developing non-Hodgkin's lymphoma than women who didn't use the dye." Jackie used the dye for twenty-four years.

Unlike Jack, who loved Jackie for her wit and her regal beauty, and Ari, who married her for her fame, Maurice loved Jackie for Jackie. Ironically, the one man who could not marry her was in the end the one most totally devoted to her. In this, the gravest crisis they faced as a couple, Maurice put his business on hold and began seeking out the leading experts in the field. He also investigated experimental procedures and treatments — all of which Jackie rejected out of hand.

It had been one of the harshest winters in memory, but Jackie insisted on braving the elements to go into the office. She confounded everyone with her irrepressible cheerfulness. "She never once complained of any pain," Moyers said. "She never once let anything show." In the office, she sometimes opted for a turban instead of a wig. "Who knows?" cracked the woman revered the world over as a cynosure of fashion. "Maybe I'll start a trend."

One of her favorite projects at this time

was a children's book by Czech illustrator Peter Sis. Jackie was such a fan of Sis's work that the previous winter she had flown to Prague just to meet him. When Sis gave Jackie a drawing, remembered Doubleday Associate Publisher Marly Russoff, "she was so excited she wanted it framed right away. We went to a frame shop. She picked out the frame, and when the shopkeeper was writing up the bill, she said, 'My name is Jacqueline Onassis — O-N-A-S-S-I-S.' "

Still determined to snag a celebrity to write a memoir, Jackie called Frank Sinatra again. She may also have just wanted to hear her old friend's voice one last time. He turned her down, but sent flowers with a note:

You are America's Queen.
God bless you, always.

Love, Frank

One of the friends she saw during this period was Peter Duchin, who had lunch with Jackie at 1040 Fifth. They talked about the memoirs that he had just begun to write. "Peter," she said, "you're about to embark on a very difficult journey. I could never do a book like this. It would be too painful."

Duchin's father was the bandleader Eddy Duchin, and his mother, Marjorie, had died in childbirth. When he asked Jackie what she remembered about his parents from her own childhood in the Hamptons, she provided a revealing glimpse into her own fragile psyche.

She told Duchin she remembered his parents "only indirectly. But I'll never forget the night my mother and father both came into my bedroom all dressed up to go out. I can still smell the scent my mother wore and feel the softness of her fur coat as she leaned over to kiss me good night. In such an excited voice she said, 'Darling, your father and I are going dancing tonight at the Central Park Casino to hear Eddy Duchin.' I don't know why the moment has stayed with me all these years. Perhaps because it was one of the few times I remember seeing my parents together. It was so romantic. So hopeful."

Her illness had obviously made her more thoughtful, reflective. "You know, Peter," Jackie went on, "we both live and do very well in this world of WASPs and old money and society. It's all supposed to be so safe and continuous. But you and I are not really *of* it. Maybe because I'm Catholic and because my parents were divorced when I was young — a terribly radical thing at the time — I've always felt an outsider in that world. Haven't you?"

"Yes and no," Duchin answered.

Jackie studied him for a moment. "That's not," she said, smiling, "a bad place to be."

That March, as snowstorms bore down on the Northeast, Caroline brought the children by every afternoon. Grand Jackie still delighted in leading Rose, Tatiana, and Jack on "fantasy adventures" around her apartment. One frigid weekend Maurice and Jackie ventured into Central Park with all the Schlossbergs and took part in a spirited snowball fight. At one point, Jackie grabbed a sled rope and pulled her granddaughters across the snow. "I haven't seen her looking that happy," said a neighbor, "in months."

Even as temperatures dipped into the teens, Jackie insisted on her daily strolls through the park. Most of the time she was accompanied by Maurice. Occasionally John, who had taken a room at the nearby Surrey Hotel to be closer to Jackie, would don his hooded parka and take his mother's arm as they strode across Fifth Avenue. Clouds of vapor billowing from their lips, they talked hopefully about the future. Although she had lived there nearly all her life, Jackie paused more than once to marvel at the magnificent Manhattan skyline that soared over the barren treetops — a skyline she, through her efforts at saving New York's architectural masterpieces, had helped to preserve.

When she was feeling strong enough, she and Maurice would catch a movie. *Schindler's List*, Steven Spielberg's Academy Award–winning film about Holocaust survivors, would be her last.

By mid-March, tests revealed that the cancer had spread to Jackie's brain and spinal cord. Now, on top of the highly debilitating chemo treatments, she began radiation therapy.

Friends from the past continued to inquire about her, and invariably it was Jackie who cheered *them* up. The local baker near her cottage in Virginia's horse country, Jim Stein, sent a batch of her favorite cookies to New York. Television journalist Charlayne Hunter-Gault, another Martha's Vineyard summer resident, said she wrote Jackie a note telling her "how much the way she had lived her life with such style, grace, and beauty meant to me. She wrote back in her humble way saying that she was surprised." In Jackie's warm, "joyful" reply, Hunter-Gault sensed nothing of her desperate situation. "You could just see her smiling."

In her note, Hunter-Gault wrote "I look forward to seeing you on the Vineyard this summer."

"Definitely," Jackie replied. "This summer."

For now, however, it was enough that blossoms were beginning to appear on the trees in Central Park. "Isn't it something?" said Jackie. "One of the most glorious springs I can remember. And after such a terrible winter." Jackie told one friend, "I'm almost glad it happened, because it's given me a second life. I laugh and enjoy things so much more."

She spent her last Easter in New Jersey, making fanciful Easter bonnets for her grandchildren to wear in the local Easter parade. Jackie, wearing one of her brightly colored turbans, laughed and clapped as Rose and Tatiana scampered across the lawn with Jack toddling behind.

"She was definitely up, actually quite cheerful," said another friend she saw during this time, author Edna O'Brien. Pete Duchin recalled that Jackie "behaved the way you would have expected her to behave — as if she intended to beat this thing." "She stayed strong-minded," confirmed another friend. "She did not contemplate the thought that she might not beat this, that she might not be around. It is not true that she had accepted the situation, come to terms with it. No. She never accepted it. It was only at the very end that she realized . . ."

The façade began to crumble on April 14 when Jackie collapsed at her apartment. She was rushed by ambulance to New York Hospital, where she was operated on for a perforated ulcer, a not-uncommon side effect of chemotherapy. Before she went into surgery, she realized she was missing her appointment with one of her authors, Peter Sis. "Please call Peter Sis," she pleaded, "and tell him I won't be able to make it."

In a strange twist of fate, stroke victim Richard Nixon was at New York Hospital at the same time. Jack's onetime friend-turned-bitter-rival for the presidency, whose own destiny seemed oddly intertwined with Jackie's, died April 22, 1994.

Whether she was making her way to the park or merely to the ladies' room at the hospital, Maurice was a constant, comforting presence at her side. "He was very tender with her, very gentle," Aileen Mehle said of Tempelsman. Unlike Jack, Maurice had always been demonstrative in public — but never more than now. When he wasn't holding her hand, he had his arm around her or gently stroked her back. "He was there for her," said Mehle, "every second of every day."

Once out of the hospital, she resumed the charade. "She was so sure, she was so strong, and she was carrying on as if this were just a minor nuisance," Scott Moyers said. She scribbled a note to Louis Auchincloss on her pale blue stationery. "All will be well," she wrote. "I promise."

The brave front was just that. "She's suffering," Maurice confided to a friend. "You don't know how she's suffering." While her mind was still sharp, she sat down and wrote notes to the children, who now filled her with pride. They were to be opened and read only after her death.

To Caroline, she wrote: "The children have been a wonderful gift to me and I'm thankful to have once again seen our world through their eyes. They restore my faith in the family's future. You and Ed have been so wonderful to share them with me so unselfishly."

In her note to John, Jackie made it clear that he was to be Camelot's standard-bearer. "I understand the pressure you'll forever have to endure as a Kennedy, even though we brought you into this world as an innocent," she wrote. "You, especially, have a place in history.

"No matter what course in life you choose, all I can ask is that you and Caroline continue to make me, the Kennedy family and yourself proud.

"Stay loyal to those who love you. Especially Maurice. He's a decent man with an abundance of common sense. You will do well to seek his advice."

By May, the pain was unbearable. According to John's friend Steven Styles, "she telephoned John and, sobbing, she told him, 'I don't think I can take it anymore.' "

On Sunday, May 15, 1994, Jackie knew when she took Maurice's arm for a walk through her beloved Central Park that it would be her last. She wore a brown wig, tan slacks, a long-sleeved pink sweater, and a scarf around her neck. Caroline went a few steps ahead, holding little Jack in her arms, as they slowly made their way toward the 840 acres of winding paths and lawns and woods that Jackie had known since she was a toddler.

This time, the characteristically restrained Maurice lost his temper and angrily chased away the waiting paparazzi. Sadly, Jackie, her face contorted in pain, clung to Maurice for support. The woman who only seven months before was trotting briskly around the reservoir now managed only a few halting steps into her emerald domain before turning back.

Disoriented and weak, her speech slightly slurred, Jackie returned to the hospital the next day. She was diagnosed with pneumonia and immediately put on antibiotics. The cancer, doctors told her, had advanced to her liver and there was nothing more they could do but treat her pneumonia.

Their patient wasn't interested in lingering. Her death, as her life, would be carried out on her terms. When she was first confronted with her diagnosis, Jackie had her lawyers draw up a living will specifying that no heroic measures be taken to keep her alive once death was a foregone conclusion. She instructed her doctors to stop treating her pneumonia, and on Wednesday discharged herself from the hospital.

With Maurice holding her hand, Jackie was taken by ambulance to 1040 Fifth Avenue and transported by stretcher to her apartment. Family members and a few close friends were summoned to Jackie's bedside. By nightfall, hundreds of photographers, reporters, camera crews, and well-wishers pressed against the blue police barricades set up on the sidewalk about Jackie's apartment building.

That night and throughout the next day, Maurice, John, and Caroline seldom left her bedside. (Daryl Hannah, on hand to provide John with moral support, tried to keep in the background.) As Jackie slipped in and out of consciousness, they shared treasured memories with one another and read aloud passages from her most cherished books of poetry. Jackie had asked that several books by her favorite authors be placed at her bedside — including the works of Isak Dinesen, Jean Rhys, and Colette.

Lee arrived that evening, followed by Ted Kennedy and his second wife, Victoria Reggie. When she emerged hours later, Lee was in tears. Solemn-faced as he left for the night, Teddy told reporters: "All the members of the family love her very deeply. We wanted to be with her this evening." Why were he and Mrs. Onassis's children leaving the building? someone asked. "It's late and she thought she'd sleep a little bit — and she wanted everyone else to do that, too."

Shortly after noon on Thursday, May 19, Monsignor Georges Bardes of St. Thomas More Church administered the last rites of the Roman Catholic Church. When he was finished, she looked into the priest's eyes and smiled. "She was physically weak," he said, "but spiritually strong." Reminiscent of the night Bobby lay dying, visitors were permitted in in groups of two — Eunice and Sargent Shriver, Pat Lawford, and of course the ultimate "Rah-Rah Girl," Ethel.

Several Kennedy cousins, including William Kennedy Smith, Massachusetts Congressman Joe Kennedy II, and Maria Shriver, also filed into Jackie's book-filled room ("like walking into a library," said one visitor), along with close friends Carly Simon and Bunny Mellon. Nearly everyone left the room, if not the building, in tears.

Yusha Auchincloss had driven at breakneck speed from Newport, praying he would reach New York in time. "I made it in time to spend most of the evening there, but first I had to compose myself. I didn't want Jackie to see me upset. I went in and out of her room for short visits over the next few hours — sitting by her bed, holding her hand, whispering some memories of our childhood. Then I kissed her good-bye . . . Jackie had lived life to the fullest, she had no regrets . . ."

That night, several family members stood quietly in the living room, murmuring to one another and occasionally wiping away a tear. In her bedroom, bathed in the gentle glow from three antique lamps, Jackie struggled for breath even in her morphine-induced sleep. Periodically, a doctor came in to check her vital signs and, in accordance with her wishes, administer even heavier doses of morphine to ease her into as painless a death as possible. Maurice slumped in a chair beside the bed; Caroline and John were in the next room.

Maurice, emotionally and physically drained, left for just a moment. By the time he returned, Jackie had slipped into a final coma. An hour later, at 10:15 P.M., on May 19, 1994, Jackie's heart stopped. Caroline, John, and Maurice were at her bedside. No one blamed Jackie for hastening her own death. There was only relief that at last the pain was over.

It had all happened with such mind-spinning swiftness — it had been only four months since the public learned of her illness — that it hardly seemed real. The woman closest to her, Nancy Tuckerman, was numb. "She just," Tuckerman said, struggling to understand what had happened, "sort of slipped away . . ."

The next morning, John stepped before the small army of cameramen and reporters encamped outside the building where he had been raised. "Last night, at around 10:15, my mother passed on," he said. "She was surrounded by her friends and family and her books and the people and things that she loved. And she did it in her own way, and we all feel lucky for that, and now she's in God's hands.

"There's been an enormous outpouring of good wishes from everyone in both New York and beyond," he continued. "And I speak for all our family when we say we're extremely grateful. And I hope now that you know, we can just have these next couple of days in relative peace."

They didn't, of course. Later that day, onlookers jostled to catch a glimpse of John, Caroline, and Maurice as they climbed into a limousine that would take them the short distance to the Frank E. Campbell Funeral Chapel. There they picked out Jackie's mahogany coffin and discussed funeral arrangements.

No sooner did they return to the apartment than Jackie's children began squabbling with their uncle Ted about the size of the funeral. Ted argued passionately for a large public funeral instead of the private affair Caroline insisted upon. The woman who had so meticulously planned Jack's state funeral had given her children substantial latitude in arranging hers; she specified only that she wanted the service to be conducted at St. Ignatius Loyola Church, and that she be interred next to Jack at Arlington National Cemetery.

Showing the backbone she had inherited from both her parents, strong-willed Caroline prevailed. She did, however, make one small concession: Speakers would be set up outside the church so that people gathered on the street would be able to hear the service. John was given the assignment of compiling the guest list and other arrangements.

That Sunday, more than one hundred mourners arrived at the apartment to pay their respects at a hastily arranged wake. No one wept; events were happening with such astonishing speed that the enormity of the loss had not yet sunk in. Meanwhile, as limousine after limousine pulled up to disgorge the many celebrities, the crowd outside 1040 Fifth swelled with well-wishers and the curious. When John appeared on the fourteenth floor balcony with Daryl Hannah to wave to the throng below, the crowd burst into a spontaneous rendition of

"The Battle Hymn of the Republic."

On a bright, sunny, Monday morning, Jackie returned to St. Ignatius Loyola, the church where she had been baptized and confirmed. The heavy casket was carried up the steps of the church by eight pallbearers: seven of Jackie's Kennedy and Radziwill nephews — and Jack Walsh, the Secret Service agent who had protected her children and once saved her from drowning off the Irish coast.

Hillary Rodham Clinton and Lady Bird Johnson were among the hundreds of politicians, writers, artists, business leaders, social lions, and entertainment figures gathered inside the church. "Getting those one thousand people through security and into their seats was one of those logistic miracles," said Jackie's friend Frederick Papert. "It's sad but true that the Kennedys know how to do this. They've had too much practice."

The ceremony was planned around readings from the Scriptures and poems that John hoped would "capture my mother's essence. Three things come to mind over and over again and ultimately dictated our selections. They were her love of words, the bonds of home and family, and her spirit of adventure."

The Reverend Walter F. Modrys conducted the Mass, and her old friend and sometime-escort Mike Nichols read a passage from the Bible. Opera diva Jessye Norman sang "Ave Maria." Caroline read from a book of Edna St. Vincent Millay's poetry that was presented to Jackie on her graduation from Miss Porter's. The slim volume was her prize for winning the school's literary award. The poem Caroline selected was a particular favorite, "Memory of Cape Cod."

Let me listen to the wind in the ash.
It sounds like surf on the shore.

Ted Kennedy delivered the eulogy. "No one else looked like her, spoke like her, wrote like her, or was so original in the way she did things. No one we knew ever had a better sense of self . . . During those four endless days in 1963, she held us together as a family and a country. In large part because of her, we could grieve and then go on. She lifted us up, and in the doubt and darkness, she gave her fellow citizens back their pride as Americans. She was then thirty-four years old. Jackie was too young to be a widow in 1963, and too young to die now."

The Senator added that Jackie herself "never wanted public notice — in part, I think, because it brought back painful memories of an unbearable sorrow, endured in the glare of a million lights."

Nothing during the eighty-minute-long

service was more moving than Maurice's emotion-laden reading of "Ithaka," by Constantine P. Cavafy:

As you set out for Ithaka
  hope your road is a long one,
  full of adventure, full of discovery . . .

To the poem's ending, he added one of his own — his own personal words of tribute to the woman he loved:

And now the journey is over.
  Too short, alas too short.
It was filled with adventure and wisdom
  laughter and love, gallantry and grace.
So farewell, farewell.

From the church, the cortege made its way through Manhattan traffic and on to La Guardia Airport, where the funeral party boarded a chartered plane. President Clinton was on the tarmac at National Airport to meet the 737 jetliner bearing Jackie's body when it arrived in Washington at 1:30 P.M. From there, the motorcade of minibuses, limousines, and police motorcycles escorted the hearse through the black iron gates of Arlington.

The casket, covered with ferns and a cross of white lilies of the valley, was placed next to Jack's. On either side lay their stillborn daughter and their infant son Patrick, whose death had brought Jackie and Jack closer than they had ever been only months before Dallas.

The Eternal Flame Jackie had lit thirty-one years before flared in the brilliant sunlight as President Clinton spoke. "God gave her very great gifts and imposed upon her great burdens," the President said. "She bore them all with dignity and grace and uncommon common sense. In the end, she cared most about being a good mother to her children, and the lives of Caroline and John leave no doubt that she was that, and more. May the flame she lit so long ago burn ever brighter here and always brighter in our hearts. God bless you, friend, and farewell."

Caroline and John each gave brief readings. Then, as sixty-four bells — one for every year of Jackie's phenomenal life — rang out from the Washington National Cathedral across the Potomac, they knelt down and kissed their mother's coffin. Then John walked the few steps over to where JFK lay and, leaning forward, touched his father's gravestone.

The pain had been etched in Caroline's face for days, but John had revealed nothing of his feelings. Now, as they turned from the graves, it finally hit him. It had always been the three of them against the world, and now she was gone. Forever. With the right hand that had saluted his father more than thirty years before, John Fitzgerald Kennedy Jr. reached up and brushed a tear from his cheek.

Jackie bore the last ordeal with characteristic gallantry.

— *Arthur Schlesinger Jr.*

Jackie would have preferred to be herself. But the world insisted that she be a legend, too.

— *Senator Edward Kennedy*

ELEVEN

Thanks to the wise counsel of Maurice Tempelsman, Jackie was believed to be worth in the neighborhood of $200 million at the time of her death. Maurice and her lawyer Alexander Folger were named as executors, with the bulk of the estate going to Caroline and John.

To her closest friend, Nancy Tuckerman, she left $250,000. Lee's children, Tony and Tina Radziwill, received $500,000 each in trust. Another niece, Janet Auchincloss Rutherford's daughter Alexandra, was bequeathed $100,000, and to her longtime Washington maid Providencia "Provi" Paredes, $50,000. In what many interpreted to be a final swipe at her envious sister, Jackie made no provision for Lee "because I have already done so during my lifetime." Maurice was left a single, cherished antiquity — a "Greek alabaster head of a woman" she had once purchased for Jack.

That first summer following Jackie's death, the City of New York paid tribute to its most famous citizen by naming the Central Park reservoir after her. She had spent countless hours on the 1.57-mile path around the reservoir, and the runners, joggers, walkers, and strollers who knew her applauded the decision. "She was as much a part of this park," said one park worker, "as this body of water."

Two years later, tribute of a different sort was paid when some 1,195 lots from the Estate of Jacqueline Kennedy Onassis went under the gavel at Sotheby's in New York. The historic auction brought another $34,461,495 into John's and Caroline's coffers. "I'm sure Jackie," said her friend Dina Merrill, "would have been *thrilled*."

She held no high office, wrote no great books, created no masterpieces, performed no heroic feats. She invented nothing, discovered nothing. She had no interest in acting and could barely carry a tune. Yet she was the most celebrated American woman of the twentieth century.

To be sure, Jacqueline Bouvier Kennedy Onassis was the consummate class act: regally beautiful, impossibly chic, intelligent, cultured, and charming — the quintessence of style and grace. These might have amounted to very little were it not for her most important quality of all — courage. For it was that which shone through most brightly when she was thrust by fate into the vortex of history.

A child of privilege and bitter divorce,

Jackie was willing to pay the price, as she said, "to be part of a great man's life." She had shared in Jack's triumphs and enhanced them with her dazzling presence. But she had also suffered the illnesses and infidelities, a miscarriage, a stillbirth, and the death of an infant — only to have it all end in one blinding instant in Dallas.

Ted Kennedy was right: During those four endless days in 1963, she *had* held us together as a nation. What the world did not know is that when her countrymen had recovered, she fell to pieces in private. She concealed her inconsolable grief for years — until another senseless tragedy forced her to take action that she felt might well save her children's lives. It was a measure of the world's love for Jack and Jackie that she was vilified here and abroad for marrying Aristotle Onassis.

At the time, newspapers everywhere proclaimed the death of Camelot. Yet over the ensuing years Jackie's mystique not only endured but flourished — even as she joined, albeit in her own fashion, the ranks of working women. Of all her accomplishments, she was proudest of her children, and deservingly so. That they could emerge as two decent adults from the ceaseless maelstrom of publicity would strike most people as nothing less than miraculous.

After November 22, 1963, Jackie created

the myth of Camelot to keep the memory of her husband's youthful idealism alive. As the embodiment of a passage in American history that was both magical and tragic, it was Jackie herself who came to symbolize the era and all that went after.

Above all else, Jackie was an *American* daughter, sister, wife, mother, grandmother. A month before her death, Jackie was taking one of her walks in the park when someone asked her which of all the places she had visited was her favorite. "What's wrong with America?" she replied.

As she lies in her final resting place alongside Jack and their two dead children, John F. Kennedy's wife is no longer merely the keeper of his Eternal Flame. It burns no less brightly for Jackie.

ACKNOWLEDGMENTS

When *Jack and Jackie: Portrait of an American Marriage* was published in 1996, there was no way of knowing that it would strike a chord with countless readers, both here and abroad. Neither searing indictment nor cloying valentine, *Jack and Jackie* merely sought to tell the whole truth about one of history's most remarkable couples. What emerged was the story of two complex, vulnerable, flawed, but exceptional human beings whose lives affected us all.

As I pointed out in *Jack and Jackie*, even though they were of my parents' generation and I grew up not on the East Coast but in the San Francisco Bay Area, our paths had somehow crossed several times over the years. On September 12, 1953, my family was taking a drive through Newport, Rhode Island, when we suddenly found our red-and-white Ford station wagon stuck in the middle of Jack and Jackie's wedding procession. Nine years later, I shook hands with President Kennedy when he spoke at the University of California's Berkeley campus. The following year, we were driving through Hyannis when once again we were caught up in a JFK motorcade — only this time, the President was returning from the hospital where his newborn son Patrick was waging a losing battle for life.

Living and working in New York City as a Time Incorporated writer and senior editor, I had other random encounters with Jackie over the years — at Shirley MacLaine's Palace Theater opening, at the glittering party honoring the late James Jones, on a street corner as she hailed a cab, and at Doubleday's headquarters. There I happened to be examining the cover of my new book with the art director when Jackie, then a Doubleday editor, suddenly materialized at my side wearing black pants and a black turtleneck.

Jack and Jackie is the biography of a relationship. *Jackie After Jack* is the story of one remarkable woman's struggle to survive emotionally in the wake of soul-crushing tragedy, of her quest for a love to rival the one she had known, and of her fierce desire to protect her children from being destroyed by the adulation that history has heaped upon them. In this regard, the parallels with the Princess of Wales were apparent even to Diana herself.

A tremendous amount of research is necessary for any comprehensive biography, and this was especially true in the case of *Jackie*

After Jack. Much time was spent interviewing hundreds of sources: friends, family members, neighbors, classmates, employees, colleagues, lovers, and journalists and photographers who covered Jackie in all her various incarnations — not to mention her children's teachers, friends, and co-workers. Only a handful of these asked not to be identified, and I respected their wishes. When I spoke to Nancy Tuckerman, Jackie's closest confidante and lifelong friend, she regretfully declined — as she has always done and vows she will always do — to be interviewed at length. However, she was most supportive when we discussed what I had hoped to accomplish with *Jack and Jackie* and *Jackie After Jack*, and once more I thank her for her kind words of encouragement.

Once again, I am fortunate enough to be working with some of the finest talents in publishing. I am particularly grateful to my editor, Paul Bresnick, and to his assistant Ben Schafer, as well as the whole Morrow family — especially Bill Wright, Paul Fedorko, Betty Kelly, Jacqueline Deval, Sharyn Rosenblum, Rebecca Goodhart, Brad Foltz, Debra Weaver, Lisa Queen, Fritz Metsch, Deborah Weiss Geline, and Camille McDuffie of Goldberg-McDuffie Communications. Additional thanks to my editor on *Jack and Jackie*, Will Schwalbe.

Yet again, my limitless gratitude goes to Ellen Levine — brilliant literary agent, friend. I am also indebted, as ever, to Ellen's gifted associates Diana Finch and Louise Quayle.

Mining the rich vein of archival information contained within the walls of Boston's John F. Kennedy Presidential Library would have been impossible without the aid of historian Michael Foster. I am also indebted to Northeastern University Professor Ray Robinson and to author Laurence Leamer for introducing me to Michael, and to the library's William Johnson, Ron Whealen, Megan Desnoyers, Maura Porter, and June Payne.

My thanks to noted British television producer and documentary filmmaker Charles Furneaux, for his kindness and generous assistance to me as I embarked on *Jack and Jackie*, which led inevitably to *Jackie After Jack*.

My daughters, Kate and Kelly, each contributed to the process, alternately providing inspiration and comic relief. I thank my parents, Jeanette and Edward Andersen, for a lifetime of support and their knowledge — like most members of their generation, they have forgotten more than the rest of us ever knew. To my wife, Valerie — irreverent as she is wise — my love and my thanks for making the last twenty-six years so much *fun*.

Additional thanks to: Pierre Salinger, David Halberstam, John Kenneth Galbraith, Gore Vidal, Charles "Chuck" Spalding, Hugh D. "Yusha" Auchincloss, Aileen Mehle, Nancy Dickerson Whitehead, Kitty Carlisle Hart, Charles Bartlett, Letitia Baldridge, Theodore "Ted" Sorensen, George Plimpton, Paul "Red" Fay, Jamie Auchincloss, Peter Duchin, Senator George Smathers, Oleg Cassini, Jacques Lowe, Arthur Schlesinger Jr., Roswell Gilpatric, John Husted, Priscilla McMillan, Evelyn Lincoln, John Marion, Roy Cohn, Joan Fontaine, Rosemary McClure, Vincent Russo, Tony Bradlee, Gloria Swanson, Robert Drew, Cleveland Amory, Doris Lilly, Betty Beale, Ham Brown, Charles Collingwood, Patricia Lawford, Paula Dranov, Helen Thomas, Stephen Corsaro, the late Theodore H. White, Bill Moyers, Dorothy Schoenbrun, Wendy Leigh, William Johnson, Carolina Herrera, Betsy Loth, the late Truman Capote, Clare Boothe Luce, Tobias Markowitz, James E. O'Neill, Dorothy Oliger, Tom Freeman, Godfrey McHugh, Alfred Eisenstaedt, Lawrence R. Mulligan, Charles Whitehouse, Barry Schenck, Susan Crimp, Earl Blackwell, Jeanette Peterson, Diana

Brooks, Linus Pauling, Jean Chapin, Cranston Jones, Richard Copeland, Martine Copeland, Charles Damore, Steve Michaud, Norman Curry, Yvette Reyes, Debbie Goodsite, Michael Shulman, Suzanne Goldstein, Jonathan Green, Joy Wansley, Steve Karten, Dudley Freeman, Bob Cosenza, Valerie Wimmer, William vanden Heuvel, Hazel Southam, Linda Hanson, Angier Biddle Duke, Lee Wohlfert, Donna Smerlas, Dale Sider, Frank Rigg, Terry L. Birdwhistell, Ronald Grele, Dale Sider, Diane Tucker, Drew Middleton, Perri Peltz, David McGough, Dr. Janet Travell, Larry Newman, Sister Joanne Frey, Sandy Richardson, Molly Fosburgh, Albert V. Concordia, Shirley Bombaci, Ray Whelan Sr., Gary Gunderson, Frank Rigg, Kathy Dolce, the John F. Kennedy Memorial Library, the Columbia University Rare Book and Manuscript Library, the Butler Library, the Seeley G. Mudd Manuscript Library at Princeton University, the Houghton Library at Harvard University, the Leukemia Society of America, the Library of Congress, the United States Secret Service, the Boston University Library, the Stanford University Archives, the University of Kentucky Library, the Federal Bureau of Investigation, the Choate School Archives, the New York Public Library, the Schlesinger Library, Barraclough Carey Productions, Channel Four Television

Ltd., Columbia University Oral History Project, the Barnstable Public Library, the Redwood Library and Athenaeum of Newport, the Gunn Memorial Library, the New Milford Library, the Southbury Library, Sotheby's, the Bancroft Library at the University of California at Berkeley, Vassar College Library, the Winterthur Museum, the Silas Bronson Library, the Brookfield Library, the Amherst College Library, the Lyndon Baines Johnson Library, the Archdiocese of Boston, Corbis-Bettmann, Archive Photos, Rex U.S.A. Ltd., Globe Photos, DMI, Reuters, the Woodbury Library, the Boston Public Library, Miss Porter's School, AP-Wide World, Movie Star News, the Associated Press, the *New Bedford Standard Times*, and the Georgetown University Library.

SOURCES AND
CHAPTER NOTES

The following chapter notes are compiled to give a general view of the sources drawn upon in preparing *Jack and Jackie*, but they are by no means all-inclusive. The author has respected the wishes of many interview subjects to remain anonymous and accordingly has not listed them, either here or elsewhere in the text. The archives and oral history collections of, among other institutions, the John Fitzgerald Kennedy Library, the Lyndon Baines Johnson Library, the libraries of Harvard University, Stanford University, Columbia University, Yale University, and Princeton University yielded a wealth of information, some of which has been released only since Jacqueline Kennedy Onassis's death in May of 1994. In addition, there have been thousands of news reports and articles concerning Jackie published over the past five decades that serve as source material for this book — including press accounts of the assassination of John F. Kennedy and its aftermath, the assassination of Robert F. Kennedy, Jackie's marriage to Aristotle Onassis, the manner in which she chose to raise Caroline and John Jr., Jackie's career in publishing, her various causes and battles with the paparazzi, her long-term love affair with Maurice Tempelsman, and her final battle with cancer. These reports have appeared in such publications as *The New York Times*, *The Washington Post*, *The Boston Globe*, *The Wall Street Journal*, *The Los Angeles Times*, *Time*, *Life*, *Newsweek*, *The Sunday Times of London*, *The New Yorker*, *Look*, *Vanity Fair*, and *Paris Match*, and carried on the Associated Press, Reuters, Knight-Ridder, Gannett, and United Press International wires.

CHAPTER 1

Interview subjects included Arthur Schlesinger Jr.; George Smathers; Pierre Salinger; Hugh D. "Yusha" Auchincloss; Charles "Chuck" Spalding; Letitia "Tish" Baldridge; Jamie Auchincloss; Charles Bartlett; Godfrey McHugh; Theodore Sorensen; Charles Furneaux; Nancy Dickerson Whitehead; Jacques Lowe; Jack Valenti; Dr. Janet Travell; Willard K. Rice; and Jack Anderson. The author also drew on numerous oral histories, including those given by Nancy Tuckerman, Robert F. Kennedy, Richard Cardinal Cushing, Eunice Kennedy Shriver,

Dean Rusk, Admiral George G. Burkley, Pamela Turnure, Paul "Red" Fay, Peter Lawford, Ted Sorenson, Hugh Sidey, Maud Shaw, Walt Rostow, William Walton, Angier Biddle Duke, Peter Lisagor, Hale Boggs, Father John C. Cavanaugh, Charles Stanton, Torbert MacDonald, Tazewell Shepard, Douglas Dillon, Liz Carpenter, Jon Galvin, Mark Dalton, and Arthur Krock.

Secret Service, Federal Bureau of Investigation, and National Security Agency files, newly released through the Freedom of Information Act, were of considerable value — as were White House staff files, the Jacqueline Kennedy Onassis papers, the John Fitzgerald Kennedy papers, the Robert Francis Kennedy papers, and the papers of Rose Fitzgerald Kennedy, Theodore H. White, Dave Powers, Kenneth O'Donnell, Paul "Red" Fay, Lawrence O'Brien, John Kenneth Galbraith, Dean Rusk, Sir Alec Douglas-Home, Kirk LeMoyne "Lem" Billings, and William vanden Heuvel. Literally, millions of words have been written about the assassination of JFK; thousands of articles from newspapers and magazines published in the United States and abroad were consulted here. William Manchester's landmark work, *The Death of a President* (New York: Harper & Row, 1967), remains the definitive account of the events in Dallas and their immediate aftermath. Other important sources for this period include Jim Bishop's *The Day Kennedy Was Shot* (New York: Funk & Wagnalls, 1968); *The Warren Commission Report* (Washington, D.C.: U.S. Government Printing Office); *"Johnny, We Hardly Knew Ye"*, by Kenneth P. O'Donnell and David F. Powers with Joe McCarthy (Boston: Little, Brown, 1970); *Kennedy*, by Theodore Sorensen (New York: Harper & Row, 1965); "The Assassination of President Kennedy," *Life*, November 29, 1963; and *A Good Life* by Ben Bradlee (New York: Simon & Schuster, 1995).

CHAPTER 2

For this chapter, the author drew on conversations with John Kenneth Galbraith, Pierre Salinger, George Plimpton, Arthur Schlesinger Jr., Jack Anderson, George Smathers, Theodore H. White, Oleg Cassini, Sister Joanne Frey, Larry Newman, Jamie Auchincloss, Priscilla McMillan, Yusha Auchincloss, Robert Drew, John Husted, Paul "Red" Fay, Charles Collingwood, Cleveland Amory, Melvin Belli, Evelyn Lincoln, Letitia "Tish" Baldridge, Angier Biddle Duke, Charles Damore, William Johnson, Dorothy Schoenbrun, and Betty Beale. Oral histories include Janet Lee Bouvier Auchincloss, J. B. West, Godfrey

McHugh, Tom Wicker, Maud Shaw, Leonard Bernstein, William Walton, Pamela Turnure, Joseph Alsop, Nancy Tuckerman, Lorraine Cooper, Helen Thomas, Albert Gore, Pope Paul VI, Stanley Tretick, Peter Lawford, Claiborne Pell, and John Sherman Cooper.

Jacqueline Kennedy Onassis's oral history was done by Terry L. Birdwhistell in New York on May 13, 1981, as part of the John Sherman Cooper Oral History Project of the University of Kentucky Library. John C. Cavanaugh's oral history can be found in the Andrew Mellon Library Oral History Collection of the Choate School and in the JFK Library's oral history collection. Liz Carpenter's and Katharine Graham's oral histories are courtesy of the Lyndon Baines Johnson Library. Some material regarding Max Jacobson's relationship to the Kennedys is from Jacobson's unpublished memoir. Theodore White's papers regarding the assassination and his handwritten notes of the historic "Camelot" interview with Jackie were released in full only in 1995, exactly one year after the death of Jacqueline Kennedy Onassis.

Among the published sources consulted: Robert Sam Anson, *"They've Killed the President!": The Search for the Murderers of John F. Kennedy* (New York: Bantam, 1975);

Theodore Sorensen, "If Kennedy Had Lived," *Look*, October 19, 1965; Gerri Hirshey, "The Last Act of Judith Exner," *Vanity Fair*, April 1990; Lady Bird Johnson, *A White House Diary* (New York: Holt, Rhinehart & Winston, 1970); Jack Anderson, *Washington Exposé* (Washington, D.C.: Public Affairs Press, 1967). Correspondence between Jacqueline Kennedy and Lyndon Baines Johnson courtesy of the LBJ Library.

CHAPTERS 3 TO 5

Interview subjects for this material include George Plimpton, Kitty Carlisle Hart, Peter Duchin, Aileen Mehle, Yusha Auchincloss, Charles Addams, Chuck Spalding, Roswell Gilpatric, Gore Vidal, John Marion, Arthur Schlesinger Jr., Nancy Dickerson Whitehead, John Kenneth Galbraith, Larry Newman, Jacques Lowe, Earl Blackwell, Pierre Salinger, Ham Brown, Roy Cohn, Jamie Auchincloss, Theodore White, Truman Capote, Charles Bartlett, Billy Baldwin, Sister Joanne Frey, Shana Alexander, the Countess of Romanones, Cranston Jones, Jack Anderson, Patricia Lawford Stewart, Mollie Fosburgh, Clare Boothe Luce, and Oleg Cassini. The author also drew on the John F. Kennedy Library's oral histories of Rose Fitzgerald Kennedy, Averell Harriman, Hubert H. Humphrey, Robert McNamara, Stanley

Tretick, Louella Hennessey, George McGovern, Jacob Javits, Lucius Clay, Nicholas Katzenbach, Admiral George Burkley, Laura Knebel, Neil MacNeil, Dave Powers, Rafer Johnson, Luis Muñoz-Marin, and Leonard Bernstein. From Columbia University's oral history collection: Bennet Cerf, William Attwood, Larry O'Brien, Toots Shor, and Sarah McClendon.

Among those documents consulted were a handwritten and typewritten manuscript by underworld figure Joe Valachi, as well as the papers of William Walton, Frank Mankiewicz, William vanden Heuvel, Tad Szulc, Arthur Krock, John Kenneth Galbraith, and Frederick Papert. In addition to hundreds of articles relating to the Manchester affair and the assassination of Robert F. Kennedy, published materials included: Philip Nobile and Ron Rosenblum, "The Curious Aftermath of JFK's Best and Brightest Affair," *New York Times Magazine*, July 9, 1976; Rita Dallas and Jeanina Ratcliffe, *The Kennedy Case* (New York: G. P. Putnam's Sons, 1975); Shana Alexander, " 'Congratulations,' Whispered Jackie, 'And Thanks for My Birthday Letter,' " *Life*, September 4, 1964; Mary Barelli Gallagher, *My Life with Jacqueline Kennedy* (New York: David McKay, 1969); William Manchester, *Controversy and Other Essays in Journalism, 1950–1975* (Boston: Little, Brown, 1976);

Jeffrey Potter, *Men, Money, and Magic: The Story of Dorothy Schiff* (New York: Coward, McCann, Geoghegan, 1976); Kitty Kelley, *Jackie Oh!* (Secaucus, N.J.: Lyle Stuart, 1979); Robert Ajemian, "A Man's Week to Reckon," *Life*, July 3, 1964; Ovid Demaris, *The Last Mafioso: The Treacherous World of Jimmy Fratianno* (New York: Times Books, 1981); Judith Exner, *My Story* (New York: Grove Press, 1977); " 'Widow Kennedy' Wasn't for Jackie," Associated Press, May 27, 1995; Arthur Schlesinger Jr., *Robert Kennedy and His Times* (Boston: Houghton Mifflin, 1978); Marlon Brando, *Songs My Mother Taught Me* (New York: Random House, 1995); "Steam from the Bubble Bath," *Time*, July 29, 1966; C. David Heymann, *A Woman Named Jackie* (New York: Lyle Stuart/Carol Communications, 1989); Peter Evans, *Ari: The Life and Times of Aristotle Onassis* (New York: Summit Books, 1986); Curt Gentry, *J. Edgar Hoover: The Man and the Secrets* (New York: Norton, 1991); Joan Braden, *Just Enough Rope* (New York: Villard, 1989); Richard Lee, "Ethel Kennedy Today," *Washingtonian*, June 1983.

CHAPTERS 6 AND 7

Author interviews included Arthur Schlesinger Jr., Kitty Carlisle Hart, George Plimpton, Aileen Mehle, Jamie Auchincloss,

Gore Vidal, Peter Duchin, Doris Lilly, Charles Furneaux, David McGough, Truman Capote, Lee Wohlfert, Roy Cohn, Halston, Priscilla McMillan, Roswell Gilpatric, Chuck Spalding, Susan Crimp, Brad Darrach, Pierre Salinger, Mary Gallagher, Louis Nizer, Earl Blackwell, Marvin Mitchelson, Gloria Swanson, and Letitia "Tish" Baldridge. Those whose oral histories proved especially valuable for these chapters were Jim Whittaker, Wes Barthelmes, Louella Hennessey, Tom Wicker, Richard Cardinal Cushing, and Aaron Shikler.

Articles and other published sources for this period included " 'Very Happy' Mrs. Kennedy and Onassis Married," *New York Times*, October 21, 1968; Susan Sheehan, "The Happy Jackie, The Sad Jackie, The Bad Jackie, The Good Jackie," *New York Times Magazine*, May 31, 1970; Fred Sparks, *The $20,000,000 Honeymoon* (New York: Bernard Geis Associates, 1970); "From Camelot to Elysium (Via Olympic Airways)," *Time*, October 25, 1968; "Vatican Newspaper Describes Mrs. Onassis as Public Sinner," *New York Times*, November 7, 1968; "Mrs. Kennedy Knew It Was Illegal, Says Vatican," *The Times*, London, October 22, 1968; Ingeborg Dedichen, *Onassis, Mon Amour* (Paris: Editions Pygmalion, 1975); Frank Brady, *Onassis: An Extravagant Life* (New York: Prentice-Hall, 1977); Arianna Stassinopoulos, *Maria Callas* (New York: Simon & Schuster, 1981); Louis Harris, "Public Split on Jackie's Marriage," *New York Post*, November 18, 1968; "Jackie vs. the Jackie Watcher," *Life*, March 31, 1972.

CHAPTERS 8 AND 9

Information for these chapters was based in part on conversations with David Halberstam, Arthur Schlesinger Jr., Pierre Salinger, John Sargent, George Smathers, Ted Sorensen, Letitia "Tish" Baldridge, John Marion, Sandy Richardson, Jamie Auchincloss, Betsy Bloomingdale, Peter Duchin, Alfred Eisenstaedt, Barry Schenck, Shirley Clurman, Betty Beale, Aileen Mehle, Shirley MacLaine, Doris Lilly, Wendy Leigh, Joan Fontaine, Jeanette Peterson, Cranston Jones, Steve Rubell, Bobby Zarem, Carolina Herrera, Lee Wohlfert, Christopher Makos, Roy Cohn, Earl Blackwell, Alex Gotfryd, Malcolm Forbes, Blair Brown, Jack Anderson, and James Young.

Among the published sources consulted: Louis Auchincloss, "Belles Lettres," *Quest*, May 1997; Joyce Maynard, "Jacqueline Onassis Makes a New Debut," *New York Times*, January 14, 1977; Laurence Leamer, *The Kennedy Women: The Saga of an American Family* (New York: Villard, 1994);

"Onassis Plotted Against Jackie," Associated Press, April 22, 1989; Deirdre Carmody, "Mrs. Onassis Resigns Editing Post; Cites Novel on an Assassination," *New York Times*, October 15, 1977; Jack Anderson, "Jackie's Money: The Real Story," *New York Post*, April 12, 1975; Stephen Birmingham, "The Public Event Named Jackie," *New York Times Magazine*, June 20, 1976; Sybil Baker, "Jackie Reveals Her Still-Radiant Faith in JFK," *New York Daily News*, October 18, 1973; Liz Smith, "P. Davis and Jackie O: Is It Really a Romance?" *Baltimore Sun*, September 19, 1978; Sally Quinn, "A New Image or Not, Jacqueline Onassis Is an Event," *Washington Post*, November 14, 1975; David Behrens, "A Long Way from Camelot," *Newsday*, July 26, 1979; Helen Lawrenson, "Jackie at 50," *Boston Herald*, July 30, 1979; "Jackie Onassis Builds a $3 Million Hideaway," Associated Press, October 25, 1981.

CHAPTERS 10 AND 11

Author interviews include Jamie Auchincloss, Yusha Auchincloss, Aileen Mehle, George Plimpton, David Halberstam, John Kenneth Galbraith, Pierre Salinger, John Marion, Peter Duchin, Jeanette Walls, John Sargent, Michael Gross, Howie Montaug, Ted Sorensen, Bob Michaelson, Norman

Winter, Rosemary McClure, Erika Bell, Stephanie Mansfield, Steve Rubell, James Young, Oleg Cassini, and Arthur Schlesinger Jr.

Published sources included Charlotte Curtis, "Mrs. Onassis, On the Go," *New York Times*, February 25, 1986; Marie Brenner, "Jackie Tops at Shunning Limelight," *Los Angeles Times*, October 23, 1983; Mimi Kazon, "Jackie and Me," *New York Live*, October 4, 1992; Robert D. McFadden, "Jacqueline Kennedy Onassis Has Lymphoma," *New York Times*, February 11, 1994; Tony Burton, "Indians Battling Jackie," *New York Daily News*, January 29, 1989; John F. Baker, *Publishers Weekly*, April 10, 1993; Cindy Adams, "Family Gathers: Decision to Leave Was Hers, Says the Hospital," *New York Post*, May 19, 1994; Edward Klein, "Jackie: Her Friends Finally Talk," *Good Housekeeping*, November 1989; Caryl S. Avery, "Jackie: A Mother's Journey," *Ladies' Home Journal*, March 1989; Wendy Leigh, "Caroline's Precious Legacy: What She Learned from Her Mother," *McCalls*, September 1994; *The Estate of Jacqueline Kennedy Onassis Auction Catalogue*, Sotheby's, April 23, 1996; "Farewell, Jacqueline," *Newsday*, May 21, 1994; Marylou Tousignant and Malcolm Gladwell, "In Somber Ceremony Jacqueline Kennedy

Onassis Is Laid to Rest," *Washington Post*, May 24, 1994; Frank Rich, "The Jackie Mystery," *New York Times*, May 26, 1994; Michael M. Thomas, "Jackie's Quiet Elegance Ennobled the Nation," *New York Observer*, May 30, 1994; Taki Theodoracopulos, "Jackie O: A Perfect Mom," *New York Post*, May 23, 1994; Annette Tapert, "Jackie's Dearest Wish," *Good Housekeeping*, July 1994; James Barron, "Ooh, Aahs and Millions in Frenzy to Buy Camelot," *New York Times*, April 26, 1996; Tina Brown, "A Woman in Earnest," *New Yorker*, September 15, 1997.

SELECTED BIBLIOGRAPHY

Acheson, Dean. *Power and Diplomacy*. Cambridge, Massachusetts: Harvard University Press, 1958.

Adams, Cindy, and Susan Crimp. *Iron Rose: The Story of Rose Fitzgerald Kennedy and Her Dynasty*. Beverly Hills, California: Dove Books, 1995.

Amory, Cleveland. *The Proper Bostonians*. New York: E. P. Dutton & Company, Inc., 1947.

Andersen, Christopher. *Jack and Jackie: Portrait of an American Marriage*. New York: William Morrow and Company, Inc., 1996.

——. *Madonna Unauthorized*. New York: Simon & Schuster, 1991.

Anson, Robert Sam. *"They've Killed the President!": The Search for the Murderers of John F. Kennedy*. New York: Bantam, 1975.

Anthony, Carl Sferrazza. *As We Remember Her*. New York: HarperCollins, 1997.

Baldridge, Letitia. *Of Diamonds and Diplomats*. Boston: Houghton Mifflin, 1968.

Baldwin, Billy. *Billy Baldwin Remembers*. New York: Harcourt Brace Jovanovich, 1974.

Beschloss, Michael R. *Kennedy and*

Roosevelt: The Uneasy Alliance. New York: W. W. Norton, 1980.

———. *Taking Charge: The Johnson White House Tapes, 1963–1964.* New York: Simon & Schuster, 1997.

Birmingham, Stephen. *Jacqueline Bouvier Kennedy Onassis.* New York: Grosset & Dunlap, 1978.

———. *Real Lace: America's Irish Rich.* New York: Harper & Row, 1973.

Bishop, Jim. *The Day Kennedy Was Shot.* New York: Funk & Wagnalls, 1968.

Blair, Joan, and Clay Blair Jr. *The Search for JFK.* New York: Berkeley, 1976.

Bouvier, Jacqueline and Lee Bouvier. *One Special Summer.* New York: Delacorte Press, 1974.

Bouvier, Kathleen. *To Jack, with Love. Black Jack Bouvier: A Remembrance.* New York: Kensington, 1979.

Braden, Joan. *Just Enough Rope.* New York: Villard, 1989.

Bradlee, Ben. *A Good Life.* New York: Simon & Schuster, 1995.

———. *Conversations with Kennedy.* New York: Norton, 1975.

Brady, Frank. *Onassis.* Englewood Cliffs, New Jersey: Prentice-Hall, 1977.

Brando, Marlon, with Robert Lindsey. *Songs My Mother Taught Me.* New York: Random House, 1995.

Bryant, Traphes, and Frances Spatz

Leighton. *Dog Days at the White House.* New York: Macmillan, 1975.

Buck, Pearl S. *The Kennedy Women: A Personal Appraisal.* New York: Harcourt, 1969.

Burke, Richard E. *My Ten Years with Ted Kennedy.* New York: St. Martin's Press, 1992.

Burns, James MacGregor. *Edward Kennedy and the Camelot Legacy.* New York: Norton, 1976.

——. *John Kennedy: A Political Profile.* New York: Harcourt, 1960.

Cameron, Gail. *Rose: A Biography of Rose Fitzgerald Kennedy.* New York: Putnam, 1971.

Cassini, Oleg. *A Thousand Days of Magic.* New York: Rizzoli, 1995.

——. *In My Own Fashion: An Autobiography.* New York: Simon & Schuster, 1987.

Cheshire, Maxine. *Maxine Cheshire, Reporter.* Boston: Houghton Mifflin, 1978.

Clarke, Gerald. *Capote.* New York: Simon & Schuster, 1988.

Cohn, Roy. *McCarthy.* New York: New American Library, 1968.

Collier, Peter, and David Horowitz. *The Kennedys: An American Drama.* New York: Summit Books, 1984.

Damore, Leo. *The Cape Cod Years of John Fitzgerald Kennedy.* Englewood Cliffs, New Jersey: Prentice-Hall, 1967.

Davis, John. *The Bouviers: Portrait of an American Family*. New York: Farrar, Straus, 1969.

Davis, John. *The Kennedys: Dynasty and Disaster*. New York: McGraw-Hill, 1984.

Dempster, Nigel. *Heiress: The Story of Christina Onassis*. London: George Weidenfeld & Nicolson, 1989.

DuBois, Diana. *In Her Sister's Shadow: An Intimate Biography of Lee Radziwill*. Boston: Little, Brown and Company, 1995.

Duchin, Peter. *Ghost of a Chance*. New York: Random House, 1996.

Evans, Peter. *Ari: The Life and Times of Aristotle Socrates Onassis*. New York: Summit Books, 1986.

Exner, Judith, as told to Ovid Demaris. *My Story*. New York: Grove Press, 1977.

Fay, Paul B. Jr. *The Pleasure of His Company*. New York: Harper & Row, 1966.

Fisher, Eddie. *Eddie: My Life, My Loves*. New York: Harper & Row, 1981.

Fontaine, Joan. *No Bed of Roses: An Autobiography*. New York: William Morrow, 1978.

Frank, Gerold. *Zsa Zsa Gabor, My Story*. New York: World, 1960.

Fraser, Nicolas, Phillip Jacobson, Mark Ottaway, Lewis Chester. *Aristotle Onassis*. Philadelphia: Lippincott, 1977.

Frischauer, Willi. *Jackie*. London: Michael Joseph, 1967.

——. *Onassis*. New York; Meredith Press, 1968.

Galbraith, John Kenneth. *Ambassador's Journal: A Personal Account of the Kennedy Years*. Boston: Houghton Mifflin, 1969.

Gallagher, Mary Barelli. *My Life with Jacqueline Kennedy*. New York: David McKay, 1969.

Giancana, Antoinette, and Thomas C. Renner. *Mafia Princess: Growing Up in Sam Giancana's Family*. New York: William Morrow, 1984.

Goodwin, Doris Kearns. *The Fitzgeralds and the Kennedys: An American Saga*. New York: Simon & Schuster, 1987.

Granger, Stewart. *Sparks Fly Upward*. New York: Putnam, 1981.

Halberstam, David. *The Best and the Brightest*. New York: Random House, 1969.

Hall, Gordon Langley, and Ann Pinchot. *Jacqueline Kennedy*. New York: Frederick Fell, Inc., 1964.

Hamilton, Nigel. *JFK: Reckless Youth*. New York: Random House, 1992.

Heymann, C. David. *A Woman Named Jackie: An Intimate Biography of Jacqueline Bouvier Kennedy Onassis*. New York: A Lyle Stuart Book/Carol Communications, 1989.

Kelley, Kitty. *His Way: The Unauthorized Biography of Frank Sinatra*. New York: Bantam, 1986.

——. *Jackie Oh!* Secaucus, New Jersey: Lyle Stuart, 1979.

——. *Nancy Reagan: The Unauthorized* Biography. New York: Simon & Schuster, 1991.

Kennedy, John F. *Profiles in Courage.* New York: Harper & Row, 1965.

——. *Why England Slept.* New York: Wilfred Funk, 1940.

Kennedy, Rose Fitzgerald. *Times to Remember.* New York: Doubleday, 1974.

Kessler, Ronald. *Inside the White House.* New York: Pocket Books, 1995.

Koskoff, David E. *Joseph P. Kennedy: A Life and Times.* Englewood Cliffs, N.J.: Prentice-Hall, Inc., 1974.

Krock, Arthur. *Memoirs: Sixty Years on the Firing Line.* New York: Funk and Wagnalls, 1968.

Kunhardt, Philip B. Jr., editor. *Life in Camelot.* Boston: Little, Brown, 1988.

Lash, Joseph P. *Eleanor and Franklin.* New York. W. W. Norton, 1971.

Latham, Caroline, with Jeannie Sakol. *The Kennedy Encyclopedia.* New York: New American Library, 1989.

Lawford, Patricia Seaton, with Ted Schwarz. *The Peter Lawford Story.* New York: Carroll & Graf, 1988.

Lawliss, Charles. *Jacqueline Kennedy Onassis.* New York: J. G. Press, 1994.

Leamer, Laurence. *The Kennedy Women:*

The Saga of an American Family. New York: Villard, 1994.

Leigh, Wendy. *Prince Charming: The John F. Kennedy Jr. Story*. New York: Signet, 1994.

Lilly, Doris. *Those Fabulous Greeks: Onassis, Niarchos, and Livanos*. New York: Cowles Book Co., 1970.

Lowe, Jacques. *Jacqueline Kennedy Onassis: A Tribute*. New York: A Jacques Lowe Visual Arts Project, 1995.

——. *JFK Remembered*. New York: Random House, 1993.

McCarthy, Joe. *The Remarkable Kennedys*. New York: The Dial Press, 1960.

Mailer, Norman. *Of Women and Their Elegance*. New York: Simon & Schuster, 1980.

——. *Marilyn*. New York: Grosset and Dunlap, 1973.

Manchester, William. *The Death of a President*. New York: Harper & Row, 1967.

——. *Portrait of a President: John F. Kennedy in Profile*. Boston: Little, Brown, 1962.

Martin, Ralph. *A Hero for Our Time*. New York: Ballantine, 1984.

Montgomery, Ruth. *Hail to the Chiefs: My Life and Times with Six Presidents*. New York: Coward-McCann, 1970.

O'Connor, Edwin. *The Last Hurrah*. New York: Bantam Books, 1970.

O'Donnell, Kenneth P., and David F.

Powers, with Joe McCarthy. *"Johnny, We Hardly Knew Ye."* Boston: Little, Brown, 1970.

Ogden, Christopher. *Life of the Party: The Biography of Pamela Digby Churchill Hayward Harriman.* New York: Warner Books, 1994.

O'Neill, Tip, with William Novak. *Man of the House: The Life and Political Memoirs of Speaker Tip O'Neill.* New York: Random House, 1987.

Oppenheimer, Jerry. *The Other Mrs. Kennedy.* New York: St. Martin's Press, 1994.

Parker, Robert. *Capitol Hill in Black and White.* New York: Dodd, Mead, 1987.

Parmet, Herbert S. *J.F.K.: The Presidency of John F. Kennedy.* New York, Dial, 1983.

——. *Jack: the Struggles of John F. Kennedy.* New York: Dial Press, 1980.

Pepitone, Lena, and William Stadiem. *Marilyn Monroe Confidential.* New York: Pocket Books, 1979.

Reeves, Richard. *President Kennedy: Profile of Power.* New York: Simon & Schuster, 1993.

Reeves, Thomas C. *A Question of Character: A Life of John F. Kennedy.* Rocklin, California: Prima Publishing, 1992.

Salinger, Pierre. *P.S.: A Memoir.* New York: St. Martin's Press, 1995.

——. *With Kennedy.* Garden City, New York: Doubleday, 1966.

Schlesinger, Arthur M. Jr. *A Thousand*

Days. Boston: Houghton Mifflin, 1965.

Shaw, Maud. *White House Nannie: My Years with Caroline and John Kennedy, Jr.* New York: New American Library, 1965.

Shulman, Irving. *"Jackie!": The Exploitation of a First Lady*. New York: Trident Press, 1970.

Sidey, Hugh. *John F. Kennedy, President*. New York: Atheneum, 1964.

Sorensen, Theodore C. *Kennedy*. New York: Harper & Row, 1965.

Spada, James. *Peter Lawford: The Man Who Kept the Secrets*. New York: Bantam, 1991.

Spignesi, Stephen. *The J.F.K. Jr. Scrapbook*. Secaucus, New Jersey: Carol Publishing, 1997.

Stack, Robert, with Mark Evans. *Straight Shooting*. New York: Macmillan, 1980.

Storm, Tempest, with Bill Boyd. *Tempest Storm: The Lady Is a Vamp*. Atlanta: Peachtree, 1987.

Summers, Anthony. *Goddess: The Secret Lives of Marilyn Monroe*. New York: Macmillan Publishing Co., 1985.

Swanson, Gloria. *Swanson on Swanson*. New York: Random House, 1980.

ter Horst, J. F., and Ralph Albertazzie. *The Flying White House*. New York: Coward, McCann & Geoghegan, 1979.

Thayer, Mary Van Rensselaer. *Jacqueline Bouvier Kennedy*. Garden City, New York: Doubleday, 1961.

Thomas, Bob. *Golden Boy: The Untold Story of William Holden*. New York: St. Martin's Press, 1983.

Thomas, Helen. *Dateline: White House*. New York: Macmillan, 1975.

Tierney, Gene, with Mickey Herskowitz. *Self-Portrait*. New York: Simon & Schuster, 1979.

Travell, Janet. *Office Hours: Day and Night*. New York: World, 1968.

Vidal, Gore. *Palimpsest: A Memoir*. New York: Random House, 1995.

Warhol, Andy. *The Andy Warhol Diaries*. New York: Warner Books, 1989.

Warren Report, The. New York. Associated Press, 1964.

Watney, Hedda Lyons. *Jackie*. New York: Leisure Books, 1971.

West, J. B., with Mary Lynn Kotz. *Upstairs at the White House*. New York: Coward, McCann & Geoghegan, Inc., 1973.

White, Theodore H. *In Search of History*. New York: Warner Books, 1978.

———. *The Making of the President 1960*. New York: Atheneum, 1961.

Wills, Garry. *The Kennedy Imprisonment*. Boston: Atlantic-Little Brown, 1981.

The employees of Thorndike Press hope you have enjoyed this Large Print book. All our Large Print titles are designed for easy reading, and all our books are made to last. Other Thorndike Press Large Print books are available at your library, through selected bookstores, or directly from us.

For information about titles, please call:

(800) 257-5157

To share your comments, please write:

Publisher
Thorndike Press
P.O. Box 159
Thorndike, Maine 04986